New Perspectives on

HTML and XHTML

5th Edition

Introductory

New Perspectives on

HTML and XHTML

5th Edition

Introductory

Patrick Carey

COURSE TECHNOLOGY
CENGAGE Learning

Australia • Brazil • Japan • Korea • Mexico • Singapore • Spain • United Kingdom • United States

COURSE TECHNOLOGY
CENGAGE Learning™

New Perspectives on HTML and XHTML, 5th Edition—Introductory

Executive Editor: Marie L. Lee

Senior Product Manager: Kathy Finnegan

Product Manager: Erik Herman

Associate Acquisitions Editor: Brandi Henson

Associate Product Manager: Leigh Robbins

Editorial Assistant: Patrick Frank

Director of Marketing: Cheryl Costantini

Marketing Manager: Ryan DeGrote

Marketing Specialist: Jennifer Hankin

Developmental Editor: Mary Kemper

Senior Content Project Manager: Jennifer Goguen McGrail

Composition: GEX Publishing Services

Text Designer: Steve Deschene

Art Director: Marissa Falco

Cover Designer: Elizabeth Paquin

Cover Art: Bill Brown

Copyeditor: Suzanne Huizenga

Proofreader: Kathy Orrino

Indexer: Alexandra Nickerson

Some of the product names and company names used in this book have been used for identification purposes only and may be trademarks or registered trademarks of their respective manufacturers and sellers.

Microsoft and the Office logo are either registered trademarks or trademarks of Microsoft Corporation in the United States and/or other countries. Course Technology, Cengage Learning is an independent entity from the Microsoft Corporation, and not affiliated with Microsoft in any manner.

Disclaimer: Any fictional data related to persons or companies or URLs used throughout this book is intended for instructional purposes only. At the time this book was printed, any such data was fictional and not belonging to any real persons or companies.

ISBN-13: 978-1-4239-2545-3

ISBN-10: 1-4239-2545-9

Course Technology
25 Thomson Place
Boston, Massachusetts 02210
USA

Cengage Learning is a leading provider of customized learning solutions with office locations around the globe, including Singapore, the United Kingdom, Australia, Mexico, Brazil, and Japan. Locate your local office at:
international.cengage.com/region

Cengage Learning products are represented in Canada by Nelson Education, Ltd.

For your lifelong learning solutions, visit **course.cengage.com**

Visit our corporate website at **cengage.com**

Printed in the United States of America
1 2 3 4 5 6 7 8 9 12 11 10 09 08

Preface

The New Perspectives Series' critical-thinking, problem-solving approach is the ideal way to prepare students to transcend point-and-click skills and take advantage of all that the World Wide Web has to offer.

Our goal in developing the New Perspectives Series was to create books that give students the software concepts and practical skills they need to succeed beyond the classroom. With this new edition, we've updated our proven case-based pedagogy with more practical content to make learning skills more meaningful to students.

With the New Perspectives Series, students understand *why* they are learning *what* they are learning, and are fully prepared to apply their skills to real-life situations.

"This text is filled with excellent explanations and activities. My students vary in their abilities, and this text covers exactly what they need in a logical, incremental fashion. It's a great reference book that students will find useful for years."
—Kenneth Wade
Champlain College

About This Book

This book provides thorough coverage of HTML and XHTML, and includes the following:

- Up-to-date coverage of using HTML and XHTML to create and design Web sites
- Instruction on how to storyboard large and complex Web sites, create and use client-side image maps, and work with inline styles
- Expanded and in-depth coverage of CSS design styles and positioning styles, resolving browser conflicts, using CSS with printed media and mobile output devices, and HTML tables and CSS table-related styles
- Reinforcement of code compliance with strict applications of HTML and XHTML and compliance with Section 508 accessibility guidelines
- Web demos, which give students an interactive approach to HTML topics
- An Online Companion, which provides supplemental information related to the content of each tutorial as well as access to the data files students need to complete the tutorials
- Updated business case scenarios throughout, which provide a rich and realistic context for students to apply the concepts and skills presented

System Requirements

This book assumes that students have an Internet connection, a text editor, and a current Web browser that supports HTML 4.0 and XHTML 1.1 standards. The following is a list of the most recent versions of the major browsers at the time this text was published: Windows—Firefox 2.0, Internet Explorer 7.0, Opera 9.25, and Safari 3.0; Macintosh—Safari 3.0. All Web browsers interpret HTML and CSS code in slightly different ways. It is highly recommend that students have several different browsers installed on their systems, for comparison purposes. Students might also want to run older versions of these browsers to highlight compatibility issues, but the code in this book is designed to support those browser versions. The screenshots in this book were produced using Internet Explorer 7.0 running on Windows Vista, unless otherwise noted. If students are using a different browser or operating system, their screens will vary slightly from those shown in the book; this does not present any problems for students in completing the tutorials.

www.course.com/NewPerspectives

The New Perspectives Approach

Context
Each tutorial begins with a problem presented in a "real-world" case that is meaningful to students. The case sets the scene to help students understand what they will do in the tutorial.

Hands-on Approach
Each tutorial is divided into manageable sessions that combine reading and hands-on, step-by-step work. Colorful screenshots help guide students through the steps. **Trouble?** tips anticipate common mistakes or problems to help students stay on track and continue with the tutorial.

InSight

InSight Boxes
New for this edition! InSight boxes offer expert advice and best practices to help students better understand how to work with HTML and XHTML. With the information provided in the InSight boxes, students achieve a deeper understanding of the concepts behind the features and skills presented.

Tip

Margin Tips
New for this edition! Margin Tips provide helpful hints and shortcuts for more efficient use of HTML and XHTML. The Tips appear in the margin at key points throughout each tutorial, giving students extra information when and where they need it.

Reality Check

Reality Checks
New for this edition! Comprehensive, open-ended Reality Check exercises give students the opportunity to practice skills by completing practical, real-world tasks, such as creating a personal Web site and creating and posting an online resume.

Review

In New Perspectives, retention is a key component to learning. At the end of each session, a series of Quick Check questions helps students test their understanding of the concepts before moving on. Each tutorial also contains an end-of-tutorial summary and a list of key terms for further reinforcement.

Apply

Assessment
Engaging and challenging Review Assignments and Case Problems have always been a hallmark feature of the New Perspectives Series. Colorful icons and brief descriptions accompany the exercises, making it easy to understand, at a glance, both the goal and level of challenge a particular assignment holds.

Reference Window

Task Reference

Reference
While contextual learning is excellent for retention, there are times when students will want a high-level understanding of how to accomplish a task. Within each tutorial, Reference Windows appear before a set of steps to provide a succinct summary and preview of how to perform a task. In addition, a complete Task Reference at the back of the book provides quick access to information on how to carry out common tasks. Finally, each book includes a combination Glossary/Index to promote easy reference of material.

Our Complete System of Instruction

Brief
Introductory
Comprehensive

Coverage To Meet Your Needs

Whether you're looking for just a small amount of coverage or enough to fill a semester-long class, we can provide you with a textbook that meets your needs.

- Brief books typically cover the essential skills in just 2 to 4 tutorials.
- Introductory books build and expand on those skills and contain an average of 5 to 8 tutorials.
- Comprehensive books are great for a full-semester class, and contain 9 to 12+ tutorials.

So if the book you're holding does not provide the right amount of coverage for you, there's probably another offering available. Visit our Web site or contact your Course Technology sales representative to find out what else we offer.

Online Companion

This book has an accompanying Online Companion Web site designed to enhance learning. This Web site includes:

- Supplemental information tied directly to the content of each tutorial, for further student exploration and reference
- Student Data Files

COURSECASTS

CourseCasts – Learning on the Go. Always available…always relevant.

Want to keep up with the latest technology trends relevant to you? Visit our site to find a library of podcasts, CourseCasts, featuring a "CourseCast of the Week," and download them to your mp3 player at http://coursecasts.course.com.

Ken Baldauf, host of CourseCasts, is a faculty member of the Florida State University Computer Science Department where he is responsible for teaching technology classes to thousands of FSU students each year. Ken is an expert in the latest technology trends; he gathers and sorts through the most pertinent news and information for CourseCasts so your students can spend their time enjoying technology, rather than trying to figure it out. Open or close your lecture with a discussion based on the latest CourseCast.

Visit us at http://coursecasts.course.com to learn on the go!

Instructor Resources

We offer more than just a book. We have all the tools you need to enhance your lectures, check students' work, and generate exams in a new, easier-to-use and completely revised package. This book's Instructor's Manual, ExamView testbank, PowerPoint presentations, data files, solution files, figure files, and a sample syllabus are all available on a single CD-ROM or for downloading at www.course.com.

Blackboard

Skills Assessment and Training

SAM 2007 helps bridge the gap between the classroom and the real world by allowing students to train and test on important computer skills in an active, hands-on environment. SAM 2007's easy-to-use system includes powerful interactive exams, training or projects on critical applications such as Word, Excel, Access, PowerPoint, Outlook, Windows, the Internet, and much more. SAM simulates the application environment, allowing students to demonstrate their knowledge and think through the skills by performing real-world tasks. Powerful administrative options allow instructors to schedule exams and assignments, secure tests, and run reports with almost limitless flexibility.

Online Content

Blackboard is the leading distance learning solution provider and class-management platform today. Course Technology has partnered with Blackboard to bring you premium online content. Content for use with *New Perspectives on HTML and XHTML, 5th Edition, Introductory* is available in a Blackboard Course Cartridge and may include topic reviews, case projects, review questions, test banks, practice tests, custom syllabi, and more. Course Technology also has solutions for several other learning management systems. Please visit http://www.course.com today to see what's available for this title.

Acknowledgments

I would like to thank the people who worked so hard to make this book possible. Special thanks to my developmental editor, Mary Kemper, for her hard work and valuable insights, and to my Product Manager, Kathy Finnegan, who has worked tirelessly in overseeing this project and made my task so much easier with her enthusiasm and good humor. Other people at Course Technology who deserve credit are Marie Lee, Executive Editor; Leigh Robbins, Associate Product Manager; Patrick Frank, Editorial Assistant; Jennifer Goguen McGrail, Senior Content Project Manager; Christian Kunciw, Manuscript Quality Assurance (MQA) Supervisor; and Serge Palladino, Danielle Shaw, Teresa Storch, and Susan Whalen, MQA testers.

Feedback is an important part of writing any book, and thanks go to the following reviewers for their helpful ideas and comments: Heith Hennel, Valencia Community College; Angela McFarland, B.T. Washington High School, Escambia; and Brian Morgan, Marshall University. My thanks as well to the members of the New Perspectives HTML Advisory Board for their insights and suggestions for this new edition: Lisa Macon, Valencia Community College; Don Mangione, Baker College of Muskegon; Chuck Riden, Arizona State University; and Kenneth Wade, Champlain College.

Writing a book is like giving birth and I have the stretch marks to prove it, so I want to thank my wife Joan for her love, encouragement, and patience. This book is dedicated to my six children: Catherine, Stephen, Michael, Peter, Thomas, and John.

– Patrick Carey

Brief Contents

HTML and XHTML—Level I Tutorials

HTML and XHTML—Level II Tutorials

Table of Contents

HTML and XHTML—Level II Tutorials

Developing a Web Page

Creating a Product Page for a Startup Company

Case | Dave's Devil Sticks

Dave Vinet is a machinist in Auburn, Maine. In his spare time, Dave builds and juggles devil sticks—juggling props used in circuses and by street performers. In recent years, he has made customized sticks for his friends and colleagues. Encouraged by their enthusiasm for his work, Dave has decided to start a business called Dave's Devil Sticks. So far his customers have come through word of mouth; now Dave wants to advertise his business on the Web. To do that, Dave needs to create a Web page that describes his company and its products. He has the text describing his company in a flyer that he hands out at juggling conventions. He has also contacted a graphic artist to design a logo. He wants to use this material in his Web page.

He has come to you for help in designing a Web page and writing the code. He wants the Web page to contain the same information and graphics contained in his flyer. To create Dave's Web page, you'll have to learn how to work with HTML, the markup language used to create documents on the World Wide Web.

Starting Data Files

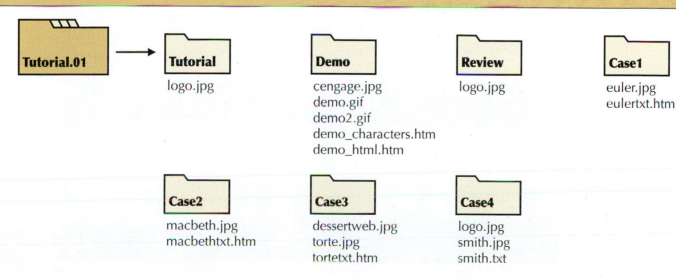

Tutorial.01 → Tutorial
logo.jpg

Demo
cengage.jpg
demo.gif
demo2.gif
demo_characters.htm
demo_html.htm

Review
logo.jpg

Case1
euler.jpg
eulertxt.htm

Case2
macbeth.jpg
macbethtxt.htm

Case3
dessertweb.jpg
torte.jpg
tortetxt.htm

Case4
logo.jpg
smith.jpg
smith.txt

Session 1.1

Exploring the History of the World Wide Web

Before you start creating a Web page for Dave, it's helpful to first look at the history of the Web and how HTML was developed. You'll start by reviewing networks.

Networks

A **network** is a structure that links several points called **nodes** allowing for the sharing of information and services. For computer networks, each node is a device such as a computer or a printer or a scanner, capable of sending and receiving data electronically over the network. A computer node is also called a **host** to distinguish it from other node devices.

As the network operates, nodes are either providing data to other nodes on the network or requesting data. A node that provides information or a service is called a **server**. For example, a **print server** is a network node that provides printing services to the network; a **file server** is a node that provides storage space for saving and retrieving files. A computer or other device that requests services from a server is called a **client**. Networks can follow several different designs. One of the most commonly used designs is the **client-server network** in which several clients access information provided by one or more servers. You might be using such a network to access your data files for this tutorial.

Networks can also be classified based on the range they cover. A network confined to a small geographic area, such as within a building or department, is referred to as a **local area network** or **LAN**. A network that covers a wider area, such as several buildings or cities, is called a **wide area network** or **WAN**. Wide area networks typically consist of two or more local area networks connected together.

The largest WAN is the Internet. The origins of the Internet can be traced backed to a WAN called the **ARPANET**, which started with two network nodes located at UCLA and Stanford connected by a single phone line. Today, the **Internet** has grown to an uncountable number of nodes involving computers, cell phones, PDAs, MP3 players, gaming systems, and television stations. The physical structure of the Internet uses fiber-optic cables, satellites, phone lines, wireless access points, and other telecommunications media, enabling a worldwide community to communicate and share information. See Figure 1-1. It is within this expansive network that Dave wants to advertise his devil sticks business.

Figure 1-1 ▶ **Structure of the Internet**

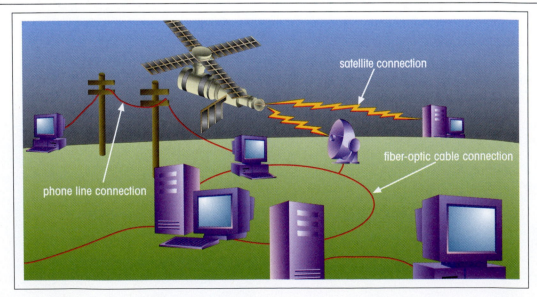

satellite connection

fiber-optic cable connection

phone line connection

Locating Information on a Network

One of the biggest obstacles to effectively using a network is not mechanical—it's the human element. Users must be able to easily navigate the network and locate the information and services they need. Most of the early Internet tools required users to master a bewildering array of terms, acronyms, and commands. Because network users had to be well versed in computers and network technology, Internet use was limited to universities and departments of the government. To make the Internet accessible to the general public, it needed a simpler interface. This interface proved to be the World Wide Web.

The foundations for the **World Wide Web**, or the **Web** for short, were laid in 1989 by Timothy Berners-Lee and other researchers at the CERN nuclear research facility near Geneva, Switzerland. They needed an information system that would make it easy for their researchers to locate and share data with minimal training and support. To meet this need, they developed a system of hypertext documents that enabled users to easily navigate from one topic to another. **Hypertext** is a method of organization in which information is not presented linearly, but in whatever order is requested by the user. For example, if you read the operating manual for your car starting with page 1 and proceeding to the end, you are processing the information linearly and in the order determined by the manual's author. A hypertext approach would place the same information in a series of smaller documents, with each document dedicated to a single topic, allowing you—and not the author—to choose the order and selection of topics you'll view.

The key to hypertext is the use of **links**, which are the elements in a hypertext document that allow you to jump from one topic or document to another, usually by clicking a mouse button. Hypertext is ideally suited to use with networks because the end user does not need to know where a particular document, information source, or service is located—he or she only needs to know how to activate the link. In the case of an expansive network like the Internet, documents can be located anywhere in the world; but that is largely unseen by the user because of the hypertext structure. The fact that the Internet and the World Wide Web are synonymous in many users' minds is a testament to the success of the hypertext approach.

The original Web supported only textual documents, but the use of hypertext links has expanded through the years to encompass information in any form, including video, sound, interactive programs, conferencing, and online gaming. While the Web has greatly expanded to include these services, the basic foundation is still the same: a collection of interconnected documents linked through the use of hypertext.

Web Pages and Web Servers

Each document on the World Wide Web is referred to as a **Web page**. Web pages are stored on **Web servers**, which are computers that make Web pages available to any device connected to the Internet. To view a Web page, the end user's device needs a software program called a **Web browser**, which retrieves the page from the Web server and renders it on the user's computer or other device. See Figure 1-2.

Figure 1-2 | **Using a browser to view a Web document from a Web server**

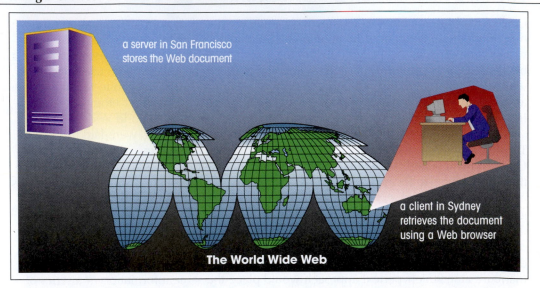

The earliest browsers, known as **text-based browsers**, were limited to displaying only text. Today's browsers are capable of displaying text, images, video, sound, and animations. In the early days of the Internet, Web browsing was limited to computers. Now browsers are installed on cell phones, PDAs (personal digital assistants), MP3 players, and gaming systems. How does a Web page work with so many combinations of browsers and clients and devices? To understand, you need to look at how Web pages are created.

Introducing HTML

A Web page is actually a text file written in **Hypertext Markup Language** or **HTML**. We've already discussed hypertext, but what is a markup language? A **markup language** is a language that describes the content and structure of a document. If this tutorial were written using a markup language, the language would identify the parts of the document, indicating which sections correspond to paragraphs, figure captions, tables, page headings, and so forth.

There are several things that HTML is not. While Web pages often contain interactive programs, HTML is not a programming language. In addition, while HTML can describe the content of a document, it is not a formatting language because it does not necessarily describe how content should be rendered. This is a necessary facet of HTML: the Web page author has no control over what device is used to view the Web page, so the browser—not the HTML—determines how the Web page will look. The end user might be using a large-screen television monitor, a cell phone, or even a device that renders Web pages in Braille or in aural speech.

If you want to format your document, the preferred method is to use styles. **Styles** are formatting rules written in a separate language from HTML telling the browser how to render each element for particular devices. A Web page author can write a style that displays page headings one way for computer monitors and another way for printed output. You'll explore some basic styles as you create your first Web pages.

The History of HTML

HTML evolved as the Web itself evolved. Thus in order to fully appreciate the nuances of HTML, it's a good idea to review the language's history. The first popular markup language was the **Standard Generalized Markup Language** (**SGML**). Introduced in the 1980s, SGML is device- and system-independent, meaning that it can be applied to almost any type of document stored in almost any format. While powerful, SGML is also quite complex; and for this reason SGML is limited to those organizations that can afford the cost and overhead of maintaining complex SGML environments. However, SGML can also be used to create other markup languages that are tailored to specific tasks and are simpler to use and maintain. HTML is one of the languages created with SGML.

In the early years after HTML was created, no single organization was responsible for the language. Web developers were free to define and modify HTML in whatever ways they thought best. Eventually, competing browsers, seeking to dominate the market, added new features called **extensions** to the language. The two major browsers during the 1990s, Netscape Navigator and Microsoft Internet Explorer, added the most extensions to HTML. Netscape provided an extension to add background sounds to documents, while Internet Explorer added an extension to provide marquee-style text that would scroll automatically across the page. These extensions and others provided Web page authors with more options, but at the expense of complicating Web page development. A Web page that took advantage of extensions might work in one browser but not in another.

Thus Web page authors faced the challenge of determining which browser or browser version supported a particular extension, and they had to create a workaround for browsers that did not. By adding this layer of complexity to Web design, extensions, while often useful, diminished the promise of simplicity that made HTML so attractive in the first place.

Ultimately, a group of Web developers, programmers, and authors called the **World Wide Web Consortium**, or the **W3C**, created a set of standards or specifications that all browser manufacturers were to follow. The W3C has no enforcement power; but because a uniform language is in everyone's best interest, the W3C's recommendations are usually followed, though not always right away. The W3C also provides online tutorials, documentation, and quizzes that you can use to test your knowledge of HTML and other languages. For more information on the W3C and the services it offers, see its Web site at *www.w3c.org*.

Figure 1-3 summarizes the various versions of HTML that the W3C has released over the past decade. While you may not grasp all of the details of these versions yet, it's important to understand that HTML doesn't come in only one version.

Figure 1-3   History of HTML and XHTML

Version	Date of Release	Description
HTML 1.0	1989	The first public version of HTML which included browser support for inline images and text controls.
HTML 2.0	1995	The first version supported by all graphical browsers. It introduced interactive form elements such as option buttons and text boxes. A document written to the HTML 2.0 specification is compatible with almost all browsers on the World Wide Web.
HTML 3.0	1996	A proposed replacement for HTML 2.0 that was never widely adopted.
HTML 3.2	1997	This version included additional support for creating and formatting tables and expanded the options for interactive form elements. It also supported limited programming using scripts.
HTML 4.01	1999	This version added support for style sheets to give Web designers greater control over page layout. It added new features to tables and forms and provided support for international features. This version also expanded HTML's scripting capability and added increased support for multimedia elements.
HTML 5.0	not yet released	This version supports elements that reflect current Web usage, including elements for Web site navigation and indexing for use with search engines. This version also removes support for purely presentational elements because those effects can be better handled with styles.
XHTML 1.0	2001	This version is a reformulation of HTML 4.01 in XML and combines the strength of HTML 4.0 with the power of XML. XHTML brings the rigor of XML to Web pages and provides standards for more robust Web content on a wide range of browser platforms.
XHTML 1.1	2002	A minor update to XHTML 1.0 that allows for modularity and simplifies writing extensions to the language.
XHTML 2.0	not yet released	The latest version, designed to remove most of the presentational features left in HTML. XHTML 2.0 is not backward compatible with XHTML 1.1.
XHTML 5.0	not yet released	A version of HTML 5.0 written under the specifications of XML, unlike XHTML 2.0, XHTML 5.0 will be backward-compatible with XHTML 1.1.

Tip

You can learn more about deprecated features by examining the documentation available at the W3C Web site and by viewing the source code of various pages on the Web.

When you work with HTML, you should keep in mind not only what the W3C has recommended, but also what HTML features the browser market actually supports. This might mean dealing with a collection of approaches: some browsers are new and meet the latest W3C specifications, while some are older but still widely supported. Older features of HTML are often **deprecated**, or phased out, by the W3C. While deprecated features might not be supported in current or future browsers, that doesn't mean that you won't encounter them—indeed, if you are supporting older browsers that recognize only early versions of HTML, you might need to use them. Because it's hard to predict how quickly deprecated features will disappear from common usage, it's crucial to be familiar with them.

Current Web developers are increasingly using **XML** (**Extensible Markup Language**), a language for creating markup languages, like SGML, but without SGML's complexity and overhead. Using XML, developers can create documents that obey specific rules for their content and structure. This is in contrast with a language like HTML, which supported a wide variety of rules but did not include a mechanism for enforcing those rules.

Indeed, one of the markup languages created with XML is **XHTML** (**Extensible Hypertext Markup Language**), a stricter version of HTML. XHTML is designed to confront some of the problems associated with the various competing versions of HTML and to better integrate HTML with other markup languages like XML. The current version of XHTML is XHTML 1.1, which is mostly (but still not completely) supported by all browsers. Because XHTML is an XML version of HTML, most of what you learn about HTML can be applied to XHTML.

Another version of XHTML, **XHTML 2.0**, is still in the draft stage and has proved to be controversial because it is not backward-compatible with earlier versions of HTML and XHTML. In response to this controversy, another working draft of HTML called **HTML 5.0** is being developed. It provides greater support for emerging online technology while still providing support for older browsers. HTML 5 is also being developed under the XML specifications as **XHTML 5.0**. At the time of this writing, none of these versions has moved beyond the development stage nor has been adopted by the major browsers. This book discusses the syntax of HTML 4.01 and XHTML 1.1, but also brings in deprecated features and browser-supported extensions where appropriate.

Writing HTML Code	InSight

Part of writing good HTML code is being aware of the requirements of various browsers and devices as well as understanding the different versions of the language. Here are a few guidelines for writing good HTML code:

- Become well versed in the history of HTML and the various versions of HTML and XHTML. Unlike other languages, HTML's history does impact how you write your code.
- Know your market. Do you have to support older browsers, or have your clients standardized on one particular browser or browser version? Will your Web pages be viewed on a single device like a computer, or do you have to support a variety of devices?
- Test your code on several different browsers and browser versions. Don't assume that if your page works in one browser it will work on other browsers or even on earlier versions of the same browser. Also check on the speed of the connection. A large file that performs well under a high-speed connection might be unusable under a dial-up connection.
- Read the documentation on the different versions of HTML and XHTML at the W3C Web site and review the latest developments in new versions of the languages.

In general, any HTML code that you write should be compatible with the current versions of the following browsers: Internet Explorer (Windows), Firefox (Windows and Macintosh), Netscape Navigator (Windows), Opera (Windows), and Safari (Macintosh).

Tools for Creating HTML Documents

Because HTML documents are simple text files, you can create them with nothing more than a basic text editor such as Windows Notepad. Specialized HTML authoring programs, known as HTML converters and HTML editors, are also available to perform some of the rote work of document creation. An **HTML converter** is a program that translates text written in another language into HTML code. You can create the source document with a word processor such as Microsoft Word, and then use the converter to save the document as an HTML file. Converters free you from the laborious task of typing HTML code; and because the conversion is automated, you usually do not have to worry about introducing coding errors into your document. However, converters tend to create large and complicated HTML files resulting in "bloated" code, which is more difficult to edit if you need to make changes. So while a converter can speed up Web page development, you will probably still have to invest time in cleaning up the code.

An **HTML editor** is a program that helps you create an HTML file by inserting HTML codes for you as you work. HTML editors can save you a lot of time and can help you work more efficiently. Their advantages and limitations are similar to those of HTML converters. Like converters, HTML editors allow you to set up a Web page quickly, but you will still have to work directly with the underlying HTML code to create a finished product.

Creating an HTML Document

Now that you've had a chance to explore some of the history of the Web and HTML's role in its development, you are ready to work on the Web page for Dave's Devil Sticks. It's always a good idea to plan your Web page before you start coding it. You can do this by drawing a sketch or by creating a sample document using a word processor. The preparatory work can weed out errors or point to potential problems. In this case, Dave has already drawn up a flyer he's passed out at juggling and circus conventions. The handout provides information about Dave's company and his products. Figure 1-4 shows Dave's current flyer.

Figure 1-4   **Elements of the Dave's Devil Sticks flyer**

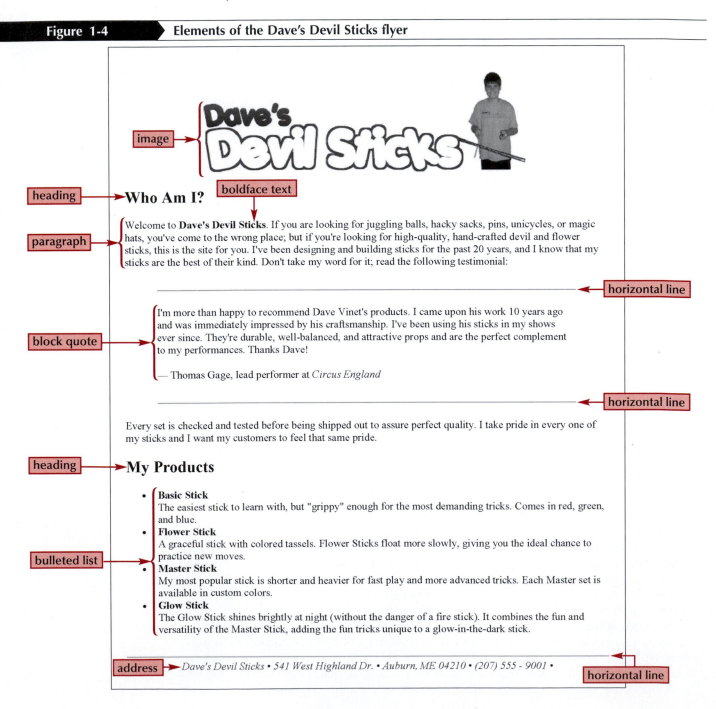

When you sketch a sample document, it is a good idea to identify the document's various elements. An **element** is a distinct object in the document, like a paragraph, a heading, or the page's title. Even the whole document is considered an element. Dave's flyer includes several elements: an image displays his company's logo, several headings break his flyer into sections, the text in his flyer is laid out in paragraphs, a bulleted list describes his products, and the address of his company is at the bottom of the flyer. Note that some elements are marked by their appearance in the text. For example, the name of his company is displayed in boldface text at the top of the flyer to set it off from other text in the opening paragraph. Italics are also used in several locations on the page. As you recreate this flyer as a Web page, you should periodically refer to Figure 1-4.

Marking Elements with Tags

The core building block of HTML is the **tag**, which marks the presence of an element. If the element contains content such as text or another element, it is marked using a **two-sided tag** in which an **opening tag** indicates the beginning of the content and a **closing tag** indicates the content's end. The syntax of a two-sided tag is:

```
<element>content</element>
```

where *element* is the name of the element and *content* is any content contained within the element. For example, the following code is used to mark a paragraph element within a document:

```
<p>Welcome to Dave's Devil Sticks.</p>
```

In this example, the <p> tag marks the beginning of the paragraph, the text "Welcome to Dave's Devil Sticks." constitutes the content of the paragraph element and the </p> tag marks the end of the paragraph.

Note that an "element" is an object in the Web document, and a "tag" is the part of the HTML code that marks the element. So you would mark a paragraph element in a document by enclosing the paragraph content within opening and closing paragraph tags.

Elements can also contain other elements. For example, the paragraph tags in the following code

```
<p>Welcome to <b>Dave's Devil Sticks</b>.</p>
```

enclose both the text of the paragraph as well as another set of tags <b> ... </b> that are used to mark content that should be treated by the browser as boldface text. Note that the <b> tags have to be completely enclosed or nested within the <p> tags. It's improper syntax to have tags overlap as in the following code sample:

```
<p>Welcome to <b>Dave's Devil Sticks.</p></b>
```

In this example, the closing </b> tag is placed *after* the closing </p> tag, which is improper because the boldface text marked with these tags must be completely enclosed *within* the paragraph.

The Structure of an HTML Document

All documents written in a markup language need to have a **root element** that contains all of the elements used in the document. For HTML documents, the root element is marked using the <html> tag as follows

```
<html>
 document content
</html>
```

where *document content* is the content of the entire document, including all other elements. The presence of the opening <html> tag in the first line of the file tells any device reading the document that this file is written in HTML. The closing </html> tag signals the end of the document and should not be followed by any other content or markup tags.

Web pages are divided into two main sections: a head and a body. The **head element** contains information about the document—for example, the document's title or a list of key-words that would aid a search engine on the Web identifying this document for other users. The **body element** contains all of the content that will appear on the Web page. Taken together, the syntax of the entire HTML file including the head and body elements is

```
<html>
    <head>
        head content
    </head>
    <body>
        body content
    </body>
</html>
```

where *head content* and *body content* are the content you want to place within the document's head and body. Note that the body element is always placed after the head element and that no other elements can be placed between the html, head, and body elements.

Tip

Enter your tags using all lowercase letters. For example, use <html> rather than <HTML>. While many browsers accept uppercase tag names, XHTML code requires tag names to be lowercase.

Reference Window | **Creating the Basic Structure of an HTML Document**

- Enter the following HTML tags
  ```
  <html>
      <head>
          head content
      </head>
      <body>
          body content
      </body>
  </html>
  ```
  where *head content* and *body content* are the content you want to place within the document's head and body.
- To specify the page title, enter the following tag within the head section
  ```
  <title>content</title>
  ```
  where *content* is the text of the Web page title.

Now that you've learned about the basic structure of an HTML file, you can start writing the HTML code for Dave's Web page.

To create the basic structure of an HTML document:

▶ **1.** Start your text editor, opening it to a blank document.

Trouble? If you don't know how to start or use your text editor, ask your instructor or technical support person for help.

▶ **2.** Type the following lines of code in your document. Press the **Enter** key after each line. Press the **Enter** key twice for a blank line between lines of code. See Figure 1-5.

```
<html>

<head>
</head>

<body>
</body>

</html>
```

Basic structure of an HTML document ◀ Figure 1-5

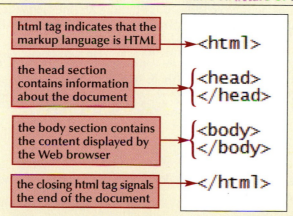

html tag indicates that the markup language is HTML → `<html>`

the head section contains information about the document → `<head>` `</head>`

the body section contains the content displayed by the Web browser → `<body>` `</body>`

the closing html tag signals the end of the document → `</html>`

▶ **3.** Save the file as **dave.htm** in the tutorial.01\tutorial folder included with your Data Files.

Trouble? If you are using the Windows Notepad text editor to create your HTML file, make sure you don't save the file with the extension .txt, which is the default file extension for Notepad. Instead, make sure you save the file with the file extension .htm or .html. Using the incorrect file extension might make the file unreadable to Web browsers, which require file extensions of .htm or .html.

Tip

To make it easier to link to your Web pages, follow the Internet convention in which HTML filenames and folder names use only lowercase letters with no spaces.

InSight | **Converting an HTML Document into XHTML**

There is considerable overlap between HTML and XHTML. You can quickly change an HTML document into an XHTML document just by altering the first three lines of code. To convert an HTML file into an XHTML file, replace the opening <html> tag with the following three lines of code:

```
<?xml version="1.0" encoding="UTF-8" standalone="no" ?>
<!DOCTYPE html PUBLIC "-//W3C//DTD XHTML 1.0 Strict//EN"
   "http://www.w3.org/TR/xhtml1/DTD/xhtml11-strict.dtd">
<html xmlns="http://www.w3.org/1999/xhtml">
```

Each line has an important role in converting the HTML document into XHTML. XHTML documents are written in XML, so the first line notifies the browser that the document is an XML file. The version number—1.0—tells the browser that the file is written in XML 1.0.

XHTML files differ from HTML files in that XHTML files have to be tested against a set of rules that define exactly which markup tags are allowed and how they can be used. To reference the set of rules, you have to include a DOCTYPE declaration in the second line of the file, indicating the collection of rules to be used. XHTML documents can be tested against several different rules. The code sample above assumes a strict interpretation of the rules is being enforced.

The third line of the file contains the opening <html> tag. In XHTML, the <html> tag must include what is known as a namespace declaration indicating that any markup tags in the document should, by default, be considered part of the XHTML language. This is necessary because XML documents can contain a mixture of several different markup languages and there must be a way of defining the default language of the document.

With these three lines in place, browsers recognize the file as an XHTML rather than an HTML document. After these three lines, there is little difference between the code in an HTML file and in an XHTML file.

Defining the Page Title

One of the elements you can add to the document head is the document title. The syntax of the document title is

```
<title>document title</title>
```

where *document title* is the text of the document title. The document title is not displayed within the page, but is usually displayed in the browser's title bar. The document title is also used by search engines like Google or Yahoo! to report on the contents of the file.

To add a title to a Web page:

▶ **1.** Click at the end of the <head> tag, and then press the **Enter** key to insert a new line in your text editor.

▶ **2.** Press the **Spacebar** three times to indent the new line of code, and then type **<title>Dave's Devil Sticks</title>** as shown in Figure 1-6.

Tip

Indent your markup tags and insert extra blank spaces as shown in this book to make your code easier to read. It does not affect how the page is rendered by the browser.

Defining the page title | Figure 1-6

```
<html>

<head>
    <title>Dave's Devil Sticks</title>
</head>

<body>
</body>

</html>
```

Web page title

Adding Comments

As you create a Web page, you might want to add notes or comments about your code. These comments might include the name of the document's author and the date the document was created. Such notes are not intended to be displayed by the browser, but are instead used to help explain your code to yourself and others. To add notes or comments, insert a **comment tag** with the syntax

```
<!-- comment -->
```

where *comment* is the text of the comment or note. For example, the following code inserts a comment describing the page you'll create for Dave's business:

```
<!-- Page created for Dave Vinet's devil stick business -->
```

A comment can also be spread out over several lines as follows:

```
<!-- Dave's Devil Sticks
     A Web page created for Dave Vinet -->
```

Because they are ignored by the browser, comments can be added anywhere within the HTML document.

Adding an HTML Comment | Reference Window

- To insert an HTML comment anywhere within your document, enter
    ```
    <!-- comment -->
    ```
  where *comment* is the text of the HTML comment.

You'll add a comment to the head of Dave's file indicating its purpose, author, and date created.

To add a comment to Dave's file:

1. Click at the end of the <head> tag, and then press the **Enter** key to insert a new line directly above the title element you've just entered.

2. Type the following lines of code, as shown in Figure 1-7

```
<!-- Dave's Devil Sticks
     Author: your name
     Date:   the date
-->
```

where *your name* is your name and *the date* is the current date.

Figure 1-7 | Adding a comment tag

Displaying an HTML File

As you continue modifying the HTML code, you should occasionally view the page with your Web browser to verify that you have not introduced any errors. You might even want to view the results using different browsers to check for compatibility. In this book Web pages are displayed using the Windows Internet Explorer 7.0 browser. Be aware that if you are using a different browser or a different operating system, you might see slight differences in the layout and appearance of the page.

To view Dave's Web page:

▶ 1. Save your changes to the **dave.htm** file.

▶ 2. Start your Web browser. You do not need to be connected to the Internet to view local files stored on your computer.

Trouble? If you start your browser and are not connected to the Internet, you might get a warning message. Click the OK button to ignore the message and continue.

▶ 3. After your browser loads its home page, open the **dave.htm** file from the tutorial.01\tutorial folder.

Trouble? If you're not sure how to open a local file with your browser, check for an Open or Open File command under the browser's File menu. If you are still having problems accessing the dave.htm file, talk to your instructor or technical resource person.

Your browser displays the Web page shown in Figure 1-8. Note that the page title appears in the browser's title bar; and if your browser supports tabs, it also appears in the tab title. The page itself is empty because you have not yet added any content to the body element.

Viewing a page title in the browser window | **Figure 1-8**

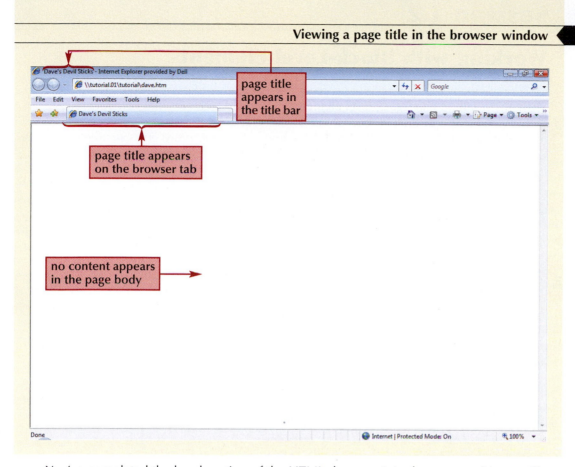

You've completed the head section of the HTML document. In the next session, you'll define the elements that are displayed in the body section. For now, you can close your files and Web browser if you want to take a break before starting the next session.

Session 1.1 Quick Check | Review

1. What is a hypertext document?
2. What is a Web server? What is a Web browser? Describe how they work together.
3. How do HTML documents differ from documents created with a word processor such as Word or WordPerfect?
4. What is a deprecated feature?
5. What element do you use to mark the beginning and end of an HTML document?
6. What code would you enter in your document to set the page title to "Technical Support"? Where would you enter this code?
7. Specify the code needed to add the comment "Page Updated on 4/15/2011" to an HTML file.
8. What error was made in the following HTML code?:

```
<head>
   <title>Customer Comments Form
   </head>
</title>
```

Session 1.2

Working with Block-Level Elements

You're now ready to begin entering content into the body of Dave's Web page. The first elements you'll add are **block-level elements**, which are elements that contain content that is viewed as a distinct block within the Web page. When rendered visually, block-level elements start on a new line in the document. Paragraphs are one example of a block-level element. To explore block-level and other HTML elements, a demo page has been prepared for you.

To open the HTML Tags demo page:

▶ 1. Use your browser to open the **demo_html.htm** file from the tutorial.01\demo folder.

▶ 2. If your browser prompts you to allow code on the Web page to be run, click the **OK** button.

Working with Headings

The first block-level elements you'll explore are heading elements. **Heading elements** are elements that contain the text of main headings on the Web page. They are often used for introducing new topics or dividing the page into topical sections. The syntax to mark a heading element is

```
<hn>content</hn>
```

where *n* is an integer from 1 to 6. Content marked with the <h1> tag is considered a major heading and is usually displayed in large bold text. Content marked with <h2> down to <h6> tags is used for subheadings and is usually displayed in progressively smaller bold text. To see how these headings appear on your computer, use the demo page.

Reference Window | **Marking Block-Level Elements**

- To mark a heading, enter
  ```
  <hn>content</hn>
  ```
  where *n* is an integer from 1 to 6 and *content* is the text of heading.
- To mark a paragraph, enter
  ```
  <p>content</p>
  ```
- To mark a block quote, enter
  ```
  <blockquote>content</blockquote>
  ```
- To mark a generic block-level element, enter
  ```
  <div>content</div>
  ```

To view heading elements:

▶ 1. Click in the blue box on the bottom left of the demo page, type **<h1>Dave's Devil Sticks</h1>** and then press the **Enter** key to go to a new line.

▶ 2. Type **<h2>Auburn, ME 04210</h2>**.

3. Click the **Preview Code** button located below the blue code window. Your browser displays a preview of how this code would appear in your Web browser (see Figure 1-9).

Marking an h1 and h2 element | Figure 1-9

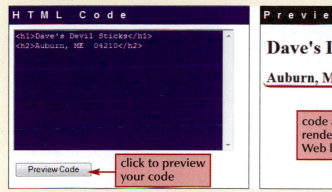
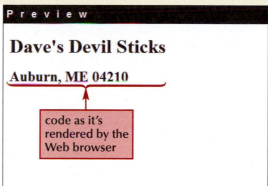

Trouble? If you are using a browser other than Internet Explorer 7.0 running on Windows Vista, your screen might look slightly different from that shown in Figure 1-9.

4. To see how an h3 heading would look, change the opening and closing tags for the store's city and state information from <h2> and </h2> to **<h3>** and **</h3>**. Click the **Preview Code** button again.

Your browser renders the code again, this time with the city and state information displayed in a smaller font. If you continued to change the heading element from h2 down to h6, you would see the text in the Preview box get progressively smaller.

It's important not to treat markup tags as simply a way of formatting the Web page. The h1 through h6 elements are used to identify headings, but the exact appearance of these headings depends on the browser and the device being used. Remember that the headings might not even be displayed visually. A browser that renders content aurally might convey an h1 heading using increased volume preceded by an extended pause.

Now that you've seen how to mark page headings, you can add some to Dave's Web page. Dave has three headings he wants to add to his document. The first is an h1 heading that will contain the company's name. The other two are h2 headings that preface two different sections of the document: one titled "Who Am I?" and the other titled "My Products."

To add headings to Dave's document:

1. Return to the **dave.htm** file in your text editor.

2. Between the opening and closing <body> tags, insert the following code:

```
<h1>Dave's Devil Sticks</h1>
<h2>Who Am I?</h2>
<h2>My Products</h2>
```

Indent your code to make it easy to read, as shown in Figure 1-10.

Figure 1-10 ▷ **Adding <h1> and <h2> markup tags**

```
<body>
    <h1>Dave's Devil Sticks</h1>
    <h2>Who Am I?</h2>
    <h2>My Products</h2>
</body>
```

▶ 3. Save your changes to the file, and then reload or refresh the **dave.htm** file in your Web browser. Figure 1-11 shows the revised Web page.

Figure 1-11 ▷ **Headings on the Web page**

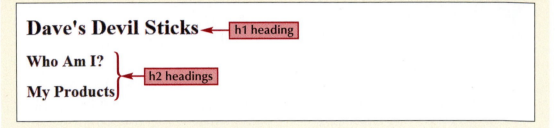

The next block-level elements you'll add are paragraphs about Dave's company and its wares.

Marking Paragraph Elements

As you saw earlier, you can mark a paragraph element using the <p> tag

`<p>content</p>`

where *content* is the content of the paragraph. When rendered in a browser, paragraphs are started on a new line. In older HTML code, you might occasionally see paragraphs marked with only the opening <p> tag but without a closing tag. In those situations, the <p> tag marks the start of each new paragraph. While this convention is still accepted by many browsers, it does violate HTML's syntax rules; if you want XHTML-compliant code, you must include the closing tags.

To add two paragraphs to Dave's Web page:

▶ 1. Return to the **dave.htm** file in your text editor.

▶ 2. Directly below the Who Am I? h2 heading, insert a new line, and then type the following code, as shown in Figure 1-12:

```
<p>Welcome to Dave's Devil Sticks. If you are looking for juggling
balls, hacky sacks, pins, unicycles, or magic hats, you've come
to the wrong place; but if you're looking for high-quality,
hand-crafted devil and flower sticks, this is the site for you.
I've been designing and building sticks for the past 20 years,
and I know that my sticks are the best of their kind.</p>

<p>Every set is checked and tested before being shipped out to
   assure perfect quality. I take pride in every one of my sticks
   and I want my customers to feel that same pride.</p>
```

Marking paragraph elements | Figure 1-12

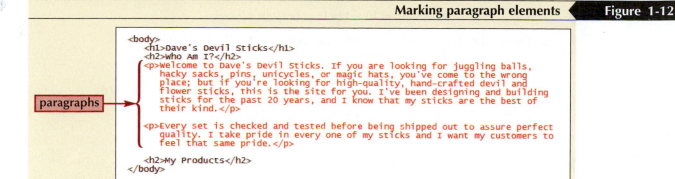

```
<body>
  <h1>Dave's Devil Sticks</h1>
  <h2>Who Am I?</h2>
  <p>Welcome to Dave's Devil Sticks. If you are looking for juggling balls,
     hacky sacks, pins, unicycles, or magic hats, you've come to the wrong
     place; but if you're looking for high-quality, hand-crafted devil and
     flower sticks, this is the site for you. I've been designing and building
     sticks for the past 20 years, and I know that my sticks are the best of
     their kind.</p>

  <p>Every set is checked and tested before being shipped out to assure perfect
     quality. I take pride in every one of my sticks and I want my customers to
     feel that same pride.</p>

  <h2>My Products</h2>
</body>
```

Trouble? Don't worry if your lines do not wrap at the same locations shown in Figure 1-12. As you'll see shortly, line wrap in the HTML code does not affect how the page is rendered by the browser.

3. Save your changes to the file and then refresh the **dave.htm** file in your Web browser. Figure 1-13 shows the new paragraphs added to the Web page.

Paragraphs added to Dave's Web page | Figure 1-13

Dave's Devil Sticks

Who Am I?

Welcome to Dave's Devil Sticks. If you are looking for juggling balls, hacky sacks, pins, unicycles, or magic hats, you've come to the wrong place; but if you're looking for high-quality, hand-crafted devil and flower sticks, this is the site for you. I've been designing and building sticks for the past 20 years, and I know that my sticks are the best of their kind.

Every set is checked and tested before being shipped out to assure perfect quality. I take pride in every one of my sticks and I want my customers to feel that same pride.

My Products

White Space and HTML

If you compare the paragraph text from the HTML code in Figure 1-12 to the way it's rendered on the Web page in Figure 1-13, you'll notice that the line returns in the code are not reflected in the Web page. When the browser renders HTML code, it ignores the presence of white space within the HTML text file. **White space** consists of blank spaces, tabs, and line breaks. As far as the browser is concerned, there is no difference between a blank space, a tab, or a line break. To explore this issue further, you'll experiment with the HTML demo page.

To explore how white space is treated by the Web browser:

▶ 1. Return to the **demo_html.htm** file in your Web browser.

▶ 2. Delete the HTML code in the left box and replace it with the following:

```
<p>Dave's Devil Sticks</p>

<p>Dave's                Devil                Sticks</p>

<p>Dave's
    Devil
    Sticks</p>
```

▶ 3. Click the **Preview Code** button. Figure 1-14 shows how the browser renders the three paragraphs of code.

Figure 1-14 | **Viewing the effects of white space on HTML code**

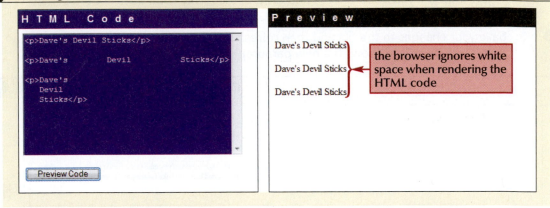

Each paragraph is rendered exactly the same by the browser. Notice that even adding blank spaces within the paragraph does not change the appearance of the text. This is because the browser ignores extra blank spaces. Consequently, you are free to use white space however you wish as you lay out the HTML code to make it easier for you to read—without impacting the appearance of the Web page.

Tip

To force the browser to retain the extra blank spaces, tabs, and line breaks from your HTML code, enclose the white space within a set of opening and closing <pre> tags.

Marking a Block Quote

The next element that Dave wants you to enter into his document is a quote from a satisfied customer. Dave wants the quote, shown earlier in Figure 1-4, to be indented from the surrounding paragraphs to make it stand out more. However, as you just saw, any indenting you do in the HTML file will be ignored by the browser. So how do you achieve this effect? Remember that HTML is used to mark up document content, and so you need a markup tag that identifies quoted material. The syntax for marking an extended quote is

```
<blockquote>content</blockquote>
```

where *content* is the text of the quote. Most browsers will by default indent block quotes on the Web page, so you'll still achieve the visual effect that Dave wants. Note that some browsers might display block quotes differently, and the only way to ensure that block quotes are always indented is by using styles. You'll explore how to apply styles shortly.

To create a block quote:

▶ **1.** Return to the **dave.htm** file in your text editor.

▶ **2.** At the end of the first paragraph, directly *before* the closing </p> tag, insert a space and then type the following text:

```
Don't take my word for it; read the following testimonial:
```

▶ **3.** Between the closing </p> tag from the first paragraph and the opening <p> tag of the second paragraph, insert the following code, as shown in Figure 1-15:

```
<blockquote>

   <p>I'm more than happy to recommend Dave Vinet's products. I came
   upon his work 10 years ago and was immediately impressed by his
   craftsmanship. I've been using his sticks in my shows ever since.
   They're durable, well-balanced, and attractive props and are
   the perfect complement to my performances. Thanks Dave!</p>

   <p>Thomas Gage, lead performer at Circus England</p>

</blockquote>
```

Marking a block quote   **Figure 1-15**

```
<p>Welcome to Dave's Devil Sticks. If you are looking for juggling balls,
   hacky sacks, pins, unicycles, or magic hats, you've come to the wrong
   place; but if you're looking for high-quality, hand-crafted devil and
   flower sticks, this is the site for you. I've been designing and building
   sticks for the past 20 years, and I know that my sticks are the best of
   their kind. Don't take my word for it; read the following testimonial:</p>

<blockquote>
   <p>I'm more than happy to recommend Dave Vinet's products. I came upon his
      work 10 years ago and was immediately impressed by his craftsmanship.
      I've been using his sticks in my shows ever since. They're durable,
      well-balanced, and attractive props and are the perfect complement to
      my performances. Thanks Dave!</p>

   <p>Thomas Gage, lead performer at Circus England</p>
</blockquote>

<p>Every set is checked and tested before being shipped out to assure perfect
   quality. I take pride in every one of my sticks and I want my customers to
   feel that same pride.</p>
```

block quote ◀

▶ **4.** Save your changes to the file, and then reload **dave.htm** in your Web browser. Figure 1-16 shows the revised page with the quoted material.

Dave's Web page with customer comment   **Figure 1-16**

Dave's Devil Sticks

Who Am I?

Welcome to Dave's Devil Sticks. If you are looking for juggling balls, hacky sacks, pins, unicycles, or magic hats, you've come to the wrong place; but if you're looking for high-quality, hand-crafted devil and flower sticks, this is the site for you. I've been designing and building sticks for the past 20 years, and I know that my sticks are the best of their kind. Don't take my word for it; read the following testimonial:

> I'm more than happy to recommend Dave Vinet's products. I came upon his work 10 years ago and was immediately impressed by his craftsmanship. I've been using his sticks in my shows ever since. They're durable, well-balanced, and attractive props and are the perfect complement to my performances. Thanks Dave!
>
> Thomas Gage, lead performer at Circus England

block quote ◀

Every set is checked and tested before being shipped out to assure perfect quality. I take pride in every one of my sticks and I want my customers to feel that same pride.

Note that the customer quote also included two paragraph elements nested within the blockquote element. The indentation applied by the browser to the block quote was also applied to any content within that element, so those paragraphs were indented even though browsers do not indent paragraphs by default.

Marking a List

Dave has a list of products that he wants to display on his Web page. This information is presented on his flyer as a bulleted list. He wants something similar on the Web site. HTML supports three kinds of lists: ordered, unordered, and definition.

Ordered Lists

Use an **ordered list** for items that must appear in a numeric order. The beginning of an ordered list is marked by the <ol> (ordered list) tag. Each item within that ordered list is subsequently marked using the <li> (list item) tag. The syntax of an ordered list is therefore

```
<ol>
    <li>item1</li>
    <li>item2</li>
...
</ol>
```

where *item1*, *item2*, and so forth are the items in the list. To explore creating an ordered list, return to the HTML demo page.

To create an ordered list:

1. Return to the **demo_html.htm** file in your Web browser.

2. Delete the HTML code in the left box and replace it with the following:

   ```
   <ol>
       <li>First Item</li>
       <li>Second Item</li>
       <li>Third Item</li>
   </ol>
   ```

3. Click the **Preview Code** button. Figure 1-17 shows how the browser renders the ordered list contents.

Figure 1-17 ▶ **Viewing an ordered list**

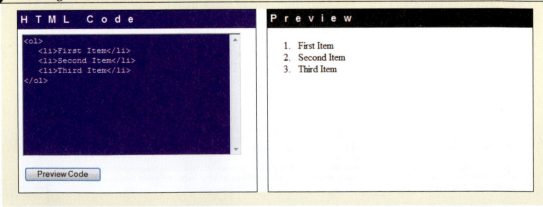

By default, entries in an ordered list are numbered, with the numbers supplied automatically by the browser.

Unordered Lists

To mark a list in which the items do not need to occur in any special order, create an **unordered list**. The structure of ordered and unordered lists is the same, except that the list contents are contained with a set of <ul> (unordered list) tags:

```
<ul>
    <li>item1</li>
    <li>item2</li>
...
</ul>
```

Try creating an unordered list with the demo page.

To create an unordered list:

1. Delete the HTML code in the left box and replace it with the following:

```
<ul>
    <li>Basic Stick</li>
    <li>Flower Stick</li>
    <li>Master Stick</li>
    <li>Glow Stick</li>
</ul>
```

2. Click the **Preview Code** button. Figure 1-18 shows how the browser renders the unordered list.

Viewing an unordered list — **Figure 1-18**

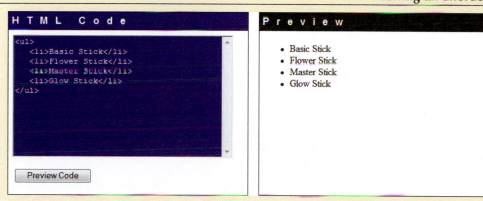

Trouble? On some browsers, the list appears with diamond shapes rather than circular bullets.

By default, unordered lists appear as bulleted lists. The exact bullet marker depends on the browser. Most browsers use a filled-in circle.

Marking Lists

- To mark an ordered list, enter

```
<ol>
    <li>item1</li>
    <li>item2</li>
...
</ol>
```

  where *item1*, *item2*, and so forth are the items in the list.
- To mark an unordered list, use

```
<ul>
    <li>item1</li>
    <li>item2</li>
...
</ul>
```

- To mark a definition list, use

```
<dl>
    <dt>term1</dt>
    <dd>description1</dd>
    <dt>term2</dt>
    <dd>description2a</dd>
    <dd>description2b</dd>
...
</dl>
```

  where *term1*, *term2*, etc. are the terms in the list and *description1*, *description2a*, *description2b*, etc. are the descriptions associated with each term.

Nesting Lists

You can place one list inside of another to create several levels of list items. The top level of the nested list contains the major items, with each sublevel containing items of lesser importance. Most browsers differentiate the various levels by using a different list symbol. Use the demo page to see how this works with unordered lists.

To create an unordered list:

1. Click at the end of the <li>Basic Stick</li> line, and then press the **Enter** key to insert a new blank line.

2. Insert the following code between the <li>Basic Stick</li> and <li>Flower Stick</li> lines:

```
<ul>
    <li>Red</li>
    <li>Blue</li>
    <li>Green</li>
</ul>
```

3. Click the **Preview Code** button. Figure 1-19 shows the result of creating a nested list.

Viewing a nested list | **Figure 1-19**

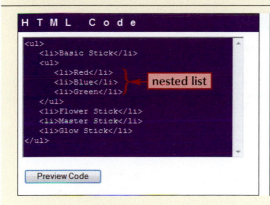
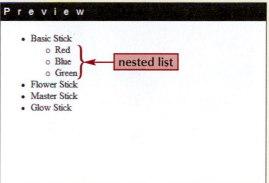

Trouble? Depending on your browser, the sublist of basic stick colors might appear with solid bullets rather than open circles.

The lower level of items is displayed using an open circle as the list bullet and indented on the page. Once again, the exact choice of formatting a nested list is left to the browser at this point. As you continue your study of HTML you'll learn how to specify the appearance of nested lists using styles.

Definition Lists

A third type of list is the **definition list**, which contains a list of terms, each followed by the term's description. The syntax for creating a definition list is

```
<dl>
    <dt>term1</dt>
    <dd>description1</dd>
    <dt>term2</dt>
    <dd>description2a</dd>
    <dd>description2b</dd>
...
</dl>
```

where *term1*, *term2*, etc. are the terms in the list and *description1*, *description2a*, *description2b*, etc. are the descriptions associated with each term. Note that definition lists must follow a specified order, with each dt (definition term) element followed by one or more dd (definition description) elements.

To create a definition list:

▶ 1. Replace the code in the left box of the HTML demo page with:

```
<dl>
    <dt>Basic Stick</dt>
    <dd>Easiest stick to learn</dd>
    <dt>Flower Stick</dt>
    <dd>A graceful stick with tassels</dd>
    <dt>Master Stick</dt>
    <dd>Our most popular stick</dd>
</dl>
```

▶ 2. Click the **Preview Code** button. Figure 1-20 shows the appearance of the definition list in the browser.

Figure 1-20 ▶ **Viewing a definition list**

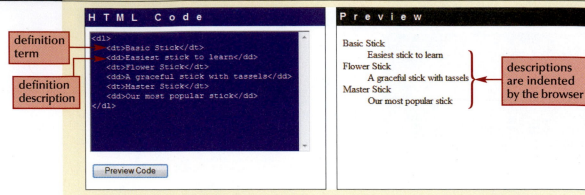

The demo page shows each term followed by a description that is placed in a new block below the term and indented on the page. If you had included multiple dd elements, each description would have been contained within its own block and indented.

Now that you've experimented with the three types of HTML lists, you'll add an unordered list of products to Dave's Web page. By default, the product names will appear as a bulleted list.

To add an unordered list to Dave's Web page:

▶ **1.** Return to the **dave.htm** file in your text editor.

▶ **2.** Directly below the <h2>My Products</h2> heading, insert the following code, as shown in Figure 1-21:

```
<ul>
   <li>Basic Stick</li>
   <li>Flower Stick</li>
   <li>Master Stick</li>
   <li>Glow Stick</li>
</ul>
```

Figure 1-21 ▶ **Adding an unordered list**

```
<h2>My Products</h2>
<ul>
   <li>Basic Stick</li>
   <li>Flower Stick</li>
   <li>Master Stick</li>
   <li>Glow Stick</li>
</ul>
</body>
```

▶ **3.** Save your changes to the file, and then refresh the **dave.htm** file in your Web browser. As shown in Figure 1-22, the list of products appears as a bulleted list at the bottom of the page.

Product list on Dave's Web page | Figure 1-22

Dave's Devil Sticks

Who Am I?

Welcome to Dave's Devil Sticks. If you are looking for juggling balls, hacky sacks, pins, unicycles, or magic hats, you've come to the wrong place; but if you're looking for high-quality, hand-crafted devil and flower sticks, this is the site for you. I've been designing and building sticks for the past 20 years, and I know that my sticks are the best of their kind. Don't take my word for it; read the following testimonial:

> I'm more than happy to recommend Dave Vinet's products. I came upon his work 10 years ago and was immediately impressed by his craftsmanship. I've been using his sticks in my shows ever since. They're durable, well-balanced, and attractive props and are the perfect complement to my performances. Thanks Dave!

> Thomas Gage, lead performer at Circus England

Every set is checked and tested before being shipped out to assure perfect quality. I take pride in every one of my sticks and I want my customers to feel that same pride.

My Products

- Basic Stick
- Flower Stick
- Master Stick
- Glow Stick

bulleted list of products

Exploring Other Block-Level Elements

HTML supports several other block-level elements you'll find useful. Dave wants to display the company's address at the bottom of the body of his page. Contact information like addresses can be marked using the <address> tag

```
<address>content</address>
```

where *content* is the contact information. Most browsers render addresses in italics, and some also indent or right-justify addresses. You'll use the address element to display the address of Dave's company.

To add an address to the bottom of Dave's Web page:

1. Return to the **dave.htm** file in your text editor.

2. Directly above the </body> tag, insert the following code, as shown in Figure 1-23:

```
<address>Dave's Devil Sticks
        541 West Highland Dr.
        Auburn, ME 04210
        (207) 555 - 9001
</address>
```

Adding an address element | Figure 1-23

```
<address>Dave's Devil Sticks
        541 West Highland Dr.
        Auburn, ME 04210
        (207) 555 - 9001
</address>
</body>

</html>
```

3. Save your changes to the file, and then refresh **dave.htm** in your Web browser. Figure 1-24 shows the revised page with the address text.

Figure 1-24 | Address text on Dave's Web page

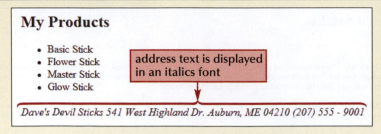

The address text appears in italics at the bottom of the page. Note that the company name, street address, city, state, and phone number all appear to run together. Remember that the browser ignores the occurrence of line breaks, tabs, and other white space in your text document. In the next session, you'll learn how to make this text more readable. For now, you'll leave the address text as it is.

At this point, you're done adding block-level elements to Dave's Web page. Figure 1-25 summarizes the properties and uses of HTML's block-level elements, including information on some block-level elements you did not add to Dave's document.

Figure 1-25 | Block-level elements

Block-Level Element	Marks	Usual Visual Appearance
`<address> ... </address>`	Contact information	*Italicized text*
`<blockquote> ... </blockquote>`	An extended quotation	Plain text indented from the left and right
`<center> ... </center>`	Text horizontally centered with the block (**deprecated**)	Plain text, centered
`<dd> ... </dd>`	A definition description	Plain text
`<dir> ... </dir>`	A multicolumn directory list (**deprecated**)	Plain text
`<div> ... </div>`	A generic block-level element	Plain text
`<dl> ... </dl>`	A definition list	Plain text
`<dt> ... </dt>`	A definition term from a definition list	Plain text
`<hn> ... </hn>`	A heading where n is a value from 1 to 6 with h1 as the most prominent heading and h6 the least prominent	**Boldfaced text of various font sizes**
`<li> ... </li>`	A list item from an ordered or unordered list	Bulleted or numbered text
`<menu> ... </menu>`	A single column menu list (**deprecated**)	Plain text
`<ol> ... </ol>`	An ordered list	Plain text
`<p> ... </p>`	A paragraph	Plain text
`<pre> ... </pre>`	Preformatted text, retaining all white space and special characters	`Fixed width text`
`<ul> ... </ul>`	An unordered list	Plain text

Working with Inline Elements

Block-level elements place their content starting on a new line within the page. Another type of element is an **inline element**, which marks a section of text within a block-level element. If you think of a block-level element as a paragraph, an inline element is like a phrase or a collection of characters within that paragraph. Inline elements do not start out on a new line or block, but instead flow "in-line" with the rest of the characters in the block.

Character Formatting Elements

Inline elements are often used to format characters and words. For example, you can use an inline element to make a name or title appear in **boldface** letters or *italics*. Inline elements used in this fashion are referred to as **character formatting elements**. Figure 1-26 describes some of the inline elements supported by HTML.

Inline elements ▸ **Figure 1-26**

Inline Element	Marks	Usual Visual Appearance
`<abbr> ... </abbr>`	An abbreviation	Plain text
`<acronym> .. </acronym>`	An acronym	Plain text
`<b> ... </b>`	Boldfaced text	**Boldfaced text**
`<big> ... </big>`	Big text	Larger text
`<cite> ... </cite>`	A citation	*Italicized text*
`<code> ... </code>`	Program code	`Fixed width text`
`<del> ... </del>`	Deleted text	~~Strikethrough text~~
`<dfn> ... </dfn>`	A definition term	*Italicized text*
`<em> ... </em>`	Emphasized content	*Italicized text*
`<i> ... </i>`	Italicized text	*Italicized text*
`<ins> ... </ins>`	Inserted text	Underlined text
`<kbd> ... </kbd>`	Keyboard-style text	`Fixed width text`
`<q> ... </q>`	Quoted text	"Quoted text"
`<s> ... </s>`	Strikethrough text (**Deprecated**)	~~Strikethrough text~~
`<samp> ... </samp>`	Sample computer code	`Fixed width text`
`<small> ... </small>`	Small text	Smaller text
`<span> ... </span>`	A generic inline element	Plain text
`<strike> ... </strike>`	Strikethrough text (**Deprecated**)	~~Strikethrough text~~
`<strong> ... </strong>`	Strongly emphasized content	**Boldfaced text**
`<sub> ... </sub>`	Subscripted text	Subscripted text
`<sup> ... </sup>`	Superscripted text	Superscripted text
`<tt> ... </tt>`	Teletype text	`Fixed width text`
`<u> ... </u>`	Underlined text (**Deprecated**)	Underlined text
`<var> ... </var>`	Programming variables	*Italicized text*

To see how to use inline elements in conjunction with block-level elements, you'll return to the HTML demo page.

To explore the use of inline elements:

▶ **1.** Return to the **demo_html.htm** file in your Web browser.

▶ **2.** In the left box, enter the HTML code:

```
<p>Welcome to Dave's Devil Sticks, owned and operated by David
Vinet.</p>
```

▶ **3.** Click the **Preview Code** button to display this paragraph in the Preview box.

To mark "Dave's Devil Sticks" as boldface text, you can enclose that phrase within a set of <b> tags.

▶ **4.** Insert a **<b>** tag directly before the word "Dave's" in the box on the left. Insert the closing **</b>** tag directly after the word "Sticks." Click the **Preview Code** button to confirm that "Dave's Devil Sticks" is now displayed in bold.

You can use the <i> tag to mark italicized text. Try this now by enclosing "David Vinet" within a set of <i> tags.

▶ **5.** Insert an **<i>** tag directly before the word "David" and insert the closing **</i>** tag directly after "Vinet". Click the **Preview Code** button to view the revised code. Figure 1-27 shows the result of applying the <b> and <i> tags to the paragraph text.

Figure 1-27 ▶ **Using the <b> and <i> tags**

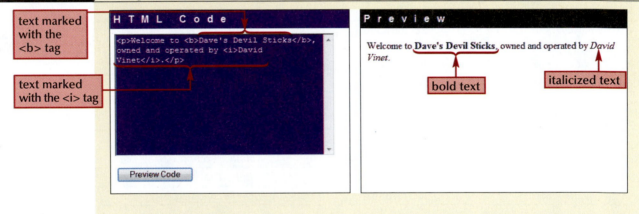

▶ **6.** Close the HTML demo page.

You can nest inline elements to mark text with more than one character-formatting element. The code

```
<p>Welcome to <b><i>Dave's Devil Sticks</i></b>.</p>
```

displays "Dave's Devil Sticks" in a ***bold italic*** font.

Dave wants to use the <b> and <i> tags in several locations in his document. He wants to display the name of his company and the names of all of his devil stick products in bold. He would also like to display the name of the juggling troupe, *Circus England*, in italics. Make these changes to his document now.

Marking Inline Elements

- To mark boldface text, enter
  `<b>`*content*`</b>`
  where *content* is the text to be displayed in boldface.
- To mark italicized text, use
  `<i>`*content*`</i>`
- To mark text with a generic inline element, use
  `<span>`*content*`</span>`

To mark boldface and italicized text:

▶ **1.** Return to the **dave.htm** file in your text editor.

▶ **2.** Go to the first paragraph of the body section and enclose the text "Dave's Devil Sticks" within a set of opening and closing <b> tags.

▶ **3.** Go to the second paragraph within the blockquote element and enclose the text "Circus England" within a set of opening and closing <i> tags.

▶ **4.** Go to the unordered list and enclose each product item within a set of opening and closing <b> tags. Nest the <b> tags within the <li> tags. Figure 1-28 highlights the revised code of Dave's document.

Marking bold and italicized text ◀ **Figure 1-28**

```
<body>
   <h1>Dave's Devil Sticks</h1>
   <h2>Who Am I?</h2>
   <p>Welcome to <b>Dave's Devil Sticks</b>. If you are looking for juggling balls,
      hacky sacks, pins, unicycles, or magic hats, you've come to the wrong
      place; but if you're looking for high-quality, hand-crafted devil and
      flower sticks, this is the site for you. I've been designing and building
      sticks for the past 20 years, and I know that my sticks are the best of
      their kind. Don't take my word for it; read the following testimonial:</p>

   <blockquote>
      <p>I'm more than happy to recommend Dave Vinet's products. I came upon his
         work 10 years ago and was immediately impressed by his craftsmanship.
         I've been using his sticks in my shows ever since. They're durable,
         well-balanced, and attractive props and are the perfect complement to
         my performances. Thanks Dave!</p>

      <p>Thomas Gage, lead performer at <i>Circus England</i></p>
   </blockquote>

   <p>Every set is checked and tested before being shipped out to assure perfect
      quality. I take pride in every one of my sticks and I want my customers to
      feel that same pride.</p>

   <h2>My Products</h2>
   <ul>
      <li><b>Basic Stick</b></li>
      <li><b>Flower Stick</b></li>
      <li><b>Master Stick</b></li>
      <li><b>Glow Stick</b></li>
   </ul>

   <address>Dave's Devil Sticks
            541 West Highland Dr.
            Auburn, ME 04210
            (207) 555 - 9001
   </address>
</body>
```

▶ **5.** Save your changes to the file.

▶ **6.** Refresh the **dave.htm** file in your Web browser. Figure 1-29 shows the revised appearance of the Web page.

Figure 1-29 **Dave's revised Web page**

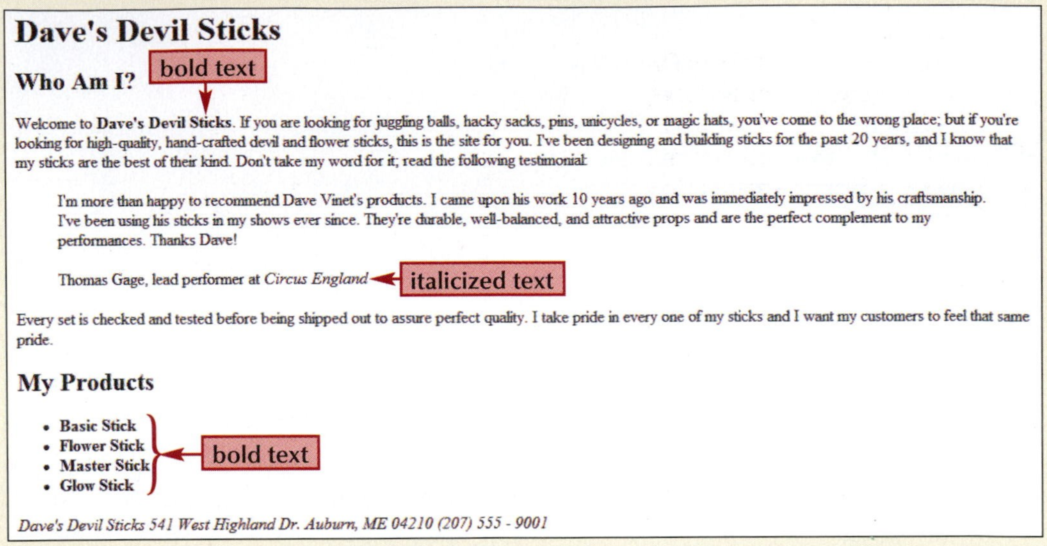

7. If you want to take a break before starting the next session, you can close your browser and any open files now.

Using the Generic Elements: div and span

Most of the block-level and inline elements you've examined have a specific meaning or purpose in your document. Sometimes you will want an element that represents a text block or a string of inline text without it having any other meaning. HTML supports two types of generic elements: div and span. The div element is used to mark general block-level content and has the syntax

```
<div>content</div>
```

The span element, used to mark general inline content, has the syntax

```
<span>content</span>
```

Browsers recognize both elements but do not assign any default format to content marked with those elements. Web authors like using the div and span elements because they know they can completely control the appearance of the content through the use of styles. This is not the case with elements such as addresses or headings, which have default formats assigned to them by the Web browser.

Logical Elements vs. Physical Elements | InSight

As you learn more HTML, you'll notice some overlap in how certain elements are displayed by the browser. To display italicized text, you could use the <dfn>, <em>, <i>, or <var> tags, or if you want to italicize an entire block of text, you could use the <address> tag. It's important to distinguish between how a browser displays an element and the element's purpose in the document. Page elements can be organized into two types: logical elements and physical elements. A logical element, marked with tags like <cite> or <code>, describes the nature of the enclosed content but not necessarily how that content should appear. A physical element, on the other hand, marked with tags like <b> or <i>, describes how content should appear but doesn't indicate the content's nature.

While it can be tempting to use logical and physical elements interchangeably, your HTML code benefits in several ways when you respect the distinction. For one, different browsers can and do display logical elements differently. For example, both Netscape's browser and Internet Explorer display text marked with the <cite> tag in italics, but the text-based browser Lynx displays the citation text using a fixed width font. An aural browser that doesn't render pages visually might increase the volume when it encounters cited text. In addition, Web programmers can also use logical elements to extract information from a page. For example, a program could automatically generate a bibliography from all of the citations listed within a Web site.

In general, you should use a logical element that accurately describes the enclosed content whenever possible, letting the browser determine the appearance based on its function, and use physical elements only for general content.

You're finished working with block-level elements and inline elements. In the next session you'll learn how to add images to the document as well as how to use styles to control the appearance of your Web pages.

Session 1.2 Quick Check | Review

1. What is the difference between a block-level element and an inline element?
2. If you want to add an extra blank line between paragraphs on your Web page, why can't you simply add an extra blank line to the HTML file?
3. Specify the code to mark the main heading on your Web page.
4. Specify the tag to mark an extended quotation. How would that quotation be rendered in most visual browsers?
5. Specify the code you would use to display the seasons of the year (Winter, Spring, Summer, and Fall) as an unordered list.
6. The following is a dialog from Shakespeare's *Hamlet*. Indicate how you would use a definition list to mark up this text, distinguishing between the speaker and the lines spoken.

    HAMLET

    There's ne'er a villain dwelling in all Denmark; but he's an arrant knave.

    HORATIO

    There needs no ghost, my lord, come from the grave to tell us this.
7. What code would you enter to display the following text as a paragraph in your Web page? Include both the block-level and inline element tags.

    Hamlet, a play by William Shakespeare.
8. What are the two generic page elements?

Session 1.3

Using Element Attributes

So far you've used markup tags only to create Dave's Web page. However, many markup tags contain **attributes** that control the use, behavior, and in some cases the appearance of elements in the document. You apply an attribute to an element by adding it to the element's markup tag using the syntax

```
<element attribute1="value1" attribute2="value2" ...>content</element>
```

where *attribute1*, *attribute2*, etc. are the names of attributes associated with the element and *value1*, *value2*, etc. are the values of those attributes. You can list attributes in any order, but you must separate them from one another with white space.

One attribute that is associated with most elements is the id attribute, which uniquely identifies the element in the Web page. The following code assigns the id value of "mainhead" to the h1 heading "Dave's Devil Sticks," distinguishing it from other h1 headings that might exist in the document:

```
<h1 id="mainhead">Dave's Devil Sticks</h1>
```

You'll learn more about the id attribute in the next tutorial. For a list of attributes associated with each element, you can also refer to the appendices.

Tip

Attribute names should be entered in lowercase letters to be completely compliant with the syntax rules of XHTML. Attribute values must be enclosed within single or double quotation marks.

Reference Window | **Adding an Attribute to an Element**

- To add an element attribute, enter
  ```
  <element attribute1="value1" attribute2="value2" ...>content
  </element>
  ```
  where *attribute1*, *attribute2*, etc. are the names of attributes associated with the element and *value1*, *value2*, etc. are the values of those attributes.

The Style Attribute

Another important attribute is the style attribute. As you've seen, an element's appearance on the Web page is determined by the browser. If you want to change how the browser displays an element, you can use the style attribute. The syntax of the style attribute is

```
<element style="rules" ...>content</element>
```

where *rules* is a set of style rules. Style rules are entered by specifying a style name followed by a colon and then a style value. You can have multiple style rules with each style name/value pair, separated from each other by a semicolon. The general form of the style attribute is therefore

```
style="name1:value1; name2:value2; ..."
```

where *name1*, *name2*, etc. are style names and *value1*, *value2* and so forth are the values of those styles.

As you proceed in your study of HTML you'll learn more about styles and how to apply them. For now you'll focus only on a few basic ones. The first is a style to align text. As you may have noticed, Web page text is usually aligned with the page's left margin. To choose a different alignment, you can apply the following text-align style to the element

```
style="text-align: alignment"
```

where *alignment* is left, right, center, or justify. For example, to center an h1 heading, you would enter the following markup tag:

```
<h1 style="text-align: center"> ... </h1>
```

A second style you'll explore defines the text color used in an element. Most browsers display text in a black font. To apply a different text color, use

```
style="color: color"
```

where *color* is a color name such as red, blue, green, and so forth. Applying the following attribute to an h1 heading causes the browser to render the heading text in a red font:

```
<h1 style="color: red"> ... </h1>
```

You can both center the text and change its font color to red by combining the two styles in one style attribute:

```
<h1 style="text-align: center; color: red"> ... </h1>
```

Applying the Style Attribute | Reference Window

- To add the style attribute, in the opening tag enter
  ```
  style="name1:value1; name2:value2; ..."
  ```
  where *name1*, *name2*, etc. are style names and *value1*, *value2* and so forth are the values of those styles.
- To center text horizontally, use
  ```
  style="text-align: alignment"
  ```
  where *alignment* is left, right, center, or justify.
- To set the font color, use
  ```
  style="color: color"
  ```
  where *color* is a color name.

To explore how to apply these two styles to a page element, you'll return to the HTML demo page.

To explore the style attribute:

1. Return to the **demo_html.htm** file in your Web browser.

2. Enter the following code in the left box, and then click the **Preview Code** button:

   ```
   <h1>Dave's Devil Sticks</h1>
   ```

   The demo page displays Dave's Devil Sticks as an h1 heading in the Preview box. Now you'll change the font color to red and center this heading in the box.

3. Within the opening <h1> tag, insert a space after "h1," and then type the attribute

   `style="text-align: center; color: red"`

4. Click the **Preview Code** button. As shown in Figure 1-30, the h1 heading is now centered and displayed in a red font.

Figure 1-30 ▶ **Applying styles to an element**

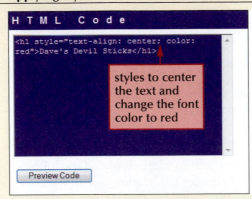

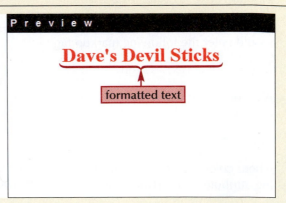

5. Continue exploring the text-align and color styles by creating headings right-aligned or centered in a blue, green, and gray-colored text.

6. Close the HTML demo page when you are finished exploring these two styles.

Dave has had a chance to examine your progress on his Web page and suggests that you center the address text at the bottom of the page. Now that you've explored the uses of the style attribute, you can make this change to his document.

To apply a style to the address element:

1. Return to the **dave.htm** file in your text editor.

2. Locate the address element at the bottom of the file and insert the following style attribute, as shown in Figure 1-31:

   `style="text-align: center"`

Figure 1-31 ▶ **Apply the text-align style to an address**

```
<address style="text-align: center">Dave's Devil Sticks
         541 West Highland Dr.
         Auburn, ME 04210
         (207) 555 - 9001
</address>
</body>

</html>
```

3. Save your changes to the file and refresh the **dave.htm** file in your Web browser. Verify that the address text is centered horizontally at the bottom of the page.

Presentational Attributes

You learned in the first session that early versions of HTML were used mostly by scientists and researchers. HTML was intended to be a language that described the structure but not necessarily the appearance of documents. Scientists and researchers didn't need flashy graphics, various fonts, or even much color on a page. The earliest Web pages weren't fancy and did not require much from the browsers that displayed them. This changed as the Web became more popular and attracted the attention of graphic designers and artists.

One way that HTML changed to accommodate this new class of users was to introduce **presentational attributes**, which are attributes that specifically describe how any element should be rendered. Rather than using styles, early versions of HTML would align text using the align attribute

```
<element align="alignment">content</element>
```

where *alignment* is either left, right, center, or justify. Thus to center an h1 heading you could use either of the following:

```
<h1 style="text-align: center">Dave's Devil Sticks</h1>
```

or

```
<h1 align="center">Dave's Devil Sticks</h1>
```

Almost all presentational attributes are now deprecated in favor of styles, but you will still see them used. Many HTML editors and converters use presentational attributes in place of styles. Even though using a deprecated attribute like align will probably not cause your Web page to fail, you should still use styles because that will ensure compatibility with future browser versions and with XHTML.

Working with Empty Elements

As he examines your work on the Web page, Dave notices that the product list you created in the last session lacks descriptions of the items. Dave wants you to take the information from his original flyer and add it to the Web page.

To add a description of each item in the product list:

1. Return to the **dave.htm** file in your text editor.

2. Locate the first closing </b> tag in the unordered list directly after the text "Basic Stick." Press the **Enter** key and type the following text, indenting it to make the code easier to read:

   ```
   The easiest stick to learn with, but "grippy" enough for the most
   demanding tricks. Comes in red, green, and blue.
   ```

3. Insert the following description for the Flower Stick, directly after the closing </b> tag for that product name:

   ```
   A graceful stick with colored tassels. Flower Sticks float more
   slowly, giving you the ideal chance to practice new moves.
   ```

4. Add the following description for the Master Stick after the closing </b> tag:

   ```
   My most popular stick is shorter and heavier for fast play and more
   advanced tricks. Each Master set is available in custom colors.
   ```

5. Finally, add the following description for the Glow Stick:

```
The Glow Stick shines brightly at night (without the danger of a fire
stick). It combines the fun and versatility of the Master Stick,
adding the fun tricks unique to a glow-in-the-dark stick.
```

Figure 1-32 highlights the newly added product descriptions.

Figure 1-32 ▶ **Adding product descriptions**

```
<h2>My Products</h2>
<ul>
    <li><b>Basic Stick</b>
            The easiest stick to learn with, but "grippy" enough for the most demanding
            tricks. Comes in red, green, and blue.</li>
    <li><b>Flower Stick</b>
            A graceful stick with colored tassels. Flower Sticks float more slowly, giving
            you the ideal chance to practice new moves.</li>
    <li><b>Master Stick</b>
            My most popular stick is shorter and heavier for fast play and more advanced
            tricks. Each Master set is available in custom colors.</li>
    <li><b>Glow Stick</b>
            The Glow Stick shines brightly at night (without the danger of a fire stick).
            It combines the fun and versatility of the Master Stick, adding the fun tricks
            unique to a glow-in-the-dark stick.</li>
</ul>
```

6. Save your changes to the file and then refresh the **dave.htm** file in your Web browser. Figure 1-33 shows the new product descriptions as they appear in the browser.

Figure 1-33 ▶ **Product descriptions on the Web page**

My Products

- **Basic Stick** The easiest stick to learn with, but "grippy" enough for the most demanding tricks. Comes in red, green, and blue.
- **Flower Stick** A graceful stick with colored tassels. Flower Sticks float more slowly, giving you the ideal chance to practice new moves.
- **Master Stick** My most popular stick is shorter and heavier for fast play and more advanced tricks. Each Master set is available in custom colors.
- **Glow Stick** The Glow Stick shines brightly at night (without the danger of a fire stick). It combines the fun and versatility of the Master Stick, adding the fun tricks unique to a glow-in-the-dark stick.

Dave thinks the revised product list is difficult to read and suggests that you place the descriptions on a new line directly below the product name. To do that you'll have to insert a line break into the Web page. The line break element is an example of an **empty element** because it contains no content. Empty elements appear in code as **one-sided tags** using

```
<element />
```

where *element* is the name of the empty element. As with other markup tags, one-sided tags can also contain attributes that define how the element is used in the document. The one-sided tag to mark a line break is

```
<br />
```

Line breaks need to be placed within block-level elements such as paragraphs or headings. Some browsers accept line breaks placed anywhere within the body of the Web page, but this is not good coding technique. XHTML in particular will reject code in which an inline element like the br element is not placed within a block-level element.

Use the br element now to mark a line break between the names and descriptions in Dave's product list.

To create line breaks between the product names and descriptions:

▶ 1. Return to the **dave.htm** file in your text editor.

▶ 2. Insert a **
** tag directly after the closing </b> tag for the Basic Stick product description.

▶ 3. Add a **
** tag after the closing </b> tag for each of the remaining three product names. Figure 1-34 shows the revised HTML code.

Adding line breaks to the Web page ◀ **Figure 1-34**

```
<h2>My Products</h2>
<ul>
   <li><b>Basic Stick</b><br />
      The easiest stick to learn with, but "grippy" enough for the most demanding
      tricks. Comes in red, green, and blue.</li>
   <li><b>Flower Stick</b><br />
      A graceful stick with colored tassels. Flower Sticks float more slowly, giving
      you the ideal chance to practice new moves.</li>
   <li><b>Master Stick</b><br />
      My most popular stick is shorter and heavier for fast play and more advanced
      tricks. Each Master set is available in custom colors.</li>
   <li><b>Glow Stick</b><br />
      The Glow Stick shines brightly at night (without the danger of a fire stick).
      It combines the fun and versatility of the Master Stick, adding the fun tricks
      unique to a glow-in-the-dark stick.</li>
</ul>
```

forces the browser to insert a line break before rendering the next line of text

▶ 4. Save your changes to the file and then refresh the Web page in your browser. Verify that each of the four product descriptions is displayed on a new line directly below the product name.

Marking a Horizontal Rule

Another useful empty element is the hr or horizontal rule element, which places a horizontal line across the Web page. The syntax of the hr element is

```
<hr />
```

The exact appearance of the horizontal rule is left to the browser. Most browsers display a gray-shaded line a few pixels in height. Horizontal rules are considered block-level elements because they are displayed starting on a new line in the Web page. The hr element can be nested either within the <body> tag, in which case the horizontal rule will extend across the width of the Web page, or within a blockquote element, in which case the horizontal rule will be indented like other contents of the block quote.

Horizontal rules are useful in breaking up a long Web page into topical sections. Dave suggests that you place a horizontal rule above and one below the customer quotation and a third at the bottom of the page directly above the company address.

To create three horizontal rules:

▶ 1. Return to the **dave.htm** file in your text editor.

▶ 2. Directly below the opening <blockquote> tag, press the **Enter** key to insert a blank line, and then insert an **<hr />** tag.

▶ 3. Insert one **<hr />** tag directly above the closing </blockquote> tag and another above the opening <address> tag. Figure 1-35 highlights the revised code.

Figure 1-35   Marking horizontal rules with the <hr /> tag

```
<blockquote>
    <hr />
    <p>I'm more than happy to recommend Dave Vinet's products. I came upon his
       work 10 years ago and was immediately impressed by his craftsmanship.
       I've been using his sticks in my shows ever since. They're durable,
       well-balanced, and attractive props and are the perfect complement to
       my performances. Thanks Dave!</p>

    <p>Thomas Gage, lead performer at <i>Circus England</i></p>
    <hr />
</blockquote>

<p>Every set is checked and tested before being shipped out to assure perfect
   quality. I take pride in every one of my sticks and I want my customers to
   feel that same pride.</p>

<h2>My Products</h2>
<ul>
    <li><b>Basic Stick</b><br />
        The easiest stick to learn with, but "grippy" enough for the most demanding
        tricks. Comes in red, green, and blue.</li>
    <li><b>Flower Stick</b><br />
        A graceful stick with colored tassels. Flower Sticks float more slowly, giving
        you the ideal chance to practice new moves.</li>
    <li><b>Master Stick</b><br />
        My most popular stick is shorter and heavier for fast play and more advanced
        tricks. Each Master set is available in custom colors.</li>
    <li><b>Glow Stick</b><br />
        The Glow Stick shines brightly at night (without the danger of a fire stick).
        It combines the fun and versatility of the Master Stick, adding the fun tricks
        unique to a glow-in-the-dark stick.</li>
</ul>

<hr />

<address style="text-align: center">Dave's Devil Sticks
         541 West Highland Dr.
         Auburn, ME 04210
         (207) 555 - 9001
</address>
</body>
```

4. Save your changes to the file and then refresh the Web page in your browser. As shown in Figure 1-36, three horizontal rules have been added to the document, visually breaking the Web page into sections.

Figure 1-36   Adding horizontal rules to the Web page

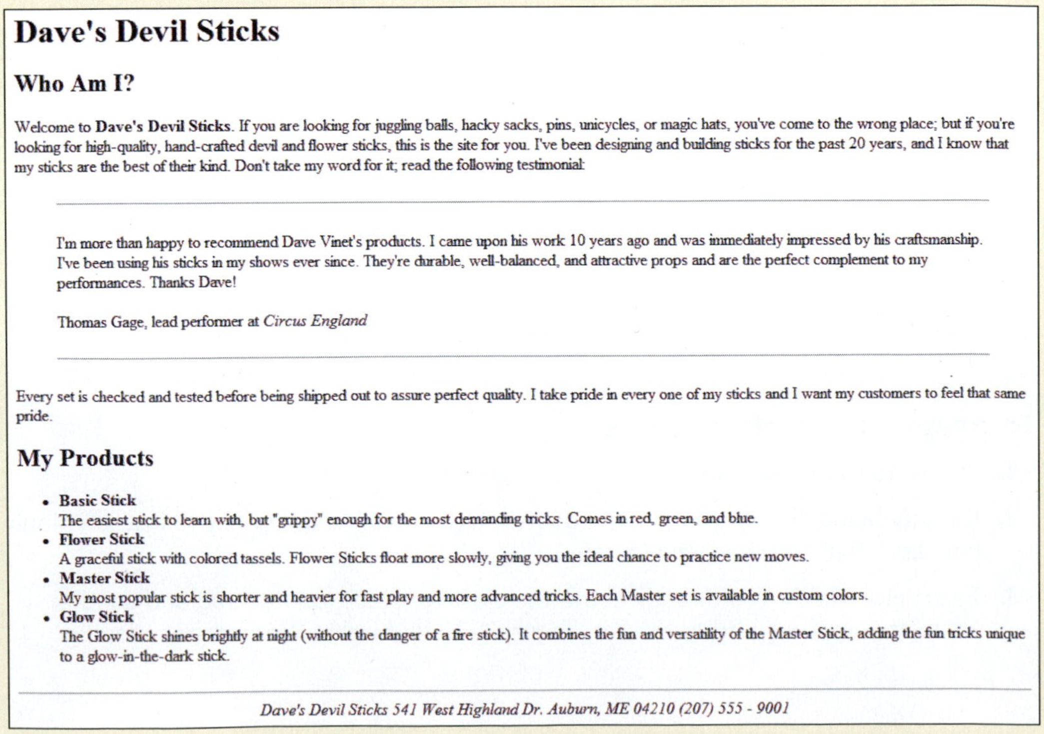

Dave's Devil Sticks

Who Am I?

Welcome to **Dave's Devil Sticks**. If you are looking for juggling balls, hacky sacks, pins, unicycles, or magic hats, you've come to the wrong place; but if you're looking for high-quality, hand-crafted devil and flower sticks, this is the site for you. I've been designing and building sticks for the past 20 years, and I know that my sticks are the best of their kind. Don't take my word for it; read the following testimonial:

I'm more than happy to recommend Dave Vinet's products. I came upon his work 10 years ago and was immediately impressed by his craftsmanship. I've been using his sticks in my shows ever since. They're durable, well-balanced, and attractive props and are the perfect complement to my performances. Thanks Dave!

Thomas Gage, lead performer at *Circus England*

Every set is checked and tested before being shipped out to assure perfect quality. I take pride in every one of my sticks and I want my customers to feel that same pride.

My Products

- **Basic Stick**
  The easiest stick to learn with, but "grippy" enough for the most demanding tricks. Comes in red, green, and blue.
- **Flower Stick**
  A graceful stick with colored tassels. Flower Sticks float more slowly, giving you the ideal chance to practice new moves.
- **Master Stick**
  My most popular stick is shorter and heavier for fast play and more advanced tricks. Each Master set is available in custom colors.
- **Glow Stick**
  The Glow Stick shines brightly at night (without the danger of a fire stick). It combines the fun and versatility of the Master Stick, adding the fun tricks unique to a glow-in-the-dark stick.

Dave's Devil Sticks 541 West Highland Dr. Auburn, ME 04210 (207) 555 - 9001

You show the revised page to Dave and he's pleased with the addition of the horizontal rules. They have made the text easier to read and have nicely highlighted Thomas Gage's tribute.

Inserting an Inline Image

Dave wants you to replace the name of the company with the company logo centered at the top of the page. Because HTML files are simple text files, nontextual content like graphics must be stored in separate files, which are then loaded by the browser as it renders the page. The location of the graphic is marked as an **inline image** using the one-sided tag

```
<img src="file" alt="text" />
```

where *file* is the name of the graphic image file and *text* is text displayed by the browser in place of the graphic image. In this tutorial, you'll assume that the graphic image file is located in the same folder as the Web page, so you don't have to specify the location of the file. In the next tutorial, you'll learn how to reference files placed in other folders or locations on the Web.

As the name implies, inline images are another example of an inline element and thus must be placed within a block-level element such as a heading or a paragraph. Inline images are most widely stored in one of two formats: GIF (Graphics Interchange Format) or JPEG (Joint Photographic Experts Group). You can use an image editing application such as Adobe Photoshop to convert images to either of these two formats. Dave has already created such a graphic and stored it with the filename **logo.jpg**, located in the tutorial.01\tutorial folder included with your Data Files.

Tip

Always include alternate text for inline images. The alt attribute is required in XHTML code and is highly recommended as a way of accommodating users running nonvisual Web browsers.

Marking Empty Elements | Reference Window

- To mark a line break, use
  ```
  <br />
  ```
- To mark a horizontal rule, use
  ```
  <hr />
  ```
- To mark an inline image, use
  ```
  <img src="file" alt="text" />
  ```
  where *file* is the name of the graphic image file and *text* is text displayed by the browser in place of the graphic image.

To insert Dave's logo centered at the top of the page:

1. Return to the **dave.htm** file in your text editor.

2. Go to the h1 heading element at the top of the body section and insert the following attribute into the opening <h1> tag:
   ```
   style="text-align: center"
   ```

3. Delete the text **Dave's Devil Sticks** from between the opening and closing <h1> tags and replace it with
   ```
   <img src="logo.jpg" alt="Dave's Devil Sticks" />
   ```
   Figure 1-37 shows the revised code in the **dave.htm** file.

Figure 1-37 | Adding an inline image to a Web page

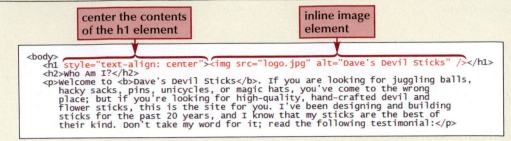

4. Save your changes to the file, and then refresh the Web page in your browser. Figure 1-38 shows the new heading with the logo centered across the page.

Figure 1-38 | Viewing Dave's logo

Working with Character Sets and Special Characters

Dave likes the work you've done so far on the Web page. He has only one remaining concern: he feels that the address information at the bottom of the page is difficult to read and would like you to add a solid circular marker separating the different sections of the address. However, this marker is not represented by any keys on your keyboard. How then do you insert this symbol into the Web page?

Character Sets

To add dots to Dave's address, you must reference a symbol that your browser will be able to display but is not found on your keyboard. This is done by using a collection of characters and symbols called a **character set**. Character sets come in a wide variety of sizes, based on the number of symbols required for communication in the chosen language. For English, no more than about 127 characters are needed to represent all of the upper- and lowercase letters, numbers, punctuation marks, spaces, and special typing symbols in the English language. Other languages, such as Japanese or Chinese, require character sets containing thousands of symbols.

Each character set has a name. The character set representing the alphabet of English characters is called **ASCII** (**American Standard Code for Information Interchange**). A more extended character set called **Latin-1** or the **ISO 8859-1** character set supports 255 characters and can be used by most languages that employ the Latin alphabet, including English, French, Spanish, and Italian. The most extended character set is **Unicode**, which can be used for any of the world's languages, supporting up to 65,536 symbols. The most commonly used character set on the Web is **UTF-8**, which is a compressed version of Unicode and is probably the default character set assumed by your browser. You can learn more about character sets by visiting the W3C Web site and the Web site for the Internet Assigned Numbers Authority at *www.iana.org*.

Numeric Character References

To store a character set, browsers need to associate each symbol with a number in a process called **character encoding**. The number is called the **numeric character reference**. For example, the copyright symbol © from the UTF-8 character set has the number 169. If you know the numeric reference, you can insert the number directly into your code to display the symbol. The syntax to insert a numeric character reference is

`&#code;`

where *code* is the reference number. Thus to display the © symbol in your Web page, you would enter

`&#169;`

into your HTML file. To render a numeric character reference correctly, the browser needs to know the character set and encoding being used in the Web page. This information is typically sent by the Web server as it transfers the HTML page to the browser; and unless you are working with specialized international documents, you usually do not have to worry about specifying the character set for the browser.

Character Entity References

Another way to insert a special symbol is to use a **character entity reference**, in which a short memorable name is used in place of the numeric character reference. The syntax to insert a character entity reference is

`&char;`

where *char* is the character's name. The character entity reference for the copyright symbol is "copy," so to display the © symbol in your Web page you could also insert

`&copy;`

into your HTML code. One of the advantages of character entity references is that browsers can use them without knowing the character set or encoding. A disadvantage is that older browsers might not recognize the character entity reference and will thus display the reference name but not the symbol it represents.

Reference Window | **Inserting Character Codes**

- To insert a character based on a numeric character reference, use
  `&#code;`
  where *code* is the character code number.
- To insert a character based on the character entity reference, use
  `&char;`
  where *char* is the name assigned to the character.
- To insert a nonbreaking space, use
  ` `
- To insert the < symbol, use
  `&lt;`
- To insert the > symbol, use
  `&gt;`

To explore various numeric character references and character entity references, you can view a demo page supplied with your Data Files.

To view the demo page:

1. Use your Web browser to open the **demo_characters.htm** file from the tutorial.01\demo data folder.

2. Type **£** in the input box at the top of the page, and then click the **Show** button. The Web browser displays the £ symbol in the ivory-colored box below. As you can see, to display the British pound symbol (£), you can use the &#163 numeric character reference.

3. Now try to display a special symbol using a character entity reference. Replace the value in the input box with **®** and then click the **Show** button. The browser now displays the ® symbol, which is the symbol for registered trademarks.

   You can view a collection of numeric character references and character entity references by selecting a table from the list box on the page.

4. Verify that General Symbols is displayed in the selection list box, and then click the **Show Table** button. As shown in Figure 1-39, the browser displays a list of 35 symbols with the character entity reference and numeric references displayed beneath each symbol.

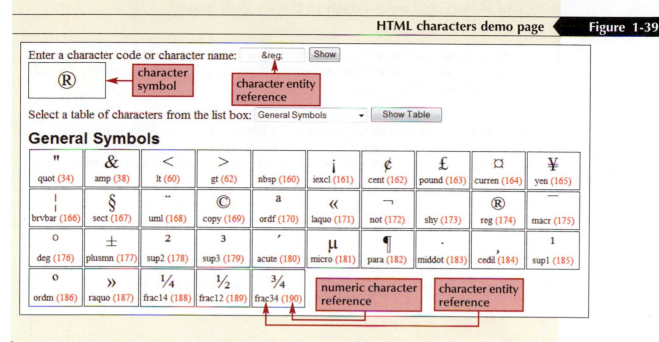

HTML characters demo page ◄ Figure 1-39

5. Take some time to explore the variety of numeric references and character entity references supported by your browser. Close the demo when you're finished, but leave your browser open.

Special Characters

One use of character codes is to insert text about HTML itself. For example, if you want your Web page to describe the use of the <h1> tag, you cannot simply type

```
The <h1> tag is used to mark h1 headings.
```

because the browser will interpret the <h1> text as marking the beginning of an h1 heading! Instead, you have to use the < and > entity references to insert the < and > symbols. The text would then be

```
The &lt;h1&gt; tag is used to mark h1 headings.
```

Another use of character codes is to add extra spaces to your Web page. Remember that browsers ignore extra blank spaces in the HTML file. To insert additional spaces, use the   entity reference ("nbsp" stands for nonbreaking space), which forces the browser to insert extra spaces.

On Dave's Web page, you decide to use the bullet symbol to break up the address text into sections. The symbol has the numeric character code value of 8226 and the entity character reference name "bull." Dave suggests you also add a long horizontal line called an em-dash to mark Thomas Gage's name as the author of the recommendation for Dave's business. The character code and entity reference for an em-dash are 8212 and "mdash," respectively.

> **Tip**
>
> Use the   character entity reference to fine-tune the layout of your documents by adding extra blank spaces to your text.

To add bullets and an em-dash to Dave's Web page:

1. Return to the **dave.htm** file in your text editor.

2. Locate the paragraph within the blockquote element containing the name of Thomas Gage. Directly after the opening <p> tag, insert the following numeric character code, followed by a space:

   `&#8212;`

3. Scroll down to the address element at the bottom of the file. At the end of each line within the address element (except the last line), insert a space and then type the **•** character entity reference. Figure 1-40 highlights the newly added code in the file.

Figure 1-40 Adding character references to the HTML file

```
<blockquote>
    <hr />
    <p>I'm more than happy to recommend Dave Vinet's products. I came upon his
       work 10 years ago and was immediately impressed by his craftsmanship.
       I've been using his sticks in my shows ever since. They're durable,
       well-balanced, and attractive props and are the perfect complement to
       my performances. Thanks Dave!</p>

    <p>&#8212; Thomas Gage, lead performer at <i>Circus England</i></p>
    <hr />
</blockquote>

<p>Every set is checked and tested before being shipped out to assure perfect
   quality. I take pride in every one of my sticks and I want my customers to
   feel that same pride.</p>

<h2>My Products</h2>
<ul>
    <li><b>Basic Stick</b><br />
        The easiest stick to learn with, but "grippy" enough for the most demanding
        tricks. Comes in red, green, and blue.</li>
    <li><b>Flower Stick</b><br />
        A graceful stick with colored tassels. Flower Sticks float more slowly, giving
        you the ideal chance to practice new moves.</li>
    <li><b>Master Stick</b><br />
        My most popular stick is shorter and heavier for fast play and more advanced
        tricks. Each Master set is available in custom colors.</li>
    <li><b>Glow Stick</b><br />
        The Glow Stick shines brightly at night (without the danger of a fire stick).
        It combines the fun and versatility of the Master Stick, adding the fun tricks
        unique to a glow-in-the-dark stick.</li>
</ul>

<hr />

<address style="text-align: center">Dave's Devil Sticks &bull;
        541 West Highland Dr. &bull;
        Auburn, ME 04210 &bull;
        (207) 555 - 9001 &bull;
</address>
</body>
```

numeric character reference → `&#8212;`

character entity reference → `&bull;`

4. Close the file, saving your changes.

5. Refresh the **dave.htm** file in your Web browser. Figure 1-41 shows the final version of Dave's Web page.

Dave's completed Web page | Figure 1-41

Who Am I?

Welcome to **Dave's Devil Sticks**. If you are looking for juggling balls, hacky sacks, pins, unicycles, or magic hats, you've come to the wrong place; but if you're looking for high-quality, hand-crafted devil and flower sticks, this is the site for you. I've been designing and building sticks for the past 20 years, and I know that my sticks are the best of their kind. Don't take my word for it; read the following testimonial:

I'm more than happy to recommend Dave Vinet's products. I came upon his work 10 years ago and was immediately impressed by his craftsmanship. I've been using his sticks in my shows ever since. They're durable, well-balanced, and attractive props and are the perfect complement to my performances. Thanks Dave!

— Thomas Gage, lead performer at *Circus England*

Every set is checked and tested before being shipped out to assure perfect quality. I take pride in every one of my sticks and I want my customers to feel that same pride.

My Products

- **Basic Stick**
  The easiest stick to learn with, but "grippy" enough for the most demanding tricks. Comes in red, green, and blue.
- **Flower Stick**
  A graceful stick with colored tassels. Flower Sticks float more slowly, giving you the ideal chance to practice new moves.
- **Master Stick**
  My most popular stick is shorter and heavier for fast play and more advanced tricks. Each Master set is available in custom colors.
- **Glow Stick**
  The Glow Stick shines brightly at night (without the danger of a fire stick). It combines the fun and versatility of the Master Stick, adding the fun tricks unique to a glow-in-the-dark stick.

Dave's Devil Sticks • 541 West Highland Dr. • Auburn, ME 04210 • (207) 555 - 9001 •

6. If you plan on taking a break before working on the end of tutorial problems, you can close your Web browser and any other open files or programs.

You show the completed Web page to Dave. He's pleased that you were able to duplicate much of what was on his original flyer. As you and Dave grow in your understanding of HTML and the Web, you'll add more pages to his site; but for now, this is a good start on giving him a presence on the Internet.

| InSight | Publishing Your Page on the Web |

Once you've completed your Web page, your next step is to research ways of getting it on the Web. You first need to find a Web server to host the page. Some of the issues you'll need to consider are how much you want to pay, how much space you need, and how important it is for you to have a highly trafficked Web site. You might first look toward the company that provides your Internet access. Most **ISPs (Internet Service Providers)** offer space on their Web server as part of their regular service or for a small fee. However, they usually limit the amount of space available to you, unless you pay an extra fee to host a larger site. There are also free Web hosts, which provide space on servers for personal or noncommercial use. Once again, the amount of space you get is limited. Free Web hosting services make their money from selling advertising space on your site, so you should be prepared to act as a billboard in return for space on their server.

Web sites are identified by their domain names. If you're planning to create a commercial site to advertise a product or service, you want the domain name to reflect your business. Free Web hosts usually include their names in your Web address. Thus instead of having a Web address like

> davesdevilsticks.com

you might have something like

> freewebhosting.net/members/~davesdevilsticks.html

If you're running a site for personal use, this might not be a problem—but it would look unprofessional on a commercial site. If you are planning a commercial site and simply want to advertise your product by publishing an online brochure, you can usually find an inexpensive host and pay a nominal yearly fee to reserve a Web address that reflects your company's name. On the other hand, if you intend to run an e-commerce site where users can purchase products online, you will need to invest in software and storage space to manage customer orders and inventory. You will also need to invest in getting your Web site noticed in the increasingly crowded Internet market. Commercial pages require careful planning and good design so that the investment in publishing the site is not wasted.

| Review | Session 1.3 Quick Check |

1. Specify the code you would enter to display the text "Product List" as an h2 heading, centered horizontally on the page.
2. What is a presentational attribute? What is a reason for using presentational attributes? What is a reason for avoiding them?
3. Specify the code you would enter to mark the text "Hamlet by William Shakespeare" as a centered h1 heading with a line break after the word "Hamlet."
4. You want to add the graphic file portrait.gif to your Web page as an inline image. For nonvisual browsers, your page should display the text "David Vinet" in place of the image. Specify the code to do this.
5. What is ISO-8859-1?
6. The trademark symbol ™ has the Unicode number 8482. How would you enter this symbol into your Web page?
7. The Greek letter b has the character entity name of "beta." How would you enter this symbol into your Web page?
8. Specify the code you would enter to add three consecutive blank spaces to your Web page.
9. Specify the code you would enter to display the text "<h2>Hamlet</h2>" on your Web page.

Tutorial Summary | Review

In this tutorial you learned how to create a basic Web page using HTML. The tutorial began by examining concepts and history surrounding networks and the development of the World Wide Web. It then explored the history of HTML, explaining how the development of HTML was a key component in the development of the Web. The first session concluded with the creation of a simple Web page consisting only of the page head. Work on designing the page body began in the second session by first exploring how to mark block-level elements. The discussion of block-level elements included work with headings, paragraphs, block quotes, and lists. The second session concluded with coverage of inline elements and discussed the issue of physical elements versus logical elements. The third session began by exploring element attributes, showing how to use the style attribute to center the contents of a block-level element. Because Web pages often need to display nontextual content, the third session then examined how to use empty elements such as line breaks, horizontal rules, and inline images. The session and the tutorial concluded by discussing character sets and explored how to insert special character symbols into a Web page.

Key Terms

ARPANET
ASCII
attribute
block-level element
body element
character encoding
character entity reference
character formatting
   element
character set
client
client-server network
closing tag
comment tag
definition list
deprecated
element
empty element
Extensible Hypertext
   Markup Language
Extensible Markup
   Language
extensions
file server
head element
heading element
host
HTML

HTML 5.0
HTML converter
HTML editor
hypertext
Hypertext Markup
   Language
inline element
inline image
Internet Service Provider
ISO-8859-1
ISP
LAN
Latin-1
link
local area network
logical element
markup language
network
node
numeric character
   reference
one-sided tag
opening tag
ordered list
physical element
presentational attribute
print server

root element
server
SGML
Standard Generalized
   Markup Language
style
tag
text-based browser
two-sided tag
Unicode
unordered list
UTF-8
W3C
WAN
Web
Web browser
Web page
Web server
white space
wide area network
World Wide Web
World Wide Web
   Consortium
XHTML
XHTML 2.0
XHTML 5.0
XML

Practice	Review Assignments

Practice the skills you learned in the tutorial using the same case scenario.

Data File needed for the Review Assignments: logo.jpg

Dave has found a host for his Web page and has published the document you helped him create on the Internet. He wants to start adding more pages to his Web site. He's come to you for help in creating a page describing his basic stick. He's already written the text for the Web page; he needs you to translate that text into HTML code. Figure 1-42 shows a preview of the page you'll create for Dave.

Figure 1-42

The Basic Stick

The Basic Stick is the perfect stick for beginners. The stick rotates slowly to provide extra time for performing stick tricks, but is flashy enough to impress your friends.

Patented Dura-Coat®️ finish ensures sticks can withstand all weather conditions. More durable than other sticks, these props will keep looking like new for as long as you own them.

Enhanced stick flexibility provides more bounce, allowing for better tricks. A soft rubber core adds a whole new element to the sticking experience that you have to feel to believe!

Full customization will give you the chance to own a pair of sticks unlike any others out there. I make exactly what you want, with your colors and your designs.

A personal touch through both my customization options and hand-crafted designs.

Specifications

- Main Stick
  - Weight: 7 oz.
  - Length: 24 inches
  - Tape: Dura-Coat®️ finish with laser-style color choices
- Handle Sticks (one pair)
  - Weight: 2 oz.
  - Length: 18 inches
  - Tape: Soft ivory tape with rubber core

Dave's Devil Sticks ♦ 541 West Highland Dr. ♦ Auburn, ME 04210 ♦ (207) 555 - 9001

Complete the following:

1. Use your text editor to create a new file named **basic.htm**, and save it in the tutorial.01\review folder included with your Data Files.
2. Within the basic.htm file, insert the structure of the HTML file, including the head and body sections.
3. Within the head section, insert a comment containing
   Dave's Devil Sticks
   Basic Stick
   Author: *your name*
   Date: *the date*
   where *your name* is your name and *the date* is the current date.

4. Add the page title **Basic Sticks** to the head section.

5. Within the body section, insert an h1 heading centered horizontally on the page and containing the inline image file **logo.jpg**, located in the tutorial.01\review folder included with your Data Files. Specify the following alternate text for the image: **Dave's Devil Sticks: The Basic Stick**.

6. Add two h2 headings containing the text **The Basic Stick** and **Specifications**. Set the font color of the heading 2 text to red.

7. Directly below the first h2 heading, insert a paragraph containing the text: **The Basic Stick is the perfect stick for beginners. The stick rotates slowly to provide extra time for performing stick tricks, but is flashy enough to impress your friends.**

8. Directly below the paragraph but above the second h2 heading, insert a block quote that contains the following:

   a. Place a horizontal rule at the top and the bottom of the block quote.

   b. Between the two horizontal rules, insert the following four paragraphs:

   Patented Dura-Coat finish ensures sticks can withstand all weather conditions. More durable than other sticks, these props will keep looking like new for as long as you own them.

   Enhanced stick flexibility provides more bounce, allowing for better tricks. A soft rubber core adds a whole new element to the sticking experience that you have to feel to believe!

   Full customization will give you the chance to own a pair of sticks unlike any others out there. I make exactly what you want, with your colors and your designs.

   A personal touch through both my customization options and hand-crafted designs.

   c. Change the first few words of each of the four paragraphs to a bold font, as indicated in Figure 1-42.

9. Directly below the second h2 heading, insert an unordered list. The list should contain two items: **Main Stick** and **Handle Sticks (one pair)**.

10. Directly below the Main Stick list item, insert an unordered list containing the following items:

    Weight: 7 oz.

    Length: 24 inches

    Tape: Dura-Coat finish with laser-style color choices

11. Directly below the Handle Sticks (one pair) list item, insert an unordered list containing:

    Weight: 2 oz.

    Length: 18 inches

    Tape: Soft ivory tape with rubber core

12. Locate the two occurrences of "Dura-Coat" in the document. Directly after the word "Dura-Coat," insert the registered trademark symbol ®. The character entity name of the ® symbol is "reg." Display the ® symbol as a superscript by placing the character within the sup inline element.

13. At the bottom of the body section, insert the company's address:

    Dave's Devil Sticks

    541 West Highland Dr.

    Auburn, ME 04210

    (207) 555 - 9001

14. Center the address on the page.

15. Separate the different sections of the address using a solid diamond ♦ (character code 9830).

16. Add a horizontal rule directly above the address element.

17. Save your changes to the file, and then open it in your Web browser to verify that the content and layout are correct.

18. Submit your completed files to your instructor.

| Apply | **Case Problem 1** |

Apply your knowledge of HTML to create a Web page for a mathematics department at a university.

Data Files needed for this Case Problem: euler.jpg and eulertxt.htm

Mathematics Department, Coastal University Professor Lauren Coe of the Mathematics Department of Coastal University in Anderson, South Carolina, is preparing material for a course on the history of mathematics. As part of the course, she has written biographies of famous mathematicians. Lauren would like you to use content she's already written to create Web pages that students can access on Coastal University's Web server. You'll create the first one in this exercise. Figure 1-43 shows a preview of this page, which profiles the mathematician Leonhard Euler.

Figure 1-43

Leonhard Euler (1707-1783)

The greatest mathematician of the eighteenth century, **Leonhard Euler** was born in Basel, Switzerland. There, he studied under another giant of mathematics, **Jean Bernoulli**. In 1731 Euler became a professor of physics and mathematics at St. Petersburg Academy of Sciences. Euler was the most prolific mathematician of all time, publishing over *800 different books and papers*. His influence was felt in physics and astronomy as well. Euler's work on mathematical analysis, *Introductio in analysin infinitorum* (1748) remained a standard textbook for well over a century. For the princess of Anhalt-Dessau he wrote *Lettres à une princesse d'Allemagne* (1768-1772), giving a clear non-technical outline of the main physical theories of the time.

One can hardly do math without copying Euler. Notations still in use today, such as e and π, were introduced in Euler's writings. He is perhaps best known for his research into mathematical analysis. Euler's formula

$$\cos(x) + i\sin(x) = e^{(ix)}$$

demonstrates the relationship between algebra, complex analysis, and trigonometry. From this equation, it's easy to derive the equation

$$e^{(\pi i)} + 1 = 0$$

which relates the fundamental constants: 0, 1, π, e, and i in a single beautiful and elegant statement.

Leonhard Euler died in 1783, leaving behind a legacy perhaps unmatched, and certainly unsurpassed, in the annals of mathematics.

Math 895: The History of Mathematics

Complete the following:

1. Open the **eulertxt.htm** file from the tutorial.01\case1 folder included with your Data Files. Save the file as **euler.htm** in the same folder.

2. Add opening and closing <html> tags to the file. Insert a head section and enclose Lauren's text on Euler within a body element.

3. Within the head section, insert a comment containing

   History of Math 895: Leonhard Euler

   Author: *your name*

   Date: *the date*

   where *your name* is your name and *the date* is the current date.

4. Add the page title **History of Math 895: Leonhard Euler** to the head section.

5. Directly below the opening <body> tag, insert a paragraph containing the inline image file **euler.jpg**, located in the tutorial.01\case1 folder included with your Data Files. Specify "Portrait of Leonhard Euler" as the alternative text.

6. Mark the next line containing "Leonhard Euler (1707 - 1783)" as an h1 heading.

7. Mark the five blocks of text describing Euler's life as paragraphs.

8. Mark the two equations as block quotes. Change the font color of the two block quotes to red.

9. Mark the name of the course title at the bottom of the file as an address.

10. Insert horizontal rules directly above the h1 heading and the address element.

⊕ **EXPLORE**

11. Within the first paragraph, display the names "Leonhard Euler" and "Jean Bernoulli" in boldface. Mark the phrase "800 different books and papers" as emphasized text using the em element. Mark the phrase "Introduction in analysin infinitorum" as a citation.

12. In the phrase, "Lettres a une princesse d'Allemagne" replace the one-letter word a with à (the character entity name is "agrave"). Mark the entire publication as a citation.

13. In the second paragraph, italicize the notation for *e* and replace "pi" with the character π (the character name is "pi").

14. In the first equation, italicize the letters *e*, *x*, and *i* (but do not italicize the "i" in "sin"). Display the term (*ix*) as a superscript.

15. In the second equation, replace "pi" with the character π. Italicize the letter *e* and *i*. Display (πi) as a superscript.

16. In the last paragraph, italicize the notations for *e* and *i* and replace "pi" with π.

17. Save your changes to the file, and then verify that the page appears correctly in your Web browser.

18. Submit your completed files to your instructor.

| Apply | **Case Problem 2** |

Apply your knowledge of HTML to create a page showing text from a scene of a Shakespeare play.

Data Files needed for this Case Problem: macbeth.jpg and macbethtxt.htm

Mansfield Classical Theatre Steve Karls is the director of Mansfield Classical Theatre, a theatre company for young people located in Mansfield, Ohio. This summer the company is planning to perform the Shakespeare play *Macbeth*. Steve wants to put the text of the play on the company's Web site and has asked for your help in designing and completing the Web page. Steve wants to have a separate page for each scene from the play. A preview of the page you'll create for Act I, Scene 1 is shown in Figure 1-44. Steve has already typed the text of the scene. He needs you to supply the HTML code.

Figure 1-44

ACT I

SCENE 1.

Summary A thunderstorm approaches and three witches convene. They agree to confront the great Scot general Macbeth upon his victorious return from a war between Scotland and Norway. Soon, heroic Macbeth will receive the title of Thane of Cawdor from King Duncan. However, Macbeth learns from the witches that he is fated for greater things and he will be led down to the path of destruction by his unquenchable ambition.

A desert place.

Thunder and lightning. Enter three Witches.

First Witch
    When shall we three meet again
    In thunder, lightning, or in rain?
Second Witch
    When the hurlyburly's done,
    When the battle's lost and won.
Third Witch
    That will be ere the set of sun.
First Witch
    Where the place?
Second Witch
    Upon the heath.
Third Witch
    There to meet with Macbeth.
First Witch
    I come, Graymalkin!
Second Witch
    Paddock calls.
Third Witch
    Anon.
ALL
    Fair is foul, and foul is fair:
    Hover through the fog and filthy air.

Exeunt

Go to Scene 2 ⇒

Text provided by Online Shakespeare

Complete the following:

1. Open the **macbethtxt.htm** file from the tutorial.01\case2 folder included with your Data Files. Save the file as **macbeth.htm** in the same folder.
2. Enclose the entire Macbeth text within the structure of an HTML document.
3. Within the head section, insert a comment containing the following text:
   Macbeth: Act I, Scene 1
   Author: *your name*
   Date: *the date*
4. Add the page title **Macbeth: Act I, Scene 1** to the head section.
5. Directly below the opening <body> tag, insert an h1 heading containing the inline image file **macbeth.jpg** (located in the tutorial.01\case2 folder included with your Data Files) with **Macbeth** as the alternate text for nonvisual browsers. Add a horizontal rule directly below the h1 heading.
6. Mark the text "ACT I" as an h2 heading. Mark "SCENE 1." as an h3 heading.

7. Mark the summary of the scene as a paragraph. Display the word "Summary" in bold.

8. In the text of the play, mark the descriptions of setting, scene, and exits as separate paragraphs, and italicize the text, as shown in Figure 1-44.

EXPLORE

9. Mark the dialog as a definition list, with each character's name marked as a definition term and each speech marked as a definition description. Where the speech goes over one line, use a line break to keep the speech on separate lines, as shown in the figure.

10. Directly below the Exeunt paragraph, insert the line **Go to Scene 2.** Mark this line as a div element and align it with the right page margin. (Steve will mark this as a link later.) At the end of the line, insert a right arrow character using the 8658 character number. Add horizontal rules directly above and below this statement.

EXPLORE

11. Mark the line "Text provided by Online Shakespeare" as a paragraph, with the text itself marked with the cite element. Align the text with the right page margin.

12. Save your changes to the file, and then confirm the layout and content of the page in your Web browser.

13. Submit the completed files to your instructor.

Challenge	**Case Problem 3**

Explore how to use HTML to create a recipe page.

Data Files needed for this Case Problem: dessertweb.jpg, torte.jpg, and tortetxt.htm

dessertWEB   Amy Wu wants to take her love of cooking and sharing recipes to the World Wide Web. She's interested in creating a new Web site called *dessertWEB* where other cooks can submit and review dessert recipes. Each page within her site will have a photo and description of the dessert, the ingredients, the cooking directions, and a list of reviews. Each recipe will be rated on a 5-star scale. She already has information on one recipe: Apple Bavarian Torte. She's asked for your help in creating a Web page from the data she's collected. A preview of the completed page is shown in Figure 1-45.

Figure 1-45

Apple Bavarian Torte (★★★★)

A classic European torte baked in a springform pan. Cream cheese, sliced almonds, and apples make this the perfect holiday treat (12 servings).

INGREDIENTS

1/2 cup butter
1/3 cup white sugar
1/4 teaspoon vanilla extract
1 cup all-purpose flour
1 (8 ounce) package cream cheese
1/4 cup white sugar
1 egg
1/2 teaspoon vanilla extract
6 apples - peeled, cored, and sliced
1/3 cup white sugar
1/2 teaspoon ground cinnamon
1/4 cup sliced almonds

DIRECTIONS

1. Preheat oven to 450° F (230° C).
2. Cream together butter, sugar, vanilla, and flour.
3. Press crust mixture into the flat bottom of a 9-inch springform pan. Set aside.
4. In a medium bowl, blend cream cheese and sugar. Beat in egg and vanilla. Pour cheese mixture over crust.
5. Toss apples with sugar and cinnamon. Spread apple mixture over all.
6. Bake for 10 minutes. Reduce heat to 400° F (200° C) and continue baking for 25 minutes.
7. Sprinkle almonds over top of torte. Continue baking until lightly browned. Cool before removing from pan.

REVIEWS

★★★★ ★
I loved the buttery taste of the crust which complements the apples very nicely.
— Reviewed on Sep. 22, 2010 by MMASON.
★★ ★★★
Nothing special. I like the crust, but there was a little too much of it for my taste, and I liked the filling but there was too little of it. I thought the crunchy apples combined with the sliced almonds detracted from the overall flavor.
— Reviewed on Sep. 1, 2010 by GLENDACHEF.
★★★★★
Delicious!! I recommend microwaving the apples for 3 minutes before baking, to soften them. Great dessert - I'll be making it again for the holidays.
— Reviewed on August 28, 2010 by BBABS.

Complete the following:

1. Open the **tortetxt.htm** file from the tutorial.01\case3 folder included with your Data Files. Save the file as **torte.htm** in the same folder.
2. Add the structure of an HTML document around the recipe text. Within the head section, insert a comment containing the following text:
   Apple Bavarian Torte
   Author: *your name*
   Date: *the date*
3. Add the page title **Apple Bavarian Torte Recipe** to the head section.
4. Directly below the opening <body> tag, insert a div element containing the inline image **dessertweb.jpg** located in the tutorial.01\case3 folder included with your Data Files. Specify the alternative text **dessertWEB**. Insert a horizontal rule directly below the div element.

EXPLORE

5. Mark the text "Apple Bavarian Torte" as an h2 heading.
6. Change the text "(4 stars)" to a set of 4 star symbols (character number 9733). Enclose the star symbols in a span element, setting the font color to teal.
7. Directly below the h2 heading, insert another div element containing the inline image **torte.jpg**, located in the tutorial.01\case3 folder included with your Data Files. Specify the alternative text **Torte image**.
8. Mark the description of the dessert as a paragraph.
9. Mark "INGREDIENTS," "DIRECTIONS," and "REVIEWS" as h3 headings.
10. Enclose the list of ingredients in a block quote. Add line breaks after each item in the list.

EXPLORE

11. Mark the list of directions as an ordered list, with each direction a separate item in the list. Replace the word "degrees" with the degree symbol (character name deg).
12. Enclose the list of reviews in a block quote. Turn the list into a definition list. Mark up the definition list as follows:

EXPLORE

   a. The definition term is the number of stars assigned by each reviewer. Change the number of stars in the text file to star symbols (character number 9733). Amy wants you to display 5 stars for each review with the number of stars displayed in a teal font matching the stars given by the reviewer and the remaining stars displayed in a gray font. Use the span element to enclose the two different groups of stars.

   b. There are two definition descriptions for each review. The first encloses the text of the review. The second encloses the date of the review and the name of the reviewer.

   c. Insert an em-dash (character name "mdash") before the word "Reviewed" in each of the reviews.

13. Save your changes to the file, and then verify the layout and content of the page in your Web browser.
14. Submit the completed files to your instructor.

| Create | **Case Problem 4** |

Test your knowledge of HTML and use your creativity to design a Web page for an exercise equipment company.

Data Files needed for this Case Problem: logo.jpg, smith.jpg, and smith.txt

Body Systems   Body Systems is a leading manufacturer of home gyms. The company recently hired you to assist in developing its Web site. Your first task is to create a Web page for the LSM400, a popular weight machine sold by the company. You've been given a text file describing the features of the LSM400. You've also received two image files: one of the company's logo and one of the LSM400. You are free to supplement these files with any other resources available to you. You are responsible for the page's content and appearance.

Complete the following:

1. Create a new HTML file named **smith.htm** and save it in the tutorial.01\case4 folder included with your Data Files.
2. Add a comment to the head section of the document describing the document's content and containing your name and the date.
3. Add an appropriate page title to the document.

4. Use the contents of the **smith.txt** document (located in the tutorial.01\case4 folder) as the basis of the text in the Web page. Include at least one example of each of the following:
   - a heading
   - a paragraph
   - an ordered or unordered list
   - an inline element
   - an inline image
   - a horizontal rule
   - a special character
   - an element attribute
5. Structure your HTML code so that it will be easy for others to read and understand.
6. Save your changes to the file, and then open it in your Web browser to verify that it is readable and attractive.
7. Submit your completed files to your instructor.

Review | Quick Check Answers

Session 1.1

1. A hypertext document is an electronic file containing elements that users can select, usually by clicking a mouse, to open other documents.
2. A Web server is a computer on a network that stores a Web site and makes it available to clients. Users access the Web site by running a program called a Web browser on their computers.
3. HTML documents do not exactly specify the appearance of a document; rather they describe the purpose of various elements in the document and leave it to the Web browser to determine the final appearance. A word processor like Microsoft Word exactly specifies the appearance of each document element.
4. Deprecated features are those features that are being phased out by the W3C and might not be supported by future browsers.
5. The html element.
6. In the head section of the document you would enter the code
   `<title>Technical Support</title>`
7. `<!-- Page Updated on 4/15/2011 -->`
8. The title element was not properly nested within the head element.

Session 1.2

1. Block-level elements contain content that is displayed in a separate section within the page, such as a paragraph or a heading. An inline element is part of the same block as its surrounding content—for example, individual words or phrases within a paragraph.
2. Web browsers will strip out extra occurrences of white space and thus will ignore the extra blank line.
3. `<h1>`*content*`</h1>`
4. Use the blockquote element. Most browsers indent blockquote text.

5.
```
<ul>
    <li>Winter</li>
    <li>Spring</li>
    <li>Summer</li>
    <li>Fall</li>
</ul>
```

6.
```
<dl>
    <dt>HAMLET</dt>
    <dd> There's ne'er a villain dwelling in all Denmark; but he's
an arrant knave.</dd>
    <dt>HORATIO</dt>
    <dd> There needs no ghost, my lord, come from the grave to tell
us this.</dd>
</dl>
```

7. `<p><i>Hamlet</i>, a play by William Shakespeare</p>`

8. div and span

Session 1.3

1. `<h2 style="text-align: center">Product List</h2>`

2. Presentational attributes are HTML attributes that exactly specify how the browser should render an HTML element. Most presentational attributes have been deprecated, replaced by styles. You should use presentational attributes when you need to support older browsers.

3. `<h1 style="text-align: center">Hamlet<br /> by William Shakespeare</h1>`

4. `<img src="portrait.gif" alt="David Vinet" />`

5. ISO-8859-1 is a character set that supports 255 characters and can be used by most languages that use the Latin alphabet.

6. `&#8482;`

7. `&beta;`

8. `   `

9. `&lt;h2&gt;Hamlet&lt;/h2&gt;`

Ending Data Files

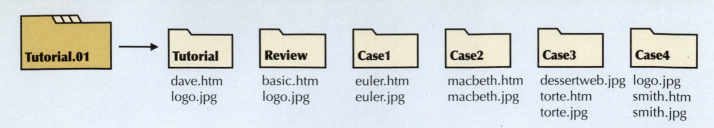

Tutorial.01 → **Tutorial**
dave.htm
logo.jpg

Review
basic.htm
logo.jpg

Case1
euler.htm
euler.jpg

Case2
macbeth.htm
macbeth.jpg

Case3
dessertweb.jpg
torte.htm
torte.jpg

Case4
logo.jpg
smith.htm
smith.jpg

Developing a Web Site

Creating a Web Site for Digital Photography Enthusiasts

Case | CAMshots

Gerry Hayward is an amateur photographer and digital camera enthusiast. He's decided to create a Web site named CAMshots, where he can offer advice and information to people who are just getting started with digital photography or who are long-time hobbyists like himself and are looking to share tips and ideas. Gerry's Web site will contain several pages, with each page dedicated to a particular topic. He has created a few pages for the Web site, but he hasn't linked them together. He has asked your help in designing his site. You'll start with only a few pages and then Gerry can build on your work as he adds more information to the site.

Starting Data Files

Tutorial.02 →

Tutorial
glosstxt.htm
hometxt.htm
tipstxt.htm
+ 3 graphic files

Demo
demo_mailto.htm
+ 3 graphic files

Review
childtxt.htm
contesttxt.htm
flowertxt.htm
scenictxt.htm
+ 22 graphic files

Case1
colleges.txt
uwlisttxt.htm
+ 1 graphic file

Case2
hometxt.htm
slide1txt.htm
slide2txt.htm
slide3txt.htm
slide4txt.htm
slide5txt.htm
slide6txt.htm
+ 18 graphic files

Case3
classtxt.htm
hometxt.htm
indextxt.htm
memtxt.htm
+ 1 graphic file

Case4
characters.txt
notes.txt
tempest.txt
+ 1 graphic file

Session 2.1

Exploring Web Site Structures

You meet with Gerry to discuss his plans for the CAMshots Web site. Gerry has already created a prototype for the Web site. He's created three Web pages: one page is the site's home page and contains general information about CAMshots; the second page contains tips about digital photography; and the third page contains a partial glossary of photographic terms. The pages are not complete, nor are they linked to one another. You'll begin your work for Gerry by viewing these files in your text editor and browser.

To view Gerry's Web pages:

▶ 1. Start your text editor, and then one at a time, open the **hometxt.htm**, **tipstxt.htm**, and **glosstxt.htm** files, located in the tutorial.02\tutorial folder included with your Data Files.

▶ 2. Within each file, go to the comment section at top of the file and add *your name* and *the date* in the space provided.

▶ 3. Save the files as **home.htm**, **tips.htm**, and **glossary.htm**, respectively, in the tutorial.02\tutorial folder.

▶ 4. Take some time reviewing the HTML code within each document so that you understand the structure and content of the files.

▶ 5. Start your Web browser, and then one at a time, open the **home.htm**, **tips.htm**, and **glossary.htm** files. Figure 2-1 shows the current layout and appearance of Gerry's three Web pages.

Figure 2-1 ▶ **Pages in the CAMshots Web site**

home.htm
the CAMshots home page

tips.htm
the CAMshots tip of the day

glossary.htm
a partial glossary of
photography terminology

Gerry wants to create links among the three pages so that users can easily navigate from one page to another. Before you write code for the links, it's worthwhile to map out exactly how you want the pages to relate to each other, using a technique known as storyboarding. A **storyboard** is a diagram of a Web site's structure, showing all the pages in the site and indicating how they are linked together. Because Web sites use a variety of structures, it's important to storyboard your Web site before you start creating your pages. This helps you determine which structure works best for the type of information your site contains. A well-designed structure ensures that users will able to navigate the site without getting lost or missing important information.

Every Web site starts with a single **home page** that acts as a focal point for the Web site. It is usually the first page that users see. Starting from the home page, you add the links to other pages in the site, creating the site's overall structure. The Web sites you commonly encounter as you navigate the Web use one of several different Web structures. Examine some of these structures to help you decide how to design your own sites.

Linear Structures

If you wanted to create an online version of a famous play, like Shakespeare's *Hamlet*, one method would be to link the individual scenes of the play in a long chain. Figure 2-2 shows the storyboard for this type of **linear structure**, in which each page is linked with the pages that follow and precede it. Readers navigate this structure by moving forward and backward through the pages, much as they might move forward and backward through the pages of a book.

A linear structure   Figure 2-2

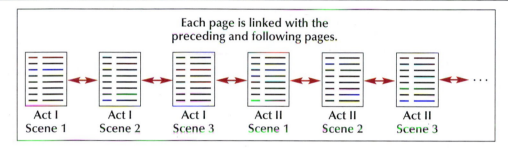

Linear structures work for Web sites with a clearly defined order of pages that are small in size. However, they can be difficult to work with as the chain of pages increases in length. An additional problem is that in a linear structure you move farther and farther away from the home page as you progress through the site. Because home pages often contain important general information about the site and its author, this is usually not the best design technique.

You can modify this structure to make it easier for users to return immediately to the home page or other main pages. Figure 2-3 shows this online play with an **augmented linear structure**, in which each page contains an additional link back to the opening page of each act.

An augmented linear structure   Figure 2-3

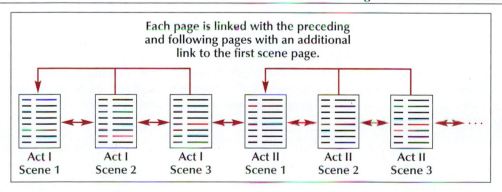

Hierarchical Structures

Another popular structure is the **hierarchical structure**, in which the pages are linked going from the home page down to pages dedicated to specific topics. Those pages, in turn, can be linked to even more specific topics. So, a hierarchical structure allows users to easily move from general to specific and back again. In the case of the online play, you can link an introductory page containing general information about the play to pages that describe each of the play's acts, and within each act you can include links to individual scenes. See Figure 2-4. With this structure, a user can move quickly to a specific scene within the page, bypassing the need to move through each scene in the play.

Figure 2-4 | A hierarchical structure

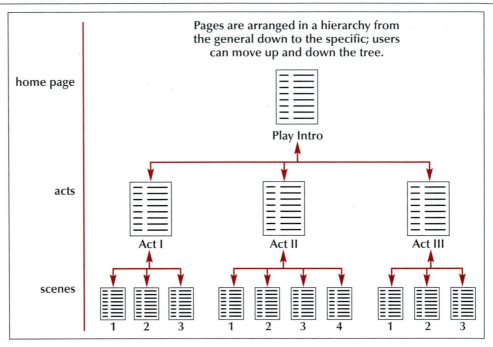

Pages are arranged in a hierarchy from the general down to the specific; users can move up and down the tree.

home page — Play Intro

acts — Act I, Act II, Act III

scenes — 1 2 3 | 1 2 3 4 | 1 2 3

Mixed Structures

With larger and more complex Web sites, you often need to use a combination of structures. Figure 2-5 shows the online play using a mixture of the three main structures. The overall form is hierarchical, as users can move from a general introduction down to individual scenes; however, users can also move through the site in a linear fashion, going from act to act and scene to scene. Finally, each individual scene contains a link to the home page, allowing users to jump to the top of the hierarchy without moving through the different levels.

A mixed structure | Figure 2-5

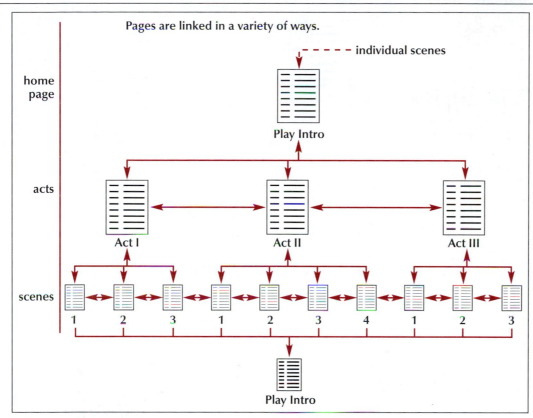

As these examples show, a little foresight can go a long way toward making your Web site easier to use. Also keep in mind that search results from a Web search engine such as Google or Yahoo! can point users to any page in your Web site—not just your home page—so they will need to quickly understand what your site contains and how to navigate it. At a minimum, each page should contain a link to the site's home page or to the relevant main topic page. In some cases, you might want to supply your users with a **site index**, which is a page containing an outline of the entire site and its contents. Unstructured Web sites can be difficult and frustrating to use. Consider the storyboard of the site displayed in Figure 2-6.

Figure 2-6 ▶ **Web site with no coherent structure**

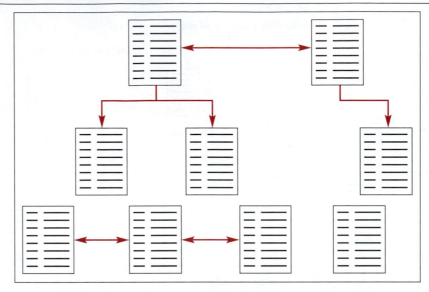

This confusing structure makes it difficult for users to grasp the site's contents and scope. The user might not even be aware of the presence of some pages because there are no connecting links, and some of the links only point in one direction. The Web is a competitive place; studies have shown that users who don't see how to get what they want within the first few seconds often leave a Web site. How long would a user spend on a site like the one shown in Figure 2-6?

Protected Structures

Sections of most commercial Web sites are off-limits except to subscribers and registered customers. As shown in Figure 2-7, these sites have a password-protected Web page that users must go through to get to the off-limits areas. The same Web site design principles apply to the protected section as the regular, open section of the site.

Figure 2-7 ▶ **A protected structure**

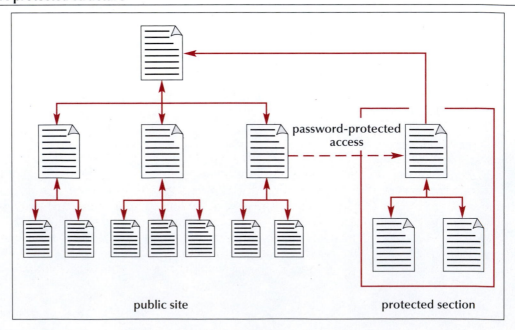

Storyboarding a protected structure is particularly important to ensure that no unmonitored "back doors" to the protected area are allowed in the site design.

Creating a Hypertext Link

Gerry wants his site visitors to be able to move effortlessly among the three documents he's created. To do that, you'll link each page to the other two pages. Figure 2-8 provides the storyboard for the simple structure you have in mind.

Storyboard for the CAMshots Web site Figure 2-8

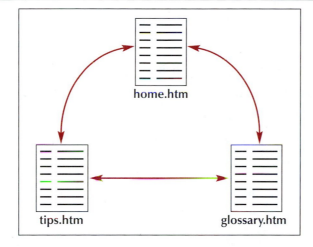

To create these links, you have to add hypertext links to each of the three documents. Hypertext links are created by enclosing some document content with a set of opening and closing <a> tags. The general syntax to create a hypertext link is

```
<a href="reference">content</a>
```

where *reference* is the location being linked to and *content* is the document content that is being marked as a link. The *reference* value can be a page on the World Wide Web, a local file, an e-mail address, or a network server. For example, to create a hypertext link to the tips.htm file, you could enter the following code:

```
<a href="tips.htm">Photography Tips</a>
```

This code marks the text "Photography Tips" as a hypertext link. When rendered by the browser, the words "Photography Tips" will be underlined, providing a visual clue to the user that the text is linked to another document. If the user clicks the text with a mouse, the browser will load the linked document (tips.htm).

Filenames are case sensitive on some operating systems, including the UNIX and Macintosh operating systems. Web servers running on those systems differentiate between a file named tips.htm and Tips.htm. For this reason, you might find that links you create on your computer do not work when you transfer your files to a Web server. To avoid this problem, the current standard is to always use lowercase filenames for all Web site files and to avoid using special characters such as blanks and slashes (/).

At the top of the home.htm, tips.htm, and glossary.htm files, Gerry has already entered the names of each of his three documents. Your first task is to mark these names as hypertext links to each of Gerry's three files. You'll start with the names in the home.htm file.

Marking a Hypertext Link

- To mark content as hypertext, use

  `<a href="`*reference*`">`*content*`</a>`

  where *reference* is the location being linked to and *content* is the document content that is being marked as a link.

To create a hypertext link to a document:

▶ 1. Return to the **home.htm** file in your text editor and locate the second div element at the top of the file.

▶ 2. Mark the text "Home" as a hypertext link using a set of <a> tags as follows:

  `<a href="home.htm">Home</a>`

▶ 3. Mark the text "Tips" as a hypertext link using the following code:

  `<a href="tips.htm">Tips</a>`

▶ 4. Mark the text "Glossary" as a hypertext link as follows:

  `<a href="glossary.htm">Glossary</a>`

Figure 2-9 highlights the revised text in the home.htm file.

Figure 2-9 ▶ **Marking hypertext links in the home.htm file**

```
<body>
    <div>
        <img src="camshots.jpg" alt="CAMshots" />
    </div>
    <hr />

    <div>
        [ <a href="home.htm">Home</a> ]
                 
        [ <a href="tips.htm">Tips</a>  ]
                 
        [ <a href="glossary.htm">Glossary</a>  ]
    </div>
```

▶ 5. Save your changes to the file.

▶ 6. The two other files have the same headings at the top of the document. Go to the **tips.htm** file in your text editor and repeat Steps 2 through 5 for the Home, Tips, and Glossary titles at the top of that file.

▶ 7. Go to the **glossary.htm** file in your text editor and repeat Steps 2 through 5 to mark the titles in that document as hypertext links as well.

Now that you've added hypertext links to each of the three documents, test those links in your browser.

▶ 8. Reload or refresh the **home.htm** file in your Web browser. As indicated in Figure 2-10, the titles at the top of the page should now be underlined, providing visual evidence that these words are treated as hypertext links.

Hypertext links in the home page ◢ Figure 2-10

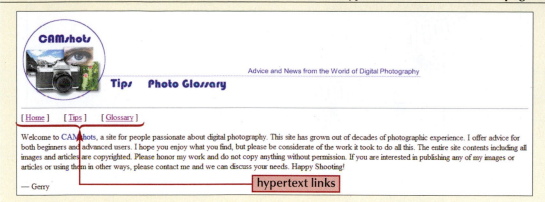

> **9.** Click the **Tips** link from the list of page names. Verify that the browser loads and displays the Tips page.

> **10.** Click the **Glossary** link. Verify that the Glossary page is opened by the browser.

> **11.** Continue to click the hypertext links from the list, confirming that you can jump from any of the three pages to each of the other two pages.

> **Trouble?** If the links do not work, check the spelling of the filenames in the href attributes of the <a> tags. Because some Web servers require you to match capitalization in a filename, you should verify this in your attributes as well.

Specifying a Folder Path

In the links you've just created, you specified only the filename and not the location of the file. When you specify only the filename, the browser searches for the file in the same folder as the document containing the hypertext link; however, large Web sites containing hundreds of documents often place those documents in separate folders to make them easier to manage.

As Gerry adds more files to his Web site, he will probably want to use folders to organize the files. Figure 2-11 shows a preview of how Gerry might employ those folders. In this case, the topmost folder is named camshots. Gerry has placed some of his HTML files within the pages folder, which he has then divided into three subfolders named tips, glossary, and articles. He has also created separate folders for the images and video clips used on his Web site. Figure 2-11 displays the location of four HTML files named index.htm, tips1.htm, tips2.htm, and glossary.htm.

Figure 2-11   A sample folder structure

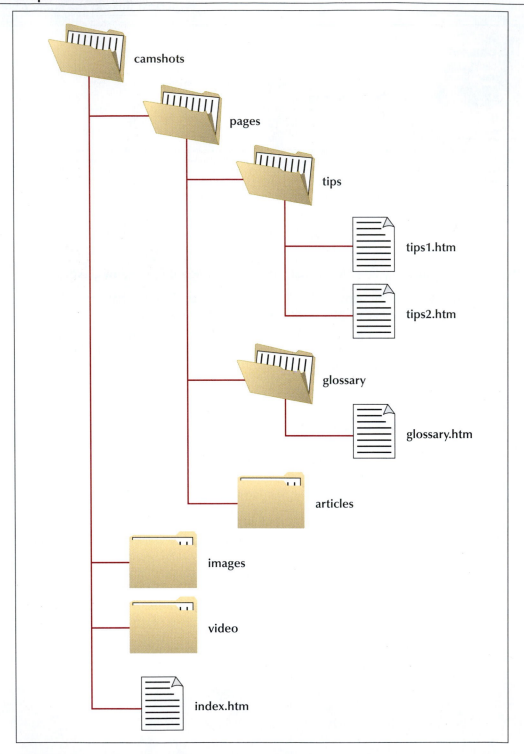

To create a link to a file located in a different folder than the current document, you must specify the file's location, or **path**, so that browsers can find it. HTML supports two kinds of paths: absolute and relative.

Absolute Paths

An **absolute path** specifies a file's precise location within a computer's entire folder structure. Absolute pathnames employ the syntax

/folder1/folder2/folder3/file

where *folder1* is the topmost folder in the computer's folder tree, followed by *folder2*, *folder3*, and so forth, down to the file you want to link to. Figure 2-12 shows how you would express absolute paths to the four files listed in Figure 2-11.

Tip

To make your Web site easier to maintain, organize your folders to match the organization of the pages on the Web site and group images and other media files within folders separate from your HTML files.

Absolute paths | Figure 2-12

Absolute Path	Interpretation
/camshots/pages/tips/tips1.htm	The tips1.htm file located in the pages/tips subfolder
/camshots/pages/tips/tips2.htm	The tips2.htm file located in the pages/tips subfolder
/camshots/pages/glossary/glossary.htm	The glossary.htm file located in the pages/glossary subfolder
/camshots/index.htm	The index.htm file located in the camshots folder

If files are located on different drives as well as in different folders, you must include the drive letter in the form

/drive||/folder1/folder2/folder3/file

where *drive* is the letter assigned to the drive. For example, the tips1.htm file located on drive C in the /camshots/pages/tips folder would have the absolute path:

```
/C|/camshots/pages/tips/tips1.htm
```

Remember that you don't have to include a drive letter if the destination document is located on the same drive as the document containing the link.

Relative Paths

When many folders and subfolders are involved, absolute pathnames can be cumbersome and confusing. For that reason, most Web designers prefer to use relative paths. A **relative path** specifies a file's location in relation to the location of the current document. If the file is in the same location as the current document, the relative path is simply the filename. If the file is in a subfolder of the current document, include the name of the subfolder without the forward slash in the form

folder/file

where *folder* is the name of the subfolder. To go farther down the folder tree to other subfolders, include those in the relative path separated by forward slashes, i.e.

folder1/folder2/folder3/file

where *folder1*, *folder2*, *folder3*, and so forth are subfolders of the current folder. Finally, a relative path can go up the folder tree by starting the pathname with a double period (..) followed by a forward slash and the name of the file. The path

../file

references the *file* document located in the parent folder of the current document. To reference a different folder on the same level of the folder tree, known as a **sibling folder**, you move up the folder tree using the double period (..) and then down using the name of the sibling folder. The general syntax is

../folder/file

where *folder* is the name of the sibling folder. Figure 2-13 shows the relative paths to the six files in the tree from Figure 2-11, starting from the camshots/pages/tips subfolder.

Figure 2-13   **Relative paths**

Relative Path from the /camshots/pages/tips Subfolder	Interpretation
tips1.htm	The tips1.htm file located in the current folder
tips2.htm	The tips2.htm file located in the current folder
../glossary/glossary.htm	The glossary.htm file located in the sibling glossary folder
../../index.htm	The index.htm file located in the parent camshots folder

Tip

You can reference the current folder using a single period (.) character.

You should almost always use relative paths in your links. If you have to move your files to a different computer or server, you can move the entire folder structure without having to change the relative pathnames you created. If you use absolute pathnames, you will probably have to revise each link to reflect the new location of the folder tree on the computer.

Changing the Base

As you've just seen, a browser resolves relative pathnames based on the location of the current document. You can change this behavior by specifying a different base or starting location for all relative paths. The code to specify a different base is

```
<base href="path" />
```

where *path* is the folder location that you want the browser to use when resolving relative paths in the current document. The base element has to be added to the head section of the HTML file and will be applied to all hypertext links found within the document.

Reference Window | **Using the Base Element to Set the Default Location of Relative Paths**

- To set the default location for a relative path, add the element
  ```
  <base href="path" />
  ```
  to the document head, where *path* is the folder location that you want the browser to use when resolving relative paths in the current document.

The base element is useful when a single document is moved to a new folder. Rather than rewriting all of the relative paths to reflect the document's new location, the base element redirects browsers to the document's old location, allowing any relative paths to be resolved as they were before.

Managing Your Web Site | InSight

Web sites can quickly grow from a couple of pages to dozens or hundreds of pages. As the size of the site increases, it becomes more difficult to get a clear picture of the site's structure and content. Imagine deleting or moving a file in a Web site that contains dozens of folders and hundreds of files. Can you easily project the effect of this change? Will all of your hypertext links still work after you move or delete the file?

To effectively manage a Web site, you should follow a few important rules. The first is to be consistent in how you structure the site. If you decide to collect all image files in one folder, you should follow that rule as you add more pages and images. Web sites are more likely to break down if files and folders are scattered throughout the server without a consistent rule or pattern. Decide on a structure early on and stick with it.

The second rule is to create a folder structure that matches the structure of the Web site itself. If the pages can be easily categorized into different groups, that grouping should also be reflected in the grouping of the subfolders. The names you assign to your files and folder should also reflect their use on the Web site. This makes it easier for you to predict how modifying a file or folder will impact other pages on the site.

Finally, you should document your work by adding comments to each new Web page. Comments are useful not only for colleagues who may be working on the site, but also for the author who has to revisit those files months or even years after creating them. The comments should include:

- The page's filename and location
- The page's author and the date the page was initially created
- A list of any supporting files used in the document, such as image and audio files
- A list of the files and their locations that link to the page
- A list of the files and their locations that the page links to

By following these rules, you can reduce a lot of the headaches associated with maintaining a large and complicated Web site.

You've completed your initial work linking the three files in Gerry's Web site. In the next session, you'll learn how to work with hypertext links that point to locations within files. If you want to take a break before starting the next session, you can close your files and your Web browser now.

Session 2.1 Quick Check | Review

1. What is storyboarding? Why is it important in creating a Web page system?
2. What is a linear structure? What is a hierarchical structure?
3. What code would you enter to link the text "Sports Info" to the sports.htm file? Assume that the current document and sports.htm are in the same folder.
4. What's the difference between an absolute path and a relative path?
5. Refer to Figure 2-11. If the current file is in the camshots/pages/glossary folder, what are the relative paths for the four files listed in the folder tree?
6. What is the purpose of the base element?

Session 2.2

Tip

In general, Web pages should not span more than one or two screen heights. Studies show that long Web pages are often skipped by busy users.

Linking to Locations within Documents

Gerry likes the links you've created in the last session and would like you to add some more links to the Glossary page. Recall that the Glossary page contains a list of digital photography terms. The page is very long, requiring users to scroll through the document to find a term of interest. At the top of the page Gerry has listed the letters A through Z. Gerry wants to give users the ability to jump to a specific section of the document by clicking a letter from the list. See Figure 2-14.

Figure 2-14 ▶ **Jumping to a location within a Web page**

clicking the letter D from the alphabetical list …

…jumps the user to the D section of the glossary

Using the id Attribute

To jump to a specific location within a document, you first need to mark that location. One way of doing this is to add an id attribute to an element at that location in the document. The syntax of the id attribute is

```
id="id"
```

where *id* is the value of the element id. For example, the following code marks the h2 element with an id value of H:

```
<h2 id="H">H</h2>
```

Note that id names must be unique. If you assign the same id name to more than one element on your Web page, the browser uses the first occurrence of the id name. XHTML documents will be rejected if they contain elements with duplicate ids. Id names are not case sensitive, so browsers do not differentiate between ids named top and TOP.

Reference Window | **Defining an Element id**

- To define the id of a specific element in a Web document, use the attribute
  id="*id*"
  where *id* is the value of the element id.

The Glossary page has only a partial list of the photography terms that Gerry will eventually add to his Web site. For now, you'll only mark sections in the glossary corresponding to the letters A through F.

To add the id attribute to h2 headings:

▶ 1. Return to the **glossary.htm** file in your text editor.

▶ 2. Scroll down the file and locate the h2 heading for the letter A. Within the opening <h2> tag, insert the following attribute:

   `id="A"`

▶ 3. Locate the h2 heading for the letter B and insert the following attribute in the opening <h2> tag:

   `id="B"`

   Figure 2-15 highlights the revised code.

Adding the id attribute to h2 headings ◀ **Figure 2-15**

```
<hr />
<h2 id="A">A</h2>
<dl>
    <dt><b>Ambient Light</b></dt>
    <dd>The natural light in a scene.</dd>
    <dt><b>Aperture</b></dt>
    <dd>The maximum size of the hole through which light enters the camera.</dd>
    <dt><b>Artifact</b></dt>
    <dd>Unwanted distortions in an image caused by image compression.</dd>
    <dt><b>Aspect Ratio</b></dt>
    <dd>The ratio between the width and height of an image.</dd>
</dl>

<hr />
<h2 id="B">B</h2>
<dl>
    <dt><b>Bit</b></dt>
    <dd>The smallest unit of computer memory.</dd>
    <dt><b>Bitmap</b></dt>
    <dd>A method of storing information that maps an image pixel bit by bit.</dd>
    <dt><b>Byte</b></dt>
    <dd>A group of 8 bits, the basic unit of information for the computer.</dd>
</dl>
```

▶ 4. Continue going down the file, adding id attributes to the opening <h2> heading tags for C, D, E, and F corresponding to the letters of those headings.

For longer documents like the Glossary page, it's also helpful to the reader to be able to jump directly from the bottom of a long page to the top of the page rather than having to scroll back up. With that in mind, you'll also add an id attribute marking the element at the top of the page.

To mark the top of the page:

▶ 1. Scroll up the **glossary.htm** file in your text editor and locate the div element directly below the opening <body> tag.

▶ 2. Insert the following attribute within the opening <div> tag, as shown in Figure 2-16:

   `id="top"`

Adding an id attribute to the div element ◀ **Figure 2-16**

```
<body>
    <div id="top">
        <img src="camshots.jpg" alt="CAMshots" />
    </div>
    <hr />
```

Linking to an id

Once you've marked an element using the id attribute, you can create a hypertext link to that element using the hypertext link

```
<a href="#id">content</a>
```

where *id* is the value of the id attribute of the element. For example, to create a link to the h2 heading for the letter A in the glossary document, you would enter the following code:

```
<a href="#A">A</a>
```

Use this code to change the entries on the Glossary page to hypertext links pointing to the section of the glossary corresponding to the selected letter.

To change the list of letters to hypertext links:

1. Locate the letter A in the list of letters at the top of the **glossary.htm** file.

2. After the [character, insert the following opening tag:

   ```
   <a href="#A">
   ```

3. Between the letter A and the] character, insert closing **</a>** tag. Figure 2-17 shows the revised code.

Figure 2-17   **Creating a hypertext link for "A"**

```
<h1 style="color: teal">Glossary</h1>
<p>
    [<a href="#A">A</a>] [B] [C]
    [D] [E] [F]
    [G] [H] [I]
    [J] [K] [L]
    [M] [N] [O]
    [P] [Q] [R]
    [S] [T] [U]
    [V] [W] [X]
    [Y] [Z]
</p>
```

4. Mark the letters B through F in the list as hypertext links pointing to the appropriate h2 headings in the document. Figure 2-18 shows the revised code for the list of letters.

Figure 2-18   **Hypertext links for the list of letters**

```
<h1 style="color: teal">Glossary</h1>
<p>
    [<a href="#A">A</a>] [<a href="#B">B</a>] [<a href="#C">C</a>]
    [<a href="#D">D</a>] [<a href="#E">E</a>] [<a href="#F">F</a>]
    [G] [H] [I]
    [J] [K] [L]
    [M] [N] [O]
    [P] [Q] [R]
    [S] [T] [U]
    [V] [W] [X]
    [Y] [Z]
</p>
```

Gerry also wants you to create a hypertext link at the bottom of the file that points to the top (using the id attribute you created in the last set of steps).

5. Scroll to the bottom of the file and locate the text "Return to Top."

6. Mark the text as hypertext, pointing to the element with an id value of top. See Figure 2-19.

Hypertext link to return to the top of the document ◄ Figure 2-19

```
<hr />
<div><a href="#top">Return to Top</a> &#8657;</div>
<hr />
<address>
    CAMShots &#8250;&#8250;&#8250; Tips and News from the World of Digital Photography
</address>
```

7. Save your changes to the file and then reload or refresh the **glossary.htm** file in your Web browser.

8. As shown in Figure 2-20, the letters A through F in the alphabetic list are displayed as hypertext links. Click the link for **F** and verify that you jump down to the end of the document, where the photographic terms starting with the letter F are listed.

Hypertext links in the glossary page ◄ Figure 2-20

Advice and News from the World of Digital Photography

Tips   Photo Glossary

[Home]   [Tips]   [Glossary]

Glossary

[A] [B] [C] [D] [E] [F] [G] [H] [I] [J] [K] [L] [M] [N] [O] [P] [Q] [R] [S] [T] [U] [V] [W] [X] [Y] [Z]

9. Click the **Return to Top** hypertext link and verify that you jump back to the top of the document.

10. Click the other links within the document and verify that you jump to the correct sections of the glossary.

    Trouble? The browser cannot scroll farther than the end of the page. So, you might not see any difference between jumping to the E section of the glossary and jumping to the F section.

InSight | **Working with Anchors**

Early browser versions might not support the use of the id attribute as a way of marking document elements. These early browser versions instead used anchors or bookmarks to mark document locations. The syntax of the anchor element is

```
<a name="anchor">content</a>
```

where *anchor* is the name of the anchor that marks the location of the document *content*. For example, to mark the h2 heading with an anchor of "A," you would enter the following code:

```
<h2><a name="A">A</a></h2>
```

Marking a location with an anchor does not change your document's appearance in any way; it merely creates a destination within your document.

You use the same syntax to link to locations marked with an anchor as you would with locations marked with id attributes. To link to the above anchor, you could use the following code:

```
<a href="#A">A</a>
```

The use of anchors is a deprecated feature of HTML and is not supported in strict applications of XHTML, but you will still see anchors used in older code and in code generated by HTML editors and converters.

Creating Links between Documents

Gerry knows that the glossary will be one of the most useful parts of his Web site, especially for novice photographers. However, he's also aware that most people do not read through glossaries. He would like to create links from the words he uses in his articles to glossary entries so that readers of his articles can quickly access definitions for terms they don't understand. His articles are not on the same page as his Glossary page, so he will have to create a link between those pages and specific glossary entries.

To create a link to a specific location in another file, enter the code

```
<a href="reference#id">content</a>
```

where *reference* is a reference to an HTML or XHTML file and *id* is the id of an element marked within that file. For example, the code

```
<a href="glossary.htm#D">"D" terms in the Glossary</a>
```

creates a hypertext link to the D section in the glossary.htm file. This assumes that the glossary.htm file is located in the same folder as the document containing the hypertext link. If not, you have to include either the absolute or relative path information along with the filename, as described in the last session.

Reference Window | **Linking to an id**

- To link to a specific location within the current file, use
  ```
  <a href="#id">content</a>
  ```
  where *id* is the id value of an element within the document.
- To link to a specific location in another file, use
  ```
  <a href="reference#id">content</a>
  ```
  where *reference* is a reference to an external file and *id* is the id value of an element in that file.

On Gerry's home page, he wants to showcase a Photo of the Month, displaying a photo that his readers might find interesting or useful in their own work. Along with the photo, he has included the digital camera settings used in taking the photo. Many of the camera settings are described on the Glossary page. Gerry suggests that you create a link between the setting name and the glossary entry. The five entries he wants to link to are: F-stop, Exposure, Focal Length, Aperture, and Flash Mode. Your first step is to mark these entries in the glossary using the id attribute.

To mark the glossary entries:

1. Return to the **glossary.htm** file in your text editor.

2. Scroll down the file and locate the Aperture definition term.

3. As shown in Figure 2-21, within the opening <dt> tag, insert the attribute

   ```
   id="aperture"
   ```

Inserting an id attribute ◀ Figure 2-21

```
<hr />
<h2 id="A">A</h2>
<dl>
    <dt><b>Ambient Light</b></dt>
    <dd>The natural light in a scene.</dd>
    <dt id="aperture"><b>Aperture</b></dt>
    <dd>The maximum size of the hole through which light enters the camera.</dd>
    <dt><b>Artifact</b></dt>
    <dd>Unwanted distortions in an image caused by image compression.</dd>
    <dt><b>Aspect Ratio</b></dt>
    <dd>The ratio between the width and height of an image.</dd>
</dl>
```

4. Scroll down the file and locate the Exposure definition term.

5. Within the opening <dt> tag, insert the following attribute:

   ```
   id="exposure"
   ```

6. Go to the F section of the glossary and mark the terms with the following ids:

   F-stop with the id f-stop

   Flash Mode with the id flash_mode

   Focal Length with the id focal_length

7. Save your changes to the **glossary.htm** file.

Next you'll go to the Home page and create links from these terms in the Photo of the Month description to their entries on the Glossary page.

To create links to the glossary entries:

1. Open the **home.htm** file in your text editor.

2. Scroll down the file and locate the F-stop term from the unordered list.

3. Mark "F-stop" as a hypertext link using the following code:

   ```
   <a href="glossary.htm#f-stop">F-stop</a>
   ```

4. Mark "Exposure" as a hypertext link with:

   ```
   <a href="glossary.htm#exposure">Exposure</a>
   ```

5. Mark the remaining three entries in the unordered list as hypertext pointing to their corresponding entries on the Glossary page. Figure 2-22 highlights the revised code in the file.

| Figure 2-22 | Linking to a location within another document |

```
                            <l>Pear Lake Reflection</l></blockquote>
<ul>
    <li>Camera:
                
        Nikon D50</li>
    <li><a href="glossary.htm#f-stop">F-stop</a>:
                  
        f/7.1</li>
    <li><a href="glossary.htm#exposure">Exposure</a>:
              
        1/200 sec.</li>                                    document file
    <li><a href="glossary.htm#focal_length">Focal Length</a>:
         
        18mm</li>
    <li><a href="glossary.htm#aperture">Aperture</a>:
                      element id
        3.6</li>
    <li><a href="glossary.htm#flash_mode">Flash Mode</a>:
           No Flash</li>
</ul>
```

▶ **6.** Save your changes to the file.

▶ **7.** Refresh the **home.htm** file in your Web browser. As shown in Figure 2-23, the settings from the Photo of the Month description are now displayed as hypertext links.

| Figure 2-23 | Linked photography terms |

Photo of the Month

Pear Lake Reflection

- Camera: Nikon D50
- F-stop: f/7.1
- Exposure: 1/200 sec.
- Focal Length: 18mm
- Aperture: 3.6
- Flash Mode: No flash

▶ **8.** Click the **F-stop** hypertext link and verify that you jump to the Glossary page with the F-stop entry displayed in the browser window.

▶ **9.** Return to the **CAMshots home page** and click the hypertext links for the other terms in the list of photo settings, verifying that you jump to the section of the glossary that displays that term's definition.

Working with Linked Images and Image Maps

A standard practice on the Web is to turn the Web site's logo into a hypertext link pointing to the home page. This gives users a quick reference point to the home page rather than searching for a link to the home page. To mark an inline image as a hypertext link, you enclose the <img> tag within a set of <a> tags as follows:

```
<a href="reference"><img src="file" alt="text" /></a>
```

Once the image has been linked, clicking anywhere within the image jumps the user to the linked file.

Introducing Image Maps

When you mark an inline image as a hypertext link, the entire image is linked to the same destination file; however, HTML also allows you to divide an image into different zones, or **hotspots,** each linked to a different destination. Therefore, a single inline image can be linked to several locations. Gerry is interested in doing this with the CAMshots logo. He would like you to create hotspots for the logo so that if the user clicks anywhere within the CAMshots circle on the left side of the logo, the user jumps to the Home page, while clicking either Tips or Photo Glossary in the logo takes the user to the Tips page or the Glossary page. See Figure 2-24.

Hotspots within the CAMshots logo ◀ Figure 2-24

home.htm   tips.htm   glossary.htm

To define these hotspots, you create an **image map** that matches a specified region of the inline image to a specific destination. HTML supports two kinds of image maps: client-side image maps and server-side image maps. You'll first study how to create a client-side image map.

Client-Side Image Maps

A **client-side image map** is an image map that is handled entirely by the Web browser running on the user's computer. Client-side image maps are defined with the map element

```
<map id="map" name="map">
   hotspots
</map>
```

where *map* is the name of the image map and *hotspots* are the locations of the hotspots within the image. Each image map has to be given an id and a name. You have to include both attributes, setting them to the same value, because HTML code requires the name attribute and XHTML requires the id attribute. As long as you include both, your code will work under all browsers. For example, the following code creates a map element named logomap:

```
<map id="logomap" name="logomap">
...
</map>
```

Map elements can be placed anywhere within the body of the Web page because they are not actually displayed by the browser, but used as references for mapping hotspots to inline images. The common practice is to place the map element below the inline image.

Defining Hotspots

The individual hotspots are defined using the area element

```
<area shape="shape" coords="coordinates" href="reference" alt="text" />
```

where *shape* is the shape of the hotspot region, *coordinates* are the list of points that define the boundaries of the region, *reference* is the file or location that the hotspot is linked to, and *text* is alternate text displayed for nongraphical browsers. Hotspots can be created in the shape of rectangles, circles, or polygons (multisided figures). So, the shape attribute can have the value rect for a rectangular hotspot, "circle" for a circular hotspot, and "poly" for a polygonal or multisided hotspot. A fourth shape option is "default," representing the remaining area of the inline image not covered by hotspots. There is no limit to the number of area elements you can add to an image map. Hotspots can also overlap. If they do and the user clicks an overlapping area, the browser opens the link of the first hotspot defined in the map.

Hotspot coordinates are measured in **pixels**, which are the smallest unit or dot in a digital image or display. Your computer monitor might have a size of 1024 x 768 pixels, which means that the display is 1024 dots wide by 768 dots tall. The CAMshots logo that Gerry uses in his Web site has a dimension of 778 pixels wide by 164 pixels tall. When used with the coords attribute of the area element, the pixel values exactly define the location and size of the hotspot region.

Each hotspot shape has a different set of coordinates that define it. To define a rectangular hotspot, enter

```
<area shape="rect" coords="x1, y1, x2, y2" ... />
```

where *x1, y1* are the coordinates of the upper-left corner of the rectangle and *x2, y2* are the coordinates of the rectangle's lower-right corner. Figure 2-25 shows the coordinates of the rectangular region surrounding the Photo Glossary hotspot.

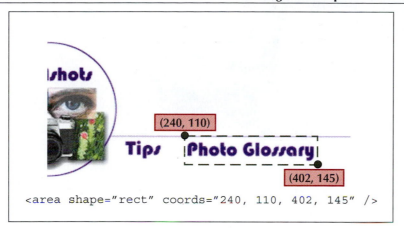

```
<area shape="rect" coords="240, 110, 402, 145" />
```

The upper-left corner of the rectangle has the coordinates (240, 110). The lower-left corner is found at the coordinates (402, 145). Coordinates are always expressed relative to the image's top-left corner. A coordinate of (240, 110) refers to a point that is 240 pixels to the right and 110 pixels down from the image's top-left corner.

Circular hotspots are defined using the area element

```
<area shape="circle" coords="x, y, r" ... />
```

where x and y are the coordinates of the center of the circle and r is the circle's radius. Figure 2-26 shows the coordinates for a circular hotspot around the CAMshots image from the Web site logo. The center of the circle is located at the coordinates (82, 78) and the circle has a radius of 80 pixels.

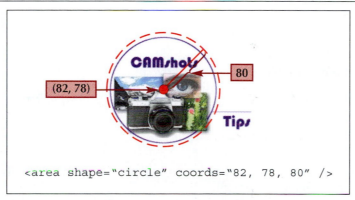

```
<area shape="circle" coords="82, 78, 80" />
```

Polygonal hotspots are defined with

```
<area shape="poly" coords="x1, y1, x2, y2, x3, y3, ..." ... />
```

where $(x1, y1)$, $(x2, y2)$, $(x3, y3)$ and so forth define the coordinates of each corner in the multisided shape. Figure 2-27 shows the coordinates for a triangular-shaped hotspot with corners at (30, 142), (76, 80), and (110, 142). With polygonal hotspots, you can create a wide variety of shapes as long you know the coordinates of each corner.

Figure 2-27 ▶ **Polygonal hotspot and area element**

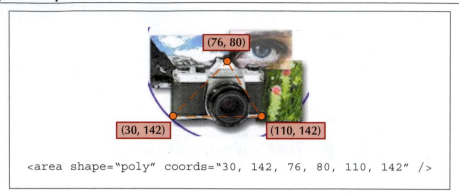

```
<area shape="poly" coords="30, 142, 76, 80, 110, 142" />
```

Finally, to define the default hotspot for the image use

```
<area shape="default" coords="0, 0, x, y" ... />
```

where *x* is the width of the inline image in pixels and *y* is the image's height. Any spot in the inline image that is not covered by another hotspot will activate the default hotspot link.

To determine the coordinates of a hotspot, you can use either a graphics program such as Adobe Photoshop or image map software that automatically generates the HTML code for the hotspots you define.

In this case, assume that Gerry has already determined the coordinates for the hotspots in his image map and provided them for you. He has three hotspots that he wants you to create, shown earlier in Figure 2-24. The first is a circular hotspot linked to the home.htm file, centered at the point (82, 78) and having a radius of 80 pixels. The second is a rectangular hotspot, linked to the tips.htm file with corners at (168, 110) and (225, 145). The third is also rectangular, linked to the glossary.htm file with corners at (240, 110) and (402, 145). You do not have to create a polygonal hotspot.

You'll name the image map containing these hotspots logomap.

To create an image map:

1. Return to **home.htm** file in your text editor.

2. Directly below the <img> tag for the CAMshots inline image, insert the following map element:

   ```
   <map id="logomap" name="logomap">
   </map>
   ```

3. Within the map element, insert a circular hotspot that points to the home.htm file using the following area element:

   ```
   <area shape="circle" coords="82, 78, 80"
       href="home.htm" alt="Home" />
   ```

4. Directly below the <area> tag for the circular hotspot, insert the following two rectangular hotspots pointing to the tips.htm and glossary.htm files:

   ```
   <area shape="rect" coords="168, 110, 225, 145"
       href="tips.htm" alt="Tips" />
   <area shape="rect" coords="240, 110, 402, 145"
       href="glossary.htm" alt="Glossary" />
   ```

   Figure 2-28 highlights the new code in the file.

Creating an image map ▶ Figure 2-28

```
<body>
  <div>
    <img src="camshots.jpg" alt="CAMshots" />
    <map id="logomap" name="logomap">
      <area shape="circle" coords="82, 78, 80"
            href="home.htm" alt="Home" />
      <area shape="rect" coords="168, 110, 225, 145"
            href="tips.htm" alt="Tips" />
      <area shape="rect" coords="240, 110, 402, 145"
            href="glossary.htm" alt="Glossary" />
    </map>
  </div>
  <hr />
```

hotspots ────────────▶ (pointing to the three `<area>` elements)

5. Save your changes to the file.

Creating a Client-Side Image Map | Reference Window

- To create a client-side image map, insert the map element
  ```
  <map name="map" id="map">
    hotspots
  </map>
  ```
  anywhere within the Web page body, where *map* is the name and id of the image map and *hotspots* is a list of hotspot areas defined within the image map.
- To add a hotspot to the image map, place the element
  ```
  <area shape="shape" coords="coordinates" href="reference"
  alt="text" />
  ```
  within the map element, where *shape* is the shape of the hotspot region, *coordinates* are the list of points that define the boundaries of the region, *reference* is the file or location that the hotspot is linked to, and *text* is alternate text displayed for nongraphical browsers.
- To define a rectangular-shaped hotspot, use the area element
  ```
  <area shape="rect" coords="x1, y1, x2, y2" ... />
  ```
  where x1, y1 are the coordinates of the upper-left corner of the rectangle and x2, y2 are the coordinates of the rectangle's lower-right corner.
- To define a circular hotspot, use
  ```
  <area shape="circle" coords="x, y, r" ... />
  ```
  where *x* and *y* are the coordinates of the center of the circle and *r* is the circle's radius.
- To define a polygonal hotspot, use
  ```
  <area shape="poly" coords="x1, y1, x2, y2, x3, y3, ..." ... />
  ```
  where (*x1, y1*), (*x2, y2*), (*x3, y3*), and so forth define the coordinates of each corner in the multisided shape.
- To define the default hotspot, use
  ```
  <area shape="default" coords="0, 0, x, y" ... />
  ```
  where *x* is the width of the inline image in pixels and *y* is the height in pixels.
- To apply an image map to an inline image, add the usemap attribute
  ```
  <img src="file" alt="text" usemap="#map" />
  ```
  to the img element, where *map* is the name or id of the map element.

Now that you've defined the image map, your next task is to apply the map to the CAMshots logo.

Applying an Image Map

To apply an image map to an image, add the usemap attribute to the inline image's <img> tag. The syntax is

```
<img src="file" alt="text" usemap="#map" />
```

where *map* is the id or name of the map element. If you place the map element in a separate file, you can reference it using the code

```
<img src="file" alt="text" usemap="reference#map" />
```

where *reference* is a reference to an HTML or XHTML file containing the map element. Unfortunately, most browsers do not support this option, so you should always place the image map in the same file as the inline image. You'll apply the logomap to the CAM-shots logo and then test it on your Web browser.

To apply the logomap image map:

1. Add the following attribute to the <img> tag for the CAMshots logo, as shown in Figure 2-29.

   ```
   usemap="#logomap"
   ```

Figure 2-29   Applying an image map

```
<body>
  <div>
    <img src="camshots.jpg" alt="CAMshots" usemap="#logomap" />
    <map id="logomap" name="logomap">
      <area shape="circle" coords="82, 78, 80"
        href="home.htm" alt="Home" />
      <area shape="rect" coords="168, 110, 225, 145"
        href="tips.htm" alt="Tips" />
      <area shape="rect" coords="240, 110, 402, 145"
        href="glossary.htm" alt="Glossary" />
    </map>
  </div>
  <hr />
```

imagemap

map element name or id

2. Save your changes to the file and reload or refresh the **home.htm** file in your Web browser.

   Trouble? Depending on your browser, you might see a border around the CAM-shots logo, which you can ignore for now. You'll remove it shortly.

3. Click anywhere within the word **Tips** in the logo image and verify that the browser opens the Tips page.

4. Return to the home page and click anywhere within the word **Photo Glossary** to verify that the browser opens the Glossary page.

Tip

If you need to be compatible with older browsers, use the attribute border="0" in place of the border-width style. Note that the border attribute has been deprecated and is not supported in strict applications of XHTML.

After changing the logo to a hypertext link, you may have noticed that you have added a border around the image. Hypertext links are usually underlined in the Web page; but with inline images, the image is displayed with a lined border. Gerry would prefer not to have a border because he feels that it detracts from the logo's appearance. He asks if you can remove the border but still keep the logo functioning as a hypertext link.

To remove the border, you can apply a border-width style to the inline image. By setting the width of the border to zero, you will effectively remove it from the logo. The style attribute to change the width of a border is

```
style="border-width: 0"
```

- To remove a border from an inline image, add the following attribute to the <img> tag:
  ```
  style="border-width: 0"
  ```

Use the border-width style to remove the border from the CAMshots logo on the three pages of Gerry's Web site.

To set the border width of the CAMshots logo to 0:

▶ 1. Return to the **home.htm** file in your text editor.

▶ 2. Add the following style attribute to the <img> tag for the logo inline image, as shown in Figure 2-30.
   ```
   style="border-width: 0"
   ```

Removing an inline image border — Figure 2-30

```
<body>
   <div>
      <img src="camshots.jpg" alt="CAMshots" usemap="#logomap" style="border-width: 0" />
      <map id="logomap" name="logomap">
         <area shape="circle" coords="82, 78, 80"
            href="home.htm" alt="Home" />
         <area shape="rect" coords="168, 110, 225, 145"
            href="tips.htm" alt="Tips" />
         <area shape="rect" coords="240, 110, 402, 145"
            href="glossary.htm" alt="Glossary" />
      </map>
   </div>
   <hr />
```

set the width of the image border to 0

▶ 3. Save your changes to the file.

▶ 4. Reload the **home.htm** file in your browser and verify that the border has been removed from the image.

Now that you've created an image map for the logo on the home page, you can create similar image maps for the logos on the Tips and Glossary pages.

To add image maps to the other Web pages:

▶ 1. Return to the **tips.htm** file in your text editor.

▶ 2. Replace the code within the div element for the logo image with the code shown earlier in Figure 2-30. (Hint: You can use the copy and paste feature of your text editor to copy the code from the home.htm file into the tips.htm file.)

▶ 3. Save your changes to the file.

▶ 4. Go to the **glossary.htm** file in your text editor.

▶ 5. As you did for the tips.htm file, replace the code within the div element for the logo image with the code from the home.htm file. Save your changes to the file.

▶ 6. Return to the **home.htm** file in your Web browser and verify that you can switch among the three Web pages by clicking the hotspots in the CAMshots logo.

▶ 7. If you want to take a break before starting the next session, close your files and programs now.

Server-Side Image Maps

The other type of image map you might encounter on the Web is a **server-side image map**, which is stored on the Web server rather than entered into the HTML code of the Web page. When you click a hotspot on a server-side image map, the coordinates of the mouse click are sent to the server, which activates the corresponding link, downloading the page to your Web browser.

The server-side image map was the original HTML standard and is still supported on the Web. However, this map has some limitations compared to client-side image maps. Because the map is located on the server, you cannot test your Web page without server access. Also, server-side image maps might be slower because information must be sent to the server with each mouse click. Finally, unlike client-side image maps, server-side image maps require the use of a mouse. This makes them unsuitable for users with disabilities or users running nongraphical browsers.

To create a server-side image map, enclose the inline image with a hypertext link such as

```
<a href="map">
   <img src="file" alt="text" ismap="ismap" />
</a>
```

where *map* is the name of a program or file running on the Web server that will handle the image map. The ismap attribute tells the Web browser to treat the inline image as an image map.

At this time, you do not foresee a need to use a server-side image map in the CAM-shots Web site. In any future projects, you'll continue to work with client-side maps.

| InSight | **Writing Effective Hypertext Links** |

To make it easier for users to navigate your Web site, you should follow a few key design tips. Write the text of your hypertext links so that they tell the reader exactly what type of document the link points to. For example, the link text

Click here for more information.

doesn't tell the user what type of document will appear when "here" is clicked. In the place of phrases like "click here," use descriptive link text such as:

For more information, view a list of frequently asked questions.

If the link points to a non-HTML file, such as a PDF document, include that information in the link text. If the linked document is extremely large and will take a while to download to the user's computer, include that information in your link text so that users can decide whether or not to initiate the transfer. The following link text informs users of the size of the video clip before they initiate the link:

Download the video clip (16 MB).

Make your link text easy to locate. Because most browsers underline hypertext links, don't use underlining for other text elements; use italic or boldface fonts instead. Users should never be confused about what is a link and what is not. Also, if you apply a color to your text, do not choose colors that will make the linked text harder to pick out against the Web page background.

Gerry is pleased with the progress you've made on his Web site. Adding the links to the glossary and within the CAMshots logo has made his site easier to navigate. However, there are many other sources of information about digital photography and digital cameras that Gerry wants to make available to his readers. In the next session you'll examine how to create links between his Web site and other sites on the World Wide Web.

Session 2.2 Quick Check | Review

1. Specify the code for marking the text "CAMshots FAQ" as an h2 heading with the id "faq."
2. Specify the code for marking the text "Read our FAQ" as hypertext linked to an element in the current document with the id "faq."
3. Specify the code for marking the text "Read our FAQ" as a hypertext link, pointing to an element with the id "faq" in the help.htm file. Assume that help.htm lies in the same folder as the current document.
4. Specify the code for placing an anchor with the name "faq" within the h2 heading "CAMshots FAQ."
5. For marking locations within a Web page, what is one advantage of using anchors rather than the id attribute? What is one disadvantage?
6. The CAMmap image map has a circular hotspot centered at the point (50, 75) with a radius of 40 pixels pointing to the faq.htm file. Specify the code to create this map element with that circular hotspot.
7. An inline image based on the logo.jpg file with the alternative text "CAMshots" needs to use the CAMmap image map. Specify the code to apply the image map to the image.
8. What attribute do you add to the inline image from the previous question to remove its border?

Session 2.3

Linking to Resources on the Internet

Gerry has a final set of tasks for you. In the tips.htm file, he has listed some of the Web sites he finds useful in his study of photography. He would like to change the entries in this list to hypertext links that his readers can click to quickly access the sites.

Introducing URLs

To create a link to a resource on the Internet, you need to know its URL. A **URL**, or **Uniform Resource Locator**, specifies the precise location of a resource on the Internet. Examples of URLs include *www.whitehouse.gov*, the home page of the President of the United States, and *www.w3.org*, the home page of the World Wide Web consortium. All URLs share the common form

```
scheme:location
```

where *scheme* indicates the type of resource referenced by the URL and *location* is the location of that resource. For Web pages, the location refers to the location of the HTML file; but for other resources, the location might simply be the name of the resource. For example, a link to an e-mail account has the e-mail address as the resource.

The name of the scheme is taken from the protocol used to access the resource. A **protocol** is a set of rules defining how information is passed between two devices. Your Web browser communicates with Web servers using the **Hypertext Transfer Protocol** or **HTTP**. Therefore, the URLs for all Web pages must start with the http scheme. This tells the browser to use http when it tries to access the Web page. Other Internet resources, described in Figure 2-31, use different communication protocols and have different scheme names.

> **Tip**
>
> Because URLs cannot contain blank spaces, avoid blank spaces in Web site file and folder names.

Figure 2-31 ▶ **Internet protocols**

Protocol	Used To
file	access documents stored locally on a user's computer
ftp	access documents stored on an FTP server
gopher	access documents stored on a gopher server
http	access Web pages stored on the World Wide Web
https	access Web pages over a secure encrypted connection
mailto	open a user's e-mail client and address a new message
news	connect to a Usenet newsgroup
telnet	open a telnet connection to a specific server
wais	connect to a Wide Area Information Server database

Linking to a Web Site

The URL for a Web page has the general form

```
http://server/path/filename#id
```

where *server* is the name of the Web server, *path* is the path to the file on that server, *filename* is the name of the file, and if necessary, *id* is the name of an id or anchor within the file. A Web page URL can also contain specific programming instructions for a browser to send to the Web server (a topic beyond the scope of this tutorial). Figure 2-32 shows the URL for a sample Web page with all of the parts identified.

Figure 2-32 ▶ **Parts of a URL**

You might have noticed that a URL like *http://www.camshots.com* doesn't include any pathname or filename. If a URL doesn't specify a path, then it indicates the topmost folder in the server's directory tree. If a URL doesn't specify a filename, the server will return to the default home page. Many servers use index.html as the filename for the default home page, so a URL like *http://www.camshots.com/index.html* would be equivalent to *http://www.camshots.com*.

Understanding Domain Names | InSight

The server name portion of the URL is also called the **domain name**. By studying the domain name you learn about the server hosting the Web site. Each domain name contains a hierarchy of names separated by periods (.), with the topmost level appearing at the end. The top level, called an **extension**, indicates the general audience supported by the Web server. For example, .edu is the extension reserved for educational institutions, .gov is used for agencies of the United States government, and .com is used for commercial sites or general-use sites.

The next lower level appearing before the extension displays the name of the individual or organization hosting the site. A domain name like camshots.com indicates a commercial or general use site owned by CAMshots. To avoid duplicating domain names, the two top-most levels of the domain have to be registered with the IANA (Internet Assigned Numbers Authority) before they can be used. You can usually register your domain name through your Internet Service Provider. Be aware that you will have to pay an annual fee to keep the domain name.

The lowest levels of the domain, which appear farthest to the left in the domain name, are assigned by the individual or company hosting the site. Large Web sites involving hundreds of pages typically divide their domain names into several levels. For example, a large company like Microsoft might have one domain name for file downloads—*downloads.microsoft.com*—and another for customer service—*service.microsoft.com*. Finally, the lowest level of the domain, the first part of the domain name, displays the name of the hard drive or resource storing the Web site files. Many companies have standardized on using "www" as the name of the lowest level in their domain.

Gerry has listed four Web pages that he wants his readers to be able to access. He's provided you with the URLs for these pages, which are shown in Figure 2-33.

Web site URLs | Figure 2-33

Web Site	URL
Apogee Photo	http://www.apogeephoto.com
Outdoor Photographer	http://www.outdoorphotographer.com
PCPhoto	http://www.pcphotomag.com
Popular Photography and Imaging	http://www.popphoto.com

To create a link to these Web sites from your document, you need to mark some text as a hypertext link, using the URL of the Web site as the value of the href attribute. So to link the text "Apogee Photo" to the Apogee Photo Web site, you would enter the following code:

```
<a href="http://www.apogeephoto.com">Apogee Photo</a>
```

Use the information that Gerry has given you to create links to all four of the Web sites listed on his tips page.

To create links to sites on the Web:

► **1.** Return to the **tips.htm** file in your text editor.

► **2.** Scroll to the bottom of the file and locate the definition list containing the list of Web sites.

3. Mark the entry for Apogee Photo as a hypertext link using the following code:

   `<a href="http://www.apogeephoto.com">Apogee Photo</a>`

4. Mark the remaining three entries in the list as hypertext links pointing to each company's Web site. Figure 2-34 highlights the revised code in the file.

| Figure 2-34 | Linking to sites on the Web |

```
<h2 style="color: blue">Photography Sites on the Web</h2>
<p>The Web is an excellent resource for articles on photography and digital cameras.
   Here are a few of my favorites.</p>
<dl>
    <dt>&#9758; <a href="http://www.apogeephoto.com">Apogee Photo</a></dt>
    <dd>An established online photography magazine with articles by top pros,
        discussion forums, workshops, and more.</dd>
    <dt>&#9758; <a href="http://www.outdoorphotographer.com">Outdoor Photographer</a></dt>
    <dd>The premier magazine for outdoor photography. The site includes extensive tips
        on photographing wildlife, action sports,
        scenic vistas, and travel sites.</dd>
    <dt>&#9758; <a href="http://www.pcphotomag.com">PCPhoto</a></dt>
    <dd>An excellent site for novices and professionals with informative reviews and
        buying guides for the latest equipment and software.</dd>
    <dt>&#9758; <a href="http://www.popphoto.com">Popular Photography and Imaging</a></dt>
    <dd>A useful and informative site with articles from the long-established
        magazine of professional and amateur photographers.</dd>
</dl>
```

5. Save your changes to the file.

6. Reload or refresh the **tips.htm** file in your Web browser. Figure 2-35 shows the revised list with each entry appearing as a hypertext link.

| Figure 2-35 | Links on the tips page |

Photography Sites on the Web

The Web is an excellent resource for articles on photography and digital cameras. Here are a few of my favorites.

☞ Apogee Photo
    An established online photography magazine with articles by top pros, discussion forums, workshops, and more.
☞ Outdoor Photographer
    The premier magazine for outdoor photography. The site includes extensive tips on photographing wildlife, action sports, scenic vistas, and travel sites.
☞ PCPhoto
    An excellent site for novices and professionals with informative reviews and buying guides for the latest equipment and software.
☞ Popular Photography and Imaging
    A useful and informative site with articles from the long-established magazine of professional and amateur photographers.

7. Click each of the links on the page and verify that the appropriate Web site opens.

   Trouble? To open these sites, you must be connected to the Internet. If you are still having problems, compare your code to the URLs listed in Figure 2-34 to confirm that you have not made a typing error. Also keep in mind that because the Web is constantly changing, the Web sites for some of these links might have changed, or a site might have been removed since this book was published.

Web pages are only one type of resource that you can link to. Before continuing work on the CAMshots Web site, you should explore how to access some of these other resources.

Linking to FTP Servers

Another method of storing and sharing files on the Internet is through FTP servers. **FTP servers** are file servers that act like file cabinets in which users can store and retrieve data files, much as they store and retrieve files from their own computer. FTP servers transfer information using a communications protocol called **File Transfer Protocol**, or **FTP** for short. The URL to access an FTP server follows the general format

`ftp://server/path/`

where *server* is the name of the FTP server and *path* is the folder path on the server that contains the files you want to access. When you access the FTP site, you can navigate through its folder tree as you would navigate the folders on your own hard disk. Figure 2-36 shows how someone can use Internet Explorer to view the FTP site and how the site appears as a collection of folders that can be opened and viewed.

FTP site appearing in the browser and in Windows Explorer ◄ Figure 2-36

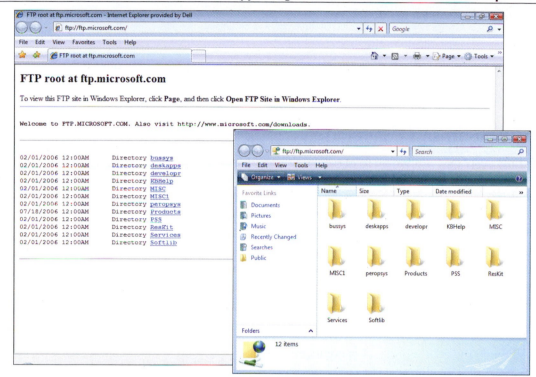

FTP servers require each user to enter a password and a username to gain access to the server's files. The standard username is anonymous and requires no password. Your browser supplies this information automatically, so in most situations you don't have to worry about passwords and usernames. However, some FTP servers do not allow anonymous access. In these cases, either your browser prompts you for the username and the password, or you can supply a username and password within the URL using the format

`ftp://username:password@server/path`

where *username* and *password* are a username and password that the FTP server recognizes. It is generally *not* a good idea, however, to include usernames and passwords in URLs, as it can allow others to view your sensitive login information. It's better to let the browser send this information or to use a special program called an **FTP client**, which can encrypt or hide this information during transmission.

Linking to a Local File

HTML is a very useful language for creating collections of linked documents. Many software developers have chosen to distribute their online help in the form of HTML files. The Web site for their help files then exist locally on the user's computer or network. If the Web site needs to reference local files (as opposed to files on the Internet or another wide area network), the URL needs to reflect this fact. The URL for a local file has the general form

`file://server/path/filename`

where *server* is the name of the local network server, *path* is the path on that server to the file, and *filename* is the name of the file. If you're accessing a file from your own computer, the server name can be omitted and replaced by an extra slash (/). So, a file from the documents/articles folder might have the URL:

```
file:///documents/articles/tips.htm
```

If the file is on a different disk within your computer, the hard drive letter would be included in the URL as follows:

```
file://D:/documents/articles/tips.htm
```

Unlike the other URLs you've examined, the "file" scheme in this URL does not imply any particular communication protocol; instead, the browser retrieves the document using whatever method is the local standard for the type of file specified in the URL.

Linking to an E-Mail Address

Many Web sites use e-mail to allow users to communicate with a site's owner, sales representative, or technical support staff. You can turn an e-mail address into a hypertext link, so that a user can click the link starting an e-mail program and automatically inserting the e-mail address into the "To" field of a new outgoing message. The URL for an e-mail address follows the form

```
mailto:address
```

where *address* is the e-mail address. To create a hypertext link to the e-mail address ghayward@camshots.com, you could use the following URL:

```
mailto:ghayward@camshots.com
```

Tip

To link to more than one e-mail address, add the addresses to the mailto link in a comma-separated list.

Although the mailto protocol is not technically an approved communication protocol, it is supported by almost every Web browser.

The mailto protocol also allows you to add information to the e-mail, including the subject line and the text of the message body. To add this information to the link, you use the form

```
mailto:address?header1=value1&header2=value2& ...
```

where *header1*, *header2*, etc. are different e-mail headers and *value1*, *value2*, and so on are the values of the headers. So to create the e-mail message

```
TO: ghayward@camshots.com
SUBJECT: Test
BODY: This is a test message
```

you would use the following URL:

```
mailto:ghayward@camshots.com?Subject=Test&Body=This%20is%20a%20test%20message
```

Notice that the spaces in the message body "This is a test message" have been replaced with %20 characters. This is necessary because URLs cannot contain blank spaces. To preserve information about blank spaces, URLs use **escape characters**, which are symbols that represent characters including nonprintable characters such as spaces, tabs, and line feeds. Escape characters use many of the same values as HTML character codes, though the syntax of escape characters is different. So, when the browser receives the following character string in a URL such as

`This%20is%20a%20test%20message`

it interprets the %20 escape character as a blank space and resolves the string as

`This is a test message`

Figure 2-37 lists some of the escape characters that can be used in any URL in place of printable or nonprintable characters.

Escape character codes — Figure 2-37

Escape Character Code	Character	Escape Character Code	Character
%20	space	%5B	[
%0D%0A	new line	%5D	]
%3C	<	%60	`
%3E	>	%3B	;
%23	#	%2F	/
%25	%	%3F	?
%7B	{	%3A	:
%7D	}	%40	@
%7C			%3D	=
%5C	\	%26	&
%5E	^	%24	$
%7E	~		

To further explore how to convert an e-mail message into a URL, you can experiment with a demo page.

To view the e-mail demo:

1. Use your Web browser to open the **demo_mailto.htm** file from the tutorial.02\demo folder included with your Data Files.

2. Scroll down the page, and in the TO: input box, enter the e-mail address **ghayward@camshots.com**.

3. Type **CAMshots Message** in the SUBJECT input box.

4. Type the following in the BODY input box:

   `This is a message generated by the CAMshots Web site for Gerry Hayward.`

5. Click the **Generate URL** button to create the URL for this e-mail message.

   As shown in Figure 2-38, the demo page generates the URL for the e-mail message. All of the blank spaces in the mail message have been replaced with the %20 escape character.

Figure 2-38 | Converting an e-mail message to a URL

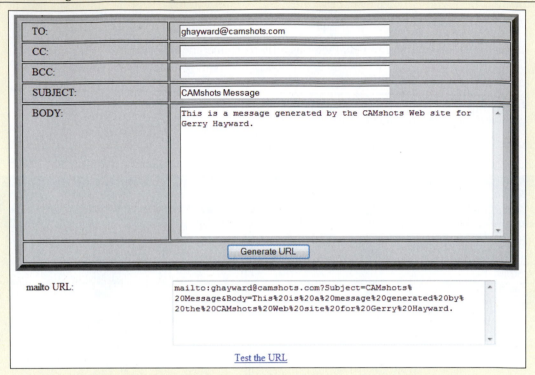

6. Click the **Test the URL** button at the bottom of the page. As shown in Figure 2-39, the browser opens the user's e-mail program, with the e-mail fields already filled in, based on the text of the URL.

Figure 2-39 | E-mail message generated by the hypertext link

Trouble? Your e-mail window might look different depending on the e-mail program installed on your computer. If you do not have access to an e-mail program, you might not see any result or you might receive an error message after clicking the Test the URL button.

7. Close the message window without saving the message.

8. Continue experimenting with the demo page, exploring the effects of different e-mail messages on the URL text. Close the demo page when you are finished.

Gerry wants you to add to a link to his e-mail address on the CAMshots home page. This gives people who read his site the ability to contact him with additional questions or ideas.

To link to an e-mail address on Gerry's home page:

1. Return to the **home.htm** file in your text editor.

2. Go to the first paragraph and locate the text "contact me."

3. Mark "contact me" as a hypertext link using the following code, as shown in Figure 2-40:

```
<a href="mailto:ghayward@camshots.com?subject=CAMshots%20Message">
   contact me
</a>
```

Adding an e-mail link to the CAMshots home page ◀ **Figure 2-40**

```
<p>Welcome to <span style="color: blue">CAMshots</span>, a site for people passionate about
   digital photography. This site has grown out of decades of photographic experience.
   I offer advice for both beginners and advanced users. I hope you enjoy what you find,
   but please be considerate of the work it took to do all this.
   The entire site contents including all images and articles are copyrighted.
   Please honor my work and do not copy anything without permission. If you are
   interested in publishing any of my images or articles or using them in other ways,
   please <a href="mailto:ghayward@camshots.com?subject=CAMshots%20Message">contact me</a>
   and we can discuss your needs. Happy Shooting!</p>
<p>&mdash; Gerry</p>
```

4. Save your changes to the file.

5. Refresh the **home.htm** file in your browser. Verify that the text "contact me" in the opening paragraph now appears as a hypertext link.

6. Click **contact me** and verify that your e-mail program displays a message with ghayward@camshots.com as the recipient and CAMshots Message as the subject.

7. Close your message window without saving the message.

InSight	E-Mail Links and Spam

Use caution when adding e-mail links to your Web site. While it may make it more convenient for users to contact you, it also might make you more vulnerable to spam. **Spam** is unsolicited e-mail sent to large numbers of people, promoting products, services, and in some cases inappropriate Web sites. Spammers create their e-mail lists by scanning discussion groups, stealing Internet mailing lists, and using programs called **e-mail harvesters** to scan HTML code for the e-mail addresses contained in mailto URLs. Many Web developers have removed e-mail links from their Web sites in order to foil these harvesters, replacing the links with Web forms that submit e-mail requests to a secure server. If you need to include an e-mail address on your Web page, you can take a few steps to reduce your exposure to spammers:

- Replace the text of the e-mail addresses with inline images that are more difficult for e-mail harvesters to read.
- Write a program to scramble any e-mail addresses in the HTML code, unscrambling the e-mail address only when it is clicked by the user.
- Replace the characters of the e-mail address with escape characters. For example, you can replace the "@" symbol with the escape sequence %40.

There is no quick and easy solution to this problem. Fighting spammers is an ongoing battle, and they have proved very resourceful in overcoming some of the defenses people have created. As you develop your Web site, you should carefully consider how to handle e-mail addresses and review the most current methods for safeguarding that information.

Reference Window	**Linking to Various Interent Resources**

- The URL for a Web page has the form
  `http://server/path/filename#id`
  where *server* is the name of the Web server, *path* is the path to a file on that server, *filename* is the name of the file, and if necessary *id* is the name of an id or anchor within the file.
- The URL for an FTP site has the form
  `ftp://server/path/filename`
  where *server* is the name of the FTP server, *path* is the folder path, and *filename* is the name of the file.
- The URL for an e-mail address has the form
  `mailto:address?header1=value1&header2=value2& ...`
  where *address* is the e-mail address; *header1*, *header2*, etc. are different e-mail headers; and *value1*, *value2*, and so on are the values of the headers.
- The URL to reference a local file has the form
  `file://server/path/filename`
  where *server* is the name of the local server or computer, *path* is the path to the file on that server, and *filename* is the name of the file. If you are accessing a file on your own computer, the server name is replaced by a third slash (/).

Tip
All of the hypertext attributes applied to the \<a> tag can also be applied to the \<area> tags within your image maps.

Working with Hypertext Attributes

HTML provides several attributes to control the behavior and appearance of your links. Gerry suggests that you study a few of these to see whether they would be effective in his Web site.

Opening a Secondary Window or Tab

By default, each page you open replaces the contents of the current page in the browser window. This means that when Gerry's readers click on one of the four external links listed on the tips page, they leave the CAMshots Web site. To return to the Web site, users would have to click their browser's Back button.

Gerry wants his Web site to stay open when a user clicks one of the links to the external Web sites. Most browsers allow users to open multiple browser windows or multiple tabs within the same browser window. Gerry suggests that links to external sites be opened in a second browser window or tab. He wants these external sites to be displayed in a second browser window or tab. This arrangement allows continual access to his Web site, even as users are browsing other sites.

To force a document to appear in a new window or tab, add the target attribute to the <a> tag. The general syntax is

```
<a href="url" target="window">content</a>
```

where *window* is a name assigned to the new browser window or browser tab. The value you use for the target attribute doesn't affect the appearance or content of the page being opened; the target simply identifies the different windows or tabs that are currently open. You can choose any name you wish for the target. If several links have the same target name, they all open in the same location, replacing the previous content. HTML also supports several special target names, described in Figure 2-41.

Target names for browser windows and tabs ◀ **Figure 2-41**

Target Name	Description
target	Opens the link in a new window or tab named *target*
_blank	Opens the link in a new, unnamed window or tab
_self	Opens the link in the current browser window or tab

Whether the new page is opened in a tab or in a browser window is determined by the browser settings. It cannot be set by the HTML code.

Opening a Link in a New Window or Tab | Reference Window

- To open a link in a new browser window or browser tab, add the attribute
  ```
  target="window"
  ```
  to the <a> tag, where *window* is a name assigned to the new browser window or tab.

Gerry suggests that all of the external links from his page be opened in a browser window or tab identified with the target name "new."

To specify a link target:

1. Return to the **tips.htm** file in your text editor.

2. Scroll to the bottom of the file and locate the four links to the external Web sites.

3. Within each of the opening <a> tags, insert the following attribute, as shown in Figure 2-42.

   ```
   target="new"
   ```

Figure 2-42 ▶ **Setting a target for a hyperlink**

```
<h2 style="color: blue">Photography Sites on the Web</h2>
<p>The Web is an excellent resource for articles on photography and digital cameras.
   Here are a few of my favorites.</p>
<dl>
   <dt>&#9758; <a href="http://www.apogeephoto.com" target="new">Apogee Photo</a></dt>
   <dd>An established online photography magazine with articles by top pros,
       discussion forums, workshops, and more.</dd>
   <dt>&#9758; <a href="http://www.outdoorphotographer.com" target="new">Outdoor Photographer</a></dt>
   <dd>The premier magazine for outdoor photography. The site includes extensive tips
       on photographing wildlife, action sports,
       scenic vistas, and travel sites.</dd>
   <dt>&#9758; <a href="http://www.pcphotomag.com" target="new">PCPhoto</a></dt>
   <dd>An excellent site for novices and professionals with informative reviews and
       buying guides for the latest equipment and software.</dd>
   <dt>&#9758; <a href="http://www.popphoto.com" target="new">Popular Photography and Imaging</a></dt>
   <dd>A useful and informative site with articles from the long-established
       magazine of professional and amateur photographers.</dd>
</dl>
```

▶ **4.** Save your changes to the file.

▶ **5.** Refresh the **tips.htm** file in your browser. Click each of the four links to external Web sites and verify that each opens in the same new browser window or tab.

▶ **6.** Close the secondary browser window or tab.

Tip

To force all hypertext links in your page to open in the same target, add the target attribute to a base element located in the document's header.

You should use the target attribute sparingly in your Web site. Creating secondary windows can clutter up the user's desktop. Also, because the page is placed in a new window, users cannot use the Back button to return to the previous page in that window; they must click the browser's program button or the tab for the original Web site. This confuses some users and annoys others. Many Web designers now advocate not using the target attribute at all, leaving the choice of opening a link in a new tab or window to the user. Note that the target attribute is not supported in strict XHTML-compliant code.

Creating a Tooltip

If you want to provide additional information about a link on your Web page, you can add a tooltip to the link. A **tooltip** is descriptive text that appears when a user positions the mouse pointer over a link. Figure 2-43 shows an example of a tooltip applied to one of Gerry's links.

Figure 2-43 ▶ **Viewing a tooltip**

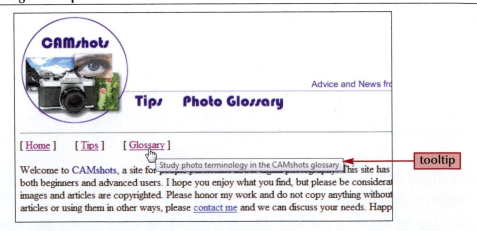

To create the tooltip, add the title attribute to the opening <a> tag in the form

```
<a href="url" title="text">content</a>
```

where *text* is the text that appears in the tooltip. To create the tooltip shown in Figure 2-43, you would enter the following HTML code:

```
<a href="glossary.htm"
   title="Study photo terminology in the CAMshots glossary">
   Glossary
</a>
```

Note that because some browsers do not support this feature, you should not place crucial information in a tooltip.

Creating a Semantic Link

The text of a hypertext link should always describe the type of document that will be called up by the link. You can also use the rel and rev attributes to add information about the link. The rel attribute describes the relation of the current document to the linked document. For example, in the link to the Glossary page, Gerry could insert the following rel attribute:

```
<a href="glossary.htm" rel="glossary">Glossary</a>
```

The rev attribute describes the reverse relationship: how the linked document views the current document. For example, if you're linking to the Glossary page from the home page, the reverse relation is "home" (because that is how the Glossary page views the home page). The HTML code would be:

```
<a href="glossary.htm" rel="glossary" rev="home">Glossary</a>
```

Links containing the rel and rev attributes are called **semantic links** because the tag contains information about the relationship between the link and its destination. This information is not designed for the user, but for the browser. A browser could display all hypertext links marked having a rel value of glossary with a special icon. The browser could also collect all of the hypertext links within the Web page and place them within a customized toolbar. Few browsers currently take advantage of these attributes, but future browsers may do so.

Although rel and rev are not limited to a fixed set of attribute values, the specifications for HTML and XHTML include a proposed list of rel and rev names. Figure 2-44 shows some of these proposed relationship values.

Figure 2-44 ▶ **Link relations for the rel and rev attributes**

Link Relation	Description
alternate	A substitute version of the current document, perhaps in a different language or in a different medium
appendix	An appendix
bookmark	A bookmark in a collection of documents
chapter	A document serving as a chapter in a collection of documents
contents	A table of contents
copyright	A copyright statement
glossary	A glossary
help	A help document
index	An index
next	The next document in a linear sequence of documents
prev	The previous document in a linear sequence of documents
section	A document serving as a section in a collection of documents
start	The first document in a collection of documents
top	The Web site's home page
stylesheet	An external style sheet
subsection	A document serving as a subsection in a collection of documents

At this point, Gerry decides against using the rel and rev attributes on his Web site. However, he'll keep them in mind as an option as his Web site expands in size and complexity.

Using the Link Element

Another way to add a hypertext link to your document is to add a link element to the document's head. Link elements are created using the one-sided tag

```
<link href="url" rel="text" rev="text" target="window" />
```

where the *href*, *rel*, *rev*, and *target* attributes serve the same purpose as in the <a> tag. For example, to use the link element to create semantic links to the three pages of Gerry's Web site, you could add the following link elements to the heading of each document:

```
<link rel="top" href="home.htm" />
<link rel="help" href="tips.htm" />
<link rel="glossary" href="glossary.htm" />
```

Because they are placed within a document's head, link elements do not appear as part of the Web page. Instead, if the browser supports them, link elements are displayed in a browser toolbar. Figure 2-45 shows how the three link elements described above would appear in the Opera's Navigation toolbar. If you click an entry on the toolbar, the browser loads the referenced page.

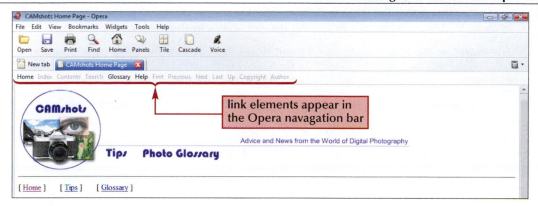

The advantage of the link element is that it places the list of links outside of the Web page, freeing up page space for other content. Also, because the links appear in a browser toolbar, they are always easily accessible to users. Currently, Opera is one of the few browsers with built-in support for the link element. Third party software exists to provide this support for Internet Explorer and Firefox. Because no single list of relationship names is widely accepted, you must check with each browser's documentation to find out what relationship names it supports. Until link elements are embraced by more browsers, you should use them only if you duplicate that information elsewhere on the page.

Working with Metadata

Gerry is happy with the work you've done on the design for his CAMshots Web site. Now he wants to start working on getting the site noticed. When someone searches for "digital photography tips" or "camera buying guide," will they find Gerry's Web site? There are thousands of photography sites on the Web. Gerry knows he needs to add a few extra touches to his home page to make it more likely that the site will be picked up by major search engines such as Yahoo! and Google.

Optimizing a Web site for search engines can be a long and involved process. For the best results, Web authors often turn to companies that specialize in making sites appear more prominently in search engines. CAMshots is a hobby site and Gerry does not want to invest any money in improving the site's visibility, but he would like to do a few simple things that would help.

Using the Meta Element

To be noticed on the Web, a site needs to include information about itself so the search engines can read it and add the site to their search indices. Information about the site is called **metadata**. You can add metadata to your Web pages by adding a meta element to the head section of the document. The syntax of the meta element is

```
<meta name="text" content="text" scheme="text" http-equiv="text" />
```

where the name attribute specifies the type of metadata, the content attribute stores the metadata value, the scheme attribute defines the metadata format, and the http-equiv attribute is used to attach metadata or commands to the communication stream between the Web server and the browser. There are three uses of the meta element:

- To store information about the document that can be read by the author, other users, or the Web server.

- To control how the browser handles the document, including forcing the browser to automatically refresh the page at timed intervals.
- To assist Web search engines in adding the document to their search index.

For example, the following meta element stores the name of the Web page's author:

```
<meta name="author" content="Gerry Hayward" />
```

For search engines, you should include metadata describing the site and the topics it covers. This is done by adding a meta element containing the site description and another meta element with a list of keywords. The following two elements would summarize the CAMshots Web site for any search engines running on the Web:

```
<meta name="description" content="CAMshots provides advice on digital
cameras and photography" />
<meta name="keywords" content="photography, cameras, digital imaging" />
```

Figure 2-46 lists some other examples of metadata that you can use to describe your document.

Figure 2-46 ▶ **Metadata**

Meta Name	Example	Description
author	`<meta name="author" content="Gerry Hayward" />`	Supplies the name of the document author
classification	`<meta name="classification" content="photography" />`	Classifies the document
copyright	`<meta name="copyright" content="&copy; 2011 CAMshots" />`	Provides a copyright statement
description	`<meta name="description" content="Digital photography and advice" />`	Provides a description of the document
generator	`<meta name="generator" content="Dreamweaver" />`	Indicates the name of the program that created the HTML code for the document
keywords	`<meta name="keywords" content="photography,cameras, digital" />`	Provides a list of keywords describing the document
owner	`<meta name="owner" content="CAMshots" />`	Indicates the owner of the document
rating	`<meta name="rating" content="general" />`	Provides a rating of the document in terms of its suitability for minors
reply-to	`<meta name="reply-to" content="ghayward@camshots.com (G. Hayward)" />`	Supplies a contact e-mail address and name for the document

In recent years, search engines have become more sophisticated in evaluating Web sites. In the process, the meta element has decreased in importance. However, it is still used by search engines when adding a site to their indexes. Because adding metadata requires very little effort, you should still include meta elements in your Web documents.

Working with Metadata | Reference Window

- To document the contents of your Web page, use the meta element
  ```
  <meta name="text" content="text" />
  ```
  where the name attribute specifies the type of metadata and the content attribute stores the metadata value.
- To add metadata or a command to the communication stream between the Web server and Web browser, use
  ```
  <meta http-equiv="text" content="text" />
  ```
  where the http-equiv attribute specifies the type of data or command attached to the communication stream and the content attribute specifies the data value or command.

Having discussed metadata issues with Gerry, he asks that you include a few meta elements to describe his new site.

To add metadata to Gerry's document:

1. Return to the **home.htm** file in your text editor.

2. Directly below the opening <head> tag, insert the following meta elements, as shown in Figure 2-47:

```
<meta name="author" content="your name" />
<meta name="description" content="A site for sharing information on
          digital photography and cameras" />
<meta name="keywords" content="photography, cameras, digital
imaging" />
```

Adding meta elements to the CAMshots home page ◄ Figure 2-47

```
<head>
    <meta name="author" content="your name" />
    <meta name="description" content="A site for sharing information on
            digital photography and cameras" />
    <meta name="keywords" content="photography, cameras, digital imaging" />
```

metadata category   metadata value

3. Close the file, saving your changes.

Applying Metadata to the Communication Stream

Describing your document is not the only use of the meta element. As you learned earlier, servers transmit Web pages using a communication protocol called HTTP. You can add information and commands to this communication stream with the meta element's http-equiv attribute. One common use of the http-equiv attribute is to force the browser to refresh the Web page at timed intervals, which is useful for Web sites that publish scoreboards or stock tickers. For example, to automatically refresh the Web page every 60 seconds, you would apply the following meta element:

```
<meta http-equiv="refresh" content="60" />
```

Another use of the meta element is to redirect the browser from the current document to a new document. This might prove useful to Gerry someday if he changes the URL of his site's home page. As his readers get accustomed to the new Web address, he can keep the old address online, automatically redirecting readers to the new site. The meta element to perform an automatic redirect has the general form

```
<meta http-equiv="refresh" content="sec;url=url" />
```

where *sec* is the time in seconds before the browser redirects the user and *url* is the URL of the new site. To redirect users after five seconds to the Web page at *http://www. camshots.com*, you could enter the following meta element:

```
<meta http-equiv="refresh" content="5;url=www.camshots.com" />
```

Another use of the http-equiv attribute is to specify the character set used by the document. (For a discussion of character sets, see Tutorial 1.) This is particularly useful for international documents in which the browser might need to know the character set being used to correctly interpret the document. The syntax to specify the character set for an HTML document is

```
<meta http-equiv="Content-Type" content="text/html;charset=char-set" />
```

where *char-set* is the character set used by the document. So to indicate that the browser uses the ISO-8859-1 character set, you would include the following meta element in the document's header:

```
<meta http-equiv="Content-Type" content="text/html;charset=ISO-
8859-1" />
```

With the Web expanding its international presence, many Web developers advocate always including metadata about the character set so there is no ambiguity in the interpretation of the character encoding used in the document.

At this point, Gerry does not need to use the meta element to send data or commands through the HTTP communication protocol. However, he will keep this option in mind if moves the site to a new address.

Gerry is happy with the Web site you've started. He'll continue to work on the site and will come back to you for more assistance as he adds new pages and elements. For now you can close any open files or applications used to create the site.

Review | **Session 2.3 Quick Check**

1. What are the five parts of a URL?
2. Specify the code to link the text "White House" to the URL *http://www.whitehouse. gov*, with the destination document displayed in a new unnamed browser window.
3. Specify the code to link the text "Washington" to the FTP server at *ftp.uwash.edu*.
4. Specify the code to link the text "President" to the e-mail address *president@whitehouse.gov*.
5. What attribute would you add to a hypertext link to display the popup title "Tour the White House"?
6. What attribute would you add to a link specifying that the destination is the next page in a linear sequence of documents?
7. Specify the code to add the description "United States Office of the President" as metadata to a document.
8. Specify the code to automatically refresh the document every 5 minutes.

Tutorial Summary | Review

In this tutorial you explored some of the issues involved in creating a Web site with several linked pages. The first session began with an overview of storyboarding as a tool for designing and maintaining complex Web site structures. The session then turned to creating a simple Web site involving three Web pages linked together with the <a> tag element. The second session focused on creating links to locations within documents, first examining how to mark a location by using the id attribute and the anchor element. It then covered how to create links to these locations from within the same document and from within another document. The second session concluded by examining how to use inline images and image maps to create links to several documents. The third session expanded the discussion of hypertext by showing how to create links to sites on the World Wide Web and non-Web locations, including FTP sites and e-mail addresses. The third session then examined how to set different hypertext attributes to control how the browser displays and reacts to hypertext links. The session and the tutorial concluded by discussing the uses of the meta element for conveying information to Web search engines.

Key Terms

absolute path	home page	relative path
augmented linear structure	hotspot	semantic link
client-side image map	HTTP	server-side image map
domain name	Hypertext Transfer	sibling folder
e-mail harvester	Protocol	site index
escape characters	image map	spam
extension	linear structure	storyboard
File Transfer Protocol	metadata	tooltip
FTP	mixed structure	Uniform Resource Locator
FTP server	protected structure	URL
hierarchical structure	protocol	

Practice the skills you learned in the tutorial using the same case scenario.

Data Files needed for the Review Assignments: child1.jpg - child3.jpg, childtxt.htm, contest0.jpg - contest3.jpg, contesttxt.htm, flower1.jpg - flower3.jpg, flowertxt.htm, scenic1.jpg - scenic3.jpg, scenictxt.htm, and thumb1.jpg - thumb9.jpg

Gerry has been working on the CAMshots Web site for a while. During that time, the site has grown in popularity with amateur photographers. Gerry wants to host a monthly photo contest to highlight the work of his colleagues. Each month Gerry will pick the three best photos from different photo categories. He's asked for your help in creating the collection of Web pages highlighting the winning entries. Gerry has already created four pages. The first page contains information about the photo contest; the next three pages contain the winning entries for child photos, scenic photos, and flower photos. Although Gerry has already entered much of the page content, he needs you to work on creating the links between and within each page. Figure 2-48 shows a preview of the photo contest's home page.

Figure 2-48

Complete the following:

1. Use your text editor to open the **contesttxt.htm**, **childtxt.htm**, **scenictxt.htm**, and **flowertxt.htm** files from the tutorial.02\review folder included with your Data Files. Enter *your name* and *the date* within each file, and then save them as **contest.htm**, **child.htm**, **scenic.htm**, and **flower.htm**, respectively, in the same folder.

2. Go to the **child.htm** file in your text editor. Locate the inline image within the first div element at the top of the file. Directly below the inline image insert an image map with the following properties:
   - Set the id and name of the image map to contestmap.
   - Add a polygonal hotspot pointing to the child.htm file containing the points (457, 84), (474, 63), (549, 63), and (566, 84). Specify "Child Photos" as the alternate text for the hotspot.
   - Add a polygonal hotspot pointing to the flower.htm file containing the points (554, 84), (571, 63), (646, 63), and (663, 84). Specify "Flower Photos" as the alternate text for the hotspot.
   - Add a polygonal hotspot pointing to the scenic.htm file containing the points (651, 84), (668, 63), (743, 63), and (760, 84). Specify "Scenic Photos" as the alternate text for the hotspot.
   - Add a circular hotspot pointing to the contest.htm file centered at the point (82, 82) and having a radius of 78 pixels. Specify "Contest Results" as the alternate text for the hotspot.

3. Apply the contestmap image map to the logo image at the top of the page. Set the width of the border to 0.

4. Locate the three h2 elements naming the three child photo winners. Assign the h2 elements the ids child1, child2, and child3, respectively.

5. Save your changes to the **child.htm** file.

6. Go to the **scenic.htm** file in your text editor. Repeat Steps 2 and 3 for the logo image at the top of the page.

7. Assign the ids scenic1, scenic2, and scenic3 to the three h2 elements located farther down in the file. Save your changes to the document.

8. Go to the **flower.htm** file in your text editor and repeat the same edits you applied to the child.htm and scenic.htm files. Assign the ids flower1 through flower3 to the three h2 headings located at the bottom of the document. Save your changes.

9. Go to the **contest.htm** file in your text editor. Repeat Steps 2 and 3 for the logo image at the top of the page.

10. Scroll to the definition list at the bottom of the file. Mark the definition term "Child Photos" as a hypertext link pointing to the child.htm file. Mark the definition term "Flower Photos" as a link to the flower.htm file. Mark the term "Scenic Photos" as a link to the scenic.htm file.

11. Following each definition term is a definition description containing three thumbnail images of the winning photos. Mark the nine thumbnail images as hypertext links pointing to the larger images (contained in the child.htm, flower.htm, and scenic.htm files). For example, mark the first child photo (thumb1.jpg) as a hypertext link pointing to the h2 element with the id child1 in the child.htm file. Set the border width of each of the nine thumbnail images to 0.

12. Scroll up and locate the fourth paragraph. Mark the text "Gerry Hayward" as a hypertext link to an e-mail message sent to *ghayward@camshots.com* with the subject line "Photo Contest."

13. Go to the sixth paragraph and mark the text "BetterPhoto.com" as a hypertext link pointing to the URL *http://www.betterphoto.com*. Set the attribute of the link so that it opens in a new browser window or tab.

14. Save your changes to the **contest.htm** file.

15. Open **contest.htm** in your Web browser. Verify that the e-mail link opens a new mail message window with the subject line "Photo Contest." Verify that the link to BetterPhoto.com opens that Web site in a new browser window or tab. Verify that the three links to the photo pages are connected to the child.htm, scenic.htm, and flower.htm files. Finally, click each of the nine thumbnail images at the bottom of the page and verify that they connect to the larger image of the photo.

16. Open **child.htm** in your Web browser. Verify that the Scenic Photos link at the top of the page is connected to the scenic.htm file. Navigate forward and backward through the three photo pages by clicking the links at the top of each page. Verify that on each page you can return to the contest page by clicking the contest logo.

17. Submit your completed files to your instructor.

Apply	Case Problem 1

Apply your knowledge of hypertext links to create a directory of universities and colleges.

Data Files needed for this Case Problem: colleges.txt, highered.jpg, and uwlisttxt.htm

HigherEd Adella Coronel is a guidance counselor for Eagle High School in Waunakee, Wisconsin. She wants to take her interest in helping students choose colleges to the Web by starting a Web site called *HigherEd*. She's come to you for help in creating the site. The first page she wants to create is a simple directory of Wisconsin colleges and universities. She's created the list of schools, but has not yet marked the entries in the list as hypertext links. Also, the list is very long, so she has broken it down into three categories: private colleges and universities, technical colleges, and public universities. Because of the length of the page, she wants to include hypertext links that allow students to jump down to a specific college category. Figure 2-49 shows a preview of the page you'll create for Adella.

Figure 2-49

Higher ♦ Ed

The Directory of Higher Education Opportunities

Wisconsin Colleges and Universities

[Private Colleges and Universities]   [Technical College System]   [University of Wisconsin System]

Private Colleges and Universities

Alverno College
Beloit College
Cardinal Stritch University
Carroll College
Concordia University Wisconsin
Edgewood College
Lakeland College
Lawrence University
Marian College
Medical College of Wisconsin
Milwaukee Institute of Art and Design
Milwaukee School of Engineering

Complete the following:

1. In your text editor, open the **uwlisttxt.htm** file from the tutorial.02\case1 folder included with your Data Files. Enter *your name* and *the date* in the comment section of the file. Save the file as **uwlist.htm** in the same folder.

2. Mark each of the school entries on the page as a hypertext link. Use the URLs provided in the colleges.txt file. (Hint: Use the copy and paste feature of your text editor to efficiently copy and paste the URL text.)

⊕ EXPLORE 3. Adella wants the links to the school Web sites to appear in a new tab or window. Because there are so many links on the page, add a base element to the document header specifying that all links will open by default in a new browser window or tab named "collegeWin."

4. Add the id names "private," "technical," and "public" to the three h2 headings that categorize the list of schools.

5. Create hyperlinks from the entries in the category list at the top of the page to the three headings.

⊕ EXPLORE 6. For each of the hypertext links you marked in Step 5, set the link to open in the current browser window and not in a new browser window or tab.

7. Save your changes to the file.

8. Open **uwlist.htm** in your Web browser and verify that the school links all open in the same browser window or tab and that the links within the document to the different school categories bring the user to those locations on the page but not in a new window tab.

9. Submit your completed files to your instructor.

Apply	**Case Problem 2**

Apply your knowledge of HTML to create a slide show Web site.

Data Files needed for this Case Problem: back.jpg, end.jpg, fiddler.jpg, forward.jpg, home.jpg, hometxt.htm, slide1.jpg - slide6.jpg, slide1txt.htm - slide6txt.htm, start.jpg, and thumb1.jpg - thumb6.jpg

Lakewood School Tasha Juroszek is a forensics teacher at Lakewood School, a small private school in Moultrie, Georgia. Tasha has just finished directing her students in *Fiddler on the Roof Jr.* and wants to place a slide show of the performances on the Web. She has already designed the layout and content of the pages, but needs help to finish the slide show. She has asked you to add hypertext links between the slide pages and the site's home page. Figure 2-50 shows a preview of one of the slide pages on the Web site.

Figure 2-50

Matchmaker (L:R) Karen Unger, Rachel Paulson, Lucy Davis, Judy French, Catherine Lewis

Complete the following:

1. Use your text editor to open the **hometxt.htm**, and **slide1txt.htm** through **slide6txt.htm** files from the tutorial.02\case2 folder included with your Data Files. Enter *your name* and *the date* in the comment section of each file. Save the files as **home.htm** and **slide1.htm** through **slide6.htm,** respectively.

2. Return to the **slide1.htm** file in your text editor. At the top of the page are five buttons used to navigate through the slide show. Locate the inline image for the home button (home.jpg) and mark it as a hypertext link pointing to the home.htm file.

3. There are six slides in Tasha's slide show. Mark the start button as a hypertext link pointing to the slide1.htm file. Mark the end button as a link to the slide6.htm file. Link the back button to slide1.htm, the first slide in the show. Link the forward button to the slide2.htm file.

4. Directly below the slide show buttons are thumbnail images of the six slides. Link each thumbnail image to its slide page.

5. Set the border width of each linked image to 0, *except* the thumbnail image for slide1. Set the border width of that thumbnail to 5.

6. Save your changes to the file.

⊕ **EXPLORE**   7. Repeat Steps 2 through 6 for the five remaining slide pages. Within each page, set the navigation buttons to go back and forth through the slide show. For the slide6.htm file, the forward button should point to the slide6.htm file since it is the last slide in the show. The border width of each linked image should be set to 0 *except* the border width of the current slide, which should be set to 5.

8. Go to the **home.htm** file in your text editor. Go to the second paragraph and mark the text "slide show" as a hypertext link pointing to the slide1.htm file.

⊕ **EXPLORE**   9. Go to the end of the second paragraph and mark the phrase "contact me" as a hypertext link pointing to the following e-mail message:
TO: tashajur@lakewood.edu
SUBJECT: Photo CD
BODY: Please send me a copy of the photos.

10. Save your changes to the file.

11. Load the **home.htm** file in your Web browser. Test the links in the Web site and verify that they work correctly.

12. Submit your completed files to your instructor.

| Challenge | **Case Problem 3** |

Broaden your knowledge of HTML by exploring how to use anchors and pop-up titles in a Web site for a health club.

Data Files needed for this Case Problem: classtxt.htm, diamond.jpg, hometxt.htm, indextxt.htm, and memtxt.htm

Diamond Health Club, Inc. You work for Diamond Health Club, a health club in Boise, Idaho that has been serving active families for 25 years. The director, Karen Padilla, has asked you to help work on their Web site. The site contains three pages: the home page describing the club, a page listing classes offered, and a page describing the various membership options. You need to add links within the main page and add other links connecting the pages. Because this Web site will need to support older browsers, you will have to use the anchor tag to mark specific locations in the three documents. Karen would also like you to create pop-up titles for some of the links in the site to supply additional information about the links to the users.

Finally, this new site will replace the old company Web site. Karen wants to keep the old Web site address and redirect users automatically to the new home page. She wants you to insert the code required to do this.

Figure 2-51 shows a preview of the completed home page.

Figure 2-51

Welcome

At Diamond Health Club, you can stay healthy year-round and have fun doing it! We offer something for everyone. Our state-of-the-art facilities can challenge the most seasoned athlete, while remaining friendly to our first-time users. Be sure to check out our great classes for everyone from children and teens to adults and seniors. No matter who you are, DHC offers a class for you.

DHC also provides several different membership options. You can register as an individual or a family. We also provide special couples plans. Planning to visit Seattle a few days, weeks, or a month? Our great temporary plans are tailored to meet the needs of any visitor. Temporary memberships also make great Christmas gifts.

Facilities

- 2 workout rooms
- Olympic size pool with at least 3 lanes always open
- Warm, 3-foot deep therapeutic pool
- 2 gymnasiums with full size basketball courts
- Five exercise rooms for private and class instruction
- Climbing gym
- 3 racquetball courts
- On-site child care

Hours

Mon. - Fri. : 5 a.m. to 11 p.m.
Sat. : 7 a.m. to 8 p.m.
Sun. : 8 a.m. to 5 p.m.

For More Information, E-mail our Staff

Ty Stoven, General Manager
Yosef Dolen, Assistant Manager
Sue Myafin, Child Care
James Michel, Health Services
Ron Chi, Membership
Marcia Lopez, Classes

Diamond Health Club ♦ 4317 Alvin Way ♦ Boise, ID 83701 ♦ (208) 555-4398
Your Year-Round Source for Fun Family Health

Complete the following:

1. Use your text editor to open the **hometxt.htm**, **indextxt.htm**, **classtxt.htm**, and **memtxt.htm** files from the tutorial.02\case3 folder included with your Data Files. Enter *your name* and *the date* in the comment section of each file. Save the files as **home.htm**, **index.htm**, **classes.htm**, and **members.htm** respectively.

⊕ EXPLORE

2. Go to the **index.htm** file. Use the <a> tag to add the anchor names fac, hours, and staff to the h3 headings "Facilities," "Hours," and "For More Information, E-mail our Staff."

⊕ EXPLORE

3. Scroll up to the top of the file. Below the logo image at the top of the page, add an image map with the following properties:
   - Give the image map a name and id of diamondmap.
   - Create a rectangular hotspot with the coordinates (225, 7) and (333, 40). Point the hotspot to the classes.htm file with the alternate text "Classes." Add the tooltip "View our classes."

- Create a rectangular hotspot with the coordinates (258, 44) and (437, 82). Point the hotspot to the members.htm file with the alternate text "Memberships." Add the tooltip "View our membership options."
- Create a default hotspot for the inline image. (*Hint:* the image is 548 pixels wide and 150 pixels tall.) Point the default hotspot to the index.htm file with the alternate text "Home Page." Add the tooltip "Return to the Home Page."

4. Apply the diamondmap hotspot to the logo image. Remove the border around the inline image.

5. In the list at the top of the page, mark "Facilities" as a link pointing to the fac anchor within the index.htm document. Mark "Staff" as a link pointing to the staff anchor within the index.htm file. Mark "Hours" as a link pointing to the hours anchor within the index.htm file.

EXPLORE

6. Add the tooltip "Learn more about our facilities" to the Facilities link. Add the tooltip "Meet the DHC staff" to the Staff link. Add the tooltip "View the DHC hours of operation" to the Hours link.

7. Go to the staff list at the bottom of the page. Format each name as a link that points to the individual's e-mail address. The e-mail addresses are:

   Ty Stoven: tstoven@dmond-health.com
   Yosef Dolen: ydolen@dmond-health.com
   Sue Myafin: smyafin@dmond-health.com
   James Michel: jmichel@dmond-health.com
   Ron Chi: rchi@dmond-health.com
   Marcia Lopez: mlopez@dmond-health.com

8. Save your changes to the file.

9. Go to the **members.htm** file in your text editor and repeat Steps 3 through 6.

10. Use the <a> tag to add anchors named "ind" to the "Individual memberships" h3 heading, "fam" to the "Family memberships" h3 heading, and "temp" to the "Temporary memberships" h3 heading.

11. Format the phrase "e-mail Ron Chi" in the first paragraph as a link pointing to Ron Chi's e-mail address. Save your changes to the file.

12. Go to the **classes.htm** file in your text editor and repeat Steps 3 through 6 for the entries at the top of that page.

13. Use the <a> tag to add the following anchors to h3 headings in the file: "senior" for "Senior Classes," "adult" for "Adult Classes," "teen" for "Teen Classes," and "child" for "Children's Classes."

14. Format the phrase "e-mail Marcia Lopez" in the first paragraph as a link pointing to Marcia Lopez's e-mail address. Save your changes to the file.

15. Return to the **index.htm** file in your text editor. Within the first paragraph, link the word "children" to the child anchor in the classes.htm file. Link the word "teens" to the teen anchor in the classes.htm file. Link the word "adults" to the adult anchor in classes.htm. Finally, link "seniors" to the senior anchor in classes.htm.

16. Within the second paragraph of index.htm, link the word "individual" to the ind anchor in the members.htm file. Link the word "family" to the fam anchor in members.htm. Finally, link the first occurrence of the word "temporary" to the temp anchor in members.htm.

17. Go to the head section of the document and add the following metadata directly below the opening <head> tag:
    - The description: "The Diamond Health Club is your year-round source for fun family health."
    - The keywords: health club, exercise, family, seattle

18. Save your changes to the file.

⬦ EXPLORE

19. Go to the **home.htm** file in your text editor. Within the head section, insert a meta element to redirect the browser to the index.htm file after a 5 second delay.

20. Mark the phrase "this link to our new Web site" as a hypertext link pointing to the index.htm file. Save your changes to the file.

21. Open the **home.htm** file in your Web browser. Verify that the browser loads the index.htm file after a 5 second delay.

22. Once the index.htm file is loaded, verify that all of your links work correctly, including the links that point to sections within documents and the links within the image map. Verify that tooltips appear as you move your mouse pointer over the links at the top of each page. (Note: Internet Explorer does not currently support tooltips found within image map hotspots.)

23. Submit your completed files to your instructor.

Create | **Case Problem 4**

Test your knowledge of HTML and use your creativity to design a Web site documenting a Shakespeare play.

Data Files needed for this Case Problem: characters.txt, notes.txt, tempest.jpg, and tempest.txt

Mansfield Classical Theatre   Steve Karls continues to work as the director of Mansfield Classical Theatre in Mansfield, Ohio. The next production he plans to direct is *The Tempest*. Steve wants to put the text of this play on the Web, but he also wants to augment the dialog of the play with notes and commentary. However, he doesn't want his commentary to get in the way of a straight-through reading of the text, so he has hit on the idea of linking his commentary to key phrases in the dialog. Steve has created text files containing an excerpt from *The Tempest* as well as his commentary and other supporting documents. He would like you to take his raw material and create a collection of linked pages.

Complete the following:

1. Create HTML files named **tempest.htm**, **commentary.htm**, and **cast.htm** and save them in the tutorial.02\case4 folder included with your Data Files. Add comment tags to the head section of each document containing *your name* and *the date*. Add an appropriate page title to each document.

2. Using the contents of the tempest.txt, notes.txt, and characters.txt text files, create the body of the three Web pages in Steve's Web site. The design of these pages is left to your imagination and skill. Make the pages easy to read and visually interesting. You can supplement the material on the page with appropriate material you find on your own.

3. Use the **tempest.jpg** file as a logo for the page. Create an image map from the logo pointing to the tempest.htm, commentary.htm, and cast.htm files. The three rectangular boxes on the logo have the following coordinates for their upper-left and lower-right corners:
   - The Play: (228, 139) (345, 173)
   - Commentary: (359, 139) (508, 173)
   - The Cast: (520, 139) (638, 173)

   Use this image map in all three of the Web pages from this Web site.

4. Create links between the dialog on the play page and the notes on the commentary page. The notes contain line numbers to aid you in linking each line of dialog to the appropriate note.

5. Create a link between the first appearances of each character's name from the tempest.htm page with the character's description on the cast.htm page.

6. Include a link to Steve Karl's e-mail address on the tempest.htm page. Steve's e-mail address is *stevekarls@mansfieldct.com*. E-mail sent to Steve's account from this Web page should have the subject line "Comments on the Tempest."

7. Add appropriate meta elements to each of the three pages documenting the page's contents and purpose.

8. Search the Web for sites that would provide additional material about the play. Add links to these pages on the tempest.htm page. The links should open in a new browser window or tab.

9. Submit your completed files to your instructor.

Review | Quick Check Answers

Session 2.1

1. Storyboarding is the process of diagramming a series of related Web pages, taking care to identify all links among the various pages. Storyboarding is an important tool in creating Web sites that are easy to navigate and understand.

2. A linear structure is one in which Web pages are linked from one to another in a direct chain. Users can go to the previous page or the next page in the chain, but not to a page in a different section of the chain. A hierarchical structure is one in which Web pages are linked from general to specific topics. Users can move up and down the hierarchy tree.

3. `<a href="sports.htm">Sports Info</a>`

4. An absolute path indicates the location of the file based on its placement in the computer. A relative path indicates the location of the file relative to the location of the current document.

5. glossary.htm
   ../tips/tips1.htm
   ../tips/tips2.htm
   ../../index.htm

6. The base element specifies the default location that the browser should use to resolve all relative paths.

Session 2.2

1. `<h2 id="faq">CAMshots FAQ</h2>`

2. `<a href="#faq">Read our FAQ</a>`

3. `<a href="help.htm#faq">Read our FAQ</a>`

4. `<h2><a name="faq">CAMshots FAQ</a></h2>`

5. Anchors are supported by older browsers. Some older browsers do not support using the id attribute to mark a location in a document. However, use of anchor tags has been deprecated, so it is not supported in strict applications of XHTML. Also, because it is deprecated, use of the anchor tag may be phased out in future browser releases.

6. ```
   <map name="CAMmap" id="CAMmap">
        <area type="circle" coords="50, 75, 40" href="faq.htm" />
   </map>
   ```

7. ```
   <img src="logo.jpg" alt="CAMshots" usemap="#CAMmap"/>
   ```

8. ```
   style="border-width: 0"
   ```

Session 2.3

1. The protocol, the hostname, the folder name, the filename, and the anchor name or id.

2. ```
   <a href="http://www.whitehouse.gov target="_blank">White House</a>
   ```

3. ```
   <a href="ftp://ftp.uwash.edu">Washington</a>
   ```

4. ```
   <a href="mailto:president@whitehouse.gov">President</a>
   ```

5. ```
   title="Tour the White House"
   ```

6. ```
   rel="next"
   ```

7. ```
   <meta name="description" content=" United States Office of the President" />
   ```

8. ```
   <meta http-equiv="refresh" content="300" />
   ```

Ending Data Files

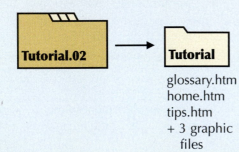

Tutorial.02 →

Tutorial
glossary.htm
home.htm
tips.htm
+ 3 graphic
files

Review
child.htm
contest.htm
flower.htm
scenic.htm
+ 22 graphic
files

Case1
uwlist.htm
+ 1 graphic
file

Case2
home.htm
slide1.htm
slide2.htm
slide3.htm
slide4.htm
slide5.htm
slide6.htm
+ 18 graphic
files

Case3
classes.htm
home.htm
index.htm
members.htm
+ 1 graphic
file

Case4
cast.htm
commentary.htm
tempest.htm
+ 1 graphic file

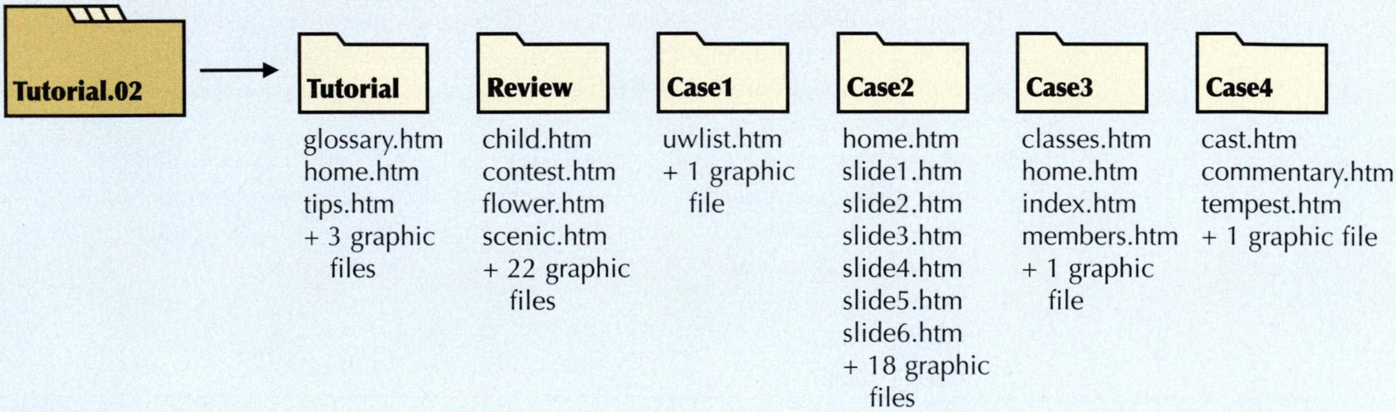

Reality Check

The Web has become an important medium for advertising products and one's self. By making your resume available online, you can quickly get prospective employers information they need to make a hiring decision. There are many sites that will assist you in writing and posting your resume. They will also, for a fee, present your online resume to employers in your chosen field. Assuming you don't want to pay to use such a site, you can also create your own Web site containing your employment history and talents. In this exercise, you'll use the skills and tasks you learned in Tutorials 1 and 2 to design your own Web site and create an online resume.

1. Collect material on yourself that would be useful in an online resume. You should include material for a page on your employment history, talents and special interests, a general biography, and a summary of the main points of your resume.

2. Create a storyboard outlining the pages on your Web site. Clearly indicate the links between the pages. Make sure that your site is easy to navigate no matter which page the user starts on.

3. Collect or create graphical image files to make your site interesting to the viewer. If you obtain graphics from the Web, be sure to follow all copyright restrictions on the material.

4. Start designing your site's home page. It should include an interesting and helpful logo. The home page should be brief and to the point, summarizing the main features of your resume. Its height should not be greater than two screens.

5. Add other pages containing more detailed information. Each page should have a basic theme and topic. The pages should follow a unified theme and design.

6. Use boldface fonts and italics to highlight important ideas. Do not overuse these page elements; doing so can distract from your page's readability rather than enhancing it.

7. Use numbered and bulleted lists to list the main points in your resume.

8. Use block quotes to highlight recommendations from colleagues and former employers.

9. Use horizontal rules to divide longer pages into topical sections.

10. If there are sites on the Web that would be relevant to your online resume (such as the Web sites of former or current employers), include links to those sites.

11. Include a link to your e-mail address. Write the e-mail address link so that it automatically adds an appropriate subject line to the e-mail message.

12. Save your completed Web site and present it to your instructor.

Working with Cascading Style Sheets

Designing a Web Site

Case | Sunny Acres

Tammy Nielsen and her husband Brent live and work at Sunny Acres, a 200-acre farm near Council Bluffs, Iowa. Over the past 25 years, the Nielsen family has expanded the farm's operations to include a farm shop, which sells fresh produce, baked goods, jams and jellies, and gifts; a pick-your-own garden, which operates from May through October and offers great produce at discounted prices; a petting barn, with over 100 animals and the opportunity to bottle-feed the baby animals; a corn maze, with over 4 miles of twisting trails through harvested corn fields; and a Halloween Festival featuring the corn maze haunted with dozens of spooks and tricks. The farm also hosts special holiday events during the winter.

Tammy created a Web site for Sunny Acres several years ago to make information about the farm easily accessible to her current customers. The Web site has become outdated, so Tammy would like to enliven it with a new design. She also wants to catch the attention of new customers via the Web. She has several pictures she wants to use on the Web site and has ideas for the look and feel of each Web page. Tammy's knowledge of HTML and Web styles is limited, so she's come to you for help in creating a new look for the Sunny Acres Web site.

Starting Data Files

Tutorial.03 →

Tutorial
farmtxt.css
haunttxt.htm
hometxt.htm
indextxt.htm
mazetxt.htm
pettingtxt.htm
producetxt.htm
+ 9 graphic files

Demo
demo_color_names.htm
demo_css.htm
demo_safety_palette.htm
+ 3 graphic files

Review
holidaytxt.htm
sunnytxt.css
+ 3 graphic files

Case1
algo.htm
crypttxt.htm
enigma.htm
history.htm
public.htm
single.htm
+ 5 graphic files

Case2
bmtourtxt.htm
wheelstxt.css
+ 4 graphic files

Case3
centertxt.css
kingtxt.htm
+ 7 graphic files

Case4
casttxt.htm
hebtxt.htm
hightxt.htm
lakestxt.htm
+ 6 graphic files

Session 3.1

Introducing CSS

You and Tammy have recently discussed the work she wants done on the new Web site. She's already entered the content for six pages of the Web site. The six pages are:

- index.htm—the page that users see when first accessing the site, currently blank
- home.htm—the home page, describing the operations and events sponsored by the farm
- maze.htm—a page describing the farm's corn maze
- haunted.htm—a page describing the farm's annual Halloween Festival and haunted maze
- petting.htm—a page describing the farm's petting barn
- produce.htm—a page describing the Sunny Acres farm shop and the pick-your-own produce garden

Figure 3-1 shows the links among these sites in the Sunny Acres storyboard. Open these files now in your text editor and browser.

Figure 3-1　　　**Storyboard of the Sunny Acres Web site**

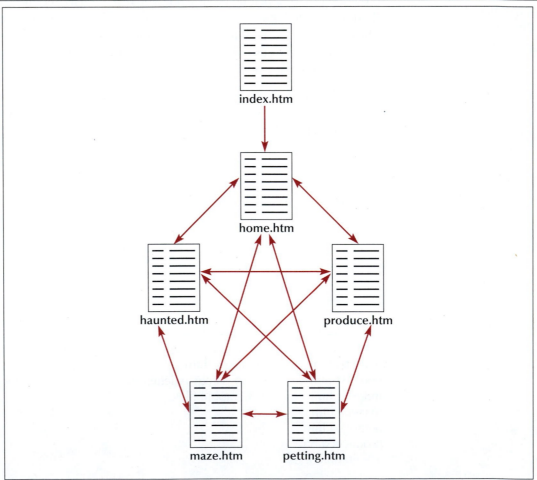

To view the Sunny Acres Web pages:

1. Use your text editor to open the **haunttxt.htm**, **hometxt.htm**, **indextxt.htm**, **mazetxt.htm**, **pettingtxt.htm**, and **producetxt.htm** files, located in the tutorial.03\tutorial folder included with your Data Files. Within each file, go to the comment section at top of the file and add *your name* and *the date* in the space provided. Save the files as **haunted.htm**, **home.htm**, **index.htm**, **maze.htm**, **petting.htm**, and **produce.htm**, respectively, in the same folder.

2. Take some time to review the HTML code within each document so that you understand the structure and content of the files.

3. Open the **home.htm** file in your Web browser, and then click the links at the top of the page to view the current appearance of the haunted.htm, maze.htm, petting.htm, and produce.htm files. Figure 3-2 shows the current layout and appearance of the Sunny Acres home page. Note that currently the index.htm file does not have any page content. You'll add that later in this tutorial.

Initial Sunny Acres home page   **Figure 3-2**

Tammy and Brent Nielsen
1973 Hwy G
Council Bluffs, IA 51503

Home The Corn Maze The Haunted Maze Petting Barn Produce

Welcome

Welcome to the home page of our family farm, Sunny Acres, where there's always something happening. With the coming of fall, we're gearing up for our big AutumnFest and Farm Show. If you haven't visited our famous Corn Maze, be sure to do so before it gets torn down on November 5. This year's maze is bigger and better than ever.

Farms can be educational and Sunny Acres is no exception. Schools and home-schooling parents, take an afternoon with us at our Petting Barn. We have over 100 friendly farm animals in a clean environment. Kids can bottle feed the baby goats, lambs, and calves while they learn about nature and the farming life. Please call ahead for large school groups.

When the sun goes down this time of year, we're all looking for a good fright. Sunny Acres provides that too with another year of the Haunted Maze. Please plan on joining us during weekends in October or on Halloween for our big Halloween Festival.

Of course, Sunny Acres is above all, a *farm*. Our Farm Shop is always open with reasonable prices and great produce. Save even more money by picking your own fruits and vegetables from our orchards and gardens.

We all hope to see you soon, down on the farm.

— Tammy & Brent Nielsen

Hours

- Farm Shop: 9 am - 5 pm Mon - Fri; 9 am - 3 pm Sat
- The Corn Maze: 11 am - 9 pm Sat; 11 am - 5 pm Sun
- The Haunted Maze: 5 pm - 9 pm Fri & Sat
- Petting Barn: 9 am - 4 pm (Mon - Fri); 11 am - 3pm (Sat & Sun)

Directions

- From Council Bluffs, proceed east on I-80
- Take Exit 38 North to the Drake Frontage Road
- Turn right on Highway G
- Proceed east for 2.5 miles
- Sunny Acres is on your left&watch for the green sign

Sunny Acres ✳ *Tammy & Brent Nielsen* ✳ *1977 Highway G* ✳ *Council Bluffs, IA 51503*

The home page has all of the content that Tammy needs, but its design needs work. In Figure 3-3 she sketches how she would like the home page to appear.

Figure 3-3 ▶ **Proposed design for the Sunny Acres home page**

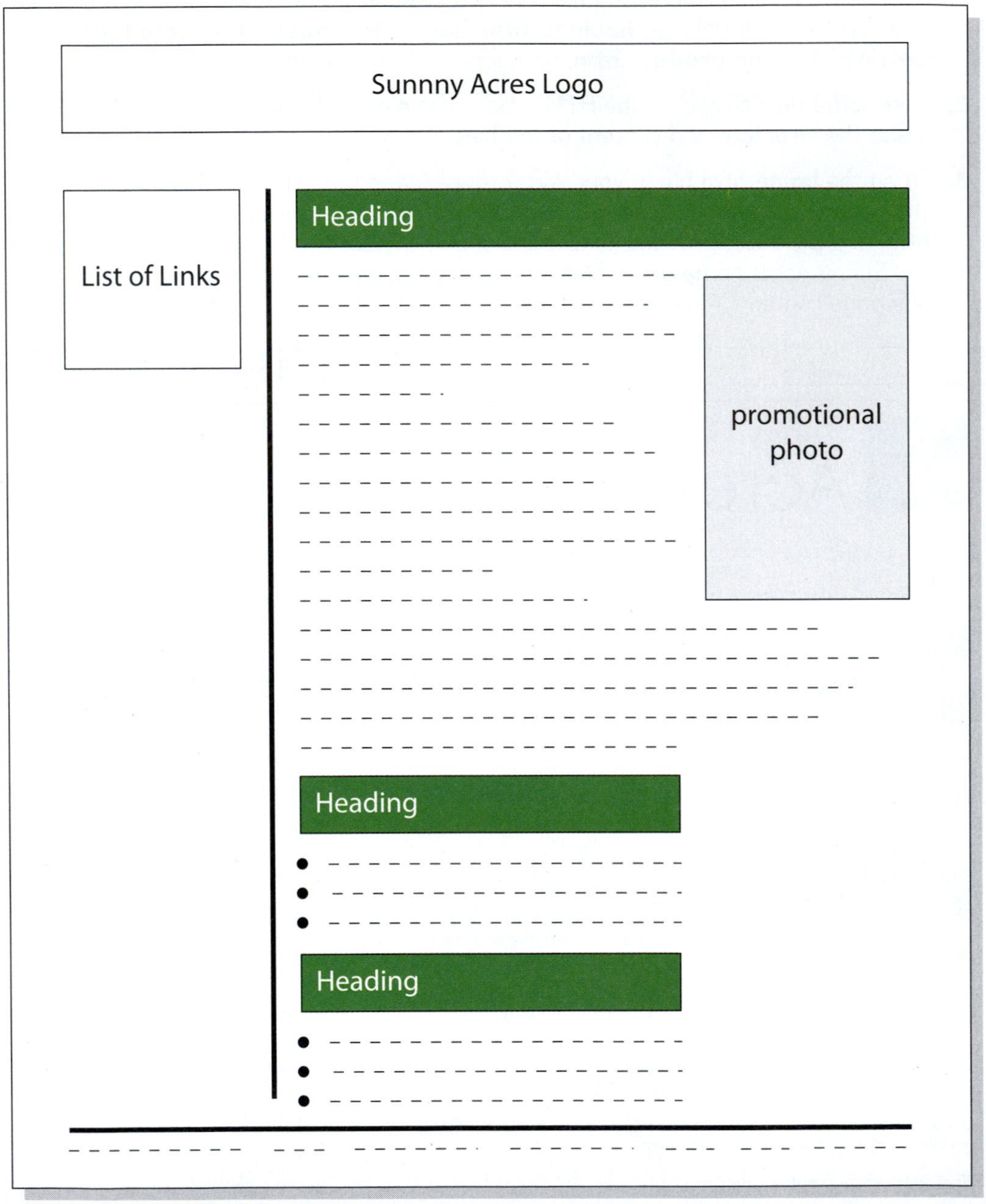

To apply this design not just to the Sunny Acres home page but also to the other pages on the Sunny Acres Web site, you'll create a page design using style sheets.

The History of CSS

A **style sheet** is a set of declarations describing the layout and appearance of a document. As you learned in Tutorial 1, HTML specifies a document's content and structure but not necessarily its appearance. To create a document design, you have to work in a different language. Several style sheet languages exist, but the most commonly used on the Web by far is the **Cascading Style Sheets** language, also known as **CSS**. You've actually been using CSS since Tutorial 1, when you used the style attribute. While the style attribute is part of the specifications for HTML and XHTML, the text of the attribute value is written in the CSS language.

Like HTML and XHTML, the specifications for CSS are maintained by the World Wide Web Consortium (W3C); and like those languages, several versions of CSS exist with varying levels of browser support. The first version of CSS, called **CSS1**, was introduced in 1996, but it was not fully implemented by any browser for another three years. CSS1 introduced styles for the following document features:

- *Fonts*: Setting font size, type, and other properties
- *Text*: Controlling text alignment and applying decorative elements such as underlining, italics, and capitalization
- *Color*: Specifying background and foreground colors of various page elements
- *Backgrounds*: Setting the background image for an element
- *Block-level elements*: Setting the margins, internal space, and borders of block-level elements

The second version of CSS, **CSS2**, was introduced in 1998. It expanded the language to support styles for:

- *Positioning*: Placing elements at specific locations on the page
- *Visual formatting*: Clipping and hiding element content
- *Media types*: Creating styles for various output devices, including printed media and aural devices
- *Interfaces*: Controlling the appearance and behavior of browser features such as scroll bars and mouse cursors

An update to CSS2, **CSS 2.1,** was introduced by the W3C in April 2002. Although the update did not add any new features to the language, it cleaned up minor errors that were introduced in the original specification. Even as browsers are implementing all of the features of CSS2, the W3C has pressed forward to the next version, **CSS3**. Still in development as of this writing, CSS3 will add styles for:

- *User interfaces*: Adding dynamic and interactive features
- *Accessibility*: Supporting users with disabilities and other special needs
- *Columnar layout*: Giving Web authors more page layout options
- *International features*: Providing support for a wide variety of languages and typefaces
- *Mobile devices*: Supporting the device requirements of PDAs and cell phones
- *Scalable vector graphics*: Making it easier for Web authors to add graphic elements to their Web pages

CSS3 will break up all of the style sheet specifications into individual modules. This approach should make it easier for developers of Web browsers to create products that support only those parts of CSS that are relevant to their products. For example, an aural browser might not need to support the CSS styles associated with printed media, so the browser's developers would need to concentrate only on the CSS3 modules that deal with aural properties. This CSS revision promises to make browser development easier; and the resulting browser products will therefore be more efficient and compact.

As with HTML, the usefulness of style sheets depends on the support of the browser community. Currently, CSS 2.1 enjoys good browser support—though there are some important differences between the major browsers that you'll explore later in this tutorial. As always, a Web page designer needs to be aware of compatibility issues that arise not just among different versions of CSS, but also among different versions of the same browser.

Applying a Style Sheet

You can apply styles to a Web site in three ways: with inline styles, with an embedded style sheet, and with an external style sheet. Each approach has its own advantages and disadvantages; you'll probably use some combination of all three in developing your Web sites. Tammy suggests that you explore each approach.

Using Inline Styles

An **inline style** is a style that is applied directly to an element through the use of the following style attribute

```
style = "style1: value1; style2: value2; style3: value3; ..."
```

where *style1*, *style2*, *style3*, and so forth are the names of the style properties, and *value1*, *value2*, *value3*, and so on are the values associated with each style property. So to center an h1 heading and display it in a red font, add the following inline style to the opening <h1> tag:

```
<h1 style="text-align: center; color: red">Sunny Acres</h1>
```

Inline styles are easy to interpret because they are applied directly to the elements they affect. However, this also makes them cumbersome. For example, if you wanted to use inline styles to make all of your headings the same font color, you would have to locate all of the h1 through h6 elements on the Web site and apply the same color style to them. This would be no small task on a large Web site containing hundreds of headings spread out among dozens of Web pages.

In addition, some developers point out that inline styles aren't consistent with the goal of separating content from style. After all, there is arguably little difference between using the inline style

```
<h1 style="text-align: center"> ... </h1>
```

and the deprecated align attribute

```
<h1 align="right"> ... </h1>
```

One goal of style sheets is to separate the development of a document's style from the development of its content. Ideally, the HTML code and CSS styles should be separate so that one person could work on content using HTML and another on design using CSS. This isn't possible with inline styles.

Using an Embedded Style Sheet

The power of style sheets becomes evident when you move style definitions away from document content. One way of doing this is to collect all of the styles used in the document in an **embedded style sheet** that is placed in the head section of the document. Embedded style sheets are created using the style element

```
<style type="text/css">
    style declarations
</style>
```

where *style declarations* are the declarations of the various styles to be applied to elements in the current document. Each style declaration has the syntax

```
selector {style1: value1; style2: value2; style3: value3; ...}
```

where *selector* identifies an element or elements within the document and the *style: value* pairs follow the same syntax that you've been using with inline styles. So to display all of the h1 headings in the documents in centered red text, add the following embedded style to the document head:

```
<style type="text/css">
   h1 {text-align: center; color: red}
</style>
```

You can apply the same style to several elements by entering the elements in a comma-separated list before the list of style properties. The following embedded style applies the centered-red font style to all of the h1 and h2 headings in the current document:

```
<style type="text/css">
   h1, h2 {text-align: center; color: red}
</style>
```

To see how to create and apply an embedded style, add one now to the home.htm file, setting the font color of all h2 and h3 headings in the document to green.

To apply an embedded style to Tammy's home page:

1. Return to the **home.htm** file in your text editor.

2. Directly above the closing </head> tag, insert the following embedded style, as shown in Figure 3-4:

   ```
   <style type="text/css">
      h2, h3 {color: green}
   </style>
   ```

Creating an embedded style sheet ◁ **Figure 3-4**

3. Save your changes to the file and refresh the **home.htm** file in your Web browser. The Welcome heading (an h2 element) and the Hours and Directions headings (both h3 elements) should now be displayed in a green font.

Styles from an embedded style sheet are applied to each of the elements listed in the style declaration—unless one of those elements has an inline style. In the case of conflicts, an inline style takes precedence over an embedded style sheet.

Using an External Style Sheet

Note that an embedded style sheet is limited to the page elements of the current document. If you wanted to use embedded styles to apply a style to an entire Web site, you would have to repeat the styles in the head section of each document. For a large Web site with many documents, this would be a cumbersome and error-prone process. Instead, you can place the style declarations in an external style sheet. An **external style sheet** is a text file that contains style declarations. The file can then be linked to any or all pages on the Web site, allowing the same styles to be applied to the entire site. The file-name extension indicates the language of the style sheet. The extension for CSS style sheets is .css. An external style sheet looks like a list of embedded styles, except that the style declarations are not enclosed within opening and closing <style> tags. The following style declaration in an external style sheet

```
h1 {text-align: center; color: red}
```

would cause all Web pages linked to that style sheet to have their h1 headings displayed in centered red text. The great advantage of external style sheets is that you can create and change the style for an entire Web site by modifying one style sheet rather than editing the code of dozens of Web pages.

Adding Style Comments

Tip

Style comments can also be added to embedded style sheets as long as they are placed between the opening and closing <style> tags.

Style sheets can be as long and complicated as HTML files. To help others interpret your style sheet code, you should document the content and purpose of the style sheet using style sheet comments. The syntax to add a style sheet comment is

```
/* comment */
```

where *comment* is the text of the comment. CSS ignores the presence of whitespace, so as with HTML code, you can place style comments and style text on several lines to make your document easier to read. For example, the following style comment extends over four lines in the style sheet:

```
/*
   Sunny Acres
   Style Sheet
*/
```

Tammy would like you to use an external style sheet for the design of her Sunny Acres Web site. She has provided a text file with the main structure of a style sheet already entered. She'd like you to start by adding a style to center the text of all the address elements.

To create an external style sheet:

1. Use your text editor to open the **farmtxt.css** file from the tutorial.03\tutorial folder included with your Data Files. Enter *your name* and *the date* in the comment section at the top of the file.

2. Below the comment section, insert the following style declaration. Figure 3-5 shows the completed style sheet.

   ```
   address {text-align: center}
   ```

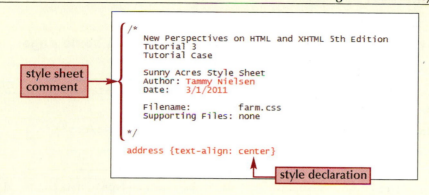

Creating an external style sheet   Figure 3-5

style sheet comment

```
/*
        New Perspectives on HTML and XHTML 5th Edition
        Tutorial 3
        Tutorial Case

        Sunny Acres Style Sheet
        Author: Tammy Nielsen
        Date:   3/1/2011

        Filename:       farm.css
        Supporting Files: none
*/

address {text-align: center}
```

style declaration

3. Save the file as **farm.css** to the tutorial.03\tutorial folder.

To apply this style to Tammy's document, you have to create a link between the home.htm file and the farm.css style sheet.

Linking to an External Style Sheet

You create a link between Web pages and external style sheets using the same link element discussed in Tutorial 2. The code to create a style sheet link is

```
<link href="url" rel="stylesheet" type="text/css" />
```

where *url* is the URL of the external style sheet. As with the link elements discussed in Tutorial 2, link elements used for style sheets must be placed in the head section of the Web page document. For example, to create a link to a styles.css style sheet, you would insert the following element into the head section of the HTML file:

```
<link href="styles.css" rel="stylesheet" type="text/css" />
```

The URL in the href attribute is interpreted in the same way as URLs for linked Web pages. In this case, you assume that the styles.css file is located in the same folder as the current document because no additional path information has been provided.

Applying a Style | Reference Window

- To apply an inline style to a page element, insert the HTML attribute
    ```
    style="style1: value1; style2: value2; style3: value3; ..."
    ```
  where *style1*, *style2*, *style3*, and so on are the names of the style properties, and *value1*, *value2*, *value3*, and so on are the values associated with each style property.
- To apply an embedded style sheet to a Web page, add to the document's head
    ```
    <style type="text/css">
      style declarations
    </style>
    ```
  where *style declarations* are lists of styles in the form
    ```
    selector {style1: value1; style2: value2; style3: value3; ...}
    ```
  with *selector* identifying the element or elements within that document receiving the style.
- To apply an external style sheet, use your text editor to create a text file containing style declarations. Use the .css filename extension. To link to the external style sheet, add
    ```
    <link href="url" rel="stylesheet" type="text/css" />
    ```
  to the document head, where *url* is the URL of the external style sheet.

You'll use the link element to create a link between Tammy's home.htm file and the farm.css style sheet.

To link the farm.css external style sheet to Tammy's home page:

▶ 1. Return to the **home.htm** file in your text editor.

▶ 2. Between the closing </style> tag and the closing </head> tag, insert the following link element, as shown in Figure 3-6:

```
<link href="farm.css" rel="stylesheet" type="text/css" />
```

Figure 3-6	Linking to an external style sheet

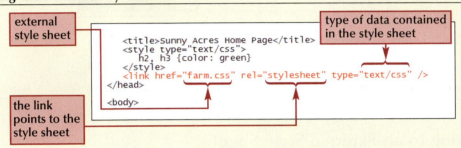

▶ 3. Save your changes to the file and then reload or refresh the **home.htm** file in your Web browser.

▶ 4. Scroll to the bottom of the page and confirm that the address text for the Sunny Acres farm is now centered horizontally on the page.

InSight | **Importing Style Sheets**

On large Web sites that involve hundreds of pages, you might decide to use different styles for different groups of pages to give a visual cue to users about where they are on the site. One way of organizing these different styles is to break them into smaller, more manageable units. The different style sheets can then be imported into a single sheet. To import a style sheet, add the following statement to either an embedded style sheet or an external style sheet file

```
@import url(url)
```

where (*url*) is the URL of an external style sheet file. For example, a company might have one style sheet named company.css that contains basic styles used in all Web pages and another style sheet named support.css that only applies to Web pages containing technical support information. The following embedded style sheet imports both files:

```
<style type="text/css">
    @import url(company.css)
    @import url(support.css)
</style>
```

The @import statement must always come before any other style declarations in the embedded or external style sheet. When the browser encounters the @import statement, it imports the content of the style sheet file directly into current style sheet, much as if you had typed the style declarations yourself.

Setting up Alternate Style Sheets

Many browsers allow Web pages to support alternative style sheets. This is particularly useful in situations with users who have special needs (such as a need for large text with highly contrasting colors). To support these users, you can create an alternate style sheet with the link element

```
<link href="url1" rel="alternate stylesheet"
      type="text/css" title="title1" />
<link href="url2" rel="alternate stylesheet"
      type="text/css" title="title2" />
```

where *url1*, *url2*, and so forth are the URLs of the style sheet files, and *title1*, *title2*, etc. are the titles of the alternate style sheets. For example, the following HTML code creates links to two style sheets named Large Text and Regular Text:

```
<link href="large.css" rel="alternate stylesheet" type="text/css"
      title="Large Text" />
<link href="regular.css" rel="alternate stylesheet" type="text/css"
      title="Regular Text" />
```

Browsers that support alternate style sheets provide a menu option for the user to select which style sheet to apply. Figure 3-7 shows how users could choose between the Large Text and the Regular Text style sheets under the Firefox browser.

Choosing between alternate style sheets in Firefox | Figure 3-7

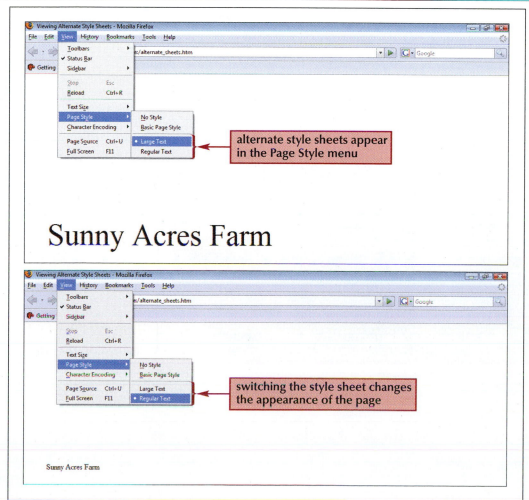

Among the major browsers, currently Netscape, Firefox, Opera, and Safari support alternate style sheets. At the time of this writing, Internet Explorer supports them only if a specialized add-in program is installed on the user's computer. Tammy wants you to be aware of alternate style sheets for the future; but for now, you will not be specifying alternate style sheets for the Sunny Acres Web site.

Understanding Cascading Order

With so many ways of applying styles to a Web site, you might wonder which style is ultimately used by the browser when the page is rendered. For example, consider a Web page that is linked to an external style sheet that sets all h1 elements in bold, red font. But the author also has an inline style for one of the h1 elements specifying centered blue font. Furthermore, the browser specifies that all h1 elements are rendered in a regular black font that is not centered on the page. Which style rule is ultimately applied to the page? To answer that question, you have to examine the principals of style precedence and style inheritance.

Style Precedence

Style precedence is the rule that determines which style is applied when one or more styles conflict. The general rule is that in the case of conflict, the more specific style has precedence over the more general style.

As shown in Figure 3-8, the most general style is the one that is built into the Web browser. Each browser has an internal style sheet that it uses for rendering page elements. The reason that most browsers indent block quotes or display h1 headings in a large font is that they are applying an internal style sheet that governs how those elements are rendered. Unless a different style is specified by the Web page author or the user viewing the page, these browser styles are used.

Figure 3-8	Levels of style precedence

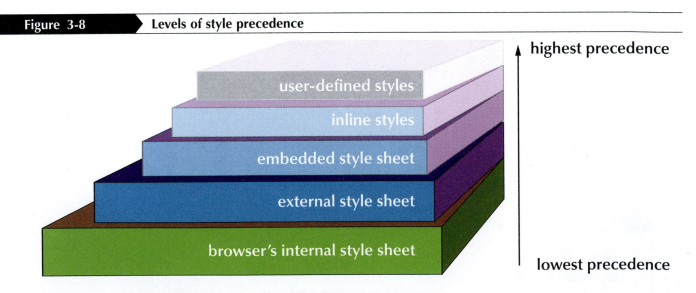

The next three levels of styles are those defined by the Web site author. The first are styles defined in an external style sheet. When linked to a Web page, those styles will have precedence over the browser's built-in styles. In the same way, an embedded style sheet applied to a specific Web page has precedence over external style sheets. Finally, inline styles applied to specific elements within a Web page have precedence over the styles defined in the embedded style sheet.

The highest level of style rules includes those defined by the user of the Web page. Most browsers allow users to modify the style sheets used by the browser and the Web page. For example, the Accessibility dialog box in Internet Explorer shown in Figure 3-9 is often used by people with disabilities to set up style sheets that meet specific needs. These user-defined styles take precedence over the browser's internal styles and any styles specified by the Web page author.

Tip

View your Web pages without the style sheets to ensure that the page is still readable even when your style sheets are not adopted by the user. The ability to understand page content should not depend on the ability to access your style sheet.

Accessibility dialog box in Internet Explorer | **Figure 3-9**

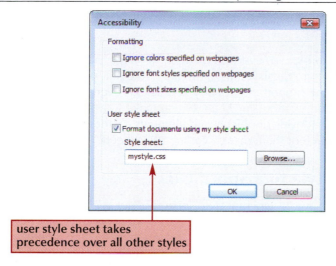

user style sheet takes precedence over all other styles

When conflicting styles are on the same level, the one declared last has precedence. For example, the following embedded style sheet

```
<style type="text/css">
   h1 {color: orange; text-align: center}
   h1 {color: blue}
</style>
```

results in h1 headings displayed in centered blue text. The text is blue because the second style declaration has precedence over the first. However, the text is still centered because the second style declaration did not alter the text-align style, so the text-align setting from the first style declaration is still in force.

You can override the precedence rules by adding the !important property to a style declaration. The style sheet

```
<style type="text/css">
 h1 {color: orange !important }
 h1 {color: blue; text-align: center }
</style>
```

results in h1 headings rendered in centered orange text because the orange style is given a higher weight than the blue style even though the blue style is declared last. The !important property is useful in situations where you want to ensure that a particular style is always enforced regardless of its location in the order of precedence.

Note that even with the !important property, any styles you specify can still be overridden by users who set up their own style sheets with their browsers.

Style Inheritance

Where there is no conflict, styles are passed down from the more general levels to the more specific in what is known as **style inheritance**. When you use an external style sheet to set the font color of h1 headings to blue, that color is assumed in all other h1 heading styles unless a different color is specified. This is also true for page elements that are nested within other page elements. For example, to set the font color of every element on the page to blue, you could enter the following style declaration:

```
body {color: blue}
```

Every element nested within the body element (that is, every element on the page) would inherit this style. This means that every h1 heading, every paragraph, every numbered list, and so forth would be displayed in blue text. To override style inheritance, you specify an alternate style for one of the descendant elements of the parent. The styles

```
body {color: blue}
p    {color: red}
```

set the text color to blue for every element on the page; paragraphs and elements contained within them are displayed in a red font. Note that you can override style inheritance using the same !important property you use for overriding style precedence.

Through style inheritance, any changes you make to a style sheet will automatically be passed down the levels of objects and elements on the Web site. This cascade of style changes is the source of the term "cascading style sheets."

Applying a Style to a Specific ID

Sometimes you'll have an external style sheet for your Web site, but will still want to apply a style to a specific element. If that is the case, you can mark the element with the id attribute, as discussed in Tutorial 2. To create a style for that marked element, apply the style declaration

```
#id {style rule}
```

where *id* is the value of the element's id attribute and *style rule* stands for the styles applied to that specific element. For example, if you have the h2 element

```
<h2 id="subtitle">A Fun Family Farm</h2>
```

in your code, you can set the font color to red using the following style:

```
#subtitle {color: red}
```

You do the same with an inline style, but using the id attribute has the advantage of moving the style declaration out of the HTML file, where it can be more easily maintained and revised.

| Reference Window | **Applying a Style to an ID** |

- To apply a style to an element marked with a specific id value, use the declaration
  `#id {style rule}`
  where *id* is the value of the element's id attribute and *style rule* stands for the styles applied to that specific element.

You'll create styles for specific element ids later in this tutorial.

Working with Color in HTML and CSS

Now that you've seen how embedded and external style sheets work, you'll begin exploring various aspects of the CSS language. You'll start by examining how to work with color. If you've worked with graphics software, you've probably made your color choices without much difficulty due to the graphical interfaces that those applications employ. Graphical interfaces, known as WYSIWYG (what you see is what you get), allow you to select colors visually. Specifying a color with CSS is somewhat less intuitive because CSS is a text-based language and requires you to define your colors in textual terms. This can be done by specifying either a color value or a color name.

Color Values

A **color value** is a numerical expression that precisely describes a color. To better understand how numbers can represent colors, it helps to review some of the basic principles of color theory and how they relate to the colors that your monitor displays.

White light is made up of three primary colors (red, green, and blue) mixed at equal intensities. By adding two of the three primary colors you can generate a trio of complementary colors: yellow, magenta, and cyan, as shown Figure 3-10.

Primary color model for light | Figure 3-10

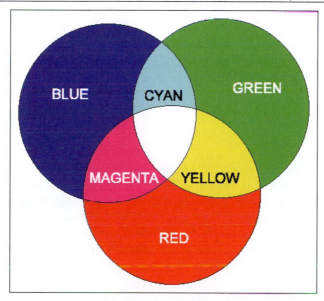

To generate a wider range of colors, you simply vary the intensity of the red, green, and blue light. For example, orange is created from a high intensity of red light, a moderate intensity of green light, and an absence of blue light. Your computer monitor generates colors by emitting red, green, and blue light at different intensities. CSS represents these intensities mathematically. Each color is represented by a triplet of numbers called an **RGB triplet**, whose values are based on the strength of its red, green, and blue components. This triplet has the form

`rgb(red, green, blue)`

where *red*, *green*, and *blue* are the intensity values of the red, green, and blue components. The intensity values range from 0 (absence of color) to 255 (highest intensity). For example, the RGB triplet for white is (255, 255, 255), indicating that red, green, and blue are equally mixed at the highest intensity. Orange has the triplet (255, 165, 0) which means it results from a mixture of high-intensity red, moderate-intensity green, and no blue. You can also enter each component value as a percentage, with 100% representing the highest intensity. In this form, you specify the color orange with

```
rgb(100%, 65%, 0%)
```

The percentage form is less commonly used than RGB values. RGB triplets can specify 256^3 (16.7 million) possible colors, which is more colors than the human eye can distinguish.

Originally, HTML required that color values be entered using the hexadecimal system. A **hexadecimal** is a number expressed in the base 16 numbering system rather than in the base 10 form you use every day. In base 10 counting, you use combinations of 10 characters (0 through 9) to represent numerical values. The hexadecimal system includes six extra characters: A (for 10), B (for 11), C (for 12), D (for 13), E (for 14), and F (for 15). For values above 15, you use a combination of those 16 characters. Therefore, to represent a number in hexadecimal terms, you convert the value to multiples of 16, plus a remainder. For example, 16 is equal to $(16 \times 1) + 0$, so its hexadecimal representation is 10. A value of 21 is equal to $(16 \times 1) + 5$, for a hexadecimal representation of 15. The number 255 is equal to $(16 \times 15) + 15$, or FF in hexadecimal format (remember that F = 15 in hexadecimal). In the case of the number 255, the first F represents the number of times 16 goes into 255 (which is 15), and the second F represents the remainder of 15. A color value represented as a hexadecimal number has the form

```
#redgreenblue
```

where *red*, *green*, and *blue* are the hexadecimal values of the red, green, and blue components. Therefore, the color yellow could be represented either by the RGB triplet

```
rgb(255,255,0)
```

or in the hexadecimal form

```
#FFFF00
```

At this point, you might be wondering whether you have to become a math major before you can start adding color to your Web pages! Fortunately, this is not the case. You can specify most colors on your Web pages with styles that use RGB triplets rather than the hexadecimal form. However, you might see HTML or CSS code that sets a color value to something like #FFA500, and now you know where such a representation comes from—even if you can't tell at a glance that it specifies the color orange.

Using Color Names

If you don't want to use color values, you can also specify colors by name. HTML and XHTML support 16 basic color names. These color names are also supported by CSS 2.1, with the addition of orange to make 17 color names. The 17 color names and their RGB and hexadecimal color values are shown in Figure 3-11.

Color Name	RGB Triplet	Hexadecimal	Color Name	RGB Triplet	Hexadecimal
Aqua	(0, 255, 255)	00FFFF	Olive	(128, 128, 0)	808000
Black	(0, 0, 0)	000000	Orange	(255, 165, 0)	FFA500
Blue	(0, 0, 255)	0000FF	Purple	(128, 0, 128)	800080
Fuchsia	(255, 0, 255)	FF00FF	Red	(255, 0, 0)	FF0000
Gray	(128, 128, 128)	808080	Silver	(192, 192, 192)	C0C0C0
Green	(0, 128, 0)	008000	Teal	(0, 128, 128)	008080
Lime	(0, 255, 0)	00FF00	White	(255, 255, 255)	FFFFFF
Maroon	(128, 0, 0)	800000	Yellow	(255, 255, 0)	FFFF00
Navy	(0, 0, 128)	000080			

Seventeen colors are not a lot, so most browsers support an extended list of 140 color names, including such colors as crimson, khaki, and peachpuff. Although this extended color list is not part of the specifications for either HTML or CSS, most browsers support it. You can view these color names in a demo page.

To view the extended list of color names:

▶ **1.** Use your browser to open the **demo_color_names.htm** file from the tutorial.03\demo folder included with your Data Files.

▶ **2.** As shown in Figure 3-12, the demo page displays the list of 140 color names along with their color values expressed both as RGB triplets and in hexadecimal form. The 17 color names supported by CSS 2.1 are highlighted in the table.

Sample	Name	RGB	Hexadecimal
	aliceblue	(240,248,255)	#F0F8FF
	antiquewhite	(250,235,215)	#FAEBD7
	aqua	(0,255,255)	#00FFFF
	aquamarine	(127,255,212)	#7FFFD4
	azure	(240,255,255)	#F0FFFF
	beige	(245,245,220)	#F5F5DC
	bisque	(255,228,196)	#FFE4C4
	black	(0,0,0)	#000000
	blanchedalmond	(255,235,205)	#FFEBCD
	blue	(0,0,255)	#0000FF
	blueviolet	(138,43,226)	#8A2BE2
	brown	(165,42,42)	#A52A2A
	burlywood	(222,184,135)	#DEB887

▶ **3.** Close the page when you are finished reviewing the extended color names list.

Depending on the design requirements of your site, you might sometimes need to use color values to get exactly the right color. However, if you know the general color that you need, you can usually enter the color name without having to look up its RGB value.

Defining Text and Background Colors

Now that you've studied how to specify a color in HTML and CSS, you can start applying it to the elements of Tammy's Web pages. CSS supports styles to define the text and background color for each element on your page. You've already worked with the color style to define text color. The style to define the background color is

```
background-color: color
```

where *color* is either a color value or a color name. If you do not define an element's color, it takes the color of the element that contains it. For example, if you specify red text on a gray background for the Web page body, all elements within the page inherit that color combination unless you specify different styles for specific elements.

Reference Window | **Setting the Background Color**

- To set the background color of an element, use
  ```
  background-color: color
  ```
  where *color* is a color name or a color value.

Tammy wants each of her pages to have a slightly different color theme. For the home page, she wants a white page background, and she wants the heading text to appear in white text on a dark green background. Although most browsers assume a white background by default, it's a good idea to make this explicit in case a browser has a differentsetting. You'll add to this style to the farm.css external style sheet because you'll eventually apply this to the entire Sunny Acres Web site. For the background color of the heading, you'll use the value

```
rgb(0, 154, 0)
```

You'll add this to an embedded style sheet in the home.htm file because Tammy doesn't intend to use the same heading background on her other pages.

To set the text and background colors on Tammy's home page:

1. Return to the **home.htm** file in your text editor.

2. As shown in Figure 3-13, change the style for h2 and h3 headings to:
   ```
   h2, h3 {color: white; background-color: rgb(0, 154, 0)}
   ```

Figure 3-13 | **Specifying text color and background colors**

```
<title>Sunny Acres Home Page</title>
<style type="text/css">
    h2, h3 {color: white; background-color: rgb(0, 154, 0)}
</style>
<link href="farm.css" rel="stylesheet" type="text/css" />
</head>
```

3. Save your changes to the file.

4. Return to the **farm.css** file in your text editor.

5. As shown in Figure 3-14, above the style declaration for the address element, insert the following style:
   ```
   body {background-color: white}
   ```

Setting the background color for the page body ◀ Figure 3-14

```
body      {background-color: white}
address   {text-align: center}
```

▶ **6.** Save your changes to the file.

▶ **7.** Reload the **home.htm** file in your Web browser. As shown in Figure 3-15, the h2 and h3 heading text should now appear as white text on a dark green background.

Formatted heading ◀ Figure 3-15

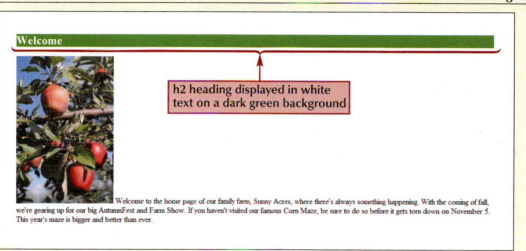

h2 heading displayed in white text on a dark green background

Welcome to the home page of our family farm, Sunny Acres, where there's always something happening. With the coming of fall, we're gearing up for our big AutumnFest and Farm Show. If you haven't visited our famous Corn Maze, be sure to do so before it gets torn down on November 5. This year's maze is bigger and better than ever.

▶ **8.** If you want to take a break before starting the next session, you can close your files and applications now.

Deprecated Approaches to Color | InSight

CSS was not part of the original HTML specifications. If you need to work with older HTML code or need to support older browser versions, you might need to use several deprecated attributes such as bgcolor and text. Both attributes require you to enter either the hexadecimal color value or a recognized color name. You use the bgcolor attribute in the <body> tag to define the background color for an entire page. To define the text color for the entire page, use the text attribute. For example, the following code changes the page background to yellow and the page's text color to sky blue with the hexadecimal value 99CCFF:

```
<body bgcolor="yellow" text="#99CCFF">
```

If you need to color a section of text on your page, enclose the text within the two-sided <font> tag. The <font> tag is a deprecated element that supports several design attributes. Among those supported is the color attribute, which you can use to specify a color name or a hexadecimal color value. For example, the following HTML code sets the text color of an h1 heading to green:

```
<h1><font color="green">Sunny Acres</font></h1>
```

Note that the bgcolor and text attributes and the font element are not part of XHTML and will be rejected by documents that require a strict application of XHTML standards.

You show Tammy the work you've done on colors. She's pleased with the ease of CSS to modify the design and appearance of elements on the Sunny Acres home page. In the next session, you'll continue to explore CSS styles, focusing on text and image styles.

| Review | **Session 3.1 Quick Check** |

1. What are inline styles, embedded styles, and external style sheets? Which would you use to create a design for an entire Web site?
2. Specify the code to enter the following comment into a CSS file:

   `Sunny Acres Style Sheet`

3. Specify the code to set the text color of every paragraph element within the Web page to red.
4. If a style sheet has the following declarations, how will address text be rendered by the browser?:

   ```
   address {color: red; text-align: left}
   address {color: blue}
   ```

5. If a style sheet has the following declarations, how will paragraph text be rendered by the browser?:

   ```
   body {background-color: ivory}
   p    {color: red}
   ```

6. What property do you add to a style to override style precedence and style inheritance?
7. Specify the style to display block quote text in a color with a red intensity of 221, a green intensity of 128, and a blue intensity of 0.

Session 3.2

Working with Fonts and Text Styles

Tammy has noticed that all of the text on her pages is displayed in the same typeface. She'd like to see more variety in the page fonts. To modify the text, you'll work with the CSS text and font styles.

Choosing a Font

By default, browsers display Web page text in a single font—usually Times New Roman. You can specify a different font for any page element using the style

`font-family: fonts`

where *fonts* is a comma-separated list of fonts that the browser can use in any element. Font names can be either specific or generic. A **specific font** is a font that is actually installed on a user's computer; examples are Times New Roman, Arial, and Garamond. A **generic font** is a name for a grouping of fonts that share a similar appearance. Browsers recognize five generic font groups: serif, sans-serif, monospace, cursive, and fantasy. Figure 3-16 shows examples of each.

Font Samples

serif	defg	defg	defg
sans-serif	defg	defg	defg
monospace	defg	defg	defg
cursive	defg	defg	defg
fantasy	defg	defg	DEFG

Note that within a font family, the actual appearance of the text might vary widely and you cannot be sure which font a given user's browser will use. For this reason, CSS allows you to specify a list of specific fonts along with a generic font. You list the specific fonts first, in order of preference, and then end the list with the generic font. If the browser cannot find any of the specific fonts listed, it uses the generic font. For example, to specify a sans-serif font, you could enter the following style:

```
font-family: Arial, Helvetica, 'Trebuchet MS', sans-serif
```

This style tells the browser to first look for the Arial font; if Arial is not available, the browser looks for Helvetica, and then Trebuchet MS. If none of those fonts is available, the browser uses a generic sans-serif font. Note that font names containing one or more blank spaces (such as Trebuchet MS) must be enclosed within single or double quotes.

To see how the generic fonts appear on your browser, you can use a demo page on text styles.

To use the demo to view your browser's generic fonts:

► 1. Use your Web browser to open the **demo_css.htm** file from the tutorial.03\demo folder included with your Data Files.

The demo page contains a collection of text styles you'll explore in this session. You can select a text style value from the drop-down lists on the left side of the demo. You can specify the text to apply the style to in the top-right box. The style as applied to the sample text appears in the middle box. The CSS code for the style appears in the bottom-right box. You press the Tab key to apply the style.

► 2. Click the top-right corner box, select and delete the text "Enter sample text here" and type **Sunny Acres**, press the **Enter** key, and then type **Corn Maze**. Press the **Tab** key to display this text in the Preview box.

► 3. In the three color input boxes, enter the RGB value

```
rgb(255, 255, 255)
```

and in the three background-color input boxes, enter

```
rgb(153, 102, 102)
```

and then press the **Tab** key.

4. Select **sans-serif** from the font-family list box. As shown in Figure 3-17, the demo page shows the effect of the styles applied to the sample text. The CSS code for these styles is shown in the Style box.

Viewing the sans-serif font

If you think users will want to print your Web pages, be aware that the general rule is to use sans-serif fonts for headlines and serif fonts for body text. For computer monitors, which have lower resolutions than printed material, the general rule is to use sans-serif fonts for headlines and body text, leaving serif fonts for special effects and large text. Tammy expects that her Web page will only be viewed on computer monitors, so you'll use a sans-serif font for all of the body text. You'll do this in the farm.css external style sheet so it can be applied to all pages on the site.

To apply a sans-serif font to the body text in Tammy's external style sheet:

1. Return to the **farm.css** file in your text editor.

2. Add the style

```
font-family: Arial, Helvetica, sans-serif
```

to the style declaration for the body element. Be sure to use a semicolon to separate this new style from the background-color style. Figure 3-18 shows the revised code.

Setting the font-family style for the body text

```
body    {background-color: white; font-family: Arial, Helvetica, sans-serif}
address {text-align: center}
```

3. Save your changes to the file and then reload the **home.htm** file in your Web browser. As shown in Figure 3-19, all of the body text in the Web page should now be displayed in a sans-serif font.

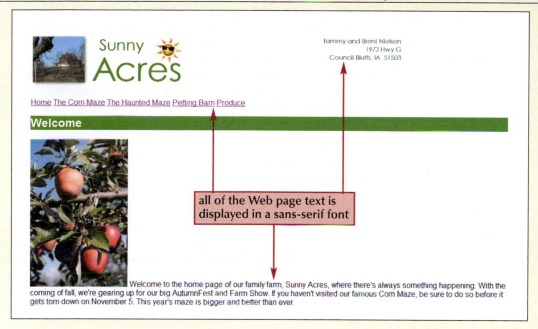

Body text in a sans-serif font | Figure 3-19

Note that the sans-serif font is applied to all page elements on the Sunny Acres home page. This is because you applied the style to the body element, and so it cascades through all the elements on the page.

Setting the Font Size

Tammy would like the Welcome heading on her home page to be displayed in slightly larger text than the rest of her site. The style to change the font size of the text within an element is

```
font-size: length
```

where *length* is a length measurement. Lengths can be specified in four different ways:

- with a unit of measurement
- with a keyword description
- as a percentage of the size of the containing element
- with a keyword expressing the size relative to the size of the containing element

If you choose to specify lengths using measurement units, you can use absolute units or relative units. Because absolute and relative units appear in several styles, it's worthwhile to spend some time understanding them. **Absolute units** are units that are fixed in size regardless of the device rendering the Web page and are specified in one of five standard units of measurement: mm (millimeters), cm (centimeters), in (inches), pt (points), and pc (picas). The points and picas measurements might not be as familiar to you as inches, millimeters, and centimeters. For comparison, there are 72 points in an inch, 12 points in a pica, and 6 picas in an inch. Size values for any of these measurements can be whole numbers (0, 1, 2 ...) or decimals (0.5, 1.6, 3.9 ...). For example, ifyou want your text to be 1/2 inch in size, you can use any of the following styles (note that you should not insert a space between the size value and the unit abbreviation):

```
font-size: 0.5in
font-size: 36pt
font-size: 3pc
```

Tip

Use absolute units only when you can predict or can fix the size and dimensions of the output device.

Absolute measurements are appropriate when you know the physical properties of the output device and want to fix the size to a specific value. Of course this is not often the case with Web pages because they can be displayed on a variety of devices, monitor sizes, and resolutions. This is one of the fundamental differences between Web page design and print design (in which you usually know the size and properties of the paper).

To cope with a wide variety of output devices and sizes, many Web page designers opt to use **relative units**, which are expressed relative to the size of other objects within the Web page. One commonly used relative unit is the **em unit**. The exact meaning of the em unit depends on its use in the style sheet. If the em unit is used for setting font size, it expresses the size relative to the font size of the parent element. For an h1 heading, the parent element is the Web page body. So the style

```
h1 {font-size: 2em}
```

sets the font size of h1 headings to twice the font size of body text. If the browser has been configured to display body text in a 12-point font, this style will cause h1 headings to be displayed in a 24-point font. On the other hand, if the h1 heading is nested within another element such as a blockquote element or div element, then the size of the h1 heading will be twice the size of text in that containing element. Context is important when interpreting the effect of the em unit.

When used for sizing objects other than fonts, the em unit is equal to a little over the width of the capital letter "M" in the font size of the current element. The style

```
h1 {width: 20em}
```

sets the width of the h1 heading to a little over the width of 20 capital Ms. Of course, the actual size of the Ms depends on the font used in the h1 heading. Because capital Ms take up the most width of any character, another way to think of the em unit is as about the length of two characters. The above style would fit about 40 characters of text in the h1 heading.

One of the great advantages of relative units like the em unit is that they can make your page **scalable**, allowing the page to be rendered the same way no matter what font size is used by the browser. For example, one user with a large monitor might have body text set to 18 points, while another user with a smaller monitor might have body text setto 10 points. Regardless of the size of the monitor, your heading text should be about 50% larger than the body text. Setting the font size of h1 headings to 1.5 em ensures that they are sized appropriately.

Another relative unit is the percentage. Like the em unit, percentages have one meaning when used for font sizes and another meaning when used to size other objects. When used for font sizes, the percentages are based on the font size of the parent element. The style

```
h1 {font-size: 200%}
```

sets the font size of h1 headings to be 200% or twice that of body text. When used to set the size of other objects, the percentage refers to the width of the parent element. So the style

```
h1 {width: 50%}
```

sets the width of the h1 heading to be 50% or half that of the body text. You'll learn more about the width style later in this tutorial.

The final unit of measurement used in Web pages is the pixel, which represents a single dot on the output device.

Be aware that the exact size of a pixel depends on the output device. Different devices have different resolutions, which are typically expressed in terms of dots per inch or dpi. For example, a 600 dpi printer has six times more pixels per inch than a typical computer monitor.

Finally, you can express font sizes using seven descriptive keywords: xx-small, x-small, small, medium, large, x-large, or xx-large. Each browser is configured to display text at a particular size for each of these keywords, but the exact size is determined by the browser's internal style sheet. You can also use the relative keywords larger and smaller to make a font one size larger or smaller than the surrounding text. For example, the following set of styles causes the body text to be displayed in a small font, while h2 text is displayed in a font one size larger (medium in this case):

```
body {font-size: small}
h2 {font-size: larger}
```

Tammy suggests that you make the h2 headings twice the size of body text. You'll add this style to the external style sheet because you want to eventually apply it to her entire Web site.

To set the font size of h2 headings in Tammy's external style sheet:

▶ 1. Return to the **farm.css** file in your text editor.

▶ 2. Directly below the style for the body element, insert the following style, as shown in Figure 3-20:

```
h2 {font-size: 2em}
```

Setting the font size of h2 headings   Figure 3-20

```
body    {background-color: white; font-family: Arial, Helvetica, sans-serif}
h2      {font-size: 2em}   ◄──── h2 headings will be twice
address {text-align: center}         the size of body text
```

▶ 3. Save your changes to the file and then reload the **home.htm** file in your Web browser. Verify that the font size used for the h2 heading at the top of the page is larger than before.

Web designers often have to work in both the em and pixel units of measure. Trying to translate between the two measuring units can be a challenge. One popular approach to defining sizes on a Web page is the so-called 62.5% hack. The idea, introduced by Richard Rutter in his Web design blog called Clagnut, is to define the default font size of the body text in a Web page as 62.5% of the width of the Web page using the following style:

```
body {font-size: 62.5%}
```

The reasoning behind the 62.5% hack is that most Web browsers display body text in a medium font, with the text at a height of 16 pixels. Taking 62.5% of this value assigns the value of 1 em to 10 pixels for body text. With these numbers, you can easily translate between the em unit and the pixel unit. The width of an element can be set to either 100 pixels or its equivalent of 10 em.

You have to be careful when using the 62.5% hack because the value of the em unit depends on its context in the document. As you nest one element within another, the em unit is expressed relative to the font size of the parent element. Several sites on the Web provide em calculators, making it easier for you to track the changing values of the em unit as you drill down through a series of nested elements.

Despite the complication with nesting, the 62.5% hack has become so popular with Web designers that it is considered a standard tool for designing challenging and visually interesting Web pages.

Controlling Spacing and Indentation

Tammy thinks that the text for the Welcome heading looks too crowded. She's wondering if you can spread it out more across the width of the page. She also would like to see more space between the first letter, "W," and the left edge of the green background.

CSS supports styles that allow you to perform some basic typographic tasks, such as kerning and tracking. **Kerning** refers to the amount of space between characters, while **tracking** refers to the amount of space between words. The styles to control an element's kerning and tracking are

```
letter-spacing: value
word-spacing: value
```

where *value* is the size of space between individual letters or words. You specify these sizes with the same units that you use for font sizing. As with font sizes, the default unit of length for kerning and tracking is the pixel (px). The default value for both kerning and tracking is 0 pixels. A positive value increases the letter and word spacing. A negative value reduces the space between letters and words. If you choose to make your pages scalable for a variety of devices and resolutions, you will want to express kerning and tracking values as percentages or in em units.

To see how modifying these values can affect the appearance of your text, return to the CSS styles demo page.

To use the demo to explore kerning and tracking styles:

1. Return to the **css_demo.htm** file in your Web browser.

2. Enter **2** in the font-size input box, and then select **em** from the corresponding unit drop-down list.

3. Select **center** from the text-align list box.

4. Enter **0.3** in the letter-spacing input box and **em** from the corresponding drop-down list. Press the **Tab** key.

5. Enter **0.8** in the word-spacing input box and **em** from the corresponding drop-down list. Press the **Tab** key. Figure 3-21 shows the revised appearance of the text after applying the letter-spacing and word-spacing styles.

Setting kerning and tracking styles | Figure 3-21

default kerning and tracking | kerning set to 0.3 em, tracking set to 0.8 em

Another typographic feature that you can set is **leading**, which is the space between lines of text. The style to set the leading for the text within an element is

```
line-height: length
```

where *length* is a specific length or a percentage of the font size of the text on those lines. If no unit is specified, most browsers interpret the number to represent the ratio of the line height to the font size. The standard ratio is 1.2:1, which means that the line height is usually 1.2 times the font size. On the other hand, the style

```
p {line-height: 2}
```

makes all paragraphs double-spaced. A common technique is to create multiline titles with large fonts and small line heights in order to give title text more impact. Use the demo page to see how this works.

To use the demo to explore leading styles:

1. Enter **0.75** in the line-height input box, and then select **em** from the corresponding unit drop-down list.

2. Press the **Tab** key to apply the line-height style. Figure 3-22 shows the revised appearance of the text.

Figure 3-22 | **Setting the line-height style**

line height set to 0.75 em

An additional way to control text spacing is to set the indentation for the first line of a block of text. The style is

```
text-indent: value
```

where *value* is a length expressed in absolute or relative units or as a percentage of the width of the text block. For example, an indentation value of 5% indents the first line by 5% of the width of the block. The indentation value can also be negative, extending the first line to the left of the text block to create a **hanging indent**.

Now you can use what you've learned about spacing to make the changes that Tammy has suggested. To make her heading text more spread out, you'll set the kerning of the h2 elements to 0.4 em. You'll also set the indentation to 1 em, moving the text of all h2 headings to the left.

To change the spacing of the h2 headings in Tammy's external style sheet:

▶ **1.** Return to the **farm.css** style sheet in your text editor.

▶ **2.** Add the following attributes to the h2 style as shown in Figure 3-23. Be sure to separate each attribute with a semicolon.

```
letter-spacing: 0.4em; text-indent: 1em
```

Applying the letter-spacing and text-indent styles to h2 headings ◀ **Figure 3-23**

```
body     {background-color: white; font-family: Arial, Helvetica, sans-serif}
h2       {font-size: 2em; letter-spacing: 0.4em; text-indent: 1em }
address  {text-align: center}
```

▶ **3.** Save your changes to the file and then refresh the Sunny Acres home page in your Web browser. Figure 3-24 shows the revised appearance of the h2 heading on that page.

Formatted h2 heading ◀ **Figure 3-24**

Welcome

Welcome to the home page of our family farm, Sunny Acres, where there's always something happening. With the coming of fall, we're gearing up for our big AutumnFest and Farm Show. If you haven't visited our famous Corn Maze, be sure to do so before it gets torn down on November 5. This year's maze is bigger and better than ever.

By increasing the kerning in the h2 heading, you've made the text appear less crowded, making it easier to read.

Applying Font Features

As you saw in the first tutorial, browsers often apply default font styles to particular types of elements. Text marked with an <address> tag, for example, usually appears in italics. This is handy when you don't have a specific design in mind for your text. However, you can also choose a specific font style, such as italics, bold, underline, and so forth. You can specify font styles using the style

```
font-style: type
```

where *type* is normal, italic, or oblique. The italic and oblique styles are similar in appearance, but might differ subtly depending on the font in use.

You have also seen that browsers render certain elements in heavier fonts. For example, most browsers render headings in a boldfaced font. You can specify the font weight for any page element using the style

```
font-weight: weight
```

where *weight* is the level of bold formatting applied to the text. You express weights as values ranging from 100 to 900, in increments of 100. In practice, however, most browsers cannot render nine different font weights. For practical purposes, you can assume that 400 represents normal (unbolded) text, 700 is bold text, and 900 represents heavy bold text. You can also use the keywords normal or bold in place of a weight value, or you can express the font weight relative to the containing element, using the keywords bolder or lighter.

Another style you can use to change the appearance of your text is

```
text-decoration: type
```

where *type* is none (for no decoration), underline, overline, line-through, or blink (to create blinking text). You can apply several decorative features to the same element by listing them as part of the text-decoration style. For example, the style

```
text-decoration: underline overline
```

places a line under and over the text in the element. Note that the text-decoration style cannot be applied to nontextual elements, such as inline images.

To control the case of the text within an element, use the style

```
text-transform: type
```

where *type* is capitalize, uppercase, lowercase, or none (to make no changes to the text case). For example, if you want to capitalize the first letter of each word in the element, you could use the style

```
text-transform: capitalize
```

Finally, you can display text in uppercase letters and a small font using the style

```
font-variant: type
```

where *type* is normal (the default) or small caps (small capital letters). Small caps are often used in legal documents, such as software agreements, in which the capital letters indicate the importance of a phrase or point, but the text is made small so as to not detract from other elements in the document.

Setting Font and Text Appearance | Reference Window

- To specify the font style, use
  `font-style: type`
  where *type* is normal, italic, or oblique.
- To specify the font weight, use
  `font-weight: type`
  where *type* is normal, bold, bolder, light, lighter, or a font weight value.
- To specify a text decoration, use
  `text-decoration: type`
  where *type* is none, underline, overline, line-through, or blink.
- To transform the text, use
  `text-transform: type`
  where *type* is capitalize, uppercase, lowercase, or none.
- To display a font variant of the text, use
  `font-variant: type`
  where *type* is normal or small-caps.

To see the impact of these styles, return to the demo page.

To use the demo to view the various font styles:

▶ 1. Return to the **CSS demo page** in your Web browser.

▶ 2. Select **bold** from the font-weight list box.

▶ 3. Select **small-caps** from the font-variant list box. Figure 3-25 shows the impact of applying the font-weight and font-variant styles.

Applying the font-weight and font-variant styles   ◀ **Figure 3-25**

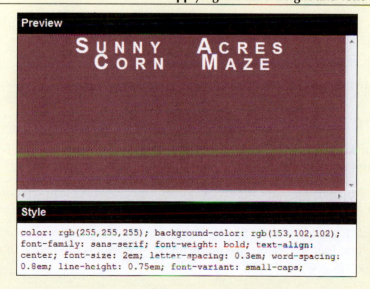

▶ 4. You've completed your work with the CSS demo page. You can continue to explore different CSS font and text styles or close the demo Web page now.

Aligning Text Vertically

In Tutorial 1, you learned how to align text horizontally using the text-align style. You can also vertically align inline elements within the content of the surrounding block. The style for setting vertical alignment is

```
vertical-align: type
```

where *type* is one of the keywords described in Figure 3-26.

Figure 3-26   **Values of the vertical-align style**

Value	Description
baseline	Aligns the element with the bottom of lowercase letters in surrounding text (the default)
bottom	Aligns the bottom of the element with the bottom of the lowest element in surrounding content
middle	Aligns the middle of the element with the middle of the surrounding content
sub	Subscripts the element
super	Superscripts the element
text-bottom	Aligns the bottom of the element with the bottom of the font of the surrounding content
text-top	Aligns the top of the element with the top of the font of the surrounding content
top	Aligns the top of the element with the top of the tallest object in the surrounding content

Instead of using keywords, you can specify a length or a percentage for the element to be aligned relative to the surrounding content. A positive value moves the element up and a negative value lowers the element. For example, the style

```
vertical-align: 50%
```

raises the element by half of the line height of the surrounding content, while the style

```
vertical-align: -100%
```

drops the element an entire line height below the baseline of the current line.

Combining All Text Formatting in a Single Style

You've learned a lot of different text and font styles. You can combine most of them into a single declaration, using the style

```
font: font-style font-variant font-weight font-size/line-height
font-family
```

where *font-style* is the font's style, *font-variant* is the font variant, *font-weight* is the weight of the font, *font-size* is the size of the font, *line-height* is the height of each line, and *font-family* is the font face. For example, the style

```
font: italic small-caps bold 16pt/24pt Arial, sans-serif
```

displays the text of the element in italics, bold, and small capital letters in Arial or another sans-serif font, with a font size of 16pt and spacing between the lines of 24pt. You do not have to include all of the properties of the font style; the only required properties are size and font-family. A browser assumes the default value for any omitted property. However, you must place any properties that you do include in the order indicated above.

Tammy thinks that the size of the address text at the bottom of the page is too large, and would like it in a smaller, non-italics, small caps, sans-serif font. You should modify the style for the address element in the farm.css style sheet so that Tammy can apply the style to any page on her Web site.

To change the style of the address element in Tammy's external style sheet:

1. Return to the **farm.css** file in your text editor.

2. Within the style declaration for the address element, add the following style attributes. See Figure 3-27.

    ```
    font: normal small-caps 0.8em sans-serif
    ```

Applying the font style to the address element ◄ **Figure 3-27**

```
body    {background-color: white; font-family: Arial, Helvetica, sans-serif}
h2      {font-size: 2em; letter-spacing: 0.4em; text-indent: 1em }
address {text-align: center; font: normal small-caps 0.8em sans-serif}
```

font style

3. Save your changes to the file.

4. Refresh the **home.htm** file in your Web browser. Scroll to the bottom of the page and verify that the style of the address element has been changed as shown in Figure 3-28.

Formatted address text ◄ **Figure 3-28**

Directions
- From Council Bluffs, proceed east on I-80
- Take Exit 38 North to the Drake Frontage Road
- Turn right on Highway G
- Proceed east for 2.5 miles
- Sunny Acres is on your left; watch for the green sign

address element

SUNNY ACRES ✳ TAMMY & BRENT NIELSEN ✳ 1977 HIGHWAY G ✳ COUNCIL BLUFFS, IA 51503

Tammy likes the way the fonts appear on her Web site. She especially likes the fact that because these changes were made in a CSS style sheet, she can apply the styles to any Web page she adds to the site in the future.

Working with Images

Tammy wants you to turn your attention to her Web site's graphic images. Graphic images can greatly increase the size of the Web page so you must balance the goal of creating an interesting and attractive page against the need to keep the size of your page and its supporting files small. Many users will turn away from Web pages that take a long time to load.

Web browsers support three graphic formats: GIF, JPEG, and PNG. Each file format has its advantages and disadvantages, and you will probably use a combination of all three formats in your Web page designs. First, you'll look at the advantages and disadvantages of using GIF image files.

Working with GIF Images

GIF (**Graphics Interchange Format**) is a common image format first developed for the CompuServe online information service. GIF files are limited to 256 colors, so they are most often used for graphics requiring fewer colors, such as clip art images, line art, logos, and icons. Images that require more color depth, such as photographs, can appear grainy when saved as GIF files. GIF image files can be large. One way to reduce the size of a GIF is to reduce the number of colors in its color palette. For example, if an image contains only 32 different colors, you can use an image editing program to reduce the palette to those 32 colors, resulting in a smaller image file that loads faster.

Another feature of GIFs is their ability to use transparent colors. A **transparent color** is a color that is not displayed when the image is viewed in an application. In place of the transparent color, a browser displays whatever is on the page background. The process by which you create a transparent color depends on the graphics software you are using. Many applications include the option to designate a transparent color when saving an image, while other packages include a transparent color tool, which you use to select the color that you want to treat as transparent.

GIFs also support animation. An **animated GIF** is composed of several images that are displayed one after the other, creating the illusion of motion. There are many online collections of animated GIFs on the Web. You can also create your own with animated GIF software, which allows you to control the rate at which an animation plays (as measured by frames per second) and to determine the number of times the animation repeats before stopping (or to set it to repeat without stopping).

Animated GIFs are a mixed blessing. They make a Web page appear more dynamic, but they are larger than static GIF files, so using them can slow down the loading of a Web page. Also, as with all formatting features, you should be careful not to overuse animated images. Animated GIFs can quickly irritate users once the novelty wears off, especially because there is no way for users to turn them off! Finally, keep in mind that like static GIF files, animated GIFs are limited to 256 colors.

One of the pages Tammy is planning for the Sunny Acres Web site is the index.htm file, which acts as a splash screen. A **splash screen** is a Web page containing interesting animation or graphics that introduces a Web site. Tammy suggests that you use an animated GIF for her splash screen. You've located a fun animated GIF of a scarecrow and another GIF that contains the Sunny Acres logo. You'll add both of these graphics as inline images to the index.htm file.

To insert GIF files into the splash screen page:

▶ 1. Open the **index.htm** file in your text editor.

▶ 2. Within the div element, insert the following inline image for the Sunny Acres logo:

```
<img src="salogo.gif" alt="Sunny Acres" /><br />
```

▶ 3. Tammy wants the animated GIF to also function as a hypertext link, pointing to the home.htm file. As shown in Figure 3-29, insert the following linked graphic directly below the Sunny Acres logo:

```
<a href="home.htm">
 <img src="scarecrow.gif" alt="animated GIF"
      style="border-width: 0" />
</a>
```

```
<body>
   <div style="text-align: center">
      <img src="salogo.gif" alt="Sunny Acres" /><br />
      <a href="home.htm"><img src="scarecrow.gif" alt="animated GIF" style="border-width: 0" /></a>
   </div>
</body>
```

4. Save your changes to the file and then open the **index.htm** file in your Web browser. As shown in Figure 3-30, an animated scarecrow appears on the Web page directly below the Sunny Acres logo.

Sunny Acres splash screen | Figure 3-30

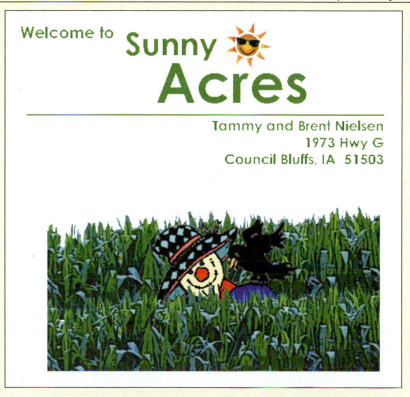

JPEG Images

The other main image file format for Web pages is JPEG. **JPEG** stands for **Joint Photographic Experts Group**. JPEGs differ from GIFs in several ways. In the JPEG format, you can create images that use all 16.7 million colors available in the color palette. Because of this, JPEG files are most often used for photographs and other images that cover a wide spectrum of color. In addition, despite the fact that JPEGs use the full color palette, the image compression algorithm used by JPEG files yields image files that are usually (though not always) smaller than their GIF counterparts. (Note that in some situations, though, the GIF format creates a smaller and better-looking image—for example, when an image contains large sections covered with a single color.) You can set the amount of compression applied to JPEGs in your imaging editing software, allowing you to balance the desire for a high-quality image versus the need to keep images compact.

As a general rule, you should use JPEGs for photos and use GIFs for illustrations that involve only a few colors. All of the photos on the Sunny Acres Web site are in JPEG format. Note that JPEGs do not support animation or transparent colors.

PNG Images

A third graphic format gaining wider acceptance is the **Portable Network Graphics** or **PNG** format. PNG files include most of the same features as GIFs (including animation and transparency) but also provide file compression and the full 16.7 million colors available with JPEGs. You can also designate several transparent colors in a PNG file, rather than the single color that GIFs support. The only problem with the PNG format is that older browsers do not support it. This is becoming less of a problem as time goes by. Figure 3-31 summarizes the features of the three major graphics formats on the Web.

Figure 3-31   **Comparison of Web graphic formats**

Feature	GIF	JPEG	PNG
Color resolution	256	16.7 million	16.7 million
Useful for line art	Yes	No	Yes
Useful for photographs	No	Yes	Yes
Interlacing/progressive encoding	Yes	Yes	Yes
Compressible	Yes	Yes	Yes
Transparent colors	Yes (1)	No	Yes (multiple)
Supported by older browsers	Yes	Yes	No

InSight | Other Image Formats

The GIF, JPEG, and PNG formats are not the only ways to add graphic images and animation to your Web site. The World Wide Web Consortium (W3C) promotes the **Scalable Vector Graphics** (**SVG**) specification, which is a graphic format written with XML that you can use to create line art composed of straight lines and curves. SVG also supports animation, and it can be used with programmable scripts that control the behavior and appearance of the animation. Because SVG files are written in XML, they are transferred as simple text files, allowing the application to interpret the SVG commands and render the graphic. Most browsers do not support SVG without the addition of specialized add-in programs.

Another popular approach is to use the Flash software program from Macromedia. You can use Flash to create interactive animations, scalable graphics, animated logos, and navigation controls for a Web site. To view a Flash animation, users must have the Flash player installed on their computers. Users can download and install the player for free, and are generally prompted to do this the first time they open a Web page that uses Flash. Flash players are available for all browsers and operating systems, so Flash is a safe and well supported method of creating animated effects and specialized graphics.

Setting the Image Size

By default, browsers display an image at its saved size. You can specify a different size by adding the HTML attributes

```
width="value" height="value"
```

to the <img /> tag, where the width and height values represent the dimensions of the image in pixels.

Changing an image's dimensions within the browser does not affect the file size. If you want to decrease the file size of an image, you should do so using an image editing application so that the image's file size is reduced in addition to its dimensions. Because of the way that browsers work with inline images, it is a good idea to specify the height and width of an image even if you're not trying to change its dimensions. When a browser encounters an inline image, it calculates the image size and then uses this information to lay out the page. If you include the dimensions of the image, the browser does not have to perform that calculation, reducing the time required to render the page. You can obtain the height and width of an image as measured in pixels using an image editing application such as Adobe Photoshop, or by viewing the properties of the graphic file in your computer's operating system.

The salogo.gif image is 599 pixels wide by 223 pixels high. The animated scarecrow graphic is 500 pixels wide by 300 pixels high. You decide to specify these dimensions in the HTML code of the index.htm file so that browsers won't have to calculate the images' dimensions when loading the page.

To set the dimensions for Tammy's splash screen images:

▶ **1.** Return to the **index.htm** file in your text editor.

▶ **2.** Within the <img> tag for the Sunny Acres logo, add the following attributes:

```
width="599" height="223"
```

▶ **3.** Within the <img> tag for the animated scarecrow graphic, add the following attributes:

```
width="500" height="300"
```

Place the attributes on a new line to make your HTML code easier to read. Figure 3-32 shows the revised code for the index.htm file.

Specifying image width and height   Figure 3-32

```
<body>
    <div style="text-align: center">
        <img src="salogo.gif" alt="Sunny Acres" width="599" height="223" /><br />
        <a href="home.htm"><img src="scarecrow.gif" alt="animated GIF"
                        width="500" height="300" style="border-width: 0" /></a>
    </div>
</body>
```

Formatting Backgrounds

Tammy has one more suggestion for the splash screen page. She would like you to change the background from its plain white color to the image shown in Figure 3-33.

Figure 3-33 ▶ **Tammy's proposed background image**

You can add a background image to any element. The style to apply a background image to an element is

```
background-image: url(url)
```

where (*url*) defines the name and location of the image file. When a browser loads the background image, it repeats the image in both the vertical and the horizontal directions until the background of the entire element is filled. This process is known as **tiling** because of its similarity to the process of filling up a floor or other surface with tiles. Let's see how Tammy's image looks in the splash screen page by adding it as a background for the entire page body. The image is saved as background.jpg.

To add a background image to the body element of Tammy's splash screen:

▶ **1.** Within the opening <body> tag, insert the following style attribute, as shown in Figure 3-34:

```
style="background-image: url(background.jpg)"
```

Figure 3-34 ▶ **Setting the background image for the page body**

```
<body style="background-image: url(background.jpg)">
   <div style="text-align: center">
      <img src="salogo.gif" alt="Sunny Acres" width="599" height="223" /><br />
      <a href="home.htm"><img src="scarecrow.gif" alt="animated GIF"
                              width="500" height="300" style="border-width: 0" /></a>
   </div>
</body>
```

▶ **2.** Close the file, saving your changes.

3. Reload the **index.htm** file in your Web browser. Verify that the Web page has the tiled background image shown in Figure 3-35.

Final splash screen page | Figure 3-35

Note that both of the GIF images on this page employ a transparent color. This allows you to see the tiled background image behind the logo and the animated scarecrow graphic.

4. If you want to take a break before starting the next session, close any open files or applications now.

Background Image Options

By default, background images are tiled both horizontally and vertically until the entire background of the element is filled up. You can specify the direction of the tiling using the style

```
background-repeat: type
```

where *type* is repeat (the default), repeat-x, repeat-y, or no-repeat. Figure 3-36 describes each of the repeat types and Figure 3-37 shows examples of the style values.

Values of the background-repeat style | Figure 3-36

Value	Description
repeat	The image is tiled both horizontally and vertically until the entire background of the element is covered
repeat-x	The image is tiled only horizontally across the width of the element
repeat-y	The image is tiled only vertically across the height of the element
no-repeat	The image is not repeated at all

Figure 3-37 | **Tiling the background image**

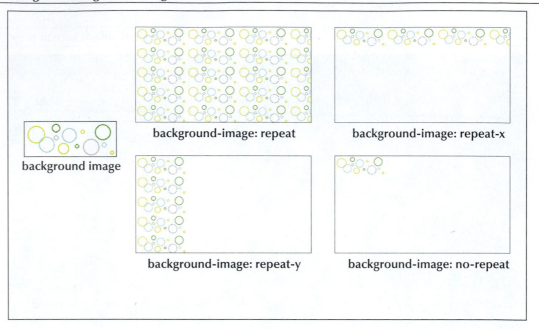

Browsers initially place a background image in an element's upper-left corner; and then if the code specifies tiling, the image is repeated from there. You can change the initial position of a background image using the style

```
background-position: horizontal vertical
```

where *horizontal* is the horizontal position of the image and *vertical* is its vertical position. You can specify a position as the distance from the top-left corner of the element, as a percentage of the element's width or height, or with a keyword. Keyword options are top, center, or bottom for vertical position, and left, center, or right for horizontal placement. For example, the style

```
background-position: 10% 20%
```

specifies an initial position for the background image 10% to the right and 20% down from the upper-left corner of the element. The style

```
background-position: right bottom
```

places the background image at the lower-right corner of the element. If you include only one position value, the browser applies that value to the horizontal position and vertically centers the image. So the style

```
background-position: 30px
```

places the background image 30 pixels to the right of the element's left border and centers it vertically.

By default, a background image moves along with its element as a user scrolls through a page. You can change this using the style

```
background-attachment: type
```

where *type* is either scroll or fixed. Scroll (the default) scrolls the image along with the element, while fixed places the image in a fixed place in the browser's display window, preventing it from moving even if the user scrolls down through the Web page. Fixed background images are often used to create the effect of a watermark, which is a translucent graphic impressed into the very fabric of paper, often found on specialized stationery.

The Background Style

Like the font style discussed in earlier in this session, you can combine the various background styles into the following single style

```
background: color url(url) repeat attachment horizontal vertical
```

where *color*, *(url)*, *repeat*, *attachment*, *horizontal*, and *vertical* are the values for the background style attributes that set the background color and control the placement and tiling of a background image. For example, the style

```
background: yellow url(logo.gif) no-repeat fixed center center
```

creates a yellow background on which the image file logo.gif is displayed. The image file is not tiled across the background, but is instead fixed in the horizontal and vertical center. You do not have to enter all of the values of the background style. However, those values that you do specify should follow the order indicated by the syntax to avoid unpredictable results.

You've completed your work with styles for the text and graphic images on the Sunny Acres Web site. You still have work to do to make the page layout interesting and attractive. In the next session you'll work with styles for block-level elements and lists.

Session 3.2 Quick Check | Review

1. Specify the style declaration to display all code elements in the Courier New font; and if that font is unavailable, use a monospace font.
2. If the font size of blockquote element text is set to 12 points, what will be the size of h2 headings nested within a blockquote if the following style declaration is applied to the Web page?

```
h2 {font-size: 1.5em}
```

3. Specify the style declaration to display all h3 headings with both an overline and an underline.
4. Specify the style declaration to set the kerning of address text to 0.5 em and tracking to 0.9 em.
5. Specify the style declaration to display the text of all definition term elements in uppercase letters.
6. Which graphic image format should you use for photographic images—GIF or JPEG—and why?
7. What attributes do you add to the <img /> tag to set the size of the image to 200 pixels wide by 100 pixels high?
8. Specify the style to use the image file mark.jpg as the background image for all blockquote elements. Fix the image at the top left of the block quote with no tiling.

Session 3.3

Floating an Element

Tammy wants you to return to work on her home page. She notices that the inline image below the Welcome heading forces a large space between the heading and the following paragraph (see Figure 3-24 from the last session). She would like the image placed alongside the right margin and the paragraph text to wrap around it. You can do this by floating the inline image.

Floating an element like an inline image causes the element to move out of the normal document flow on the page, moving to a position along the left or right margins of the parent element. The other elements on the Web page that are not floated are then moved up to occupy the position previously occupied by the floating element. Figure 3-38 shows a diagram of an element that is floated along the right margin of the page body.

Figure 3-38   **Floating an element**

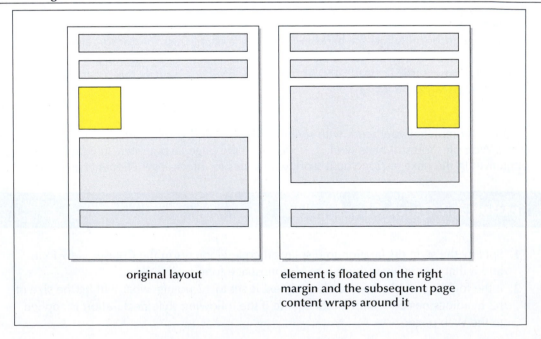

original layout

element is floated on the right margin and the subsequent page content wraps around it

To float an element, apply the style

`float: position`

where *position* is none (the default to turn off floating), left, or right. Most page elements can be floated. You can also stack floating elements to create a column effect in your page layout, as in Figure 3-39.

Floating multiple elements to create columns — Figure 3-39

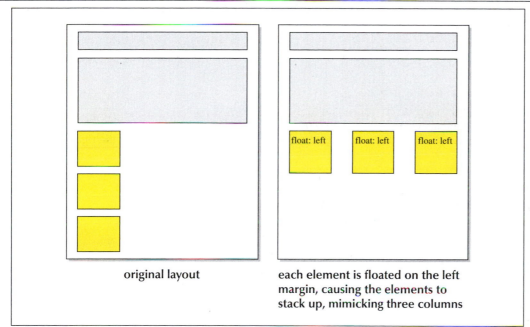

original layout

each element is floated on the left margin, causing the elements to stack up, mimicking three columns

Sometimes you will want to prevent an object from wrapping around a floating element. For example, you might not want headings to wrap around inline images. To prevent an element from wrapping, apply the clear style

`clear: position`

where *position* is none (the default), left, right, or both. For example, the style declaration

`clear: right`

causes the element not to be displayed until the right margin of the parent element is clear of floating objects. See Figure 3-40.

Figure 3-40 ▶ **Using the clear style**

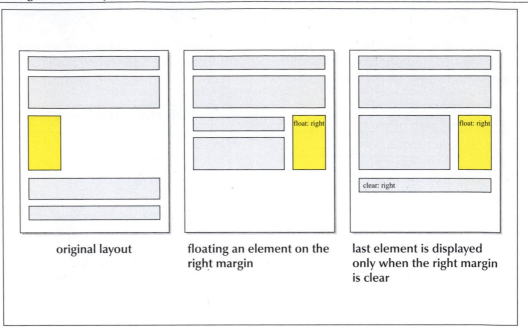

original layout

floating an element on the right margin

last element is displayed only when the right margin is clear

Reference Window | **Floating an Element**

- To float an element, use the style
  ```
  float: position
  ```
  where *position* is none (to turn off floating), left or right.
- To display an element clear of a floating element, use the style
  ```
  clear: position
  ```
  where *position* is none, left, right, or both.

Tammy wants you to use what you've learned about the floating style to float the inline image from the home page on the right margin of the paragraph that contains it. You could add the float style as an inline style directly to the <img> tag for the image, but Tammy has similar promotional photos on several of the pages from her Web site. She has given each promotional photo the id promoimage. Recall from the first session that you can create style declarations for elements based on their id values. This means you can use the farm.css style sheet to float all of these images with the following style declaration:

```
#promoimage {float: right}
```

Tammy wants you to add this style to the farm.css style sheet.

To float the promotional images on the Sunny Acres Web site:

1. Return to the **farm.css** style sheet in your text editor.
2. At the bottom of the file, add the following style as shown in Figure 3-41:
   ```
   #promoimage {float: right}
   ```

Applying the float style ◁ Figure 3-41

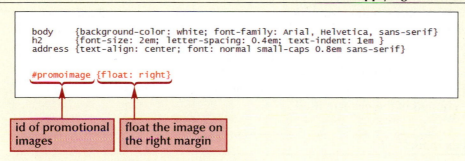

Tip

The float style floats the object on the margin of the parent element, not necessarily the margin of the Web page.

▶ **3.** Save your changes to the file.

▶ **4.** Refresh the **home.htm** file in your Web browser. As shown in Figure 3-42, the promotional inline image is now floated on the right margin of the first paragraph. The subsequent page content flows around the image.

Floating the image on the paragraph's right margin ◁ Figure 3-42

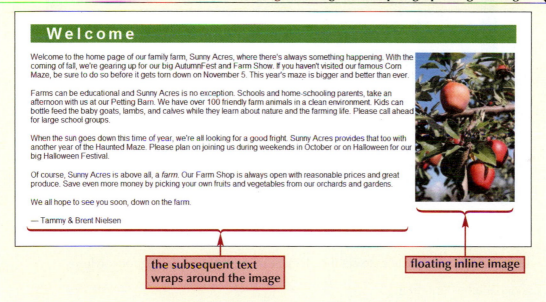

In older HTML code, you might see inline images floated using the align attribute. The general syntax of the align attribute is

```
<img align="position" ... />
```

where *position* is left or right. Note that the align attribute has been deprecated and is not supported in strict applications of XHTML.

Working with the Box Model

Floating the promotional image improved the appearance of the page. Tammy wants you to work with the size and placement of other elements on the page such as the heading and address elements. She wants a page layout that is easy to read and attractive to the eye.

A study of the technique of Web page layout starts with an appreciation of the CSS box model. The **box model** describes the structure of page elements as they are laid out on the Web page. In the box model, each element is composed of the four sections shown in Figure 3-43:

- the **margin** between the element and other page content
- the **border** of the box containing the element content
- the **padding** between the element's content and the box border
- the **content** of the element itself

Figure 3-43 **The box model**

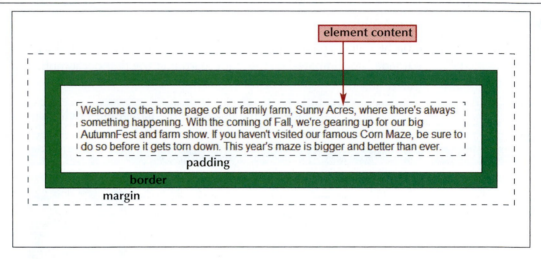

The size and appearance of these four sections determine how the element is displayed by the browser and play an important role in determining the layout of the elements on the Web page. Start exploring the box model by examining how to set the margins around an element.

Margin Styles

CSS supports several styles to set the element margin. The following four styles

```
margin-top: length
margin-right: length
margin-bottom: length
margin-left: length
```

set the sizes of the top, right, bottom, and left margins. Here *length* is a length expressed in one of the CSS units of measure discussed in the last session. You can also use the keyword auto, which leaves it to the browser to determine the margin size. The style declaration

```
h1 {margin-top: 10px; margin-right: 20px; margin-bottom: 10px;
    margin-left: 20px}
```

creates margins of 10 pixels above and below the h1 heading and margins of 20 pixels to the left and right of the heading.

These four margin styles can be combined into the single style

```
margin: top right bottom left
```

where *top*, *right*, *bottom*, and *left* are the sizes of the top, right, bottom, and left margins. (To help remember this order, think of moving clockwise around the element, starting with the top margin.) The style

```
h1 {margin: 10px 20px 10px 20px}
```

applies an identical set of margins to the longer style described above.

    You don't have to supply values for all of the margins. If you specify only three values, they are applied to the top, right, and bottom margins. If you specify only two values, they're applied to the top and bottom margins. If you specify only a single value, a browser applies that value to all four margins. So the style

```
h1 {margin: 10px 20px}
```

applies a 10-pixel margin above and below the h1 heading and a 20-pixel margin to the left and right. The style

```
h1 {margin: 10px}
```

creates a 10-pixel margin around the entire heading.

    One of the changes that Tammy suggested is to add more space between the promotional image and the surrounding text. She thinks that the text is too tight around the image and suggests that you set a 1-em margin below and to the left of the image. The top margin and the right margin can be set to 0 em units. Remember that you are making these changes to the CSS style sheet so that Tammy can apply them to any image she marks with the promotional id.

To set the margins around the promotional image in Tammy's external style sheet:

▶ 1. Return to the **farm.css** style sheet in your text editor.

▶ 2. Add the following margin style to the style declaration for the promotional image, as shown in Figure 3-44:

```
margin: 0em 0em 1em 1em
```

Setting margins around the promotional images ◄ **Figure 3-44**

```
body    {background-color: white; font-family: Arial, Helvetica, sans-serif}
h2      {font-size: 2em; letter-spacing: 0.4em; text-indent: 1em }
address {text-align: center; font: normal small-caps 0.8em sans-serif}

#promoimage {float: right; margin: 0em 0em 1em 1em}
```

▶ 3. Save your changes to the file.

▶ 4. Reload the **home.htm** file in your Web browser. Verify that the margin to the left and below the promotional image has been increased slightly.

    The margin styles can also be applied to the body element. By setting the margin around the page body to 0, you can remove the extra space many browsers insert by default between the page content and the edge of the browser window.

Padding Styles

The styles for the size of the padding in the box model are similar to the margin styles. The following four styles set the size of the padding above, to the right, below, and to the left of the element content:

```
padding-top: length
padding-right: length
padding-bottom: length
padding-left: length
```

You can also combine these four styles in a single padding style

```
padding: top right bottom left
```

where *top*, *right*, *bottom*, and *left* are the padding sizes around the element content. As with the margin style, you can specify any or all of the four padding values. When you specify a single value, it is applied to all four padding values. The style

```
h1 {padding: 5px}
```

sets the padding space around the h1 heading content to 5 pixels in each direction. By default, elements have no padding. The space between elements such as between adjacent paragraphs is set by the margins alone.

Reference Window | **Setting Margin and Padding Space in the Box Model**

- To set the margin space around an element, use
    ```
    margin: length
    ```
  where *length* is the size of the margin using one of the CSS units of measure.
- To set the padding space within an element, use
    ```
    padding: length
    ```
- To set a margin or padding for one side of the box model only, specify the direction (top, right, bottom, or left). For example, use
    ```
    margin-right: length
    ```
  to set the length of the right margin.

Border Styles

CSS supports three types of styles for the box model border. You can set the border width, the border color, or the border style. As with the margin and padding styles, there are styles that affect the top, right, bottom, and left borders or all borders at once. To define the width of the border, use

```
border-top-width: length
border-right-width: length
border-bottom-width: length
border-left-width: length
```

or the following single border-width style for setting the width for any or all of the borders:

```
border-width: top right bottom left
```

You've already worked with the border-width style in Tutorial 2, where you used it to remove the border around a linked image. The style

```
img {border-width: 0px}
```

could be used to remove the borders around all of the inline images on the Web page or Web site. Border widths can also be expressed using the keywords thin, medium, or thick. The exact meaning of these sizes depends on the browser.

The next set of styles set the color of the border (if one exists) around an element. These styles are

```
border-top-color: color
border-right-color: color
border-bottom-color: color
border-left-color: color
border-color: top right bottom left
```

where *color* is a color name, color value, or the keyword transparent to create an invisible border. For example, the following style adds a 4-pixel red border directly above the address element:

```
address {border-top-width: 4px; border-top-color: red}
```

If you don't specify a color, the browser uses the text color of the element within the box.

The final border style defines the border design. The five border styles are

```
border-top-style: type
border-right-style: type
border-bottom-style: type
border-left-style: type
border-style: top right bottom left
```

where *type* is one of the nine border style displayed in Figure 3-45.

Tip

You can create the illusion of a drop shadow by adding borders of different thicknesses around the element. Try border styles such as
`border-width: 1px 4px 4px 1px`
to create this effect.

Border style designs — **Figure 3-45**

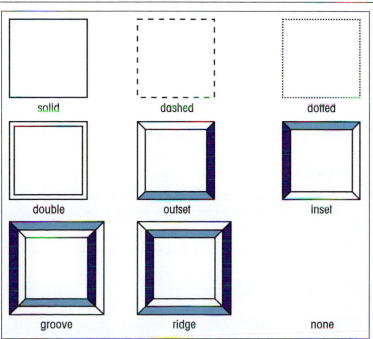

For example, to place a double border below an element, use the style:

```
border-style-bottom: double.
```

All of the border styles discussed above can be combined into a single style that defines each or all of the borders around the element. The syntax of these border styles is

```
border-top: width style color
border-right: width style color
border-bottom: width style color
border-left: width style color
border: width style color
```

where *width* is the width of the border, *style* is the style of the border, and *color* is the border color. The three properties must be entered in that order. For example, the style

```
h1 {border: 2px solid blue}
```

adds a 2-pixel wide solid blue border around every h1 heading.

Reference Window | **Setting Border Styles in the Box Model**

- To set the border width, use
    ```
    border-width: length
    ```
  where *length* is the width of the border using one of the CSS units of measure.
- To set the border color, use
    ```
    border-color: color
    ```
  where *color* is a color name or value.
- To set the border design, use
    ```
    border-style: type
    ```
  where *type* is none, solid, dashed, dotted, double, outset, inset, groove, or ridge.
- To set all of the border options in one style, use
    ```
    border: length color type
    ```
  in that order.

Having discussed the wide varieties of border styles with Tammy, she suggests you add a top border to the address element on the Sunny Acres home page. She thinks a double green border 0.5 em in height would look good. To keep the border from crowding the address text, you'll increase the padding between the text and the border to 1 em.

To create a border for the address element in Tammy's external style sheet:

1. Return to the **farm.css** style sheet in your text editor.

2. Add the following styles to the address element as shown in Figure 3-46. Place the styles on a new line to make your code easier to read. Be sure to separate all styles with a semicolon.

   ```
   border-top: 0.5em double green; padding-top: 1em
   ```

Using the border-top and padding-top styles ◄ Figure 3-46

```
body     {background-color: white; font-family: Arial, Helvetica, sans-serif}
h2       {font-size: 2em; letter-spacing: 0.4em; text-indent: 1em }
address {text-align: center; font: normal small-caps 0.8em sans-serif;
         border-top: 0.5em double green; padding-top: 1em}

#promoimage {float: right; margin: 0em 0em 1em 1em}
```

▶ **3.** Save your changes to the file.

▶ **4.** Reload the **home.htm** file in your Web browser. Scroll to the bottom of the page and verify that a double green border has been added to the top of the address element, as shown in Figure 3-47.

Adding a double top border to the address element ◄ Figure 3-47

Hours

- Farm Shop: 9 am - 5 pm Mon - Fri; 9 am - 3 pm Sat
- The Corn Maze: 11 am - 9 pm Sat; 11 am - 5 pm Sun
- The Haunted Maze: 5 pm - 9 pm Fri & Sat
- Petting Barn: 9 am - 4 pm (Mon - Fri); 11 am - 3pm (Sat & Sun)

Directions

- From Council Bluffs, proceed east on I-80
- Take Exit 38 North to the Drake Frontage Road
- Turn right on Highway G
- Proceed east for 2.5 miles
- Sunny Acres is on your left; watch for the green sign

SUNNY ACRES ☀ TAMMY & BRENT NIELSEN ☀ 1977 HIGHWAY G ☀ COUNCIL BLUFFS, IA   51503

Because of their flexibility, border styles are usually applied in place of the hr (horizontal rule) element discussed in Tutorial 1 as a way of creating section breaks on Web pages.

Width and Height Styles

The final aspect of the box model that can be controlled with CSS styles is the box's width and height. The default width and height are determined by the browser. For inline elements, the width is the width of the element content and the height is the height of a single line. Block-level elements extend across the width of their parent element with a height that expands to meet the content enclosed within the block. So a heading element will have a width than spans the width of the Web page. If the heading is nested within a blockquote element, its width will span the width of the blockquote, and so on. You can set a different width using the style

```
width: value
```

where *value* is the width of the content expressed in one of the CSS units of measure discussed in the last session. According to the CSS specifications, the width value does not take into account the size of the margins, padding space, or borders. It applies only to the actual content of the element. Most browsers follow the CSS specifications, except Internet Explorer. With Internet Explorer, the width style value is applied to element content, padding, and borders. This means that if you are using the box model for page layout, you can end up with different layouts under different browsers. For example, the style declaration

```
p {width: 500px; padding: padding: 30px; border: 10px solid green}
```

results in a paragraph that is 500 pixels wide under Internet Explorer with 420 pixels reserved for the width of the element content. Under other browsers that follow the CSS specifications (such as Firefox, Opera, and Safari), the element content is 500 pixels wide and the width of the entire box (including the padding and borders) is 580 pixels. See Figure 3-48.

Figure 3-48 **Interpretations of the box model width style**

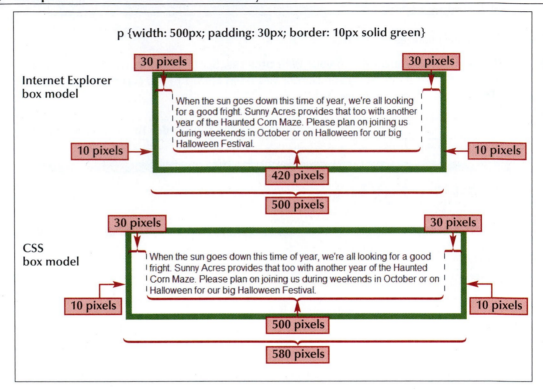

There are several ways of reconciling these interpretations of the box model that we'll discuss later. For now, you should simply be aware that this is an ongoing concern for designers trying to do precise Web page layout.

Quirks Mode and Standards Mode | InSight

Internet Explorer has two modes it can work in. One is **quirks mode**, in which the browser applies the Internet Explorer interpretation of the box model and other features of CSS. However, starting with Internet Explorer 6, you can force the IE browser to adopt the CSS interpretation of the box model styles by putting it into **standards mode**. This is done by changing the code of your Web page from HTML to XHTML by replacing the opening <html> tag with the following three lines:

```
<?xml version="1.0" encoding="UTF-8" standalone="no" ?>

<!DOCTYPE html PUBLIC "-//W3C//DTD XHTML 1.0 Strict//EN"
    "http://www.w3.org/TR/xhtml1/DTD/xhtml11-strict.dtd">

<html xmlns="http://www.w3.org/1999/xhtml">
```

When the IE browser encounters these lines, it interprets all CSS styles in accord with a strict interpretation of the CSS guidelines. Standards mode also enforces other aspects of the CSS specifications; so to be more compliant with CSS, you should use the three lines of code above to put the IE browser in standards mode. By default, Internet Explorer works in quirks mode, which is often necessary to support older HTML and CSS code written before the CSS 2.1 standards were introduced.

As long as you are not doing exact Web page design in which the difference of a few pixels can render your page unreadable, you can work in either standards or quirks mode. However, as you gain confidence in Web design and attempt more intricate layouts, you might find a need to work in standards mode. Note that all browsers, not just Internet Explorer, support a standards mode and quirks mode. You can learn more by reading the browser's technical documentation or by doing a Web search on the differences between quirks and standards models.

To set the height of the element content, use the height style

```
height: value
```

where *value* is the height of the content expressed in CSS units of measure. If you set a height value that is insufficient to display all of the element content, the browser will ignore the height value and still expand the height of the box. There are styles to override this behavior that you explore in Tutorial 4.

Setting the Width and Height in the Box Model | Reference Window

- To set the box model width, use
    ```
    width: length
    ```
  where *length* is the width of the box content in one of the CSS units of measure. (Note that Internet Explorer applies the width value to the box model content, padding space, and border.)
- To set the box model height, use
    ```
    height: length
    ```
  where *length* is the height of the box content in one of the CSS units of measure.

Tammy doesn't like the appearance of h3 headings on the home page shown earlier in Figure 3-47. The headings identify two subsections of the document: one for the hours the farm is open and the other for directions to the farm. Currently the two headings extend across the width of the Web page. Tammy suggests that the headings would look better if they were about the same width as the text of the bulleted lists they introduce. You'll also increase the size of the left padding to offset the text a few spaces from the box's left border. You'll apply this style to other h3 headings on the Sunny Acres Web site, so you'll add the style to the farm.css external style sheet.

To set the style of the h3 headings in Tammy's external style sheet:

▶ 1. Return to the **farm.css** style sheet in your text editor.

▶ 2. Insert the following style directly below the style for the h2 heading, as shown in Figure 3-49:

```
h3 {width: 20em; padding-left: 1em}
```

Figure 3-49 ▶ **Setting the width and left padding of the h3 element**

```
body     {background-color: white; font-family: Arial, Helvetica, sans-serif}
h2       {font-size: 2em; letter-spacing: 0.4em; text-indent: 1em }
h3       {width: 20em; padding-left: 1em}
address {text-align: center; font: normal small-caps 0.8em sans-serif;
         border-top: 0.5em double green; padding-top: 1em}

#promoimage {float: right; margin: 0em 0em 1em 1em}
```

▶ 3. Save your changes to the file.

▶ 4. Reload the **home.htm** file in your Web browser. Figure 3-50 shows the revised appearance of the two h3 headings.

Figure 3-50 ▶ **Reformatted h3 headings**

Hours

- Farm Shop: 9 am - 5 pm Mon - Fri; 9 am - 3 pm Sat
- The Corn Maze: 11 am - 9 pm Sat; 11 am - 5 pm Sun
- The Haunted Maze: 5 pm - 9 pm Fri & Sat
- Petting Barn: 9 am - 4 pm (Mon - Fri); 11 am - 3pm (Sat & Sun)

Directions

- From Council Bluffs, proceed east on I-80
- Take Exit 38 North to the Drake Frontage Road
- Turn right on Highway G
- Proceed east for 2.5 miles
- Sunny Acres is on your left; watch for the green sign

Controlling Page Layout with div Containers

Tammy is pleased with the layout of the Sunny Acres home page. But when she displayed it on her laptop's wide-screen monitor, she expressed concern about the text that extends across the screen. Studies show that text gets more difficult to read as the length of the line extends beyond about 30 to 50 characters per line. A page layout like that shown in Figure 3-51 is difficult enough to read that many people will skip over it.

Page layout on a wide-screen monitor | Figure 3-51

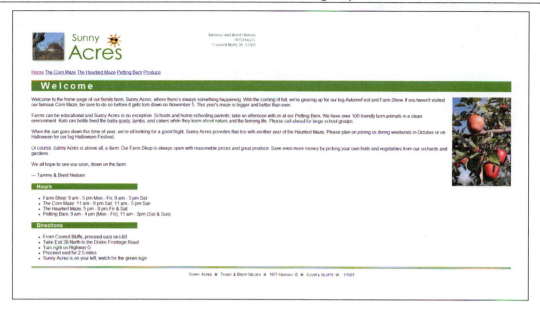

Tammy wants you to modify the page layout so that the length of the line is always kept within an acceptable limit under any monitor resolution. To do that, you'll use the style associated with the box model to set the width and margins of the different sections of the page. The technique involves placing different sections of the page within div elements called **div containers**, which you can then resize and float to create different page layouts. Recall that the div element is a generic block-level element. Browsers do not have default styles for the element's padding, border, margins, or width, so you can set all of these with your style sheet without worrying about conflicts with the browser's default settings.

The first div container that you'll add to the Sunny Acres home page will enclose the entire page content. You'll give this div container the id, outer.

To create the outer div container on Tammy's home page:

▶ **1.** Open the **home.htm** file with your text editor.

▶ **2.** Directly below the opening <body> tag, insert the following:

```
<div id="outer">
```

▶ **3.** Scroll down to the bottom of the file. Directly above the closing </body> tag, insert the following:

```
</div>
```

Figure 3-52 highlights the newly added code.

Figure 3-52 ▶ **Adding the outer div container**

```
<body>

<div id="outer">
    <h1><img src="salogo.jpg" alt="Sunny Acres" /></h1>
    <div id="links">
        <a href="home.htm">Home</a>
        <a href="maze.htm">The Corn Maze</a>
        <a href="haunted.htm">The Haunted Maze</a>
        <a href="petting.htm">Petting Barn</a>
        <a href="produce.htm">Produce</a>
    </div>

    <h2>Welcome</h2>



    <address>
        Sunny Acres  &#9728; 
        Tammy &amp; Brent Nielsen  &#9728; 
        1977 Highway G  &#9728; 
        Council Bluffs, IA    51503
    </address>

</div>
</body>
```

▶ **4.** Save your changes to the file.

Now that you've enclosed the page content within a div container, you can specify the width of the content. Rather than letting the content extend across the width of the browser window, you'll set the width to 50 em.

To set the width of the outer div container:

▶ **1.** Return to the **farm.css** style sheet in your text editor.

▶ **2.** Add the following style to the bottom of the file, as shown in Figure 3-53:

   `#outer {width: 50em}`

Figure 3-53 ▶ **Setting the width of the outer div container**

```
body    {background-color: white; font-family: Arial, Helvetica, sans-serif}
h2      {font-size: 2em; letter-spacing: 0.4em; text-indent: 1em }
h3      {width: 20em; padding-left: 1em}
address {text-align: center; font: normal small-caps 0.8em sans-serif;
         border-top: 0.5em double green; padding-top: 1em}

#promoimage {float: right; margin: 0em 0em 1em 1em}
#outer      {width: 50em}
```

▶ **3.** Save your changes to the file, and then reload **home.htm** in your Web browser. Verify that the width of the page content has been changed.

Note that by setting the width of the outer div container to 50 em, you've set the width to a defined size. Most monitors can fit this size; but if the user is using a smaller monitor, it's possible that the page width will extend beyond the browser window. If that is the case, the user will have to scroll horizontally through the browser window to view the entire page text. This is considered bad design, so you should test your Web pages on a variety of devices and resolutions to ensure this doesn't happen. Setting a page width is often a balancing act between competing needs.

Tammy has included a list of links at the top of the home page. She would like to display these links to the left of the Sunny Acres introduction. The links have been placed in a div container of their own with the id named links, so you can apply the following styles to the links div container:

- float it on the left margin of the outer div container
- set the width to 10 em
- set the background color to white
- add an outset border 0.5 em in width

You'll add this style declaration to the farm.css external style sheet so that Tammy can use it throughout her Web site.

Tip

You can set the page width by applying the width style to the body element.

To set the style for the list of links:

▶ 1. Return to the **farm.css** style sheet in your text editor.

▶ 2. As shown in Figure 3-54, add the following style:

```
#links {float: left; width: 10em; background-color: white;
       border-style: outset; border-width: 0.5em}
```

Setting the style of the links div container ◀ Figure 3-54

```
#promoimage {float: right; margin: 0em 0em 1em 1em}
#outer      {width: 50em}
#links      {float: left; width: 10em; background-color: white;
             border-style: outset; border-width: 0.5em}
```

▶ 3. Save your changes to the file, and then reload **home.htm** in your Web browser. Figure 3-55 shows the revised appearance of the Sunny Acres home page.

List of links floated on the left margin ◀ Figure 3-55

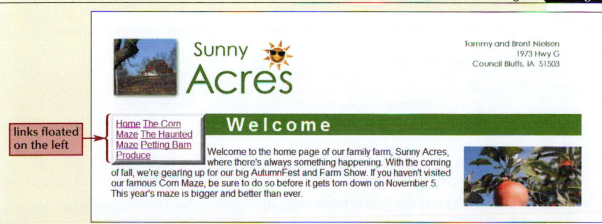

links floated on the left

Floating the list of links on the left page margin has saved some vertical space, but the layout is not attractive. Tammy thinks it would look much better if the welcoming text did not wrap around the links box, but instead was placed in a separate column. You can do this by enclosing the welcoming text within a div container of its own and then setting the left margin large enough to clear the links box.

To create the div container:

▶ 1. Return to the **home.htm** file in your text editor.

▶ 2. Directly above the opening <h2> tag for the Welcome title, insert:

```
<div id="inner">
```

▶ 3. Scroll down the file and directly above the opening <address> tag, insert:

```
</div>
```

Figure 3-56 highlights the revised text.

Figure 3-56	Adding the inner div container

```
<div id="inner">
<h2>welcome</h2>
<p>
    <img src="photo1.jpg" alt="home page photo" id="promoimage" />
    welcome to the home page of our family farm,
    Sunny Acres, where there's always something
    happening. With the coming of fall, we're gearing up for our big AutumnFest
    and Farm Show. If you haven't visited our famous Corn Maze, be sure to do
    so before it gets torn down on November 5. This year's maze is bigger and
    better than ever.
</p>
```

```
    <h3>Directions</h3>
    <ul>
        <li>From Council Bluffs, proceed east on I-80</li>
        <li>Take Exit 38 North to the Drake Frontage Road</li>
        <li>Turn right on Highway G</li>
        <li>Proceed east for 2.5 miles</li>
        <li>Sunny Acres is on your left; watch for the green sign</li>
    </ul>
    </div>
```

▶ 4. Save your changes to the file.

Now you can set the styles for the inner div container. To separate the text in the inner div container from the links box, you'll apply styles to:

• set the left margin to 12 em
• display a solid green border 0.1 em wide on the left side of the container
• set the left padding to 1 em

You want to add this style to the farm.css style sheet so that Tammy can use it in any of her pages.

To create a style for the inner div container:

1. Return to the **farm.css** style sheet in your text editor.

2. Add the following style, as shown in Figure 3-57:

```
#inner {margin-left: 12em; padding-left: 1em;
       border-left: 0.1em solid green}
```

Setting the style of the inner div container | Figure 3-57

```
#promoimage {float: right; margin: 0em 0em 1em 1em}
#outer      {width: 50em}
#links      {float: left; width: 10em; background-color: white;
             border-style: outset; border-width: 0.5em}
#inner      {margin-left: 12em; padding-left: 1em;
             border-left: 0.1em solid green}
```

3. Save your changes to the file and then reload or refresh **home.htm** in your Web browser. Figure 3-58 shows the revised layout of the Sunny Acres home page.

Layout of the inner div container | Figure 3-58

left margin is set to 12 em

The page looks much better with the two div containers separating the content on the home page.

One source of page layout conflicts come from the different ways browsers apply the padding space. One way to avoid this problem is to set the padding space to 0 and only use the margin style with nested div containers. For example, if you need to set the padding space around your paragraphs to 10 pixels, but you worry that this will adversely affect the layout for IE users, place the paragraph in a div container and set the margin around the paragraph to 10 pixels. Because margins are interpreted the same way by all browsers, you will find that the paragraph's width will be the same under the IE box model and the CSS box model.

Setting the Display Style

Tammy likes the revised page layout but still finds the list of links difficult to read. She thinks it would be better if each link were on a separate line. You could fix this by enclosing each link within its own paragraph or by inserting a line break between each link. However, Tammy wants to move as much of the formatting into style sheets as she can, rather than making these changes to document content. She also might want to explore different layouts in the future—for example, laying out the links horizontally at the top of the page—and doesn't want to have to remove paragraph tags or line breaks if she does that.

As you've seen, most page elements are classified as either inline elements or block-level elements. Browsers treat links as inline elements, which is why all of the entries in the links list run together on a single line. You can use CSS to change the display style applied to any element, allowing you to make inline elements appear as block-level elements and vice versa. The syntax of the display style is

```
display: type
```

where *type* is one of the CSS display types described in Figure 3-59.

Figure 3-59 ▶ **Values of the display style**

Display	Description
block	Display as a block-level element
inline	Display as an inline element
inline-block	Display as an inline element with some of the properties of a block (much like an inline image or frame)
inherit	Inherit the display property of the element's parent
list-item	Display as a list item
none	Do not display the element
run-in	Display as either an inline or block-level element depending on the context (CSS2)
table	Display as a block-level table
inline-table	Display as an inline table
table-caption	Treat as a table caption
table-cell	Treat as a table cell
table-column	Treat as a table column
table-column-group	Treat as a group of table columns
table-footer-group	Treat as a group of table footer rows
table-header-group	Treat as a group of table header rows
table-row	Treat as a table row
table-row-group	Treat as a group of table rows

To display all hypertext links as block-level elements rather than inline elements, apply the following style

```
a {display: block}
```

which has the same effect on page layout as turning the hypertext link into a generic div element.

Setting the Display Style | Reference Window

- To set the display style of an element, use

   display: *type*

  where *type* is the type of display. Use inline for inline elements and block for block-level elements.

You'll add this style to the farm.css style sheet. You'll also set the margin around each of the hypertext links to 0.1 em to provide more space between the links and the links box.

To set the display style for the links container:

▸ **1.** Return to the **farm.css** file in your text editor.

▸ **2.** As shown in Figure 3-60, add the following style:

   ```
   a {display: block; margin: 0.3em}
   ```

The final farm.css style sheet ◀ **Figure 3-60**

```
body    {background-color: white; font-family: Arial, Helvetica, sans-serif}
h2      {font-size: 2em; letter-spacing: 0.4em; text-indent: 1em }
h3      {width: 20em; padding-left: 1em}
address {text-align: center; font: normal small-caps 0.8em sans-serif;
         border-top: 0.5em double green; padding-top: 1em}
a       {display: block; margin: 0.3em}

#promoimage {float: right; margin: 0em 0em 1em 1em}
#outer      {width: 50em}
#links      {float: left; width: 10em; background-color: white;
             border-style: outset; border-width: 0.5em}
#inner      {margin-left: 12em; padding-left: 1em;
             border-left: 0.1em solid green}
```

▸ **3.** Save your changes to the file and then refresh **home.htm** in your Web browser. Figure 3-61 shows the final layout of the entire Sunny Acres home page.

Figure 3-61 The final layout of the Sunny Acres home page

Tammy and Brent Nielsen
1973 Hwy G
Council Bluffs, IA 51503

Home
The Corn Maze
The Haunted Maze
Petting Barn
Produce

Welcome

Welcome to the home page of our family farm, Sunny Acres, where there's always something happening. With the coming of fall, we're gearing up for our big AutumnFest and Farm Show. If you haven't visited our famous Corn Maze, be sure to do so before it gets torn down on November 5. This year's maze is bigger and better than ever.

Farms can be educational and Sunny Acres is no exception. Schools and home-schooling parents, take an afternoon with us at our Petting Barn. We have over 100 friendly farm animals in a clean environment. Kids can bottle feed the baby goats, lambs, and calves while they learn about nature and the farming life. Please call ahead for large school groups.

When the sun goes down this time of year, we're all looking for a good fright. Sunny Acres provides that too with another year of the Haunted Maze. Please plan on joining us during weekends in October or on Halloween for our big Halloween Festival.

Of course, Sunny Acres is above all, a *farm*. Our Farm Shop is always open with reasonable prices and great produce. Save even more money by picking your own fruits and vegetables from our orchards and gardens.

We all hope to see you soon, down on the farm.

— Tammy & Brent Nielsen

Hours

- Farm Shop: 9 am - 5 pm Mon - Fri; 9 am - 3 pm Sat
- The Corn Maze: 11 am - 9 pm Sat; 11 am - 5 pm Sun
- The Haunted Maze: 5 pm - 9 pm Fri & Sat
- Petting Barn: 9 am - 4 pm (Mon - Fri); 11 am - 3pm (Sat & Sun)

Directions

- From Council Bluffs, proceed east on I-80
- Take Exit 38 North to the Drake Frontage Road
- Turn right on Highway G
- Proceed east for 2.5 miles
- Sunny Acres is on your left; watch for the green sign

SUNNY ACRES ✳ TAMMY & BRENT NIELSEN ✳ 1977 HIGHWAY G ✳ COUNCIL BLUFFS, IA 51503

Compared to the initial design of this page shown earlier in Figure 3-2, you've improved the appearance of the page and made it easier to read. There are four other pages on the Sunny Acres Web site that you haven't yet formatted. However, they share a common document structure with the home page, so you can apply the same style rules you've created for the home.htm file to those files. This is why external style sheets are so powerful: You can apply the same styles to many pages without having to duplicate your work.

Tammy wants those other pages to have slightly different color schemes, so you'll have to apply some embedded styles to each of them. They already have the outer and inner div containers, so you will not have to add those elements to the files.

To apply Tammy's external style sheet to the rest of the pages on her Web site:

▶ 1. Open the **haunted.htm** file from the tutorial.03\tutorial folder included with your Data Files.

▶ 2. Directly above the closing </head> tag, insert the following code, as shown in Figure 3-62:

```
<style type="text/css">
   h2, h3 {color: white; background-color: black}
</style>
<link href="farm.css" rel="stylesheet" type="text/css" />
```

Applying the style sheet to the haunted.htm file ◀ **Figure 3-62**

```
<title>Sunny Acres Haunted Maze</title>
<style type="text/css">
   h2, h3 {color: white; background-color: black}
</style>
<link href="farm.css" rel="stylesheet" type="text/css" />
</head>
```

▶ 3. Close the file, saving your changes.

▶ 4. Open the **maze.htm** file and repeat Steps 2 and 3, using a background color value of (200, 105, 0).

▶ 5. Open the **petting.htm** file and repeat Steps 2 and 3, using a background color of blue.

▶ 6. Open the **produce.htm** file and repeat Steps 2 and 3, using a background color of red.

▶ 7. Return to the Sunny Acres home page in your Web browser, and then click the links in the links box to view the appearance of the other four Web pages to verify that you've applied a uniform design to the Web site. Figure 3-63 shows the appearance of each of the four other pages.

Revised design of the Sunny Acres Web site ◀ **Figure 3-63**

haunted.htm   maze.htm   petting.htm   produce.htm

▶ 8. Close any remaining open files or applications.

You've completed your work on the Sunny Acres Web site. Through the use of style sheets, you've managed to create a common look and feel for all of Tammy's Web pages. Style sheets also speeded up the development time as you were able to apply previously created style sheets to other pages on the site. Finally, if you or Tammy decide to make a change to the site's design style, you can make your modifications to the farm.css style sheet and have your revisions instantly applied to all of the Web site pages. Tammy will continue to work with the Web site, adding new material and making other design decisions.

Review | **Session 3.3 Quick Check**

1. An inline image has the id photoImage. Specify the style declaration you would enter to float this inline image on the left margin.
2. Specify the style declaration to set the right and bottom margins of the photoImage inline image to 5 pixels each.
3. You want your paragraphs to have a padding space above and below the paragraph equal to 10 pixels. Specify the style declaration to do this.
4. You want your block quotes to have a 20-pixel left margin and to have a solid gray 4-pixel-wide left border. Specify the style declaration to do this.
5. You want the h1 heading with the mainHeading id to be displayed in a green font with a double green border 8 pixels wide. Specify the style declaration to do this.
6. Describe the difference between how Internet Explorer and CSS calculate element widths under the box model.
7. By default, images are displayed as inline elements. Specify the style declaration you would enter to display all inline images as block-level elements.

In this tutorial, you learned how to use the CSS language to create and apply style sheets. In the first session, you learned how to apply inline styles, embedded styles, and external style sheets. You also explored the parts of style declarations and saw how they relate to elements within Web page documents. The first session concluded by examining how both foreground and background color can be described and rendered under CSS and HTML. In the second session, you began by working with the different CSS styles associated with text and fonts. You also learned about several different measuring units that can be applied to font sizes and letter, word, and line spacing. The second session also provided an overview of different image types supported by most browsers and showed how to use these images to create animated graphics and wallpaper-style backgrounds. The final session began by looking at how to float elements within a Web page layout. You then explored the box model, showing how to define an element's internal and external space. The session also showed how to add borders to any page element. The session concluded by looking at div containers, showing how they can be used as tools to create dynamic and interesting page layouts.

Key Terms

absolute unit
animated GIF
box model
Cascading Style Sheets
color value
CSS
CSS2
CSS 2.1
CSS3
div container
em unit
embedded style sheet
external style sheet
Flash
floating
generic font
GIF

Graphics Interchange
    Format
hanging indent
hexadecimal
inline style
Joint Photographic
    Experts Group
JPEG
kerning
leading
margin
padding
PNG
Portable Network
    Graphics
quirks mode
relative unit

RGB triplet
scalable
Scalable Vector Graphics
specific font
splash screen
standards mode
style inheritance
style precedence
style sheet
SVG
tiling
tracking
transparent color

Practice | Review Assignments

Practice the skills you learned in the tutorial using the same case scenario.

Data Files needed for the Review Assignments: greenbar.jpg, holiday.jpg, holidaytxt. htm, salogo.jpg, and sunnytxt.css

Tammy has been working with the Web site you designed. She's returned to you for help with another Web page. The Sunny Acres farm is planning a festival called *Holiday on the Farm* to bring people to Sunny Acres during the months of November and December. They're planning to offer sleigh rides, sledding (weather permitting), and a visit with Santa Claus. Tammy has already created the content for this page and located a few graphics she wants you to use. One is the Sunny Acres logo that she's placed at the top of the page. Another is a promotional photo that she wants placed in a box floated on the right margin of the Web page. The third graphic displays a green bar that Tammy wants to tile as a background. A preview of the page you'll create for Tammy is shown in Figure 3-64.

Figure 3-64

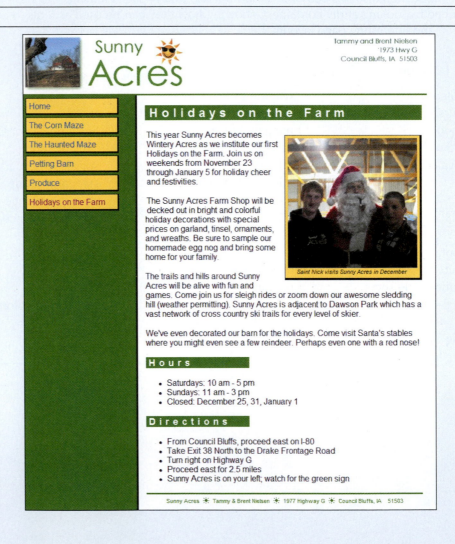

Complete the following:

1. Use your text editor to open the **holidaytxt.htm** and **sunnytxt.css** files from the tutorial.03\review folder included with your Data Files. Enter *your name* and *the date* in the comment section within each file and save them as **holiday.htm** and **sunny.css**, respectively, in the same folder. Take some time to review the content and appearance of the holiday.htm file in your text editor and Web browser.

2. Go to the holiday.htm file in your text editor. Add a div container named outer that encloses the entire page content within the opening and closing <body> tags.

3. Add a second div container named inner that encloses the page content from the h2 heading down to the address element.

4. Locate the photo inline image. Set the width and height of this image to 250 pixels.

5. Link the **holiday.htm** file to the **sunny.css** style sheet. Close the file, saving your changes.

6. Return to the **sunny.css** file in your text editor. Add the following style for the page body:
   - Set the margin to 0 pixels.
   - Set the default font face to Arial, Helvetica, or the generic sans-serif font.
   - Change the background color to white and display the background image file **greenbar.jpg** tiled in the vertical direction only starting from the top left corner of the page.

7. Display the h1 headings with a 3-pixel-wide solid green bottom border and a margin of 0 pixels.

8. Display the h2 and h3 headings in white text on a green background. Set the left padding to 5 pixels and the kerning to 7 pixels. Set the width of the h3 headings to 200 pixels.

9. Display the address text in an 8-point normal green font. Center the address text with a top padding of 5 pixels. Add a 3-pixel solid green border to the top of the address text.

10. Set the width of the outer div container to 770 pixels.

11. Set the left margin of the inner div container to 225 pixels. Set the left padding of the inner div container to 10 pixels.

12. The holiday.htm file contains the photobox paragraph, which displays the photo inline image followed by a caption for the image. Apply the following styles to the photobox paragraph:
    - Float the paragraph on the right margin.
    - Center the text horizontally within the box.
    - Display the text in an 8-point italic font.
    - Change the background color to the value (255, 215, 71).
    - Add a 10-pixel margin to the top of, below, and to the left of the box, and set the right margin to 0 pixels.
    - Add a solid black border that is 1 pixel wide on the box's top and left, and 4 pixels wide on the right and bottom.

13. Display the photo image within the photobox paragraph as a block-level element.

14. Tammy has placed a list of links within the links div container. Float this container on the left margin.

15. Display all hypertext links using the following styles:
    - Remove any underlining from the hypertext links by setting the text decoration to none.

- Display each link as a block-level element 180 pixels wide with a 5-pixel margin and 5 pixels of internal padding.
- Set the background to the color value (255, 215, 71).
- Add a solid black border that is 1 pixel wide on the top and left, and 3 pixels wide on the right and bottom.

16. Save your changes to the file and then open the **holiday.htm** file in your Web browser. Verify that the page layout appears similar to that shown in Figure 3-64. Note that Figure 3-64 displays the page as rendered by the Internet Explorer browser; you will see some slight differences under other Web browsers.

17. Submit your completed files to your instructor.

| Apply | **Case Problem 1** |

Apply your knowledge of hypertext links to create a Web page for the International Cryptographic Institute.

Data Files needed for this Case Problem: algo.htm, back1.gif, back2.gif, crypttxt.htm, enigma.htm, history.htm, locks.jpg, logo.gif, public.htm, scytale.gif, and single.htm

International Cryptographic Institute   Sela Dawes is the media representative for the ICI, the International Cryptographic Institute. The ICI is an organization of cryptographers who study the science and mathematics of secret codes, encrypted messages, and code breaking. Part of the ICI's mission is to inform the public about cryptography and data security. Sela has asked you to work on a Web site containing information about cryptography for use by high school science and math teachers. She wants the design to be visually interesting in order to help draw students into the material. Figure 3-65 shows a preview of your design.

Figure 3-65

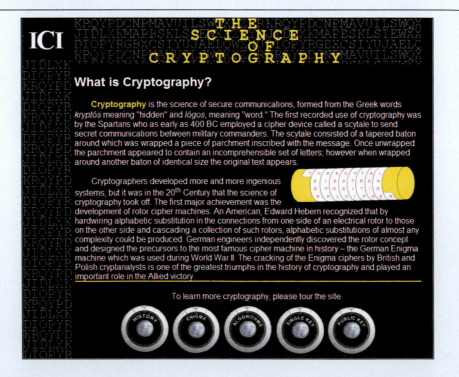

Complete the following:

1. In your text editor, open **crypttxt.htm** from the tutorial.03\case1 folder included with your Data Files. Enter *your name* and *the date* in the comment section of the file. Save the file as **crypt.htm** in the same folder.

2. Add a div container covering the page content from the h1 heading through the end of the third paragraph. Give the div element the id pageContent.

3. Add an embedded style sheet to the head section of the document. With the style sheet, create the following style for the page body:
   - Set the background color to black and the text color to white.
   - Use the file **back1.gif** as a background image tiled in the vertical direction only.
   - Sets the margin to 0 pixels.

4. Apply the following styles to the pageContent div container:
   - Set the width to 670 pixels and the left margin to 100 pixels.
   - Set the default font to Arial, Helvetica, or sans-serif.

5. Apply the following styles to the h1 element:
   - Set the font family to Courier New or monospace.
   - Set the font size to 24 points, the kerning to 10 points, and the leading to 0.7 points.
   - Center the text of the h1 heading horizontally.
   - Change the font color to yellow.
   - Use **back2.gif** as the background image.
   - Set the margin to 0 pixels.

6. Create a style to display bold text in a yellow font.

7. Create a style to indent paragraphs by 2 em units.

8. Locate the inline image for the **logo.gif** file. Set the width and height for the image to 95 pixels wide by 78 pixels high. Float the image on the left page margin.

9. Locate the **scytale.gif** image. Set the dimensions to 250 pixels wide by 69 pixels high. Float the image on the right margin.

10. Use an inline style to add a 2-pixel solid yellow border to the bottom of the second paragraph. Change the bottom padding of the paragraph to 10 pixels.

11. Use an inline style to center the contents of the third paragraph.

12. Locate the **locks.jpg** inline image and set the dimensions of the image to 510 pixels wide by 110 pixels high.

13. Directly below the locks.jpg inline image, create an image map with the name and id, locks. Add the following hotspots to the image map:
    - A circular hotspot linked to history.htm centered at the coordinate (52, 52) with a radius of 43 pixels; the alternate text should be "History"
    - A circular hotspot with a radius of 43 pixels located at the coordinate (155, 52); link the hotspot to enigma.htm and set the alternate text to "Enigma"
    - A circular hotspot with a radius of 43 pixels located at the coordinate (255, 52); link the hotspot to algo.htm and set the alternate text to "Algorithms"
    - A circular hotspot with a radius of 43 pixels located at the coordinate (355, 52); link the hotspot to single.htm and set the alternate text to "Single Key"
    - A circular hotspot with a radius of 43 pixels located at the coordinate (455, 52); link the hotspot to public.htm and set the alternate text to "Public Key"

14. Apply the locks image map to the **locks.jpg** inline image. Use an inline style to remove the border around the inline image.

15. Save your changes to the file. Load **crypt.htm** in your Web browser. Verify that the layout appears similar to that shown in Figure 3-65 and that the image map hotspots open the appropriate pages on your Web site.

16. Submit your completed files to your instructor.

| Apply | **Case Problem 2** |

Apply your knowledge of CSS to create a three-column layout for a bike touring company.

Data Files needed for this Case Problem: block.jpg, bmtourtxt.htm, body.jpg, h1back. jpg, h1title.gif, and wheelstxt.css

Mountain Wheels   Adriana and Ivan Turchenko are the co-owners of Mountain Wheels, a bike shop and touring agency in Littleton, Colorado. One of their most popular tours is the Bike the Mountains Tour, a six-day excursion over some of the highest roads in Colorado. Adriana wants to update the company's Web site, providing more information about the Bike the Mountains Tour. She envisions a three-column layout with a list of links in the first column and descriptive text in the second and third columns. She has asked for your help in working up a design. As a first step, you'll design the page containing the tour's itinerary. Adriana has already created all of the page content and provided all of the graphics needed for page backgrounds. She needs your help in working with the CSS. Figure 3-66 shows a preview of the Web page you'll create.

Figure 3-66

Bike the Mountains Tour

INTRODUCTION

The Bike the Mountains Tour rises from the town of Littleton, Colorado and explores the Colorado Front Range. Our tour crosses the Continental Divide twice, giving you the opportunity to bike the highest paved roads in the United States. This tour is a classic showcase of Colorado's Rocky Mountain scenery.

Not designed for the weekend cyclist, this tour is offered only for those fit enough to ride high mountain passes. We provide sag wagons and support. Your lodging and meals are also part of the registration fee. We guarantee tough climbs, amazing sights, sweaty jerseys, and lots of fun.

"The Bike the Mountains Tour is *amazing*. I highly recommend it and would gladly return."

This is the seventh year we've offered the Bike the Mountains Tour. It is our most popular tour and riders are returning again and again. Our experienced tour leaders will be there to guide, help, encourage, draft, and lead you every stroke of the way. Come join us!

- Home
- Learn More
- Testimonials
- Route Maps
- Register
- Lodging
- Meals
- Training
- Equipment
- Forums
- FAQs
- Contact Us

ITINERARY

Day 1

We start from the foothills above Littleton, Colorado, promptly at 9am. Be sure to fuel up at Kate's House of Pancakes before starting your ride. The first day is a chance to get your legs in shape, test your gearing, and prepare for what's to come. Be aware that there are several steep grades as we climb out of the valley into the Front Range. Optional side tours and shortcuts will be provided.

Day 2

Day 2 starts with a climb up Bear Creek Canyon to Lookout Mountain, followed by a swift and winding descent into the town of Golden. Refresh yourself at the famous Coors Brewery. You'll need the break to get yourself ready for a great climb through Golden Gate Canyon to the Peak to Peak Highway, ending in the gambling town of Blackhawk. Try your hand at poker and blackjack, but watch your wallet.

Day 3

Day 3 takes you along the Peak to Peak Highway. Established in 1918 this is Colorado's oldest scenic byway. This 55-mile route showcases the mountains of the Front Range, providing amazing vistas from Golden Gate Canyon State Park to Rocky Mountain National Park. We'll stop at Estes Park for fun and refreshment. Get a good night's sleep; you'll need it the next day.

Day 4

Now for the supreme challenge: Day 4 brings some real high-altitude cycling through Rocky Mountain National Park and up Trail Ridge Road. It's an amazing ride, high above timberline, topping out at over 11,000 feet. Stop and rest at the Alpine Visitor's Center before all of that hard work is rewarded with a fast and joyous descent into the town of Grand Lake.

Day 5

We start Day 5 on the west side of the Continental Divide. From Grand Lake, you'll bike to Winter Park, a great ski town summer resort. From Winter Park it's a steady and scenic climb over Berthoud Pass, and back to the eastern side of the Continental Divide. We'll stay at Idaho Springs, where you can enjoy the natural hot springs at the hotel.

Day 6

On Day 6 choose your pleasure or your poison. You can ride back to Littleton over Squaw Pass and Bear Creek. The ride is beautiful and enjoyable in its own right. However, if you're "up" to it, this is your opportunity to tackle Mount Evans. The 7-mile side trip to the top of Mt Evans, at over 14,000 feet, is something that can't be found anywhere else in the country. We'll provide the sag wagon, you provide the legs and lungs.

Once you're back to Littleton, please join us for a celebratory dinner as we share memories of an amazing 6 days of riding the Colorado mountains.

Bike the Mountains Tour • Littleton, CO 80123 • (303) 555 - 5499

Complete the following:

1. In your text editor, open **bmtourtxt.htm** and **wheelstxt.css** from the tutorial.03\case2 folder included with your Data Files. Enter *your name* and *the date* in the comment section of each file. Save the files as **bmtour.htm** and **wheels.css** in the same folder.

2. Review the contents and current layout of the **bmtour.htm** file in your text editor and browser. Create three div containers for the three columns that Adriana wants to use in her proposed page layout. To create the three div containers:

   - Locate the div container for the list of links at the top of the file. Give this div element the id, column1.
   - Enclose the page content starting with the h2 Introduction heading through the paragraph describing the Day 2 activities of the tour in another div container. Give this div element the id, column2.
   - Enclose the page content starting with the Day 3 heading through the last paragraph describing the Day 6 activities in a div element with the id, column3.

3. Within the head section, create a link to the external style sheet, **wheels.css**. Save your changes to the **bmtour.htm** file.

4. Go to the **wheels.css** style sheet in your text editor. Create a style for the page body containing the following style rules:

   - Set the font family to Verdana, Helvetica, or sans-serif.
   - Set the margin size to 0 pixels.
   - Set the background color to white and add a background image using the body.jpg file tiled in the vertical direction.

5. Create the following style for the first column in the layout of the **bmtour.htm** file:

   - Set the width to 140 pixels. Set the left padding to 10 pixels and the top padding to 20 pixels.
   - Float the column on the left page margin.

6. Create the following style for the second column of the **bmtour.htm** file:

   - Set the width to 40% of the width of the page body.
   - Float the column on the left margin.
   - Add a 1-pixel-wide solid black border to the left and right of the column.

7. Set the width of the third column to 40% of the width of the page body and also float this column on the left.

8. Create the following style for the h1 heading:

   - Center the contents of the heading, setting the height to 100 pixels and the margin to 0 pixels.
   - Set the background color to white with the file h1back.jpg as the background image, tiled in the horizontal direction.
   - Add a 1-pixel-wide solid black bottom border.

9. Create the following style for the h2 headings:

   - Indent the text 30 pixels.
   - Set the font color to white and the background to the color value (108, 87, 12).
   - Set the kerning to 8 points and the margin to 0 pixels.
   - Display the text in small caps.

10. Set the left margin of h3 headings to 10 pixels.

11. Set the margins of all paragraphs to 10 pixels on the top and left and 20 pixels on the right and bottom.

12. Apply the following styles to blockquote elements on the page:

    - Set the width of every blockquote element to 200 pixels with 10 pixels of padding.
    - Display the text in a 16-point white font.
    - Add a 3-pixel-wide solid black border.

- Change the background color to the value (255, 204, 0) with the image file **block.jpg** as the background, tiled in the horizontal direction.
- Set the margins around the blockquote to 5 pixels, except for the right margin, which should be set to 10 pixels.
- Float the blockquote on the right margin.

13. Apply the following styles to hypertext elements:
    - Display hypertext elements as block-level elements with 2 pixels of padding.
    - Set the top, right, and bottom margins to 5 pixels. Set the left margin to 0 pixels.
    - Set the font size to 10 points.
    - Remove underlining from the hypertext links by setting the text decoration to none.
    - Add a 1-pixel-wide solid black border.
    - Change the background color to the value (255, 255, 192).

14. Apply the following styles to the address element:
    - Center the address text.
    - Display the text in a 10-point normal font (no italics).
    - Set the background color to white.
    - Set the padding size to 10 pixels and add a 1-pixel-wide solid black top border.
    - ⊕ **EXPLORE** Display the address only when both margins are clear of floating elements.

15. Save your changes to the file.

16. Open the **bmtour.htm** file in your Web browser. Verify that the layout resembles that shown in Figure 3-66.

17. ⊕ **EXPLORE** Try to locate a wide screen monitor and view the Web page under that monitor's resolution. What aspect of your style sheet allowed the columns to be resized to fit the increased width of the monitor? This type of page layout is called a fluid or liquid layout. Explain why.

18. Submit your completed files to your instructor.

Challenge	**Case Problem 3**

Broaden your knowledge of CSS and HTML by creating an image with an irregular text wrap.

Data Files needed for this Case Problem: banner.jpg, king1.gif – king6.gif, kingtxt.htm, and centertxt.css

Center for Diversity   Stewart Tompkins is the project coordinator for the Midwest University Center for Diversity. He is currently working on a Web site titled The Voices of Civil Rights, containing Web pages with extended quotes from civil rights leaders of the past and present. He has asked you to help develop a design for the pages in the series. He has given you the text for one of the pages, which is about Dr. Martin Luther King, Jr.

Stewart has supplied a photo of Dr. King that he would like you to include on the page. He has seen how text can be made to wrap irregularly around a photo in graphic design software, and he wonders if you can do the same thing on a Web page. Although you cannot use this same technique with page elements, which are always rectangular, you can break a single image into a series of rectangles of different sizes. When the text wraps around these stacked rectangles, they provide the appearance of a single image with an irregular line wrap. Stewart asks you to try this with his Dr. King photo. Figure 3-67 shows a preview of the page you'll create. Note how the right margin of the text seems to wrap around Dr. King's image along a diagonal line, rather than a vertical one.

Figure 3-67

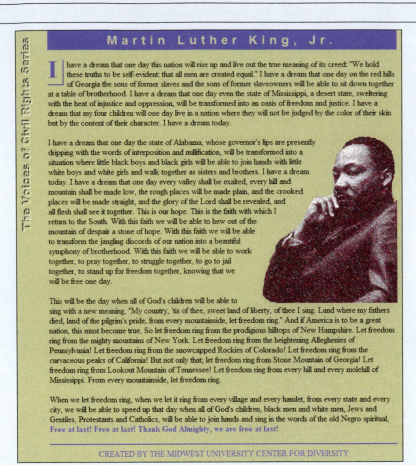

Complete the following:

1. In your text editor, open the **kingtxt.htm** and **centertxt.css** files from the tutorial.03\case3 folder included with your Data Files. Enter *your name* and *the date* in the comment section of each file. Save the files as **king.htm** and **center.css** in the same folder. Take some time to study the content and layout of the king.htm file as it appears in your text editor and Web browser.

2. Return to the **king.htm** file in your text editor. Directly below the opening <body> tag, insert a div element with the id banner. Within the div element, insert an inline image for the **banner.jpg** graphic file. Give the inline image the id, bannerImage, and specify the alternate text "The Voices of Civil Rights Series."

3. Enclose the rest of the page content, starting with the h1 heading at the top of the page through the address at the bottom of the file, in a div element with the id, pageContent.

4. Save your changes to the file.

5. In your text editor, go to the **center.css** file. Create a style for the body element that sets the font color to black, the background color to the value (204, 204, 153), and the margin to 0 em.

6. Float the banner div container on the left page margin.

7. Set the width of the pageContent div container to 42 em and the left margin to 4 em.

8. Apply the following styles to h1 headings:
   - Set the font face to Arial, Helvetica, or sans-serif.

- Set the font size to 1.5 em and the kerning to 0.5 em. Center the h1 heading text.
- Set the padding to 0.2 em.
- Set the font color to the value (204, 204, 153) and the background color to the value (102, 102, 204).

9. Display text marked as an em element in a normal bold font. Set the font color to the value (102, 102, 204).

10. Apply the following styles to the address element:
    - Set the font style to normal to remove the default italics style.
    - Display the text in uppercase letters. Set the font color to (102, 102, 204).
    - Center the address text.
    - Set the padding to 0.5 em.
    - Add a solid top border 0.1 em wide in the color value (102, 102, 204).

11. Save your changes to the **center.css** style sheet.

12. Return to the **king.htm** file in your text editor. Add a link to the center.css to the head of the document.

⊕ **EXPLORE** 13. Stewart wants the opening word from Dr. King's speech to appear as a drop cap. To create this effect, enclose the word in a span element and apply the following inline styles:
    - Float the span element on the left paragraph margin.
    - Set the font weight to bold and the font size to 3 em.
    - Set the font color to the value (102, 102, 240).
    - Set the line height to 0.8 em.
    - Add a solid border 0.05 em wide with the color value (102, 102, 204) to the right and bottom edge of the span element.
    - Set the bottom and right padding to 0.2 em.
    - Set the right margin to 0.2 em.

⊕ **EXPLORE** 14. To create an irregular line wrap around the image, you have to break the image into several files and then stack them on the left or right margin, displaying an image only when the margin is clear of the previous image. To remove the seams between the images, you have to set the top and bottom margins to 0. The Dr. Martin Luther King, Jr. graphic has been broken into six files for you. To stack them:
    - Directly below the first paragraph, insert a div element containing six inline images for the graphic files **king1.gif** through **king6.gif**. For each image, set the alternate text to an empty text string.
    - Use inline styles to set the width of the six inline images to the following values: king1.gif = 6.7 em, king2.gif = 7.85 em, king3.gif = 11.45 em, king4.gif = 14.25 em, king5.gif = 15.5 em, king6.gif = 16.6 em.

15. Scroll to the top of the file and add an embedded style sheet to the head section of the document.

16. Within the embedded style sheet, create the following styles for inline images in the document:
    - Float the images on the right margin.
    - Set the clear style so that the image is only displayed when the right margin is clear of other floating images.
    - Set the left margin to 2 em and the other margins to 0 em.

17. Directly below the style you just created, add the following styles for the inline image with the bannerImage id:
    - Set the width to 3.5 em.

- Set the value of the float style to none (to prevent this inline image from floating on the page).
- Set the margin to 0 em.

18. Save your changes to the file. Open the **king.htm** file in your Web browser and verify that it resembles the layout shown in Figure 3-67. Verify that the first letter in the speech appears as a drop cap and that the image of Dr. King is surrounded by an irregular line wrap with no seams appearing between the six stacked images.

⊕ EXPLORE 19. Using Firefox or another browser that allows the user to increase and decrease the browser's default font size, increase and decrease the font size on the Dr. King Web page. What happens to the size of the images and the general appearance of the page layout? This type of design is called an elastic layout. Can you see why? How did choosing the em unit to size the page elements and the graphic images create this effect?

20. Submit your completed files to your instructor.

| Create | **Case Problem 4** |

Test your knowledge of CSS and HTML by creating a design for a Scottish touring company's Web site.

Data Files needed for this Case Problem: castles.jpg, casttxt.htm, Hebrides.jpg, hebtxt. htm, highland.jpg, hightxt.htm, lake.jpg, lakestxt.htm, parch.jpg, and tslogo.gif

Travel Scotland!   Fiona Henderson is the owner of *Travel Scotland!*, a touring company specializing in guided tours of Scotland. She's come to you for help in creating a design for the *Travel Scotland!* Web site. Fiona has four Web pages describing four of the company's tours. She's already inserted the content and gathered some graphic images to supplement her text. She wants you to take her unformatted Web pages and create an interesting design and layout.

Complete the following:

1. In your text editor, open the **casttxt.htm**, **hebtxt.htm**, **hightxt.htm**, and **lakestxt.htm** from the tutorial.03\case4 folder included with your Data Files. Enter *your name* and *the date* in the comment section of each file. Save the files as **castles.htm**, **hebrides.htm**, **highland.htm**, and **lakes.htm** in the same folder. Take some time to study the content of these four files. You are free to supplement the content of these Web pages with additional material you find on your own. You may also edit the HTML tags and attributes within these pages if they help you achieve your final design.

2. Use your text editor to create an external style sheet named **ts.css**, placed in the tutorial.03\case4 folder. Add a comment section to the style sheet containing *your name*, *the date*, a description of the style sheet, and its purpose in the Web site.

3. Add styles to the ts.css style sheet that you'll apply to the four pages on the *Travel Scotland!* Web site. The design of the Web site is up to you, but it should include at least one example of each of the following:
   - A style that modifies the text and background colors of page elements
   - A style that modifies the font size, face, and appearance of element text
   - A style that defines an element's padding and margins, distinctly different in at least two directions
   - A style to define the border appearance of an element
   - A style that floats an inline image or element
   - A style that adds a background image to an element
   - A style applied to a div container identified by an id value

4. Each of the four Web pages should have a slightly different appearance. Add an embedded style sheet to each file that provides a slightly different color scheme for each Web page.

5. Link your Web pages to your style sheet, and then test your Web page under a variety of browsers and monitor resolutions. Correct any problems that arise from those differing environments.

6. Submit your completed files to your instructor.

| Review | | Quick Check Answers |

Session 3.1

1. Inline styles are styles applied directly to an element through the use of the style attribute in the element's tag. Embedded styles are styles placed in the head section of a document and apply to elements within that document. External style sheets are files separate from the document and can be applied to any document on a Web site. External style sheets are best for setting the styles of an entire Web site.

2. `/* Sunny Acres Style Sheet */`

3. `p {color: red}`

4. As left-aligned blue text

5. In red text with an ivory-color background

6. `!important`

7. `blockquote {color: rgb(221, 128, 0)}`

Session 3.2

1. `code {font-family: Courier New, monospace}`

2. 18 points

3. `h3 {text-decoration: overline underline}`

4. `address {letter-spacing: 0.5em; word-spacing: 0.9em}`

5. `dt {text-transform: uppercase}`

6. JPEG because the JPEG format supports a much larger color palette, while GIFs are limited to 256 colors and so will not display photographic images without dithering the colors.

7. `width = "200" height = "100"`

8. `blockquote {background-image: url(mark.jpg);`
   `            background-repeat: no-repeat;`
   `            background-position: left top;`
   `            background-attachment: fixed}`

Session 3.3

1. `#photoImage {float: left}`

2. `#photoImage {margin-right: 5px; margin-bottom: 5px}`

3. `p {padding-top: 10px; padding-bottom: 10px}`

4. `blockquote {margin-left: 20px; border-left: 4px solid gray}`

5. `#mainHeading {color: green; border: 8px double green}`

6. Internet Explorer applies the width property to the entire box, including the padding and border spaces. The CSS box model applies the width property to the content of the box, but not to the padding and margins.

7. `img {display: block}`

Ending Data Files

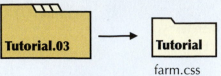

Tutorial
farm.css
haunted.htm
home.htm
index.htm
maze.htm
petting.htm
produce.htm
+ 9 graphic files

Review
holiday.htm
sunny.css
+ 3 graphic files

Case1
algo.htm
crypt.htm
enigma.htm
history.htm
public.htm
single.htm
+ 5 graphic files

Case2
bmtour.htm
wheels.css
+ 4 graphic files

Case3
center.css
king.htm
+ 7 graphic files

Case4
castles.htm
hebrides.htm
highland.htm
lakes.htm
ts.css
+ 6 graphic files

Creating Special Effects with CSS

Adding Advanced Styles to a Web Site

Case | Online Scrapbooks

Scrapbooking is the popular hobby of creating albums containing photos, memorabilia, writing, and other embellishments. This hobby has become a multimillion-dollar industry with companies that specialize in scrapbooking supplies and support. One of these companies is Online Scrapbooks.

Kathy Pridham, who leads the Web development team at Online Scrapbooks, has hired you to work on the style for the new company's Web site. The Web site's home page will have information on how to get started in scrapbooking and links to other pages that contain a wide variety of information. Because the Web site will have so many pages, Kathy is using Cascading Style Sheets to manage the layout, design, and function of the pages. She has a style sheet providing the site's basic layout and design. She would like you to add features such as graphical bullets, rollover effects, and drop caps. To make those enhancements, you'll need to use some of the special features supported by CSS.

Kathy knows that many users want to access the Web site from mobile devices, while others want to be able to print some of the site's contents. She wants the site to work with any kind of output, including mobile devices and printed output.

Starting Data Files

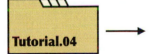

Tutorial.04 →

Tutorial
printtxt.css
samptxt.htm
scrapstxt.css
starttxt.htm
+ 4 graphic files

Demo
demo_positioning.htm
+ 5 graphic files

Review
gallerytxt.htm
printertxt.css
screentxt.css
+ 7 graphics files

Case1
h01txt.htm-h18txt.htm
printtxt.css
willettxt.css
+ 21 graphic files

Case2
cwpagetxt.htm
cwtxt.css
+ 2 graphic files

Case3
longstxt.htm
+ 11 graphic files

Case4
bizetbio.txt
bizetlist.txt
mozartbio.txt
mozartlist.txt
puccinibio.txt
puccinilist.txt

verdibio.txt
verdilist.txt
wagnerbio.txt
wagnerlist.txt
+ 5 graphic files

Session 4.1

Working with Selector Patterns

Kathy has already created a basic Web page describing how to get started in scrapbooking. She's written an article and created the basic Web page layout using an external style sheet. She's provided you with her HTML document, her graphic files, and her style sheet to study. Kathy suggests that this Web page would be a good place to start in your task of enhancing her basic design.

To view Kathy's data files:

1. In your text editor, open the **starttxt.htm** and **scrapstxt.css** files, located in the tutorial.04\tutorial folder included with your Data Files. Within the comment section at the top of each file, add *your name* and *the date* in the space provided. Save the files as **start.htm** and **scraps.css**, respectively, in the same folder.

2. Take some time to review the code in both the external style sheet file and the HTML document. Note how the CSS styles are applied to specific elements in the start.htm file to create an interesting layout and design.

3. Open **start.htm** in your Web browser. Figure 4-1 shows the current appearance of the start.htm file.

Figure 4-1 | Initial design for the Getting Started page

ONLINE
SCRAPBOOKS

- Home
- Getting Started
- Scrapbooking Tips
- Supply List
- Glossary
- Online Classes
- Sample Pages
- Online Store
- Shopping Cart
- Checkout
- Your Account
- Order Status
- Wish List
- Customer Service
- About Us
- Newsletter
- FAQ
- Contact Us

Getting Started

Scrapbooking is the practice of combining photos, memorabilia, and stories in an album, preserving memories for future generations. In recent years, scrapbooking has become a $300 million dollar industry as the public has discovered the joys of creating albums for families and friends. Online Scrapbooks is here to help you with all of your scrapbooking needs.

Preserving Your Memories

Scrapbook albums have existed since the beginning of photography. However, the sad fact is that photographs and most printed material are not permanent: they will fade and yellow with age. Scrapbookers of today are aware of these problems, and the industry is providing remedies to minimize deterioration. For the best results, avoid using materials with high acid content which can cause photos and paper to deteriorate. Another thing to avoid is lignin, a material that is the bonding element in wood fibers. Over time, paper with lignin will become yellow and brittle, so you should only use lignin-free products.

Basic Materials

- Acid-free paper, card stock, and stickers
- Acid-free pen, markers, and adhesive
- Acid-free memory book album
- Straight and pattern edge scissors
- Photos and photo corners
- Paper punches
- Journalling templates
- Decorative embellishments

Your albums should contain page protectors to shield the pages from smudges, oil, and dirt that can be transferred from your hands. You should never use albums with sticky "magnetic" pages. The sticky substance will be transferred to the photo and backing paper causing deterioration. Never crop Polaroid® photos: they will curl and fall apart. Mount all memorabilia on acid-free cardstock paper, and photocopy all newspaper clippings on acid-free paper.

ONLINE SCRAPBOOKS · 212 SUNSET DRIVE · RICHMOND, KY 40475 · (859) 555-8100

As you can see from Figure 4-1, Kathy has applied a layout in which the list of links floats on the left page margin and a box describing basic scrapbooking materials floats on the right margin. There is one main heading marked as an h1 element displayed at the top of page, providing a logo with the company name.

The three other headings—Getting Started, Preserving Your Memories, and Basic Materials—are marked as h2 elements. Kathy wants to apply a slightly different format to the Basic Materials h2 heading than the one applied to the Getting Started and Preserving Your Memories h2 headings. One way of applying a specific format to this heading is through the use of an id attribute. However, Kathy doesn't want to maintain a list of id values for all the various elements on her Web page. Instead, she would like to create styles for elements based on their location or their use in the document. She asks if this can be done with CSS.

Contextual Selectors

So far, the only styles you've worked with are ones in which the style selector references either an element (or a group of elements) or an element identified by an id. For example, the style

```
b {color: blue}
```

displays all boldface text in a blue font. What would you do, however, if you didn't want every example of boldface text to be displayed in a blue font? What if you wanted this style applied only to boldface text located within an ordered or unordered list?

Recall that on a Web page, elements are nested within other elements, forming a hierarchical tree structure. The top element on the Web page is the body element because it contains all of the content appearing in the page. From this top element, other elements descend. Figure 4-2 shows an example of such a tree structure for a Web page consisting of a few headings, a couple of paragraphs, some boldface elements, and a span element nested within a paragraph.

A sample tree hierarchy of page elements   Figure 4-2

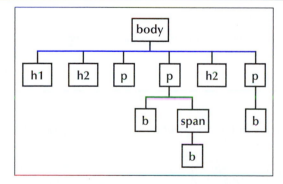

To take advantage of this tree structure, CSS allows you to create **contextual selectors** that express the location of an element within the hierarchy of elements. The general syntax of a contextual selector has the form

```
parent descendant {styles}
```

where *parent* is the parent element, *descendant* is a descendant of the parent, and *styles* are the styles to be applied to the descendant element. To apply a blue color only to boldface text found in lists, you would use the style:

```
li b {color: blue}
```

In this case, li is the parent element and b is the descendant element (because it is contained within the list item). Any bold element not nested within a list element is not affected by this style. Note that the descendant element does not have to be a direct child of the parent element; it can appear several levels below the parent element in hierarchy. For example in the code

```
<li>
   <span><b>Special</b>Orders</span> this month!
</li>
```

the bold element is a descendant of the list item, but it is a direct child only of the span element. So the word "Special" would appear in a bold font if the above style is applied to the document. Contextual selectors can be grouped with other selectors. The following style applies a blue font to h2 headings and to boldface list items, but nowhere else:

```
li b, h2 {color: blue}
```

Contextual selectors can also be applied with elements marked with a specific id. The style

```
#notes b {color: blue}
```

displays bold text in a blue font if it is nested within an element with an id of notes.

The parent/descendant form is only one example of a contextual selector. Figure 4-3 describes some of the other contextual forms supported by CSS.

Figure 4-3	Contextual selectors

Selector	Description
*	Matches any element in the hierarchy
e	Matches any element, e, in the hierarchy
e1, e2, e3, ...	Matches the group of elements: e1, e2, e3, ...
e f	Matches any element, f, that is a descendant of an element, e
e > f	Matches any element, f, that is a direct child of an element, e
e + f	Matches any element, f, that is immediately preceded by a sibling element, e

For example, the style

```
* {color: blue}
```

causes *all* of the elements in the document to appear in a blue font. On the other hand, the style

```
p > b {color: blue}
```

applies the blue font only to boldface text that is contained within a paragraph element as a child of that element and not any descendent. Figure 4-4 provides additional examples of how to select different elements of the Web page document based on the expression in the contextual selector. Selected elements are highlighted in red for each pattern. Remember that because of style inheritance, any style applied to an element is passed down the document tree. So a style applied to a paragraph element is automatically passed down to elements contained within that paragraph unless it conflicts with a more specific style.

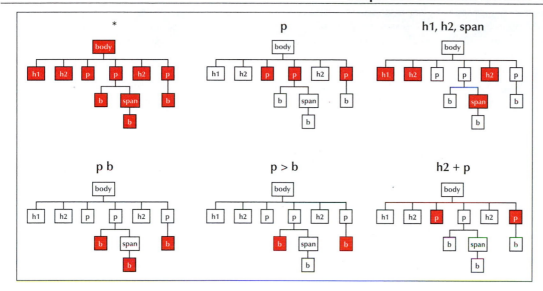

Although the contextual selectors listed in Figure 4-3 are part of the specifications for CSS2, they are not well supported by earlier versions of the Internet Explorer browser. In particular, the *e > f* and *e + f* contextual selectors should be used with caution if you need to support Internet Explorer. Other browsers, including Firefox, Opera, and Safari, do support all of the contextual selectors described in Figure 4-3.

Attribute Selectors

On occasion you might also need to select elements based on their attribute values. For example, if you want to display link text in a blue font, you might use the following declaration:

`a {color: blue}`

However, this declaration makes no distinction between <a> tags used to mark links and <a> tags used to mark document anchors (for a discussion of anchors, see Tutorial 2). HTML makes this distinction based on the presence or absence of the href attribute. To select an element based on the element's attributes, you can create an **attribute selector** that has the form

`element[att] {styles}`

where *element* is a page element, *att* is the name of an attribute associated with the element, and *styles* are the styles applied to the element. The declaration

`a[href] {color: blue}`

applies the blue font color style only to link elements that contain an href attribute. Any <a> tag used to mark anchors would not contain the href attribute, and therefore would not be affected by this style. Figure 4-5 describes some of the other attribute selectors supported by CSS.

Figure 4-5	Attribute selectors

Selector	Description	Example	Interpretation
elem[att]	The element contains the att attribute	a[href]	Matches hypertext elements containing the href attribute
elem[att="val"]	The element's att attribute equals val	a[href="gloss.htm"]	Matches hypertext elements whose href attribute equals "gloss.htm"
elem[att~="val"]	The element's att attribute value is a space-separated list of words, one of which is exactly val	a[rel~="glossary"]	Matches hypertext elements whose rel attribute contains the word "glossary"
elem[att|="val"]	The element's att attribute value is a hyphen-separated list of words beginning with val	p[id|="first"]	Matches paragraphs whose id attribute starts with the word "first" in a hyphen-separated list of words
elem[att^="val"]	The element's att attribute begins with val (CSS3)	a[rel^="prev"]	Matches hypertext elements whose rel attribute begins with "prev"
elem[att$="val"]	The element's att attribute ends with val (CSS3)	a[href$="org"]	Matches hypertext elements whose href attribute ends with "org"
elem[att*="val"]	The element's att attribute contains the value val (CSS3)	a[href*="faq"]	Matches hypertext elements whose href attribute contains the text string "faq"

Browser support for attribute selectors is mixed. For this reason, you should use attribute selectors with caution. Note that some of the attribute selectors listed in Figure 4-5 are part of the proposed specifications for CSS3 and have scattered browser support at the present time. As with contextual selectors, attribute selectors enjoy good support from Firefox, Opera, and Safari, but poor support from Internet Explorer. IE does support attribute and contextual selectors if you write your HTML code to put Internet Explorer into standards mode (for a discussion of standards mode, see Tutorial 3).

Using Selector Patterns

- To apply a style to all elements in the document, use the * selector.
- To apply a style to a single element, use the *e* selector, where *e* is the name of the element.
- To apply a selector to a descendant element, *f*, use the *e f* selector, where *e* is the name of the parent element and *f* is an element nested within the parent.
- To apply a selector to a child element, *f*, use the *e > f* selector, where *e* is the name of a parent element and *f* is an element that is a direct child of the parent.
- To apply a selector to a sibling element, use the *e + f* selector, where *e* and *f* are siblings and *f* immediately follows *e* in the document tree.

Applying a Selector Pattern

After discussing how to use selector patterns, you and Kathy decide to apply them to her Getting Started document. You decide to create a style for the h2 heading in the Basic Materials box so that you can use the style in similar boxes on other pages in the Online Scrapbooking site. You'll center this heading, change the background color to white, reduce the top margin to 0 pixels, and add a solid orange border to the bottom of the element. Because this heading appears within a div element that is identified with an id value of pullout, you'll add the following style to the style sheet:

```
#pullout h2 {text-align: center; background-color: white; margin-top:
  0px;
                border-bottom: 2px solid orange}
```

Add this style declaration to the scraps.css file.

To add a contextual selector to the style sheet:

1. Go to the **scraps.css** file in your text editor.

2. Directly below the style for the #pullout selector, insert the following style, as shown in Figure 4-6:

```
#pullout h2 {text-align: center; background-color: white;
                margin-top: 0px; border-bottom: 2px solid orange}
```

Using a contextual selector   Figure 4-6

```
#pullout          {float: right; width: 250px; margin: 0px 0px 10px 10px;
                   border: 5px outset orange; background-color: ivory;
                   font-size: 10pt; font-family: Arial, Helvetica, sans-serif}
#pullout h2       {text-align: center; background-color: white; margin-top: 0px;
                   border-bottom: 2px solid orange}
```

selector references only those h2 elements within an element with the pullout id

▶ **3.** Save your changes to the file and then reload **start.htm** in your Web browser. Figure 4-7 shows the revised appearance of the document.

Figure 4-7   Applying a style to a nested h2 element

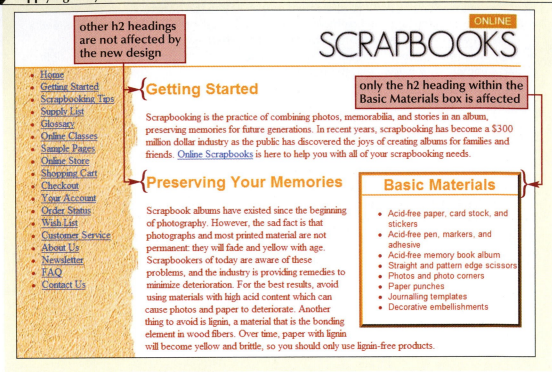

As shown in Figure 4-7, the appearance of the h2 element nested within the Basic Materials box has been modified under the new style, but h2 elements located elsewhere in the document retain their original appearance.

Several versions of the Internet Explorer browser don't follow all of the CSS specifications for selectors and styles. You can correct many of the incompatibilities by converting your HTML code to XHTML and putting IE into standards mode rather than quirks mode. However, this might not work for older versions of Internet Explorer, such as IE5 and even IE6. For those browser versions, you can use **conditional comments** that allow you to apply different HTML code for different versions of Internet Explorer. The general syntax of a conditional comment is

```
<!--[if condition IE version]><!-->
    HTML code
<!--<![endif]-->
```

where *condition* is a condition that is either true or false, *version* is the version number of an IE browser, and *HTML code* is code that will be run if *condition* is true. For example, the code

```
<!--[if lt IE 6]><!-->
    <link rel="stylesheet" type="text/css" href="old.css" />
<!--<![endif]-->
```

links the Web page to the old.css style sheet file, but only if the browser version in use is older than Internet Explorer 6. In this case, the *condition* value is lt for "less than." Other *condition* values include lte (less than or equal to), gt (greater than), gte (greater than or equal to), and ! (not equal to). If you specify no *condition* value, the *HTML code* will be run only for the specified version of Internet Explorer. You can also leave off the version number to apply the HTML code to Internet Explorer but not to other browsers. So the code

```
<!--[if IE]><!-->
    <link rel="stylesheet" type="text/css" href="ie_styles.css" />
<!--<![endif]-->
```

links the file to the ie_styles.css style sheet file, but only if Internet Explorer is being used.

Conditional comments are one of the best ways you can tailor your HTML code to match the capabilities of different versions of Internet Explorer and other browsers.

Applying Styles to Lists

Kathy has her Web page links in an unordered list that is displayed in a box floated on the left page margin. Like all unordered lists, the browser displays the items in this list with bullet markers. Kathy would like to remove the bullet markers from this list. To remove the markers you can apply one of the many CSS list styles.

Choosing a List Style Type

To specify the list marker displayed by the browser, you can apply the style

```
list-style-type: type
```

where *type* is one of the markers shown in Figure 4-8.

Figure 4-8   List style types

list-style-type	Marker (s)
disc	●
circle	○
square	□
decimal	1, 2, 3, 4, ...
decimal-leading-zero	01, 02, 03, 04, ...
lower-roman	i, ii, iii, iv, ...
upper-roman	I, II, III, IV, ...
lower-alpha	a, b, c, d, ...
upper-alpha	A, B, C, D, ...
none	no marker displayed

For example, to create a list with alphabetical markers such as

A. Home
B. Getting Started
C. Scrapbooking Tips
D. Supply List

you would apply the following list style to the ol list element:

```
ol {list-style-type: upper-alpha}
```

List style types can be used with contextual selectors to create an outline style for several levels of nested lists. Figure 4-9 shows an example in which several levels of list style markers are used in formatting an outline. Note that each marker style is determined by the location of each ordered list within the levels of the outline. The top level is displayed with uppercase Roman numerals; the bottom level, nested within three other ordered lists, uses lowercase letters for markers.

Creating an outline style | Figure 4-9

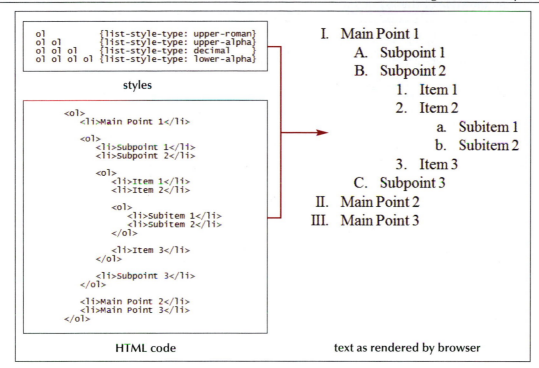

```
ol            {list-style-type: upper-roman}
ol ol         {list-style-type: upper-alpha}
ol ol ol      {list-style-type: decimal   }
ol ol ol ol   {list-style-type: lower-alpha}
```

styles

```
<ol>
    <li>Main Point 1</li>

    <ol>
        <li>Subpoint 1</li>
        <li>Subpoint 2</li>

        <ol>
            <li>Item 1</li>
            <li>Item 2</li>

            <ol>
                <li>Subitem 1</li>
                <li>Subitem 2</li>
            </ol>

            <li>Item 3</li>
        </ol>

        <li>Subpoint 3</li>
    </ol>

    <li>Main Point 2</li>
    <li>Main Point 3</li>
</ol>
```

I.   Main Point 1
    A.   Subpoint 1
    B.   Subpoint 2
       1.   Item 1
       2.   Item 2
          a.   Subitem 1
          b.   Subitem 2
       3.   Item 3
    C.   Subpoint 3
II.   Main Point 2
III.   Main Point 3

HTML code   text as rendered by browser

If you don't find the marker you want from the list-style-type style, you can supply your own in a graphic image file. To use a graphic image for the list marker, use the style

```
list-style-image: url(url)
```

where (*url*) is the URL of the graphic image file. The style

```
ul {list-style-image: url(redball.gif) }
```

displays items in an unordered list marked with the graphic image in the redball.gif file.

Kathy wants her list of links to appear without any bullet marker, but she wants the list of basic materials to appear with a bullet marker based on one of her graphic image files. She suggests that you use both the list-style-type and list-style-image attributes to modify the appearance of the two lists. To differentiate between the two lists, you'll use contextual selectors. The list of links is an unordered list nested within a div container with the id named links, while the list of basic materials is nested within the pullout div box.

To apply a list style to Kathy's list of links:

1. Return to the **scraps.css** file in your text editor.

2. Directly below the style for the #links selector, enter:

   ```
   #links ul    {list-style-type: none}
   ```

3. Directly below the style for the #pullout h2 selector, enter:

   ```
   #pullout ul {list-style-image: url(bullet.jpg)}
   ```

   Figure 4-10 shows the revised code in the style sheet.

Figure 4-10 ▶ Setting the style of the list marker

```
body          {margin: 0px; color: brown;
               background: white url(back.jpg) repeat-y}
h1, h2, h3 {font-family: Arial, Helvetica, sans-serif; color: orange}
h1           {border-bottom: 2px solid orange; background-color: white; margin: 0px; padding: 0px}
ul           {margin-top:0px}

#outer_container {width: 780px}
#head            {text-align: right}

#links        {float: left; width: 200px}
#links ul     {list-style-type: none}

#article      {margin-left: 200px}

#pullout      {float: right; width: 250px; margin: 0px 0px 10px 10px;
               border: 5px outset orange; background-color: ivory;
               font-size: 10pt; font-family: Arial, Helvetica, sans-serif}
#pullout h2   {text-align: center; background-color: white; margin-top: 0px;
               border-bottom: 2px solid orange}
#pullout ul   {list-style-image: url(bullet.jpg)}

address       {text-align: center; font-style: normal; font-variant: small-caps;
               border-top: 2px solid orange; color: orange}
```

no marker is used with the list

the graphic file bullet.jpg is used for the list marker

▶ **4.** Save your changes to the file, and then refresh **start.htm** in your Web browser. Figure 4-11 shows the revised appearance of the two lists in the document.

Figure 4-11 ▶ Formatted lists

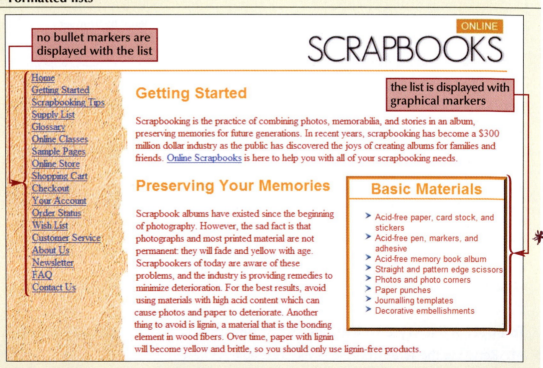

no bullet markers are displayed with the list

the list is displayed with graphical markers

Tip

Web browsers always place bullets to the left of the list text. To create a right-side bullet marker, add a background image containing the marker symbol to each list item, placing the image on the right border of the list element.

The bullet markers have been removed from the list of links and have been replaced by blue arrows in the Basic Materials list.

Defining the List Position and Layout

Kathy likes the revised markers, but she thinks there's too much empty space to the left of the lists. She would like you to modify the layout to remove the extra space. As you learned in Tutorial 1, each list is treated as a block-level element. By default, most browsers place the list marker to the left of this block, lining up the markers with each list item. You can change this default behavior by using the style

```
list-style-position: position
```

where *position* is either "outside" (the default) or "inside." Placing the marker inside of the block causes the list text to flow around the marker. Figure 4-12 shows how the list-style-position affects the appearance of a bulleted list.

Formatted lists　　**Figure　4-12**

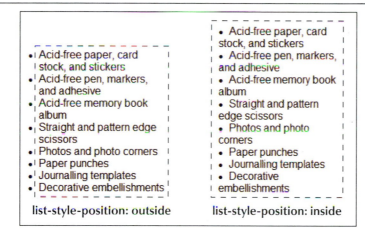

By specifying "inside" for the list-style-position value, you force both the list text and the list marker to be displayed inside of the block. With the addition of the list marker, you will have less space available for the list text.

When a browser renders a list, it offsets the list text a certain distance from the bullet marker. At this time there is no style for specifying the space between the list marker and the list text. The browser also indents the entire list a certain distance from other elements on the page. There is no commonly accepted value for the length that the entire list is indented. Browsers indent lists by setting a value for either the list's left margin or left padding. Firefox indents the list by setting the left padding value, while Opera and Internet Explorer set the size of the left margin. So to have a consistent layout across all browsers, you need to set a value for both the left padding and the left margin.

The internal style sheets for Explorer and Opera set the left margin size to 40 pixels or about 2.5 em and set the left padding space to 0 pixels. Firefox's internal style sheet does the opposite, setting the size of the left margin to 0 pixels and the left padding space to 40 pixels or 2.5 em. So if you want to reduce the indent applied by the browser, you should choose a style that reduces the sum of the left margin and left padding spaces to less than 40 pixels or 2.5 em. Finding the right combination of left padding and left margin values is often a matter of trial and error; you'll have to test your choices under different browsers and different resolutions.

Applying List Styles

- To define appearance of the list marker, use the style
    `list-style-type: type`
  where *type* is disc, circle, square, decimal, decimal-leading-zero, lower-roman, upper-roman, lower-alpha, upper-alpha, or none.
- To insert a graphic image as a list marker, use the style
    `list-style-image: url(url)`
  where *(url)* is the URL of the graphic image file.
- To set the position of the list marker, use the style
    `list-style-position: position`
  where *position* is inside or outside.
- To define all of the list style properties in a single style, use
    `list-style: type url(url) position`

After some work, you decide to indent Kathy's list of links by 15 pixels and the Basic Materials list by 25 pixels. You'll add these styles to the scraps.css external style sheet.

To change the margins and padding for the two lists:

1. Return to the **scraps.css** file in your text editor.

2. Add the following style to the style declaration for the #links ul selector:

   margin-left: 15px; padding-left: 0px

3. Add the following to the style declaration for the #pullout ul selector:

   margin-left: 25px; padding-left: 0px

   Figure 4-13 shows the revised style code.

Figure 4-13 ▸ **Setting the spacing within the lists**

```
#outer_container   {width: 780px}
#head              {text-align: right}

#links             {float: left; width: 200px}
#links ul          {list-style-type: none; margin-left: 15px; padding-left: 0px}

#article           {margin-left: 200px}

#pullout           {float: right; width: 250px; margin: 0px 0px 10px 10px;
                    border: 5px outset orange; background-color: ivory;
                    font-size: 10pt; font-family: Arial, Helvetica, sans-serif}
#pullout h2        {text-align: center; background-color: white; margin-top: 0px;
                    border-bottom: 2px solid orange}
#pullout ul        {list-style-image: url(bullet.jpg); margin-left: 25px; padding-left: 0px}
address            {text-align: center; font-style: normal; font-variant: small-caps;
                    border-top: 2px solid orange; color: orange}
```

4. Save your changes to the file, and then reload or refresh **start.htm** in your Web browser. Verify that both lists moved slightly to the left as a result of the reduced left margin and left padding values in the scraps.css style sheet.

You can combine all of the CSS styles for lists into a single style attribute. The syntax of this combined style is

`list-style: type url(url) position`

where *type* is one of the CSS marker types, *(url)* is the location of a graphic file containing a marker image, and *position* is the position of the list markers relative to the containing box.

Nongraphical browsers use the marker defined by the *type* value, while graphical browsers use the image from the graphic file. For example, the style

```
ul {list-style: circle url(dot.gif) inside}
```

displays unordered lists using the marker stored in the dot.gif file; unless a nongraphical browser is displaying the page, in which case the circle marker is applied. In both cases, the marker will be displayed on the inside of the box surrounding the list.

Working with Classes

The list of links on the Getting Started page covers three main areas: pages that teach scrapbooking, pages that sell products, and pages that provide information about the company. Although Kathy has ordered the links by area, the sections are not separated visually on the rendered page. Kathy suggests that you increase the space between the three groups so it's clear where one group ends and another starts. One method for doing this is to mark the first link in each group, and then to increase the size of the margin above those links. You can mark those links using the class attribute. The class attribute is used when you want to identify elements that share a common characteristic. It has the syntax

```
<elem class="class"> ... </elem>
```

where *elem* is an element in the body of the Web page and *class* is a name that identifies the class of objects to which the element belongs. The HTML code

```
<h2 class="subtitle">Getting Started</h2>
<h2 class="subtitle">Preserving Your Memories</h2>
```

marks both of the h2 headings—Getting Started and Preserving Your Memories—as belonging to the subtitle class. Note that unlike the id attribute, several elements can share the same class value. The class values need not be assigned to the same type of element. You can, for example, also mark h3 headings and address elements as belonging to the subtitle class if it suits your purpose. Also, unlike the id attribute, you can place several class values in a space-separated list in the class attribute. The h2 element

```
<h2 class="subtitle mainpage">Preserving Your Memories</h2>
```

belongs to both the subtitle and the mainpage classes.

The advantage of the class attribute is that you can use it to assign the same style to multiple elements sharing the same class value. The selector for the class attribute is

```
.class {styles}
```

where *class* is the name of the class and *styles* are the styles applied to that class of element. So to display all elements belonging to the subtitle class in a blue font, you could apply the following style:

```
.subtitle {color: blue}
```

Because the same class name can be used with elements of different types, you might need to specify exactly which elements of a particular class receive a defined style. This is done using the selector

```
elem.class {styles}
```

where *elem* is the element and *class* is the class. The style

```
h2.subtitle {color: blue}
```

applies a blue font to elements of the subtitle class, but only if they are h2 headings. You can also use class selectors with other selectors in more complicated expressions. The style

```
blockquote h2.subtitle {color: blue}
```

applies the blue font color only to h2 headings of the subtitle class nested within a blockquote element.

Reference Window | **Applying a Style to an Element Class**

- To assign an element to a class, add the attribute
    ```
    class="class"
    ```
    to the element's markup tag, where *class* is the name of the class.
- To apply a style to a class of elements, use the selector
    ```
    .class
    ```
    where *class* is the name of the class.
- To apply a style to an element of a particular class, use the selector
    ```
    elem.class
    ```
    where *elem* is the name of the element and *class* is the name of the class.

Now that you've seen how to create and apply a style to an element class, you can create a style for the list of links on the Getting Started page. The three links that indicate the start of a new link group are named Home, Online Store, and About Us. You need to mark these as belonging to the newGroup class and then apply a style that increases the top margin of these elements.

To create a style for a class of elements:

1. Go to the **start.htm** file in your text editor.

2. Locate the div element containing the list of links, and then insert the attribute

    ```
    class="newGroup"
    ```

    in the opening <li> tag for the Home, Online Store, and About Us links. See Figure 4-14.

Figure 4-14 | **Inserting the class attribute**

```html
<div id="links">
    <ul>
        <li class="newGroup"><a href="#">Home</a></li>
        <li><a href="#">Getting Started</a></li>
        <li><a href="#">Scrapbooking Tips</a></li>
        <li><a href="#">Supply List</a></li>
        <li><a href="#">Glossary</a></li>
        <li><a href="#">Online Classes</a></li>
        <li><a href="#">Sample Pages</a></li>
        <li class="newGroup"><a href="#">Online Store</a></li>
        <li><a href="#">Shopping Cart</a></li>
        <li><a href="#">Checkout</a></li>
        <li><a href="#">Your Account</a></li>
        <li><a href="#">Order Status</a></li>
        <li><a href="#">Wish List</a></li>
        <li><a href="#">Customer Service</a></li>
        <li class="newGroup"><a href="#">About Us</a></li>
        <li><a href="#">Newsletter</a></li>
        <li><a href="#">FAQ</a></li>
        <li><a href="#">Contact Us</a></li>
    </ul>
</div>
```

3. Save your changes to the file.

    Next you'll go to the style sheet and create a style for the class of newGroup elements.

4. Return to the **scraps.css** file in your text editor. Directly below the style for the #links ul selector, insert the following style:

```
#links li.newGroup {margin-top: 15px}
```

Note that the selector includes both the element name and the class name to make it clear that elements receive the margin-top style. Figure 4-15 shows the revised style code.

Defining a style for the newGroup class ◄ Figure 4-15

```
#links              {float: left; width: 200px}
#links ul           {list-style-type: none; margin-left: 15px; padding-left: 0px}
#links li.newGroup {margin-top: 15px}
```

5. Save your changes to the file and then refresh **start.htm** in your Web browser. As shown in Figure 4-16, the list of links is now divided into three topical areas.

Links list separated into groups ◄ Figure 4-16

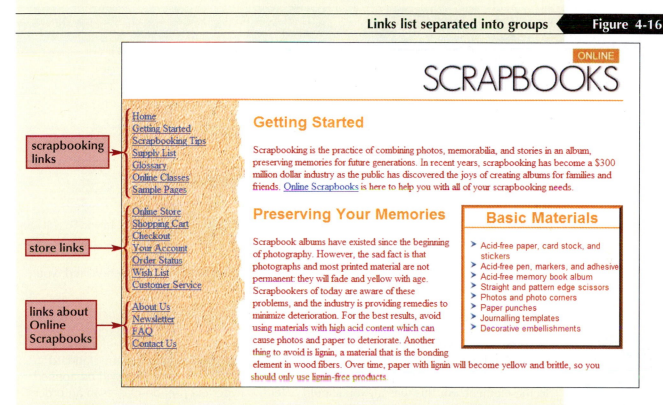

Kathy likes the layout of the list of links. Now she wants to focus on some design elements to enhance the user's interaction with those links.

Using Pseudo-Classes and Pseudo-Elements

Although she realizes that most browsers underline linked text by default, Kathy thinks that a large block of underlined text is difficult to read. She's seen sites in which links are underlined only when the mouse pointer hovers over the linked text. This type of effect is called a **rollover effect** because it is applied only when a user "rolls" the mouse pointer over an element. She would like you to make underlining a rollover effect for the list of links.

Creating a Link Rollover

Rollover effects for links can be created using pseudo-classes. A **pseudo-class** is a classification of an element based on its current status, position, or use in the document. For example, one pseudo-class indicates whether a link has been previously visited by the user. Another pseudo-class indicates whether a link is currently being activated or clicked. To create a style for a pseudo-class, use the style

```
selector:pseudo-class {styles}
```

where *selector* is an element or group of elements within a document, *pseudo-class* is the name of a pseudo-class, and *styles* are the styles you want to apply. Figure 4-17 lists some of the pseudo-classes supported by CSS.

| Figure 4-17 | Pseudo-classes |

Pseudo-class	Description	Example
link	The link has not yet been visited by the user	`a:link {color: red}`
visited	The link has been visited by the user	`a:visited {color: green}`
active	The link is in the process of being activated by the user	`a:active {color: yellow}`
hover	The mouse pointer is hovering over the link	`a:hover {color: blue}`
focus	The element has received the focus of the keyboard or mouse pointer	`input.focus {background-color: yellow}`
first-child	The element is the first child of its parent	`p:first-child {text-indent: 0}`
lang	Specifies the language to be used with the element	`q:lang(FR) {quotes: '<<' '>>'}`

If you want the font color of your links to change to red after they've been visited, you could use the following style declaration:

```
a:visited {color: red}
```

In some cases, two or more pseudo-classes can apply to the same element—for example, a link can be both previously visited and hovered over. In such situations, the standard cascading rules apply: the pseudo-class that is listed last in the style sheet will be applied to the element. For this reason, you should enter the hypertext pseudo-classes in an order that reflects how users interact with hypertext links. The link pseudo-class should come first, followed by the visited class, the hover class, and finally the active class. The link pseudo-class comes first because it represents a hypertext link that has not yet been visited or even clicked by the user. The visited pseudo-class comes next, for the link that has been previously visited or clicked. The hover pseudo-class comes next, for the situation in which the user has once again moved the mouse pointer over the hypertext link before clicking the link. The active pseudo-class is last, representing the exact instant in which the link is clicked by the user.

| Reference Window

Creating a Hypertext Rollover

- To create a rollover for a hypertext link, apply these styles to the link element
  ```
  a:link      {styles}
  a:visited   {styles}
  a:hover     {styles}
  a:active    {styles}
  ```
  where *styles* are the CSS styles applied to hypertext links that have not been visited (link), already visited (visited), have the mouse pointer over them (hover), or are actively being clicked (active).

Kathy wants to remove the underlining from all of the links on her Getting Started page. If the mouse pointer is hovering over a link, however, she wants the link text to appear in a black font and underlined. The style declarations to remove the underlining and to create this rollover effect are:

```
#links a:link {text-decoration: none}
#links a:visited {text-decoration: none}
#links a:hover {color: black; text-decoration: underline}
#links a:active {text-decoration: none}
```

Add these styles now to the scraps.css style sheet.

To create a rollover effect for hypertext links:

1. Return to the **scraps.css** file in your text editor.

2. Directly below the style for the #links li.newGroup selector, insert the following style declarations, as shown in Figure 4-18:

   ```
   #links a:link {text-decoration: none}
   #links a:visited {text-decoration: none}
   #links a:hover {color: black; text-decoration: underline}
   #links a:active {text-decoration: none}
   ```

Using pseudo-classes in a selector ◀ Figure 4-18

```
#links              {float: left; width: 200px}
#links ul           {list-style-type: none; margin-left: 15px; padding-left: 0px}
#links li.newGroup  {margin-top: 15px}
#links a:link       {text-decoration: none}
#links a:visited    {text-decoration: none}
#links a:hover      {color: black; text-decoration: underline}
#links a:active     {text-decoration: none}
```

3. Save your changes to the file, and then refresh the **start.htm** file in your Web browser.

4. Verify that the links in the list of links are no longer underlined (because you have set the text-decoration style to have a value of none).

5. Hover your mouse pointer over a link in the list and verify that when the mouse pointer hovers over the link, it appears in a black font and is underlined. See Figure 4-19.

Figure 4-19 | **Viewing a rollover effect**

ONLINE
SCRAPBOOKS

Home
Getting Started
Scrapbooking Tips
Supply List
Glossary
Online Classes
Sample Pages

Online Store
Shopping Cart
Checkout
Your Account
Order Status
Wish List
Customer Service

About Us
Newsletter
FAQ
Contact Us

Getting Started

Scrapbooking is the practice of combining photos, memorabilia, and stories in an album, preserving memories for future generations. In recent years, scrapbooking has become a $300 million dollar industry as the public has discovered the joys of creating albums for families and friends. Online Scrapbooks is here to help you with all of your scrapbooking needs.

Preserving Your Memories

Scrapbook albums have existed since the beginning of photography. However, the sad fact is that photographs and most printed material are not permanent: they will fade and yellow with age. Scrapbookers of today are aware of these problems, and the industry is providing remedies to minimize deterioration. For the best results, avoid using materials with high acid content which can cause photos and paper to deteriorate. Another thing to avoid is lignin, a material that is the bonding element in wood fibers. Over time, paper with lignin will become yellow and brittle, so you should only use lignin-free products.

Basic Materials

> Acid-free paper, card stock, and stickers
> Acid-free pen, markers, and adhesive
> Acid-free memory book album
> Straight and pattern edge scissors
> Photos and photo corners
> Paper punches
> Journalling templates
> Decorative embellishments

InSight | **Presentational Attributes for Hypertext Links**

Earlier versions of HTML did not include support for the link, visited, and active pseudo-classes. If a Web page author wanted to change the color of a hypertext link, he or she would have to add to the page's <body> tag the attributes

```
<body link="color" vlink="color" alink="color">
```

where the link attribute specifies the color of unvisited links, the vlink attribute specifies the color of visited links, and the alink attribute specifies the color of active links. Colors had to be entered either as a supported color name or as a hexadecimal color value. There is no HTML attribute for creating a rollover effect, so for older browsers you would have to use CSS (if it was supported) or a programming language such as JavaScript to display rollovers.

The link, vlink, and alink attributes have been deprecated and are not supported by strictly compliant XHTML code, but you might still see them used in the code of older Web pages.

Creating a Drop Cap

Kathy has a few more formatting changes she would like you to make to the Getting Started page. She wants you to add the following effects to the first paragraph on the page:

• The first line should be displayed in a small caps style.
• The first letter should be increased in size and displayed as a drop cap.

So far all of our selectors have been based on elements that exist somewhere in the document hierarchy. We can also define selectors based on **pseudo-elements** that are not part of the document tree, but instead are abstracted from what we know of an element's content, use, or position in the document. For example, a paragraph element is part of the document tree and is marked with the <p> tag, but the first line of that paragraph is not—there is no "first line" element even though people intuitively know what page content corresponds to the paragraph's first line. CSS's support for pseudo-elements enables you to create styles for objects such as a paragraph's first line.

The selector for a pseudo-element is similar to what we use for a pseudo-class. The syntax of the pseudo-element selector is

```
selector:pseudo-element {styles}
```

where *selector* is an element or group of elements within the document, *pseudo-element* is an abstract element based on the selector, and *styles* are the styles that you want to apply to the pseudo-element. Figure 4-20 lists some of the pseudo-elements supported by CSS.

Pseudo-elements   Figure 4-20

Pseudo-element	Description	Example
first-letter	The first letter of the element text	`p:first-letter {font-size:14pt}`
first-line	The first line of the element text	`p:first-line {text-transform: uppercase}`
before	Content inserted directly before the element	`p:before {content:"Special!"}`
after	Content appended to the element	`p:after {content:"eof"}`

For example, to display the first letter of every paragraph in a gold fantasy font, you could apply the following style:

```
p:first-letter {font-family: fantasy; color: gold}
```

The advantage of this pseudo-element is that you don't have to mark the first letter in the HTML document; its position is inferred by the browser when it applies the style.

A pseudo-element is also useful for a design element such as a drop cap. To create a drop cap, you increase the font size of an element's first letter and float it on the left margin. Drop caps also generally look better if you decrease the line height of the first letter, enabling the surrounding content to better wrap around the letter. Finding the best combination of font size and line height is a matter of trial and error; and unfortunately what looks best in one browser might not look as good in another. After trying out several combinations for the Getting Started page, you settle on a drop cap that is 400% the size of the surrounding text, with a line height of 0.8. The following style will create this effect:

```
p:first-letter {float: left; font-size: 400%; line-height: 0.8}
```

However, Kathy only wants to apply this style to the first paragraph on each page. The first paragraph on the Getting Started page has already been given the id value firstp, so the style declaration becomes

Tip

Older browsers might not support the first-letter pseudo-element. If you still want to create a drop cap for those browsers, mark the first letter with a span element and apply your style to that element.

```
#firstp:first-letter {float: left; font-size: 400%; line-height: 0.8}
```

Because Kathy also wants the first line of that paragraph to be displayed in small caps, you will also use the first-line pseudo-element in the following style:

```
#firstp:first-line {font-variant: small-caps}
```

Add both of these styles to the scraps.css style sheet.

To create the drop cap effect:

1. Return to the **scraps.css** file in your text editor.

2. Directly above the style for the #article selector, insert the following two styles involving the first-letter and first-line pseudo-elements. See Figure 4-21:

   ```
   #firstp:first-line {font-variant: small-caps}
   #firstp:first-letter {float: left; font-size: 400%; line-height: 0.8}
   ```

Figure 4-21	Specifying a style for the first-line and first-letter pseudo-elements

```
#firstp:first-line    {font-variant: small-caps}
#firstp:first-letter {float: left; font-size: 400%; line-height: 0.8}

#article              {margin-left: 200px}
```

3. Close the **scraps.css** file, saving your changes, and then refresh the **start.htm** file in your Web browser. Figure 4-22 shows the final layout of the Getting Started page.

Figure 4-22	Final appearance of the Getting Started page

4. If you want to take a break before starting the next session, close any open files or programs now.

Generating Text with Pseudo-Elements

You can use CSS to insert text into your Web page using the before and after pseudo-elements. The before pseudo-element places text directly before the element, while the after pseudo-element placed the text directly after the element. The syntax of both pseudo-elements is

```
selector:before {content: "text"}
selector:after {content: "text"}
```

where *selector* is an element to which you want to add the *text* string. For example, the style

```
em:after {content: " !"}
```

appends an exclamation point to the end of every element marked with a <em> tag. You can use the before and after pseudo-elements in conjunction with other pseudo-elements and pseudo-classes. The code

```
a:hover:before {content: "<"}
a:hover:after {content: ">"}
```

creates a rollover effect in which the < and > characters are placed around a hypertext link when a mouse pointer hovers over the link.

The content value must be entered as a text string, and you cannot use the content property to insert HTML code. The browser displays the HTML code rather than the element the code represents. For example, if you apply the style

```
em:after {content: "<b>!</b>"}
```

the browser displays the text of opening and closing <b> tags in addition to the exclamation point. Although you cannot insert an HTML element, you can insert an HTML attribute. This is useful because attribute values are usually not displayed on the Web page, but you can automatically insert an attribute value using the attr property

```
content: attr(attribute)
```

where *attribute* is an attribute of the element. For example, the following style appends every hypertext link with the link's URL (as stored in the href attribute):

```
a:after {content attr(" [" attr(href) "] ")}
```

Note that in this example, the href attribute will be enclosed within a set of opening and closing square brackets [.]. This makes your text easy to read by using spaces or brackets to offset the generated content from its surrounding text.

Using the before and after pseudo-elements, you can create truly dynamic Web pages whose content can change based on the styles stored in different style sheets. Internet Explorer does not support the before and after pseudo-elements unless your code puts the IE browser in standards mode. You will not need to use the before and after pseudo-elements in Kathy's Web site.

Kathy is pleased with the work you've done adding special effects to the Getting Started page. She feels that the use of the first-letter and first-line pseudo-elements to create the drop cap effect added a great deal to the appearance of the page. She's also pleased with your work on the rollover effect in the list of links and the graphic image used in the Basic Materials list. In the next session, you'll expand your understanding of CSS by using the styles to directly position elements on the rendered Web page.

| Review | | **Session 4.1 Quick Check** |

1. Specify the style to italicize the content of all span elements nested within paragraphs.
2. Specify the style to italicize the content of all span elements that are direct children of paragraph elements.
3. Specify the style to italicize all h2 headings that directly follow h1 headings.
4. Specify a style to display all elements that belong to the newsAlert class in boldface text.
5. Specify a style to display only span elements belonging to the newsAlert class in boldface text.
6. Specify a style in which every hypertext link is displayed with a yellow background when the mouse pointer hovers over the link.
7. Specify a style in which hovering over a hypertext link causes the Web browser to change the link's background image to the graphic file hover.jpg.
8. Specify a style that displays the first letter of every block quote in a red font.
9. Specify a style that displays the first line of every block quote in a red font.

Session 4.2

Positioning Objects with CSS

One purpose of the Online Scrapbooks Web site is to teach new scrapbookers how to create beautiful and interesting pages. Every month Kathy wants to highlight a scrapbook page that displays some noteworthy features. Figure 4-23 shows the current Samples page. (Note that because of the scraps.css style sheet, this page uses the same layout as the other pages in the Web site.) The scrapbooking sample is displayed in the main section of the document.

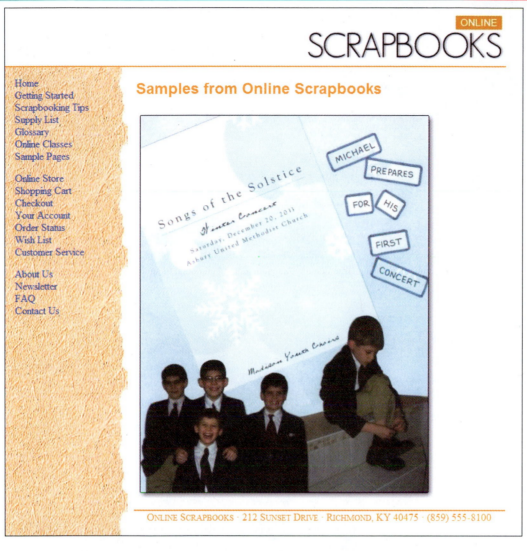

Kathy wants to augment the page by inserting callouts that highlight certain portions of the scrapbooking sample for the reader. She wants each callout to be placed close to the feature that it highlights. Kathy has drawn in the locations of the three callouts that she wants to add in the sketch shown in Figure 4-24.

| Figure 4-24 | Sketch of the Samples page |

Figure 4-25 shows the text of the three callout notes.

| Figure 4-25 | Text of the three callout notes |

Note	Text
note 1	Paste cut-out letters and words in your scrapbook to create a 3D effect. Online Scrapbooks sells professionally designed cut-out letters, words, and phrases for all occasions.
note 2	Clippings, flyers, programs, and other memorabilia are valuable sources of information that can enhance your scrapbook pages. Make sure that any material is copied to acid-free paper. Newspaper clippings are especially susceptible to deterioration.
note 3	Photographic cut-outs and textured backgrounds can add visual interest to your pages. See the online store for our wide variety of textured and embossed papers.

You'll insert each of these notes in div containers placed within the main section of the page. You'll set the id values of the three elements to note1, note2, and note3, respectively, and you'll add the class value notes to each element so that you can apply a common set of styles to all of the notes.

To insert the three notes:

1. Use your text editor to open the **samptxt.htm** from the tutorial.04\tutorial folder included with your Data Files. Enter *your name* and *the date* in the comment section of the file and save it as **samples.htm** in the same folder.

2. Directly below the h2 heading, Samples from Online Scrapbooks, insert the following div container elements, as shown in Figure 4-26:

```
<div id="note1" class="notes">
    <p>Paste cut-out letters and words in your scrapbook to create
    a 3D effect. Online Scrapbooks sells professionally  designed
    cut-out letters, words, and phrases for all occasions.</p>
</div>
<div id="note2" class="notes">
    <p>Clippings, flyers, programs, and other memorabilia are valuable
    sources of information that can enhance your scrapbook pages.
    Make sure that any material is copied to acid-free paper.
    Newspaper clippings are especially susceptible to deterioration.
    </p>
</div>
<div id="note3" class="notes">
    <p>Photographic cut-outs and textured backgrounds can add
    visual interest to your pages. See the online store for our
    wide variety of textured and embossed papers.</p>
</div>
```

Inserting text for the three notes ◀ **Figure 4-26**

```
<div id="article">
    <h2>Samples from Online Scrapbooks</h2>

    <div id="note1" class="notes">
        <p>Paste cut-out letters and words in your scrapbook to create
        a 3D effect. Online Scrapbooks sells professionally
        designed cut-out letters, words, and phrases for all occasions.</p>
    </div>
    <div id="note2" class="notes">
        <p>Clippings, flyers, programs, and other memorabilia are valuable
        sources of information that can enhance your scrapbook pages.
        Make sure that any material is copied to acid-free paper.
        Newspaper clippings are especially susceptible to deterioration.</p>
    </div>
    <div id="note3" class="notes">
        <p>Photographic cut-outs and textured backgrounds can add visual
        interest to your pages. See the online store for our wide
        variety of textured and embossed papers.</p>
    </div>

    <div id="sample_image">
        <img src="sample.jpg" alt="sample page" width="474" height="616" />
    </div>
```

Because the styles in this task will apply only to this page and no others in Kathy's Web site, you'll add an embedded style sheet to the samples.htm file to format the appearance of the three notes. Kathy wants the text to appear in a brown 8-point sans-serif font on an ivory background. She wants the note boxes to be displayed with a 3-pixel light gray inset border. The notes should be 130 pixels wide with a margin space of 5 pixels around the paragraphs.

To define a style for the three notes:

1. Scroll to the top of the samples.htm file.

2. Directly below the link element, insert the following embedded style sheet as shown in Figure 4-27:

```
<style type="text/css">
 .notes  {font-family: sans-serif; font-size: 8pt; color: brown;
         background-color: ivory;
         border: 3px inset rgb(212, 212, 212); width: 130px}
.notes p {margin: 5px}
</style>
```

Figure 4-27	Setting the styles for the notes text

```
<title>Samples from Online Scrapbooks</title>
<link href="scraps.css" rel="stylesheet" type="text/css" />
<style type="text/css">
    .notes  {font-family: sans-serif; font-size: 8pt; color: brown;
             background-color: ivory; border: 3px inset rgb(212, 212, 212);
             width: 130px}
    .notes p {margin: 5px}
    </style>
</head>
```

3. Save your changes to the file.

4. Open the **samples.htm** file in your Web browser. Figure 4-28 shows the formatted appearance of the three note boxes. Note that although the boxes are placed side-by-side in this figure to make them easier to read, they should be stacked one on top of the other at the top of your Web page.

Figure 4-28	Formatted note boxes

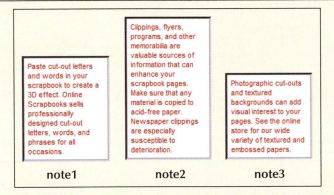

Trouble? Depending on your browser, your note boxes may look slightly different than those shown in Figure 4-28.

Now that you've entered the text and the formatting styles for the three callout notes, your next task is to position them at appropriate locations on the Samples page.

The Position Style

Positioning was one of the first enhancements to the original CSS1 specifications. Collectively, the various positioning styles were known as **CSS-Positioning**, or more commonly, **CSS-P**. CSS-P became part of the specification for CSS2, and positioning styles were some of the first CSS2 styles to be adopted by browsers.

To place an element at a specific position on the page, use the styles

```
position: type; top: value; right: value; bottom: value; left: value;
```

where *type* indicates the type of positioning applied to the element, and the top, right, bottom, and left styles indicate the coordinates of the top, right, bottom, and left edges of the element. In practice, usually only the left and top coordinates are used because the right and bottom coordinates can be inferred given the element's height and width. Coordinates can be expressed in any of the CSS measuring units.

The position style has five possible values: static, absolute, relative, fixed, and inherit. The default position is static, which enables browsers to place an element based on where it flows in the document. This is essentially the same as not using any CSS positioning at all. Any values specified for the left or top styles with a static position are ignored by the browser. You'll explore each of the other values (absolute, relative, fixed, and inherit) so that you can use them to position the notes on Kathy's Sample Pages page.

Absolute Positioning

Absolute positioning enables you to place an element at specific coordinates either on a page or within a containing element. For example, the declaration

```
position: absolute; left: 100px; top: 50px
```

places an element at the coordinates (100, 50), or 100 pixels to the right and 50 pixels down from upper-left corner of the page or the containing element. Once an element has been placed using absolute positioning, it affects the placement of other objects on the Web page. To explore how absolute positioning affects page layout, you'll use a demo containing objects that can be positioned on the Web page.

To explore absolute positioning:

1. Use your Web browser to open the **demo_positioning.htm** file from the tutorial.04\demo folder included with your Data Files.

   The demo page contains two colored boxes that you can move by changing the values in the Positioning Styles box. The boxes are initially set to their default position, which is within the flow of the other elements on the demo page. To make it easier to place the boxes at specific positions, a grid marked in pixels has been added to the page background.

2. Select **absolute** from the list box for the outer box, and then press the **Tab** key.

3. Enter **275** in the left box, and then press the **Tab** key. Enter **350** in the top box, and then press the **Tab** key again. As shown in Figure 4-29, the red outer box is placed at the page coordinates (275, 350).

Figure 4-29 **Viewing absolute positioning**

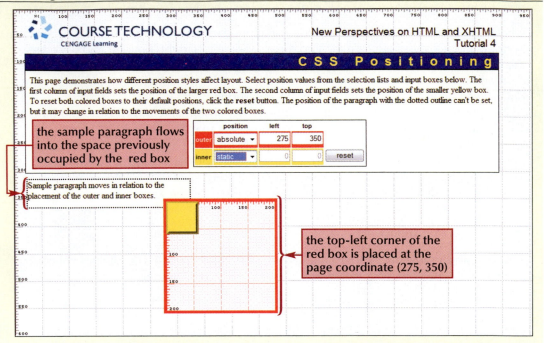

Absolute positioning takes an element out of the normal flow of a document, so that any subsequent content flows into the space previously occupied by the element. Note that on the demo page, the sample paragraph moves up into the space that was previously occupied by the red outer box.

When elements are nested within one another, the position of the element is based on the coordinates within the parent object if that object is itself placed on the page using a CSS positioning style. If the parent object is not positioned using a CSS style, then the position of the nested object is set within the next object higher up in the hierarchy of elements positioned on the page. If no other objects are positioned on the page, the top and left coordinates are based on the browser window. To see this effect, return to the demo page.

To view absolute positioning with a nested object:

1. Within the demo page, select **absolute** from the list box for the inner element.

2. Enter **90** in the left box for the inner object and **75** for the top box. As shown in Figure 4-30, the inner yellow box is placed at the (90, 75) coordinate within the outer box, not within the Web page.

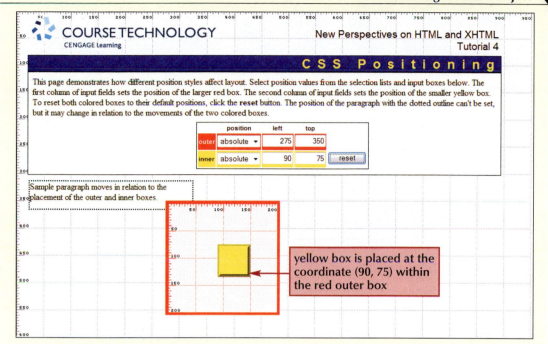

Now examine what occurs when the outer box is no longer placed on the Web page using a positioning style.

3. Select **static** from the list box for the outer element.

   As shown in Figure 4-31, the red outer box is returned to its default position on the Web page. The yellow inner box is now placed at the coordinate (90, 75), but within the Web page.

Absolute positioning within a nonpositioned element | Figure 4-31

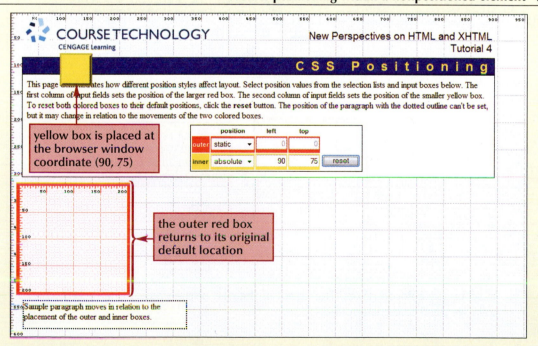

Tip

You can enter negative values for the top and left styles to move page elements up and to the left from their default locations.

▶ **4.** Continue experimenting with the demo page by entering values for the top and left coordinates and observing the effect on the placement of the boxes.

Relative Positioning

Relative positioning is used to move an element relative to its default position on the page. An element's default position is where the browser would have placed it if no positioning style was applied to it. For example, the style

```
position: relative; left: 100px; top: 50px
```

places an element 100 pixels to the right and 50 pixels down from its normal placement in a browser window. Relative positioning does not affect the position of other elements on a page, which retain their original positions as if the element had never been moved. You'll use the demo page to experiment with this.

To explore relative positioning:

▶ **1.** Click the **reset** button within the demo page to return both boxes to their default locations on the Web page.

▶ **2.** Select **relative** from the list box for the outer element, and then enter **275** for the left value and **50** for the top value. As shown in Figure 4-32, the outer box moves 275 pixels to the right and 50 pixels down from its default location.

Figure 4-32 ▶ **Relative positioning**

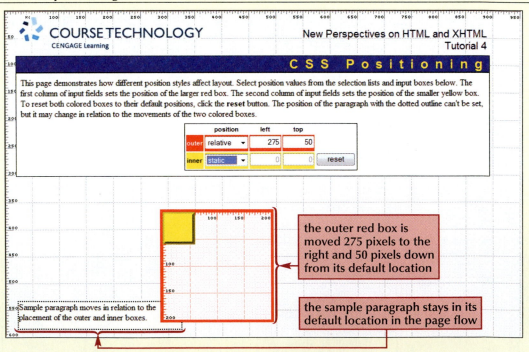

Also note that the sample paragraph does not flow into the space previously occupied by the colored boxes. The layout of the rest of the page is unaffected when relative positioning is applied.

▶ **3.** Explore other combinations of absolute and relative positioning to see their effect on the layout of the demo page.

In many Web page layouts, you might want to position any object nested within a div container, but you don't need to move the container itself. In those cases, use relative positioning to place the div container with the top and left values set to 0 pixels. The position you apply to the nested object will then be based on coordinates within the div container object.

Fixed and Inherited Positioning

An element placed with absolute or relative positioning scrolls with the rest of the document. Alternately, you can fix an element at a specific spot in the document window while the rest of the page scrolls by setting the value of the position style to fixed. Note that not all browsers support the fixed position, so you should use it with some caution if it is a crucial part of your Web page layout.

You can also assign the inherit position style to an element so that it inherits the position value of its parent element. You'll explore both positioning styles on the demo page.

To explore fixed and inherited positioning:

▶ **1.** Click the **reset** button within the demo page to return both boxes to their default locations on the Web page.

▶ **2.** Select **fixed** from the list box for the outer element, and then enter **300** for the left and top values.

The red box is placed at the window coordinates (300, 300). The sample paragraph moves up into the space previously occupied by the red box.

Trouble? If you are running an older browser, you might not see any change in the position of the red box.

▶ **3.** Select **inherit** from the list box for the inner element, and then enter **600** for the left value and **300** for the top value.

The yellow box inherits the position style of its parent. In this case it uses fixed positioning and is placed to the right of the outer red box. See Figure 4-33.

Figure 4-33 ▶ **Fixed and inherited positioning**

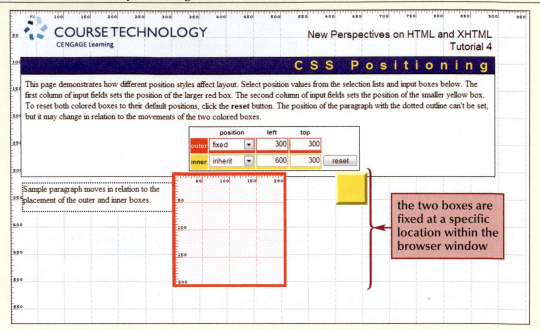

Trouble? Internet Explorer does not support the inherit position style at the time of this writing. To fix the position of the inner box, you have to choose fixed drop in the list box.

▶ 4. Resize the browser window so it's small enough to force the browser to display the vertical and horizontal scroll bars. Scroll through the document and verify that the two color boxes remain fixed at the same location within the window.

▶ 5. Continue to experiment with different positioning combinations. Close the demo page when you're finished.

Reference Window | **Positioning an Object with CSS**

- To position an object at a specific coordinate, use the style
  ```
  position: type; top: value; right: value; bottom: value;
                  left: value;
  ```
  where *type* indicates the type of positioning applied to the object (absolute, relative, static, fixed, or inherit) and the top, right, bottom, and left styles indicate the coordinates of the object.

Now that you've seen how to work with the different positioning styles of CSS, you can apply your knowledge to position the three callout notes. After trying different values, you and Kathy settle on the following coordinates using absolute positioning:

```
note1: (600, 120)
note2: (170, 400)
note3: (570, 550)
```

You'll add styles for these positions to the embedded style sheet in the samples.htm file.

To position the three notes for the Samples page:

▶ **1.** Return to the **samples.htm** file in your text editor.

▶ **2.** Add the following styles to the embedded style sheet, as shown in Figure 4-34:

```
#note1 {position: absolute; left: 600px; top: 120px}
#note2 {position: absolute; left: 170px; top: 400px}
#note3 {position: absolute; left: 570px; top: 550px}
```

Setting the position of the three note boxes | Figure 4-34

```
<style type="text/css">
    .notes    {font-family: sans-serif; font-size: 8pt; color: brown;
               background-color: ivory; border: 3px inset rgb(212, 212, 212);
               width: 130px}
    .notes p {margin: 5px}
    #note1    {position: absolute; left: 600px; top: 120px}
    #note2    {position: absolute; left: 170px; top: 400px}
    #note3    {position: absolute; left: 570px; top: 550px}
</style>
```

▶ **3.** Save your changes, and then reload the **samples.htm** file in your Web browser. Figure 4-35 shows the placement of the three sample notes.

Notes placed with absolute positioning | Figure 4-35

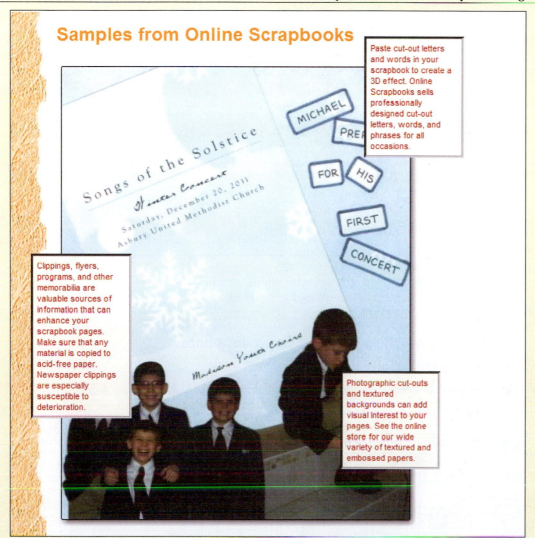

You show Kathy the revised page. She likes the position of the notes, but she points out that they are pretty big and they hide too much of the scrapbooking sample. Kathy would like you to investigate ways of making the notes less intrusive.

Working with Overflow and Clipping

Reducing the height of each note by lowering the value of its height attribute might seem like an easy solution to Kathy's first request. Unfortunately, though, this would not meet her needs because the height of each note expands to accommodate its content. If you want to force an element into a specified height and width, you have to define how the browser should handle a situation where content overflows the space allotted to the object. The syntax of the overflow style is

```
overflow: type
```

where *type* is visible (the default), hidden, scroll, or auto. A value of visible instructs browsers to increase the height of an element to fit the overflow content. The hidden value keeps an element at the specified height and width, but cuts off excess text. The scroll value keeps an element at the specified dimensions, but adds horizontal and vertical scroll bars to allow users to scroll through the overflow. Finally, the auto value keeps an element at the specified size, adding scroll bars only as they are needed. Figure 4-36 shows examples of the effect of each overflow value.

| Figure 4-36 | Values of the overflow style |

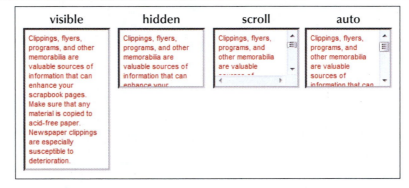

You decide to limit the height of each callout note to 90 pixels and have the browser display scroll bars as needed by setting the value of the overflow style to auto.

To define the overflow style for the callout notes:

1. Return to the **samples.htm** file in your text editor.

2. Add the following styles to the .notes selector, as shown in Figure 4-37:

   ```
   height: 90px; overflow: auto
   ```

| Figure 4-37 | Setting the overflow style for the notes |

```
<style type="text/css">
    .notes    {font-family: sans-serif; font-size: 8pt; color: brown;
               background-color: ivory; border: 3px inset rgb(212, 212, 212);
               width: 130px; height: 90px; overflow: auto}
    .notes p  {margin: 5px}
    #note1    {position: absolute; left: 600px; top: 120px}
    #note2    {position: absolute; left: 170px; top: 400px}
    #note3    {position: absolute; left: 570px; top: 550px}
</style>
```

3. Save your changes, and then refresh the **samples.htm** file in your Web browser. Figure 4-38 shows the appearance of the three callout notes with heights limited to 90 pixels and scroll bars added.

Notes with scroll bars ◄ Figure 4-38

4. Use the scroll bars to verify that the entire content of each note is still available to the user.

   Trouble? Depending on your browser, you might not see scrollbars around each note box.

5. If you want to take a break before starting the next session, you can close any open files or programs now.

Clipping an Element

Closely related to the overflow style is the clip style. The clip style allows you to define a rectangular region through which the element's content can be viewed. Anything that lies outside the boundary of the rectangle is hidden. The syntax of the clip style is

```
clip: rect(top, right, bottom, left)
```

where *top*, *right*, *bottom*, and *left* define the coordinates of the clipping rectangle. For example, a clip value of rect(10, 175, 125, 75) defines a clip region whose top and bottom edges are 10 and 125 pixels from the top of the element, and whose right and left edges are 175 and 75 pixels from the left side of the element. See Figure 4-39.

Figure 4-39   **Clipping an element**

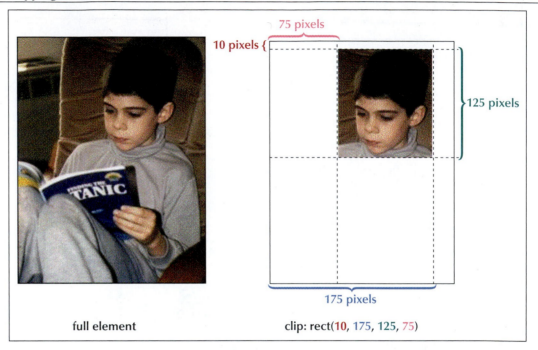

full element   clip: rect(10, 175, 125, 75)

The *top*, *right*, *bottom*, and *left* values can also be set to auto, which matches the specified edge of the clipping region to the edge of the parent element. For example, a clip value of rect(10, auto, 125, 75) creates a clipping rectangle whose right edge matches the right edge of the parent element.

Limiting Width and Height

In some page layouts, you might want to limit an element's height or width. This is often desirable when you've specified the element's size using relative units that can expand or contract depending on the size of the browser window. If the browser window is very wide, the element might become too wide to be easily readable. If the browser window is too narrow, the element might be reduced to a size that is also difficult to view. Rather than allowing these problems to occur, you can specify an element's minimum or maximum height or width using the styles

```
min-width: value
min-height: value
max-width: value
max-height: value
```

where *value* is the width or height value in one of the CSS units of measure. The min and max values are usually used alongside the height and width styles to set a possible range of values for an element. For example, the style declaration

```
div {width: 80%; min-width: 200px; max-width: 700px}
```

sets the width of the div element to 80% of the Web browser window. If the browser window is 800 pixels wide, the div element will be 640 pixels wide. However, browser windows can vary in size and many users will resize their browser windows to free up desktop space. In that case, the size of the div element will vary accordingly, but it will never be allowed to get smaller than 200 pixels or larger than 700 pixels. Using the min and max styles enables the Web page designer to have some control over the page layout and avoid problems caused by either very large or very small windows.

Max-Width and Internet Explorer | InSight

As mentioned in Tutorial 3, usability studies have shown that most users are comfortable reading text that extends no more than 60 to 70 characters per line or about 30 em. Beyond this length, reading comprehension goes down rapidly and eye fatigue increases. To deal with this problem, Web page designers often use the max-width style to ensure that their Web pages are not too wide on large monitors or screens set to high resolutions.

Internet Explorer did not fully support maximum widths until IE 7. For browser versions earlier than IE7, Web page authors have had to adopt workarounds to approximate the effect of the max-width style. One popular approach, offered by Svend Tofte, is to use a CSS command introduced and supported by Internet Explorer to automatically size the width of an element based on the width of the browser window. For example, the following set of styles defines a maximum width of 800 pixels for an object:

```
max-width:800px;
width:expression(document.body.clientWidth > 800? "800px":
"auto" );
```

In this code, browsers that support maximum widths use the max-width style in the first line to set the maximum width of the object to 800 pixels. Those browsers then ignore the next line and continue on to the rest of the style sheet. Internet Explorer on the other hand, ignores the max-width style in the first line and goes directly to the second line. The second line contains a command that tests whether the browser window is wider than 800 pixels. If it is, it sets the width of the object to 800 pixels. If the browser window is not wider than 800 pixels, the object will be automatically sized by the browser to fit into whatever space is available. The result is that the object will have a maximum width under both IE and browsers that support the max-width style.

This particular workaround can be adapted for different widths and different units of measure. For more information, you can view Svend Tofte's work at *www.svendtofte.com/ code/max_width_in_ie/* or do a Web search for IE workarounds to the max-width problem. As always, you should test any code to ensure that it works with a variety of browsers and operating systems.

Stacking Elements

Positioning elements can sometimes lead to objects that overlap each other. By default, elements that are formatted later in an HTML or XHTML document are stacked on top of earlier elements. In addition, elements placed using CSS positioning are stacked on top of elements that are not. To specify a different stacking order, use the style

z-index: *value*

where *value* is a positive or negative integer or the keyword "auto." As shown in Figure 4-40, objects are stacked based on their z-index values, with the highest z-index values placed on top. A value of auto allows the browser to determine stacking order using the default rules.

Figure 4-40 ▶ **Using the z-index style to stack elements**

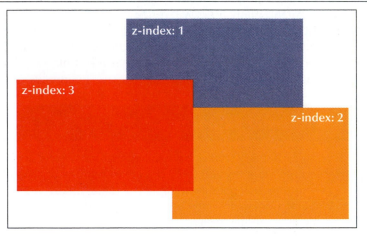

The z-index style only works for elements that are placed with absolute positioning. Also, an element's z-index value determines its position relative only to other elements that share a common parent; the style has no impact when applied to elements with different parents. Figure 4-41 shows a diagram in which the object with a high z-index value of 4 is still covered because it is nested within another object that has a low z-index value of 1.

Figure 4-41 ▶ **Nesting z-index values**

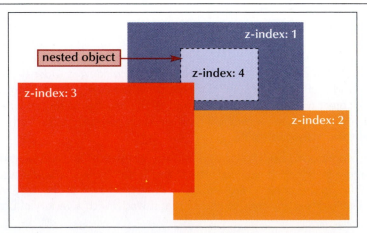

Kathy is pleased with how the notes are positioned over the scrapbooking sample, so you don't need to use the clip or z-index styles. The page looks good on computer monitors. In the next session, you'll explore styles to make your Web pages ready for print media and portable devices.

Session 4.2 Quick Check | Review

1. Specify the style to place an element with the id named logo at the coordinates (150, 75) using absolute positioning.
2. Specify a style to place the logo element 25% down from the top of the page and 10% to the right.
3. What is the style to move span elements belonging to the class highlight up 10 pixels?
4. Specify a style that moves all link elements 5 pixels down when the mouse pointer hovers over them.
5. What is the style to fix an element with the links id at the browser window coordinates (10, 50)?
6. Specify a style to set the width of all block quotes to 70% of the browser window width with a minimum width of 250 pixels and a maximum width of 650 pixels.
7. Specify a style to set the height of all block quotes to 25% of the browser window height. If the content of the block quote cannot fit within this space, include a style to add scroll bars to the block quote as needed.
8. The #title element has a z-index of 1. The #subtitle has a z-index of 5. Will the #subtitle element always be displayed on top of the #title element? Explain why or why not.

Session 4.3

Working with Different Media

Many users of the Online Scrapbooks Web site have reported to Kathy that they enjoy the monthly Samples page so much that they print the samples and store them for future reference. However, these users often find that the pages don't print well. Most users would prefer to print only the scrapbook sample, without the Online Scrapbooks header, links list, and footer. Also, they enjoy the notes that Kathy adds to the sample page, but they would like those notes to be printed on a separate page from the scrapbook sample. In Figure 4-42, Kathy has sketched the design she envisions for the printed version of the Samples page.

Figure 4-42 ▶ **Kathy's proposed printed output**

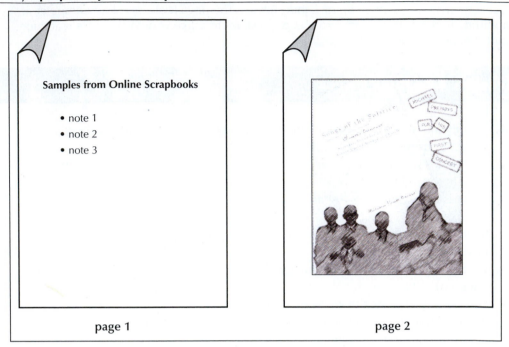

One solution to Kathy's problem would be to create two versions of the Samples page: one for computer screens and the other for printouts. However, Kathy would like to avoid having multiple versions of the same file on her Web site. She would much prefer having a separate style sheet: one that is designed for printed output. She would like you to examine how to create style sheets that are designed for specific devices such as a printer.

Media Types

By default, a style sheet is applied to all devices, and each device must determine how best to match the styles to its own requirements. For example, when you print a Web page, the Web browser and its built-in styles prepare the document for the printer. The user also has some control over that process—for example, determining the size of the page margins or the content of the printout's header or footer. However, beyond that, the user cannot control how the page is printed.

CSS2 and subsequent versions have given more control to Web page authors to specify output styles for particular devices. To do that, you use the media attribute to specify an output device in either the style element (for embedded style sheets) or in the link element (for external style sheets). The syntax of the media attribute is

```
<style type="text/css" media="type">
   ...
</style>
```

or

```
<link href="url" type="text/css" media="type" ... />
```

where *type* is the type of media used by the style sheet. Figure 4-43 lists the different values of the media attribute.

Value	Used for
all	All output devices (the default)
aural	Speech and sound synthesizers
braille	Braille tactile feedback devices
embossed	Paged Braille printers
handheld	Small or handheld devices with small screens, monochrome graphics, and limited bandwidth
print	Printers
projection	Projectors
screen	Computer screens
tty	Fixed-width devices like teletype machines and terminals
tv	Television-type devices with low resolution, color, and limited scrollability

For example, to specify that aural browsers should render your Web page using the sounds.css style sheet, you would enter the following link element in the HTML file:

```
<link href="sounds.css" type="text/css" media="aural" />
```

In the same way, you would use the following media attribute in an embedded style sheet to indicate that its styles are intended for aural devices:

```
<style type="text/css" media="aural">
    ...
</style>
```

The media attribute can also contain a comma-separated list of media types. The following link element points to a style sheet designed for both print and screen media:

```
<link href="output.css" type="text/css" media="print, screen" />
```

Style sheets cascade through the media types in the same way they cascade through a document tree. A style sheet in which the output device is not specified is applied to all devices, unless it is superseded by a style designed for a particular device. In the following set of embedded style sheets, h1 headings are displayed in a sans-serif font for all devices; however, the text color is red for computer screens and black for printed pages:

```
<style type="text/css">
    h1 {font-family: sans-serif}
</style>
<style type="text/css" media="screen">
    h1 {color: red}
</style>
<style type="text/css" media="print">
    h1 {color: black}
</style>
```

When no value is given to the media attribute, any style defined in the embedded or external style sheet is used for all media, where applicable.

The @media Rule

It's not always convenient to maintain several different style sheets for the same document. In place of several style sheets, you can use a single style sheet broken down into different sections for each media type. This is done using the rule

```
@media type {
   styles declarations
}
```

where *type* is one of the supported media types and *style declarations* are style declarations associated with that media type. For example, the following style sheet is broken into four sections with a different collection of styles for screen, print, handheld, and television media:

```
@media screen   { body {font-size: 1em}  h1 {font-size: 2em}  }
@media print    { body {font-size: 12pt} h1 {font-size: 16pt} }
@media handheld { body {font-size: 8pt}  h1 {font-size: 12pt} }
@media tv       { body {font-size: 16pt} h1 {font-size: 24pt} }
```

In this style sheet, the font size is smallest for a handheld device (which presumably has a limited screen area), and largest for a television (which is usually viewed from a greater distance). Similar to the media attribute, the @media rule also allows you to place media types in a comma-separated list, as in the following declaration:

```
@media screen, print, handheld, tv {
   h1 {font-family: sans-serif}
}
```

Both the media attribute and the @media rule come with their own benefits and disadvantages. The @media rule enables you to consolidate all of your styles within a single style sheet; however, this consolidation can result in larger and complicated files. The alternative—placing media styles in different sheets—can make those sheets easier to maintain; however, if you change the design of your site, you might have to duplicate your changes across several style sheets.

Media Groups

The distinction among the different media types is not always immediately clear. For example, how is projection media different from screen media? The difference lies in what kind of output can be sent to the media. All output media can be described based on some common properties. CSS uses **media groups** to describe how different media devices render content. There are four media groups based on the following characteristics:

- continuous or paged
- visual, aural, or tactile
- grid (for character grid devices) or bitmap
- interactive (for devices that allow user interaction) or static (for devices that allow no interaction)

Figure 4-44 shows how all output media are categorized based on the four media groups. For example, a printout is paged (because the output comes in discrete units or pages), visual, bitmap, and static (you can't interact with it). A computer screen, on the other hand, is continuous, visual, bitmap, and can be either static or interactive.

Media type	continuous/ paged	visual/aural/ tactile	grid/bitmap	interactive/ static
aural	continuous	aural	N/A	both
braille	continuous	tactile	grid	both
embossed	paged	tactile	grid	both
handheld	both	visual	both	both
print	paged	visual	bitmap	static
projection	paged	visual	bitmap	static
screen	continuous	visual	bitmap	both
tty	continuous	visual	grid	both
tv	both	visual, aural	bitmap	both

Media groups are important because the CSS2 specifications indicate which media *group* a particular style belongs to, rather than the specific media *device*. For example, the font-size style belongs to the visual media group because it describes the visual appearance of the document content; and as indicated in Figure 4-44, this means you can use the font-size style with handheld, print, projection, screen, tty, and tv media. However, it would have no meaning to—and will in fact be ignored by—devices whose output consists of Braille or aural communication. On the other hand, the pitch style, used to define the pitch or frequency of a speaking voice, belongs to the aural media group and is supported by aural and tv devices. By studying the media groups, you can choose the styles that apply to a given output device.

Creating Styles for Different Media | Reference Window

- To create a style sheet for specific media, add the attribute
  ```
  media = "type"
  ```
  to either the link element or the style element, where *type* is one or more of the following: aural, braille, embossed, handheld, print, projection, screen, tty, tv, or all. If you don't specify a media type, the style sheet applies to all media. Multiple media types should be entered in a comma-separated list.
- To create a style for specific media from within a style sheet, add to the sheet the rule
  ```
  @media type {style declarations}
  ```
  where *type* is the media type and *style declarations* are the styles that are applied to the different page elements within that media.

Now that you've seen how to define the style sheet for a particular media device, you decide to create one for printers.

To create a style sheet for print media:

1. Use your text editor to open the **printtxt.css** style sheet from the tutorial.04\tutorial folder included with your Data Files. Enter *your name* and *the date* in the comment section of the file.

2. Save the file as **print.css** in the same folder.

Kathy wants you to use the print.css style sheet for any paged visual media, which includes both printed media and projected media. You'll use the scraps.css style sheet for continuous visual media, which includes computer screens, television monitors, and ttys. In the samples.htm file, add a link to the print.css style sheet and insert the media attribute to indicate which style sheets to use for which output devices.

To link Kathy's Samples page to the print.css style sheet:

▶ 1. Return to the **samples.htm** file in your text editor.

▶ 2. Directly above the link element in the document head, insert the following link element for the print.css style sheet:

```
<link href="print.css" rel="stylesheet" type="text/css"
    media="print, projection" />
```

▶ 3. Add the following media attribute to the link element for the scraps.css file to indicate that it should be used for screen, tv, and tty media:

```
media="screen, tv, tty"
```

Figure 4-45 highlights the new code in the samples.htm file.

Figure 4-45 ▶ **Linking to external style sheets for different media**

```
<title>Samples from Online Scrapbooks</title>
<link href="print.css" rel="stylesheet" type="text/css" media="print, projection" />
<link href="scraps.css" rel="stylesheet" type="text/css" media="screen, tv, tty" />
```

The samples.htm file also includes an embedded style sheet. Like the external style sheet, you need to create two embedded sheets: one for printers and projection devices, and the other for screens, tvs, and ttys.

To create an embedded style sheet for print media:

▶ 1. Within the samples.htm file, directly above the embedded style sheet, insert the following HTML code:

```
<style type="text/css" media="print, projection">
</style>
```

▶ 2. Add the following media attribute to the opening <style> tag for the first embedded style sheet. See Figure 4-46.

```
media="screen, tv, tty"
```

Figure 4-46 ▶ **Embedded style sheets for different media**

```
<style type="text/css" media="print, projection">
</style>

<style type="text/css" media="screen, tv, tty">
    .notes    {font-family: sans-serif; font-size: 8pt; color: brown;
               background-color: ivory; border: 3px inset rgb(212, 212, 212);
               width: 130px; height: 90px; overflow: auto}
    .notes p {margin: 5px}
    #note1    {position: absolute; left: 600px; top: 120px}
    #note2    {position: absolute; left: 170px; top: 400px}
    #note3    {position: absolute; left: 570px; top: 550px}
</style>
```

3. Save your changes to the file, and then reload the **samples.htm** file in your Web browser. Confirm that the appearance of the page has not changed. (It should not change because your Web browser is treated as screen media and you haven't changed the style sheet for that media type.)

With two sets of style sheets for the different media types, you are ready to start defining the styles for printed output.

Hiding Elements

The first thing you notice when examining Kathy's sketch of the printed version of the Samples page is that many elements from the Web page—such as the list of links on the left and the address at the bottom—are missing. CSS has two styles that you can use to keep an element from being displayed in the output: the display style and the visibility style. As you've already seen in Tutorial 3, the display style supports the value "none," which causes the element to not be rendered by the output device. Alternately, you can use the visibility style, which has the syntax

```
visibility: type
```

where *type* is visible, hidden, collapse, or inherit (the default). A value of "visible" makes an element visible; the "hidden" value hides the element; a value of "collapse" is used with the tables to prevent a row or column from being displayed; and the "inherit" value causes an element to inherit the visibility style from its parent. Unlike the display style, the visibility style hides an element, but does not remove it from the flow of elements on the page. As shown in Figure 4-47, setting the display style to none not only hides an element, but also removes it from the page flow.

Comparing the visibility and display styles ◀ **Figure 4-47**

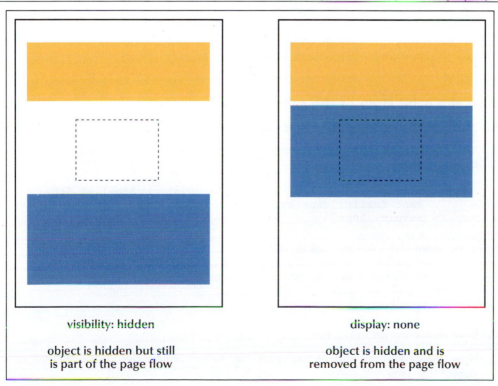

visibility: hidden

object is hidden but still
is part of the page flow

display: none

object is hidden and is
removed from the page flow

The display: none style is more appropriate for hiding elements in most cases. Use of the visibility: hidden style is usually reserved for scripts in which an element is alternatively hidden and made visible to create an animated effect. You'll use the display: none style to hide the #head, #links, and address selectors in the printed output.

To apply the display: none style:

▶ 1. Return to the **print.css** file in your text editor.

▶ 2. Add the following style declaration below the comment section:

`#head, #links, address {display: none}`

▶ 3. Kathy still wants all headings to appear in a sans-serif font in the printed version of the page. Add the following style to the sheet:

`h1, h2, h3, h4, h5, h6 {font-family: sans-serif}`

Figure 4-48 shows the code from the print.css style sheet.

Figure 4-48 | **Using the display:none style**

```
#head, #links, address {display: none}
h1, h2, h3, h4, h5, h6 {font-family: sans-serif}
```

▶ 4. Save your changes to the file.

Next, you need to modify the style for the callout notes. Kathy wants the notes to be displayed as items in a bulleted list. You can change the style of the notes to list items by applying the following display style:

`display: list-item`

Once the display style has been set to list-item, you can apply the same list styles you would use with elements marked with HTML's <li> tag. You decide to display each note with the bullet.jpg graphic image you used earlier in Session 1. You'll also set the text style to a 12-point sans-serif font with a margin of 20 pixels.

To set the print style of the callout notes:

▶ 1. Return to the **samples.htm** file in your text editor.

▶ 2. Add the following style to the embedded style sheet for printed output. See Figure 4-49.

```
.notes {display: list-item; list-style-image: url(bullet.jpg);
        font-family: sans-serif; font-size: 12pt;
        margin: 20px}
```

Figure 4-49 | **Setting the print styles for the callout notes**

```
<style type="text/css" media="print, projection">
    .notes {display: list-item; list-style-image: url(bullet.jpg);
            font-family: sans-serif; font-size: 12pt; margin: 20px}
</style>
```

▶ 3. Save your changes to the file.

Now test whether the styles you've defined have been applied to the printed version of the page.

4. Reload the **samples.htm** file in your Web browser. Verify that the appearance of the page within the browser window has *not* changed.

5. Either print the Web page from within your browser or use your browser's Print Preview command to preview the printed version of the page. Figure 4-50 shows how the page appears when printed.

Preview of the Samples page   Figure 4-50

Samples from Online Scrapbooks   Page 1 of 1

notes printed as a bulleted list

Samples from Online Scrapbooks

> Paste cut-out letters and words in your scrapbook to create a 3D effect. Online Scrapbooks sells professionally designed cut-out letters, words, and phrases for all occasions.

> Clippings, flyers, programs, and other memorabilia are valuable sources of information that can enhance your scrapbook pages. Make sure that any material is copied to acid-free paper. Newspaper clippings are especially susceptible to deterioration.

> Photographic cut-outs and textured backgrounds can add visual interest to your pages. See the online store for our wide variety of textured and embossed papers.

Kathy likes the printout you created; however, she still wants the notes to appear on a separate sheet. To do this, you'll have to place a page break in the middle of the document. Although page breaks are not supported by media types such as computer screens, they are supported in printed output and for projection devices.

Using Print Styles

CSS defines printed pages by extending the box model described in Tutorial 3 to incorporate the entire page in a **page box**. As shown in Figure 4-51, the page box is composed of two areas: the **page area**, containing the content of the document, and the **margin area**, containing the space between the printed content and the edges of the page.

Figure 4-51	The page box

As with the box model, you can specify the size of a page box, the page margins, the internal padding, and other features. The general rule to create and define a page box is

```
@page {styles}
```

where *styles* are the styles you want applied to the page. For example, the following @page rule sets the page margin for the printed output to 5 inches:

```
@page {margin: 5in}
```

A page box does not support all of the measurement units you've used with the other elements. For example, pages do not support the em or ex measurement units. In general, you should use measurement units that are appropriate to the dimensions of your page, such as inches or centimeters.

Page Pseudo-Classes and Named Pages

If your Web pages will require several pages when printed, you might want to define different styles for different pages. You can do this with pseudo-classes that reference specific pages. The syntax to apply a pseudo-class to a page uses the following rule

```
@page:pseudo-class {styles}
```

where *pseudo-class* is first (for the first page of the printout), left (for the pages that appear on the left in double-sided printouts), and right (for pages that appear on the right in double-sided printouts).

For example, if you are doing two-sided printing, you might want to mirror the margins of the left and right pages of the printout. The following styles result in pages in which the inner margin is set to 5 centimeters and outer margin is set to 2 centimeters:

```
@page:left {margin: 3cm 5cm 3cm 2cm}
@page:right {margin: 3cm 2cm 3cm 5cm}
```

To format specific pages other than the first, left, or right pages, you first must create a page name that contains a set of styles for the page. The syntax to create a page name is

```
@page name {styles}
```

where *name* is the label assigned to the page style. The following code creates the large_margins page name that defines a page box with 10-centimeter margins:

```
@page large_margins {margin: 10cm}
```

Once you define a page name, you can apply it to any block-level element in your document. The content of the block-level element will appear on its own page, with the browser automatically inserting page breaks before and after the element if required. To assign a page name to a block-level element, use the style

```
selector {page: name}
```

where *selector* is a CSS selector that points to a block-level element and *name* is the name of a defined page. For example, the style

```
blockquote {page: large_margins}
```

causes all block quotes to be displayed on their own separate pages using the styles defined for the large_margins page.

Setting the Page Size

Because printed media can vary in size and orientation, one of the styles supported by the page box is the size style that allows the Web author to define the default dimensions of the printed page as well as whether the pages should be printed in portrait or landscape orientation. The syntax of the size style is

```
size: width height orientation
```

where *width* and *height* are the width and height of the page, and *orientation* is the orientation of the page (portrait or landscape). If you don't specify the orientation, browsers assume a portrait orientation. To format a page as a standard-size page in landscape orientation with a 1-inch margin, you would apply the following style:

```
@page {size: 8.5in 11in landscape; margin: 1in}
```

If you remove the orientation value, as in the style

```
@page {size: 8.5in 11in; margin: 1in}
```

browsers print the output in portrait by default. Note that the page sizes and orientations chosen by the Web page author can still be overridden by the user, who may choose different settings when actually printing the page.

You can also replace the width, height, and orientation values with the keyword "auto" (to let the browser determine the page dimensions) or "inherit" (to inherit the page size from the parent element). If a page does not fit into the dimensions specified by the style, browsers will either rotate the page box 90 degrees or scale the page box to fit the sheet size.

Use the @page rule to define the print layout of the Samples page. Kathy suggests that you set the page size to 8.5 × 11 inches, in portrait orientation, with 0.5-inch margins.

To set the style of the printed page:

▶ **1.** Return to the **print.css** file in your text editor.

▶ **2.** As shown in Figure 4-52, add the following rule to the top of the list of style declarations:

  `@page {size: 8.5in 11in portrait; margin: 0.5in}`

Figure 4-52 ▶ **Setting the print style with the @print rule**

```
@page {size: 8.5in 11in portrait; margin: 0.5in}
#head, #links, address {display: none}
h1, h2, h3, h4, h5, h6 {font-family: sans-serif}
```

▶ **3.** Save your changes to the file.

Working with Page Breaks

When a document is sent to the printer, the printer decides the location of the page breaks unless that information is included as part of the print style. To specify a page break that occurs either before or after a page element, you apply the following styles:

```
page-break-before: type
page-break-after: type
```

The *type* style attribute has the following values:

- **always**, to always place a page break before or after the element
- **avoid**, to never place a page break
- **left**, to place a page break where the next page will be a left page
- **right**, to place a page break where the next page will be a right page
- **auto**, to allow the printer to determine whether or not to insert a page break
- **inherit**, to insert the page break style from the parent element

For example, if you want h1 headings to always be placed at the start of a new page, you would apply the following style in your style sheet:

```
h1 {page-break-before: always}
```

Or, if you want block quotes to always appear on their own page, you could place a page break before and after the block quote using the style:

```
blockquote {page-break-before: always; page-break-after: always}
```

Preventing a Page Break

Sometimes you want to keep the printer from inserting a page break inside of an element. This usually occurs when you have a long string of text that you don't want broken into two pages. You can prevent the printer from inserting a page break by using the style

```
page-break-inside: type
```

where *type* is auto, inherit, or avoid. To prevent a block quote from appearing on two separate pages, you could apply the following style:

```
blockquote {page-break-inside: avoid}
```

Note that the avoid type does not guarantee that there will not be a page break within the element. If the content of an element exceeds the dimensions of the sheet, the browser will be forced to insert a page break.

Working with Widows and Orphans

Even with the three page break styles, there will be situations where a printer will have to divide the contents of an element across two pages. Although this situation is largely unavoidable, designers can control the occurrence of widows and orphans in their printed output. A **widow** occurs when only a few ending lines of an element appear at the top of a page. An **orphan** is just the opposite: it occurs when only a few beginning lines of an element appear at the bottom of a page. Leaving one or two lines "stranded" on a page either as a widow or an orphan makes the material more difficult to read and is considered poor page design. The styles to control the appearance of widows and orphans in the printout are

```
widow: value
orphan: value
```

where *value* is the number of lines that must appear within the element before a page break can be inserted by the printer. The default value is 2, which means the widow or orphan must contain at least two lines of text. If you want to increase the size of widows and orphans to three lines for the paragraphs of your document, you could use the style declaration

```
p {widow: 3; orphan: 3}
```

and the printer will not insert a page break if less than three lines of a paragraph will be stranded at either the top or the bottom of a page. It's important to note that the widow and orphan values might not always be followed. Browsers attempt to use page breaks that obey the following guidelines:

- Insert all of the manual page breaks as indicated by the page-break-before, page-break-after styles, and page-break-inside styles.
- Avoid inserting page breaks where indicated in the style sheet.
- Break the pages as few times as possible.
- Make all pages that don't have a forced page break appear to have the same height.
- Avoid page breaking inside a block-level element that has a border.
- Avoid breaking inside a table.
- Avoid breaking inside of a floating element.

Only after attempting to satisfy these constraints are the Web page designer's recommendations for the widow and orphan styles applied.

You can combine all of the various page styles described above to provide the greatest control over the appearance of your printed document. The following set of styles shows how to create a style for the blockquote element that places each block quote on a separate 8.5 × 11 sheet of paper in landscape orientation:

```
@page quote_page {8.5in 11in landscape}
blockquote    {page: quote_page; page-break-before: always;
                                  page-break-inside: avoid;
                                  page-break-after: always}
```

Browser support for the various CSS print styles is very uneven, so you should always test your print styles on a wide variety of browsers and operating systems.

Tip

You can repeat an element across several pages as a header or footer by placing it in the printout using fixed positioning.

Reference Window | **Working with Print Styles**

- To define a page box for a printout that indicates the page size, margins, and orientation, use the declaration
  ```
  @page {styles}
  ```
  where *styles* are the styles that define the page.
- To set the page size and orientation, use the style
  ```
  size: width height orientation
  ```
  where *width* and *height* are the width and height of the page, and *orientation* is the orientation of the page (portrait or landscape).
- To insert a page break before an element, use the style
  ```
  page-break-before: type
  ```
  where *type* is always (to always place a page break), avoid (to never place a page break), left (to force a page break where the succeeding page will be a left page), right (to force a page break where the succeeding page will be a right page), auto (to allow the browser to determine whether or not to insert a page break), or inherit (to inherit the page break style of the parent element).
- To insert a page break after an element, use the style
  ```
  page-break-after: type
  ```
  where *type* has the same values as the page-break-before style.
- To apply a page break inside an element, use the style
  ```
  page-break-inside: type
  ```
  where *type* is auto, inherit, or avoid.

Now that you've seen how to insert page breaks into printed output, you are ready to insert a break into the printed version of the Samples page. Recall that Kathy wants the list of notes to appear on one page and the scrapbooking sample to appear on another. To do this, you can either place a page break after the third callout note or place a page break before the inline image of the scrapbooking sample. You decide to place a page break before the image. This will enable you to insert additional callout notes later without having to revise the page break structure. The sample image has been placed within a div container element with the id sample_image. To ensure that this container will start on a new page, you'll add the style below to the print.css style sheet. Kathy also wants the image centered horizontally on the page. The complete style for the #sample_image selector is:

```
#sample_image {page-break-before: always;
               text-align: center}
```

Kathy also wants the sample image itself resized to better fit the size of the page. She suggests you increase the size of the printed image to 7 inches wide by 9.1 inches tall. Because the img element for the sample image is nested within the #sample_image div container, you can set the size using the following style:

```
#sample_image img {width: 7in; height: 9.1in}
```

Add both of these styles to the print.css style sheet.

To complete the print.css style sheet:

▶ **1.** As shown in Figure 4-53, add the following styles to the bottom of the **print.css** style sheet:

```
#sample_image      {page-break-before: always;
                    text-align: center}
#sample_image img {width: 7in; height: 9.1in}
```

Final print.css style sheet ◀ Figure 4-53

```
@page {size: 8.5in 11in portrait; margin: 0.5in}
#head, #links, address {display: none}
h1, h2, h3, h4, h5, h6 {font-family: sans-serif}

#sample_image      {page-break-before: always;
                    text-align: center}

#sample_image img {width: 7in; height: 9.1in}
```

▶ **2.** Close the file, saving your changes.

▶ **3.** Reload the **samples.htm** file in your Web browser.

▶ **4.** Either print the Web page or use the Print Preview feature of your Web browser to view the layout and design of the printed version of the document. As shown in Figure 4-54, the printed version covers 2 pages, with the list of notes on one page and the sample image resized and centered on the second page.

Figure 4-54   **Two-page printout of the samples.htm file**

Samples from Online Scrapbooks   Page 1 of 2

Samples from Online Scrapbooks

> Paste cut-out letters and words in your scrapbook to create a 3D effect. Online Scrapbooks sells professionally designed cut-out letters, words, and phrases for all occasions.

> Clippings, flyers, programs, and other memorabilia are valuable sources of information that can enhance your scrapbook pages. Make sure that any material is copied to acid-free paper. Newspaper clippings are especially susceptible to deterioration.

> Photographic cut-outs and textured backgrounds can add visual interest to your pages. See the online store for our wide variety of textured and embossed papers.

Samples from Online Scrapbooks   Page 2 of 2

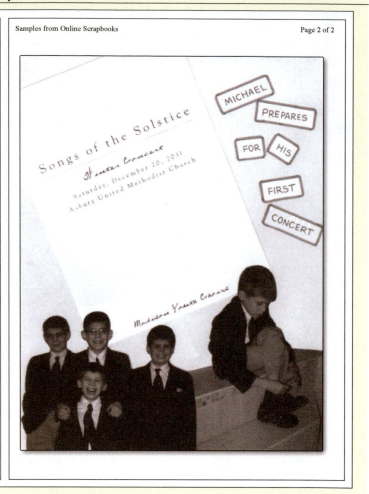

5. Close your Web browser and any other programs and files.

Styles for Handheld Devices | InSight

Although CSS allows you to create styles for handheld devices such as cell phones, PDAs, and MP3 players, effectively translating a large Web page into a smaller space is not easy. Some handheld devices support screens only up to 120 pixels wide; so you might quickly find your graphics-intensive Web page does not translate well into a portable world.

In general, if you want your Web page to be accessible to handheld devices, you should avoid using decorative images, and you should always specify alternative text for your graphic images. Also avoid floating elements. In the small, confined space of a handheld device, a floating element can behave unpredictably and ruin your page layout. Instead try to limit your page layout to a single column.

Use relative units such as the em unit and percent values to set the size of your fonts and block-level elements. If you must use pixels to specify a margin or padding size, try to keep your sizes within 5 pixels. Using larger pixel values such as 15 or 20 pixel widths can have an unpredictable effect on your page.

Finally, you have to pick and choose the features that are the most crucial to your Web page. A long list of links, while useful on a computer screen, can be distracting and difficult to navigate in a portable browser. Use the display:none style to control which elements will be sent to handheld devices.

Support for handheld browsing is still in its infancy, so don't be surprised to find a great deal of variation in the support for your HTML and CSS code among the various portable devices.

You've completed your work on the Samples page for the Online Scrapbooks Web site, and you'll be able to apply what you've learned about print styles to the other pages in the site. At the moment, most browsers support few of the page styles other than page breaking. This is sure to change in the future, however, as Web pages expand beyond the limitations of the computer screen into new media. Kathy finds this an exciting prospect, providing the opportunity to advertise the company to a whole new set of potential customers.

Session 4.3 Quick Check | Review

1. What attribute would you add to an embedded or external style sheet link to apply a style sheet to a mobile phone?
2. Which media types belong to the continuous/visual group?
3. Which media types would be most appropriate for Web browsers designed for the visually impaired?
4. What is the difference between the display:none and visibility:hidden styles?
5. Specify a style to set the page size of the printed document to 11 inches wide by 14 inches high in landscape orientation with a 1.5-inch margin.
6. Specify the style to insert a page break before every h1 heading in your document.
7. In page design, what is a widow? What is an orphan?

Review | **Tutorial Summary**

In this tutorial, you learned how to use Cascading Style Sheets to create interesting and flexible layouts and designs. The first session examined different types of CSS selectors, providing the Web author flexibility in creating and applying specific design styles. The first session also explored how to apply styles to unordered lists. It concluded by examining how to use CSS to create rollover effects and drop caps. The second session focused on CSS positioning styles and explored how to use CSS positioning to place elements in absolute and relative coordinates. The final session looked at applying styles to media other than computer screens, focusing on creating styles for printed output. In the session you learned how to work with page flow within printed materials by controlling the placement of page breaks before, after, and within page elements.

Key Terms

absolute positioning	media group	pseudo-element
attribute selector	orphan	relative positioning
conditional comment	page box	rollover effect
contextual selector	pseudo-class	widow

Practice | Review Assignments

Practice the skills you learned in the tutorial using the same case scenario.

Data Files needed for the Review Assignments: back.jpg, gallerytxt.htm, marker.gif, printertxt.css, sample1.jpg – sample4.jpg, scraps.jpg, and screentxt.css

Kathy stopped by to ask for your help in designing a new Web page to display scrapbooking samples sent in by different visitors to the Web site. The screen version of the Web page will show four new sample scrapbook pages each month, laid out on the page in a 2 × 2 grid. The print version of the same page will display enlarged versions of the four samples, printed on separate pages. Kathy also has some changes she wants you to make to the size navigation links. A preview of the design you'll apply to the Scrapbook Gallery page is shown in Figure 4-55.

Figure 4-55

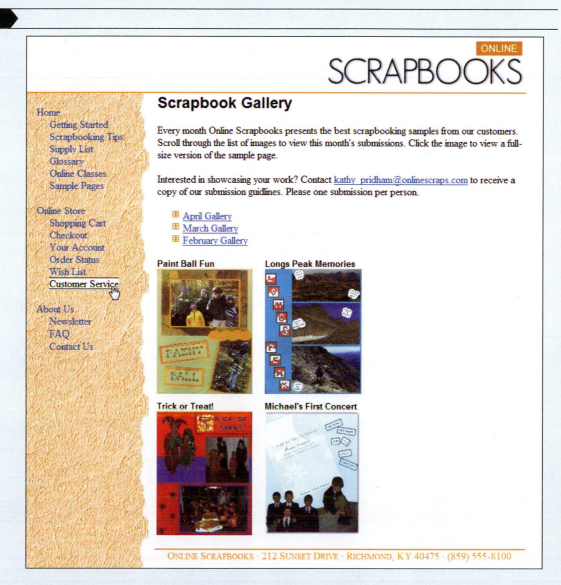

Complete the following:

1. Use your text editor to open the **gallerytxt.htm**, **printertxt.css**, and **screentxt.css** files from the tutorial.04\review folder included with your Data Files. Enter *your name* and *the date* in the comment section of each file. Save the files as **gallery.htm**, **printer.css**, and **screen.css**, respectively, in the same folder. Take some time to study the content and layout of the Gallery Web page and observe how the styles in the screen.css style sheet file affects the layout and appearance of the page as it appears in your Web browser.

2. Return to the **gallery.htm** file in your text editor. Kathy wants you to format the appearance of the list of links by indenting links belonging to a particular group or class. To define the class of links, do the following:
   - Add a class attribute to the li elements in the list of links, placing the Home, Online Store, and About Us links in the newgroup class.
   - Place the other li elements in the list of links in the subgroup class.

3. The Gallery page contains four images of scrapbook page samples chosen for the May gallery. Scroll down to the four div container elements (marked with ids sample1 through sample4) and place each of the div containers in the samples class.

4. Save your changes to the **gallery.htm** file and then go to the **screen.css** style sheet file in your text editor. This style sheet will be used to design the layout of the Gallery page as it appears on computer screens.

5. Kathy wants to remove the bullet markers from the list of links. She also wants to change the layout of the links, moving them farther to the left and indenting links belonging to the subgroup class. To apply these styles, do the following:
   - For ul elements nested within the #links selector, change the marker style to none.
   - To move the list of links to the left on the Web page, set the size of the left margin to 15 pixels and the size of the left padding to 0 pixels.
   - Set the top margin of elements belonging to the newgroup class to 20 pixels.
   - Set the left margin of elements belonging to the subgroup class to 20 pixels.

6. The Gallery page also includes links to galleries from the months of February, March, and April. These links also appear in a list nested within the content div container. Kathy would like you to replace the bullet marker on this list with a graphical marker. To apply this style, set all the ul elements nested within the #content selector to use the **marker.gif** file as their bullet marker.

7. Kathy would like you to create a rollover effect for the list of links displayed on the left margin of the Web page. To create the rollover effect, add the following styles to the style sheet:
   - For links within the #links selector, remove any underlining by setting the text-decoration style to none. Do this for the link, visited, and active pseudo-classes.
   - When the mouse pointer is hovering over those links, change the font color to black and change the background color to white, and use the text-decoration style to add an underline and an overline to the link text.

8. Kathy wants the four scrapbook samples to be reduced in size and placed in a 2 x 2 grid on the Web page. To create this effect, add the following styles to the style sheet:
   - Apply absolute positioning to all elements belonging to the samples class.
   - For all img elements nested within the samples class, set the width of the image to 150 pixels, the height to 193 pixels, and the border width to 0 pixels.

- All four scrapbook samples are nested within a div container with the id samples_ container. Place this div container on the Web page using relative positioning. Set the top and left coordinates of the element to 0 pixels. Set the height of samples_ container to 450 pixels.
- Place the #sample1 selector at the page coordinates (0, 0). Place the #sample2 selector at the coordinates (170, 0). Place the #sample3 selector at the coordinates (0, 220). Place the #sample4 selector at the coordinates (170, 220).

9. Save your changes to the **screen.css** file. Load the **gallery.htm** file in your Web browser and verify that its layout resembles that shown in Figure 4-55. Confirm that the Web browser displays the correct rollover effect when you hover your mouse pointer over any of the links in the list on the left page margin.

10. Kathy also wants you to create a style sheet for printed versions of the Gallery page in which only the four scrapbook samples and their headings are shown, each on its own page. To create this style, return to the **printer.css** file in your text editor.

11. Add the following styles to the style sheet:
    - Set the page size to 8.5 × 11 inches, in portrait orientation, with a margin of 0.5 inches.
    - Prevent the display of the #head and #links selectors as well as the address, ul, and h2 elements and paragraphs nested within the #content selector.
    - Horizontally center all elements belonging to the samples class, and add a page break after every occurrence of this class of element.
    - Set the font size of h3 headings nested within the samples class to 18 points and the font family to sans-serif.
    - Set the size of img elements nested within the samples class to 6.5 inches wide by 8.35 inches tall. Set the border width to 0 pixels.

12. Save your changes to the **printer.css** file and return to the **gallery.htm** file.

13. Edit the link element pointing to the screen.css style sheet, adding an attribute that indicates that this style sheet should only be used for screen output.

14. Add a link pointing to the printer.css style sheet with an attribute indicating that this style sheet is used for printed output.

15. Save your changes to the **gallery.htm** file and refresh the page in your Web browser. Confirm that the appearance of the page within the browser window is unchanged. Print the Web page or use your browser's Print Preview command to confirm that the printed version of the page displays only the four scrapbook samples and their headings.

16. Submit your completed files to your instructor.

Apply | Case Problem 1

Apply your knowledge of Web site design to create a Web site for a golf course.

Data Files needed for this Case Problem: h01txt.htm – h18txt.htm, hole01.jpg – hole18.jpg, next.jpg, prev.jpg, printtxt.css, willet.jpg, and willettxt.css

Willet Creek Golf Course   Willet Creek is a popular public golf course in central Idaho. You've been asked to work on the design of the course's Web site by Michael Carpenter, the head of promotion for the course. Part of the Web site contains a preview of each of the course's 18 holes, complete with yardages and shot recommendations. Each hole has been given its own Web page with a set of links to navigate from one page to another. Figure 4-56 shows a preview of the design you'll use to show one of the pages on the golf course Web site.

Figure 4-56

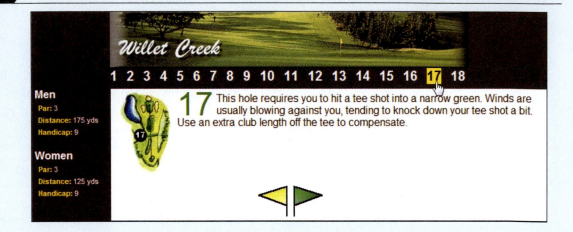

Michael also wants another style sheet designed for printed output. Figure 4-57 shows a preview of the print style used with the golf course pages.

Figure 4-57

Willet Creek Golf Course: 17th Hole

Men

- **Par:** 3
- **Distance:** 175 yds
- **Handicap:** 9

Women

- **Par:** 3
- **Distance:** 125 yds
- **Handicap:** 9

Hole 17

This hole requires you to hit a tee shot into a narrow green. Winds are usually blowing against you, tending to knock down your tee shot a bit. Use an extra club length off the tee to compensate.

1 of 1

Michael has already done a lot of work in setting up the page content and has even applied a few CSS styles to the page elements. He needs you to complete the task, getting the Web pages ready for the next round of golfers.

Complete the following:

1. In your text editor, open the files **h01txt.htm** through **h18txt.htm** from the tutorial.04\case1 folder included with your Data Files. Enter *your name* and *the date* in the comment section of each file and save the files as **h01.htm** through **h18.htm** in the same folder.

2. Use your text editor to open the **printtxt.css** and **willettxt.css** files, also from the tutorial.04\case1 folder included with your Data Files. Enter *your name* and *the date* in each file and save them as **print.css** and **willet.css**, respectively, in the same folder. Take some time to review the contents and layout of the Web pages, paying particular attention to the use of div container tags and id attributes to mark off different sections of the document. Also take some time to review the contents of the **willet.css** style sheet to examine what styles Michael has already created for the Web site.

3. Return to the **willet.css** file in your text editor. The list of links to each page in the Web site is contained within a div container with the id hole_list. Apply the following styles to the list and the links it contains:

   • Display each link in a bold, white font, with a font size of 1.25 em.
   • When a mouse pointer hovers over a link, change the background color to yellow and the font color to black.
   • Display each li element within the #hole_list selector as an inline element with a margin of 0 pixels, a padding space of 0 pixels above and below the element, and padding space of 5 pixels to the left and right.

4. The hole_stats div container stores statistical information about each hole, providing the par score, distance, and handicap value for men and women. Apply the following styles to this element:

   • Use absolute positioning to place the div container at the page coordinates (0, 115).
   • For h2 elements nested within the container, set the font size to 1 em and the left margin to 5 pixels. Set the size of the other margins to 0 pixels.
   • Remove the list markers from the unordered list within the container. Also, set the left margin of the list to 10 pixels, the left padding to 0 pixels, and the top margin to 0 pixels. Display the unordered list in a 0.7 em size font.
   • Display the contents of the strong element within the container in a yellow font.

5. The hole_summary div container contains a text summary of the hole and how to play it. Add a style to place the container at the coordinates (120, 115). Use absolute positioning.

6. The hole_image div container stores an image of the hole. Use absolute positioning to place this element at the coordinates (10, 5).

7. The hole_description div container contains a text description of the hole. Use absolute positioning to place this element at the coordinates (100, 5).

8. Within the hole_description container is a span element that contains the hole number. Michael would like this number to appear as a drop cap. Create this effect by floating the span element on the left margin with a line height of 0.75 with 2 pixels of padding on the right. Set the font color to green and the font size to 300%.

9. At the bottom of each page are a pair of flag images that can be clicked to move to the next hole on the course. The images are nested within a div container with the id flags. Apply the following styles to the div container and the images it contains:

   • Set the border width of img elements within the flags container to 0 pixels.

- Use absolute positioning to place the #prevFlag selector at the coordinates (220, 145).
- Use absolute positioning to place the #nextFlag selector at the coordinates (270, 145).

10. Save your changes to the **willet.css** file. Go to the **h01.htm** through **h18.htm** files in your text editor and link each file to the willet.css style sheet, specifying that the sheet is to be used with screen and tv media. Save your changes to each file, and then view the Web site in your browser. Verify that the layout resembles that shown in Figure 4-57 and that the list of links at the top of the page has a rollover effect.

11. Return to the **print.css** file in your text editor. Add the following styles to the style sheet:
    - Set the page size to 8.5 × 11 inches in portrait orientation.
    - Set the font family of the h1, h2, and h3 headings to sans-serif.
    - Horizontally align the contents of the #head selector.
    - Prevent the display of the #hole_list and #flags selectors.
    - Float the #hole_stats selector on the left margin with a 0.2-inch right margin and 0.1 inches of padding. Add a 0.1-inch double black border to the right and bottom of the element.
    - Set the font size of h2 elements nested within the #hole_stats selector to 12 points.
    - Use absolute positioning to place the #hole_image selector 3 inches from the top of the page and 3 inches from the page's left margin.
    - Set the width of img elements within the #hole_image selector to 3.54 inches wide by 5 inches tall.
    - Display the span element nested within the #hole_description selector as a block-level element. Display the text in a 20-point bold sans-serif font.

⊕ **EXPLORE**
    - Use the before pseudo-element to place the text "Hole" directly before the content of the span element.

12. Save your changes to the **print.css** file. Return to the **h01.htm** through **h18.htm** files in your text editor. Link each file to the print.css style sheet, indicating that this style sheet is used for print media.

13. Print **h01.htm** (or use the Print Preview feature on your Web browser) to verify that the layout of the printed Web page resembles that shown in Figure 4-57. (Note: Internet Explorer does not support the before pseudo-element, so in this browser you will not see the word "Hole" next to the hole number in the printed version of the page.)

14. Submit your completed files to your instructor.

Challenge	**Case Problem 2**

Test your knowledge of Web site design by completing a Civil War history page.

Data Files needed for this Case Problem: cwlogo.gif, cwpagetxt.htm, cwtxt.css, and tan.jpg

Civil War Studies Adanya Lynne is a professor of military history at Ridgeview State College in Bartlett, Tennessee. She has been working on a Web site for a course she is preparing in Civil War studies. Professor Lynne has already created some sample pages and done work on the design and layout, but she needs your help in completing the project. She would like to create a list of links in an outline format by nesting one ordered list inside of another. She's also interested in using CSS to create a drop-shadow effect on the main topic headings on her pages. To test your design, you'll create a style for a page containing the text of Lincoln's second inaugural address. A preview of the page you'll create for Professor Lynne is shown in Figure 4-58.

Figure 4-58

The Civil War

Lincoln's Second Inaugural

I. Background and Causes of the War
  A. Economic Development
  B. Slavery
    1. Missouri Compromise
    2. Compromise Measures of 1850
    3. Kansas-Nebraska Act
    4. Dred Scott Decision
    5. John Brown's Raid
    6. Frederick Douglass
    7. Lincoln-Douglas Debates
  C. States' Rights
  D. The Election of 1860
II. Political and Military Leaders
  A. Southern
    1. Jefferson Davis
    2. Robert E. Lee
    3. Thomas J. "Stonewall" Jackson
    4. James Longstreet
    5. Joseph E. Johnston
  B. Northern
    1. Abraham Lincoln
    2. George B. McClellan
    3. Ulysses S. Grant
    4. William Tecumseh Sherman
III. The Events of 1861 - 1862
  A. Events
    1. Secession of the Confederate

AT THIS SECOND APPEARING TO TAKE THE OATH OF THE PRESIDENTIAL OFFICE THERE IS LESS occasion for an extended address than there was at the first. Then a statement somewhat in detail of a course to be pursued seemed fitting and proper. Now, at the expiration of four years, during which public declarations have been constantly called forth on every point and phase of the great contest which still absorbs the attention and engrosses the energies of the nation, little that is new could be presented. The progress of our arms, upon which all else chiefly depends, is as well known to the public as to myself, and it is, I trust, reasonably satisfactory and encouraging to all. With high hope for the future, no prediction in regard to it is ventured.

On the occasion corresponding to this four years ago all thoughts were anxiously directed to an impending civil war. All dreaded it, all sought to avert it. While the inaugural address was being delivered from this place, devoted altogether to saving the Union without war, urgent agents were in the city seeking to destroy it without war—seeking to dissolve the Union and divide effects by negotiation. Both parties deprecated war, but one of them would make war rather than let the nation survive, and the other would accept war rather than let it perish, and the war came.

One-eighth of the whole population were colored slaves, not distributed generally over the Union, but localized in the southern part of it. These slaves constituted a peculiar and powerful interest. All knew that this interest was somehow the cause of the war. To strengthen, perpetuate, and extend this interest was

Complete the following:

1. Use your text editor to open the **cwpagetxt.htm** and **cwtxt.css** files from the tutorial.04\case2 folder included with your Data Files. Enter *your name* and *the date* in the comment section of each file. Save the files as **cwpage.htm** and **cw.css**, respectively, in the same folder. Take some time to examine the contents and structure of the HTML file and the external style sheet.

2. Return to the **cwpage.htm** file in your text editor. Create a link to the cw.css style sheet. You do not have to specify a media attribute.

3. Scroll down the file and locate the h2 heading "Lincoln's Second Inaugural." Directly below this heading, insert another h2 heading containing exactly the same text but with the class name shadow.

4. Go to the paragraphs within the article div container. Give the first paragraph the class name first_para and give the remaining paragraphs the class name following_para.

5. Save your changes to the **cwpage.htm** file and then return to the **cw.css** file in your text editor.

6. The page_content div container contains the entire contents of the Web page. Add the following styles for the container:
   - Use relative positioning to place the container with top and left coordinates of 0 pixels.
   - Set the width of the container to 95% of the width of the document window.
   - Insert styles to set the minimum width of the container to 800 pixels and the maximum width to 1000 pixels.

 EXPLORE

7. The linkList div container contains the list of links in Adanya's Web site. Use absolute positioning to place this element at the coordinates (5, 140). Set the width to 280 pixels. Add a 1-pixel-wide solid black border to the right edge of the element.

8. Remove the underlining from the links nested within the linkList container, and change the font color to black. If a mouse pointer hovers over any of the links, have the browser underline the link text.

EXPLORE 9. The links appear in a set of nested ordered lists. Adanya wants these links to appear in an outline format. To create the outline, do the following:

- Display the ol element using uppercase Roman numerals as the bullet marker. Set the font size to 0.9 em.
- Display ol elements nested within another ordered list using uppercase letters as bullet markers.
- Display ol elements nested within *two* levels of ordered lists using decimal numbers as bullet markers.

10. Use absolute positioning to place the article div container at the coordinates (320, 190).

EXPLORE 11. You can create a drop-shadow around a heading by duplicating the heading and then offsetting one heading from another. You've already duplicated the heading in the cwpage.htm file; complete the drop-shadow by applying the following styles:

- Use absolute positioning to place the h2 element at the coordinates (320, 125). Set the font color of the heading to the RGB value (237, 227, 178) and the z-index value to 2.
- Directly below the h2 style, insert a style to place the element belonging to the shadow class at the coordinates (321, 126), once again using absolute positioning. Set the font color to black and the z-index value to 1.

12. Adanya wants you to create drop caps and a special first line style for the paragraphs that contain the text of Lincoln's second inaugural address. Add the following styles to the style sheet:

- Display the first line of the paragraph belonging to the first_para class in small capital letters.
- Float the first letter of the "first_para" paragraph on the left margin of the paragraph with top and left margin values of 0 pixels and right bottom margins of 5 pixels. Set the font size to 300% and the line height to 0.75.
- Use the text-indent style to indent the paragraphs belonging to the following_para class by 10 pixels each.

13. Save your changes to the style sheet.

14. Load the **cwpage.htm** file in your Web browser and verify that the layout matches that shown in Figure 4-58. Confirm that the Lincoln's Second Inaugural heading appears with a drop-shadow. Verify that the list of links appears in outline form and that links within the outline display a rollover effect.

EXPLORE 15. If you have a large screen monitor and access to Firefox, Opera, or another Web browser that supports minimum and maximum widths, resize your browser window and verify that the width of the page content does not exceed 1000 pixels or fall below 800 pixels even as you resize the browser window. (Note: Internet Explorer does not support minimum and maximum width styles.)

16. Submit your completed files to your instructor.

Challenge | **Case Problem 3**

Broaden your knowledge of CSS styles by creating an interactive map for a national park Web site.

Data Files needed for this Case Problem: image0.jpg – image9.jpg, longstxt.htm, and lpmap.jpg

Longs Peak Interactive Map   Longs Peak is one of the most popular attractions of Rocky Mountain National Park (RMNP). Each year during the months of July, August, and September, thousands of people climb Longs Peak by the Keyhole Route to reach the 14,255-foot summit. Ron Bartlett, the head of the RMNP Web site team, has asked for your help in creating an interactive map of the Keyhole Route. The map will be installed at electronic kiosks in the park's visitor center. Ron envisions a map with 10 numbered waypoints along the Keyhole Route, displaying photos and text descriptions of each way-point when a mouse pointer hovers over its corresponding numbered point. Figure 4-59 shows a preview of the online map with the first waypoint highlighted by the user.

Figure 4-59

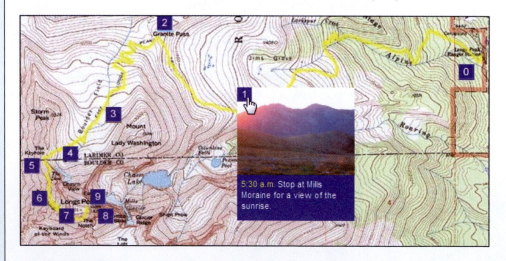

Longs Peak Online Trail Map

At 14,255 feet, Longs Peak towers above all other summits in Rocky Mountain National Park. The summer is the only season in which the peak can be climbed by a non-technical route. Early mornings break calm, clouds build in the afternoon sky, often exploding in storms of brief, heavy rain, thunder and dangerous lightning. Begin your hike early, way before dawn, to be back below timberline before the weather turns for the worse.

The Keyhole Route, Longs Peak's only non-technical hiking pathway, is a 16 mile round trip with an elevation gain of 4,850 feet. Though non-technical, the Keyhole Route is still challenging and is not recommended for those who are afraid of heights or exposed ledges. Hikers should be properly outfitted with clothing, food and water. Use caution when ascending or descending steep areas. Don't be afraid to back down when bad weather threatens.

Move your mouse pointer over the numbered landmarks in the map to preview the hike.

Ron also wants to create a print version of the waypoint descriptions. Users can print the map elsewhere on the park's Web site, so he wants the print style sheet to display just the list of waypoints in a bulleted list.

Complete the following:

1. Use your text editor to open the **longstxt.htm** file from the tutorial.04\case3 folder included with your Data Files. Enter *your name* and *the date* in the comment section at the top of the file. Save the file as **longs.htm** in the same folder. Take some time to study the contents of the file. Notice that the waypoint descriptions are nested within the online_map div container. Each waypoint description has been placed in a separate div container with the class name notes and id names ranging from point0 to point9.

2. To create a rollover effect for the nine waypoints, you need to mark the waypoint contents as hyperlinks. Within each of the nine div containers, enclose the img element and paragraph element within a single <a> tag. Point each link to the **longs.htm** file so that if a user clicks the link, it will simply refresh the current Web page.

3. Add a style to the embedded style sheet at the top of the file to remove underlining from all hypertext links.

4. Currently the online_map div container does not display the Longs Peak map. Add the following style to the embedded style sheet to display the map:
   - Set the width of the container to 600 pixels wide by 294 pixels high.
   - Add a 1-pixel-wide solid black border to the container.
   - Apply the **lpmap.jpg** graphic file as the background image.
   - Use relative positioning to place the container on the page. Set the top and left coordinates to 0 pixels.

5. In the embedded style sheet, add the following styles for all of the div containers belonging to the notes class:
   - For paragraphs nested within each note, set the font size to 8 points and the margin to 5 pixels.
   - Set the font color to yellow for each span element nested within a note.

EXPLORE

6. For each link nested within a notes class element, apply the following styles:
   - Set the width and height of the link to 20 pixels.
   - Hide any content that overflows the boundary of the link.
   - Set the background color to blue and the font color to white.
   - Set the z-index value to 1.

EXPLORE

7. When the mouse hovers over a link within a notes class element, have the browser apply the following style:
   - Change the width to 150 pixels and the height to 170 pixels.
   - Change the overflow property to visible.
   - Set the z-index value to 2.

8. Use absolute positioning to place the link nested within the #point0 selector at the coordinates (560, 60).

9. Repeat Step 8 for the nine remaining waypoints:
   - #point1 at (277, 90)
   - #point2 at (175, 0)
   - #point3 at (110, 115)
   - #point4 at (55, 165)
   - #point5 at (5, 180)

- • #point6 at (15, 222)
- • #point7 at (50, 245)
- • #point8 at (100, 245)
- • #point9 at (90, 220)

10. Go to the top of the file and add a media attribute to the embedded style sheet indicating that the sheet is designed for screen and tv media.

11. Save your changes to the file and then open **longs.htm** in your Web browser. Verify that the placement of the waypoints follows the locations shown in Figure 4-59. Confirm that when you hover your mouse over each of the nine waypoints, a description of the waypoint appears on the top of the trail map.

12. Return to the **longs.htm** file in your text editor. Create a new embedded style sheet designed for print media.

13. Scroll down to the "Longs Peak Online Trail Map" h2 heading and enclose the text "Online Trail Map" within a span element.

14. Add the following styles to the embedded print style sheet:
    - • Set the font family for the page body to sans-serif.
    - • Remove underlining from all hypertext links.
    - • Do not display the #instructions selector, the span element nested within the h2 element, or the img element nested within elements belonging to the notes class.
    - • Display the notes class of elements as list items with a disc marker. Set the margin to 20 pixels.
    - • Change the display property of paragraphs nested within the notes class of elements to inline.
    - • Display span elements nested within the notes class of elements in a bold font.

⊕ **EXPLORE** 15. Add a style that inserts the text string "Trail Itinerary" after the h2 heading.

16. Save your changes to the file.

17. Refresh the **longs.htm** file in your Web browser. By either printing the page or viewing the page within the Print Preview window, confirm that the printed page only shows a bulleted list of the waypoint descriptions. If you are running Firefox, Opera, or Safari, confirm that the heading at the top of the page reads "Longs Peak Trail Itinerary." (If you are using Internet Explorer, the title will simply read "Longs Peak.")

18. Submit your completed files to your instructor.

| Create | **Case Problem 4** |

Test your knowledge of CSS and HTML by creating a Web page design for a children's choir.

Data Files needed for this Case Problem: bizet.jpg, bizetbio.txt, bizetlist.txt, mozart.jpg, mozartbio.txt, mozartlist.txt, puccini.jpg, puccinibio.txt, puccinilist.txt, verdi.jpg, verdibio.txt, verdilist.txt, wagner.jpg, wagnerbio.txt, and wagnerlist.txt

Gresham Children's Choir Faye Dawson is an instructor for Gresham Children's Choir in Gresham, Oregon. The choir is a chance for talented youth to perform and to learn about music history. Faye is working on a Web site describing the history of opera. She's asked for your help in creating a design. Faye has provided you with information on five different composers: Bizet, Mozart, Puccini, Verdi, and Wagner. For each composer, she's given you an image file containing the composer's picture, a text file listing the composer's works, and a text file containing a biographical sketch. Use this information to design your Web site. You may supplement these files with any other material you think will enhance your site's design.

Complete the following:

1. Use your text editor to create four HTML files named **bizet.htm**, **mozart.htm**, **puccini.htm**, **verdi.htm**, and **wagner.htm**, placing them in the tutorial.04\case4 folder included with your Data Files. Enter *your name* and *the date* in a comment section of each file. Include any other comments you think will aptly document the page's purpose and history.

2. Use the provided text files and image files to create a Web page describing each composer's life and accomplishments. Include hypertext links between the five composer Web pages.

3. Create an external style sheet named **gresham.css** for your Web site. Insert a comment section in the style sheet file that includes *your name* and *the date* as well as other comments that describe the style sheet.

4. The content of the gresham.css style sheet is up to you, but it must include the following features:
   - Styles that use contextual selectors
   - A style that uses a pseudo-element and a pseudo-class
   - Styles that use positioning styles (either absolute or relative)
   - A style that creates or modifies an ordered or unordered list
   - A style to create a rollover effect

5. Create another style sheet named **printer.css** containing styles for a printed version of the pages in your Web site. Add appropriate comments to the different parts of your style sheet.

6. Test your Web site on a variety of browsers to ensure your design works under different conditions.

7. Submit your completed files to your instructor.

Review | **Quick Check Answers**

Session 4.1

1. `p span {font-style: italic}`
2. `p > span {font-style: italic}`
3. `h1 + h2 {font-style: italic}`
4. `.newsAlert {font-weight: bold}`
5. `span.newsAlert {font-weight: bold}`
6. `a:hover {background-color: yellow}`
7. `a:hover {background-image:url(hover.jpg)}`
8. `blockquote:first-letter {color: red}`
9. `blockquote:first-line {color: red}`

Session 4.2

1. `#logo {position: absolute; top: 75px; left: 150px}`
2. `#logo {position: relative; top: 25%; left: 10%}`
3. `span.highlight {position: relative; top: -10px}`
4. `a:hover {position: relative; top: 5px}`
5. `#links {position: fixed; top: 50px; left: 10px}`
6. `blockquote {width: 70%; min-width: 250px; max-width: 650px}`
7. `blockquote {height: 25%; overflow: auto}`
8. No. It will only be on top of other elements for which it shares a common parent.

Session 4.3

1. `media = "handheld"`
2. screen, tv, tty
3. aural, Braille, embossed
4. The display:none style hides the element and removes it from the document flow. The visibility:hidden style hides the element, but does not remove it from the document flow.
5. `@page {11in 14in landscape ; margin 1.5 in}`
6. `h1 {page-break-before: always}`
7. A widow occurs when a page break divides a block of text, leaving only one or two lines of text on the succeeding page. An orphan occurs when the page break occurs near the start of the block of text, leaving only one or two lines of text on the first page.

Ending Data Files

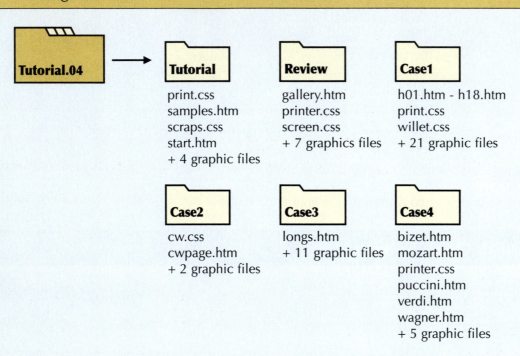

Tutorial.04 →

Tutorial
print.css
samples.htm
scraps.css
start.htm
+ 4 graphic files

Review
gallery.htm
printer.css
screen.css
+ 7 graphics files

Case1
h01.htm - h18.htm
print.css
willet.css
+ 21 graphic files

Case2
cw.css
cwpage.htm
+ 2 graphic files

Case3
longs.htm
+ 11 graphic files

Case4
bizet.htm
mozart.htm
printer.css
puccini.htm
verdi.htm
wagner.htm
+ 5 graphic files

Objectives

Session 5.1
- Explore the structure of a Web table
- Create headings and cells in a table
- Create cells that span multiple rows and columns
- Create row and column groups
- Add a caption and a summary to a table

Session 5.2
- Format a table using HTML attributes
- Format a table using CSS styles
- Collapse table borders
- Display page elements in tabular form

Session 5.3
- Create a jigsaw layout
- Explore the use of tables for page layout
- Create rounded borders

Working with Web Tables

Creating a Radio Program Schedule

Case | KPAF Radio

Kyle Mitchell is the program director at KPAF, a public radio station broadcasting out of Bismarck, North Dakota. To remain viable, it's important for the station to have a presence on the Internet. With this in mind, Kyle has begun upgrading the KPAF Web site. He envisions a site in which listeners have quick and easy access to information about the station and its programs.

The Web site needs to include pages listing the KPAF morning, afternoon, and evening schedules. Kyle decides that this information is best conveyed to the listener in a table, with each column of the table displaying one day's program schedule and each row displaying the broadcast times for the various KPAF programs. Kyle has never created a Web table, so he's come to you for help in designing a Web page describing the KPAF evening schedule. Kyle wants the table you create to be easy to read and informative. He also wants you to add table styles that will enhance the appearance of the Web page.

Starting Data Files

Tutorial.05 →

Tutorial
kpaftxt.css
newshows.css
newshows.txt
roundedtxt.css
schedtxt.htm
tablestxt.css
+ 9 graphic files

Review
kpaf.css
morningtxt.htm
programstxt.css
+ 5 graphic files

Case1
jpftxt.css
stabletxt.css
sudokutxt.htm
+ 6 graphic files

Case2
caltxt.css
ccctxt.css
febtxt.htm
+10 graphic files

Case3
dhometxt.htm
dometxt.css
dtabletxt.css
+ 14 graphic files

Case4
rooms.txt
+ 9 graphic files

Session 5.1

Introducing Web Tables

You meet with Kyle in his office at KPAF to discuss the design of the new Web site. Kyle has already created a basic Web page displaying the KPAF logo and a list of links to other pages. Open this file now.

To view Kyle's data files:

1. In your text editor, open the **schedtxt.htm** and **kpaftxt.css** files, located in the tutorial.05\tutorial folder included with your Data Files. Enter *your name* and *the date* in the comment section of each file. Save the files as **schedule.htm** and **kpaf.css** in the same folder.

2. Review the **schedule.htm** file in your text editor to become familiar with its content and structure. Insert the following link element below the opening <title> tag to link the schedule.htm file to the kpaf.css style sheet:

   ```
   <link href="kpaf.css" rel="stylesheet" type="text/css" />
   ```

3. Save your changes to the file and then open the **schedule.htm** file in your Web browser. Figure 5-1 shows the current appearance of the Web page.

Figure 5-1   Initial schedule page

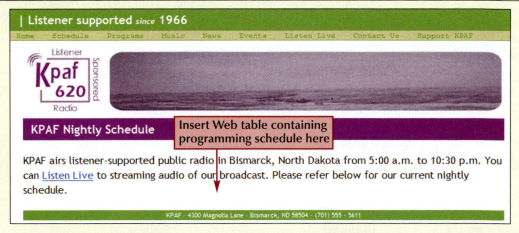

4. Go to the **kpaf.css** style sheet in your text editor. Review the styles and compare them to the elements contained within the schedule.htm file to fully understand Kyle's design for the schedule page.

5. Close the style sheet file when you're finished reviewing it.

The first thing that Kyle needs you to add to the schedule page is KPAF's nightly schedule, which covers from 6:00 p.m. to 10:30 p.m. Kyle hands you a printout of the KPAF schedule shown in Figure 5-2. At 10:30 p.m. the station goes dark and does not broadcast again until 5:00 a.m. the following day. Kyle wants you to use HTML to recreate this table.

Time	Monday	Tuesday	Wednesday	Thursday	Friday	Saturday	Sunday
6:00	National News	National News	National News	National News	National News	National News	National News
6:30	Local News	Local News	Local News	Local News	Local News	Local News	Local News
7:00	Opera Fest	Radio U	Science Week	The Living World	Word Play	Agri-Week	Folk Fest
7:30					Brain Stew	Bismarck Forum	
8:00	The Classical Music Connection				Old Time Radio	Saturday Nite Jazz	The Indie Connection
8:30					The Inner Mind		
9:00					Open Mike Nite		
9:30							
10:00	World News Feed	World News Feed	World News Feed	World News Feed	World News Feed	World News Feed	World News Feed

To create this program listing in HTML, you have to first understand the HTML table structure.

Marking Tables and Table Rows

Each table in a Web page follows a basic structure consisting of the table element and a collection of table rows nested in the table element. The general HTML code for a Web table is

```
<table>
    <tr>
    table cells
    </tr>
    <tr>
    table cells
    </tr>
...
</table>
```

where <table> marks the table element, <tr> marks each row, and *table cells* are the cells within each row. Note that the dimension of a Web table is defined by the number of rows and the number of cells within the rows. There is no HTML element to mark a table column. You'll explore how to create table cells shortly. Tables are considered block-level elements, so when rendered by a browser, they'll appear on a new line on the Web page. Like other block-level elements, you can float tables and resize them using the same styles you've already studied.

Kyle's proposed Web table has 10 rows, with the first row containing the days of the week, followed by nine rows listing the KPAF shows from 6:00 p.m. to 10:30 p.m. in half-hour intervals. For now, you'll insert tr elements for just the first three rows of the table. You'll also include a class attribute, placing the table in the schedule class of elements to distinguish it from other tables on the KPAF Web site.

To insert the table and tr elements:

▶ 1. Return to the **schedule.htm** file in your text editor.

▶ 2. Directly above the address element, insert the following code, as shown in Figure 5-3:

```
<table class="schedule">
   <tr>
   </tr>
   <tr>
   </tr>
   <tr>
   </tr>
</table>
```

Figure 5-3 ▶ **Marking a table and table rows**

```
<table class="schedule">
   <tr>
   </tr>
   <tr>                    ◀── table rows
   </tr>
   <tr>
   </tr>
</table>

<address>
   KPAF &#183;
   4300 Magnolia Lane, Bismarck ND 58504 &#183;
   (701) 555 - 5611
</address>
```

At this point you have a table with three rows but nothing within those rows. The next part of the table structure is the cells within each row.

Marking Table Headings and Table Data

There are two types of table cells: those that contain headings and those that contain data. The two tags are different so that the headings in a table are formatted differently than the rest of the cells. **Table headings**, the cells that identify the contents of a row or column, are marked using a <th> tag. You can place a <th> tag anywhere in a table, but you'll most often place one at the top of a column or at the beginning of a row. Most browsers display table headings in a bold font, centered within the table cell.

Kyle wants you to mark the cells in the first row of the radio schedule as headings because the text identifies the contents of each column. He also wants the first cells in the remaining rows displaying the time to be marked as headings. Add these cells to the first three columns of the schedule table.

To insert the table headings:

▶ 1. Return to the **schedule.htm** file in your text editor.

▶ 2. In the first table row, insert the following th elements:

```
<th>Time</th>
<th>Monday</th>
<th>Tuesday</th>
<th>Wednesday</th>
<th>Thursday</th>
<th>Friday</th>
<th>Saturday</th>
<th>Sunday</th>
```

3. Insert the heading

```
<th>6:00</th>
```

in the second table row.

4. In the third table row insert the following heading:

```
<th>6:30</th>
```

5. Figure 5-4 shows the revised code in the schedule table.

Inserting table heading cells | Figure 5-4

```
<table class="schedule">
   <tr>
                <th>Time</th>
                <th>Monday</th>
                <th>Tuesday</th>
table headings →  <th>Wednesday</th>
                <th>Thursday</th>
                <th>Friday</th>
                <th>Saturday</th>
                <th>Sunday</th>
   </tr>
   <tr>
        → <th>6:00</th>
   </tr>
   <tr>
        → <th>6:30</th>
   </tr>
</table>
```

The other type of table cells is **data cells**, which are marked with the <td> tag and are used for any content that is not considered a heading. Most browsers display table data using unformatted text, left-aligned within the cell. You'll use table data cells to insert the names of the KPAF programs. KPAF airs the national and local news at 6:00 and 6:30, respectively, every night of the week. Add these broadcasts to the schedule table.

To insert table data for the next two rows of the table:

1. Return to the **schedule.htm** file in your text editor.

2. In the second table row, insert the following td elements:

```
<td>National News</td>
<td>National News</td>
<td>National News</td>
<td>National News</td>
<td>National News</td>
<td>National News</td>
<td>National News</td>
```

3. In the third table row, insert the following elements:

```
<td>Local News</td>
<td>Local News</td>
<td>Local News</td>
<td>Local News</td>
<td>Local News</td>
<td>Local News</td>
<td>Local News</td>
```

Figure 5-5 shows the newly inserted HTML code.

| Figure 5-5 | Inserting table data cells |

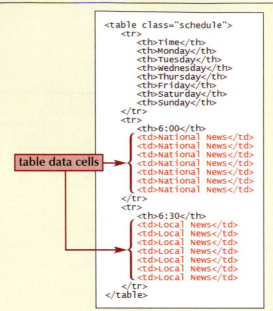

```
<table class="schedule">
    <tr>
        <th>Time</th>
        <th>Monday</th>
        <th>Tuesday</th>
        <th>Wednesday</th>
        <th>Thursday</th>
        <th>Friday</th>
        <th>Saturday</th>
        <th>Sunday</th>
    </tr>
    <tr>
        <th>6:00</th>
        <td>National News</td>
        <td>National News</td>
        <td>National News</td>
        <td>National News</td>
        <td>National News</td>
        <td>National News</td>
        <td>National News</td>
    </tr>
    <tr>
        <th>6:30</th>
        <td>Local News</td>
        <td>Local News</td>
        <td>Local News</td>
        <td>Local News</td>
        <td>Local News</td>
        <td>Local News</td>
        <td>Local News</td>
    </tr>
</table>
```

table data cells

4. Save your changes to the file, and then refresh the **schedule.htm** file in your Web browser. Figure 5-6 shows the current appearance of the programming schedule. The headings are in bold and centered, and the table data is in a normal font and left-aligned.

| Figure 5-6 | Viewing the Web table |

KPAF Nightly Schedule

KPAF airs listener-supported public radio in Bismarck, North Dakota from 5:00 a.m. to 10:30 p.m. You can Listen Live to streaming audio of our broadcast. Please refer below for our current nightly schedule.

Time	Monday	Tuesday	Wednesday	Thursday	Friday	Saturday	Sunday
6:00	National News	National News	National News	National News	National News	National News	National News
6:30	Local News	Local News	Local News	Local News	Local News	Local News	Local News

Trouble? If your table looks different than Figure 5-6, you might have inserted an incorrect number of table cells. Check your code and verify that you've inserted one table header and seven table data cells in each row.

- To mark a Web table, use the element
  ```
  <table>rows</table>
  ```
  where *rows* are the rows of the table.
- To mark a table row, use the element
  ```
  <tr>cells</tr>
  ```
  where *cells* are the table cells contained within the row.
- To mark a cell containing a row or column heading, use the element
  ```
  <th>content</th>
  ```
  where *content* is the content of the heading.
- To mark a cell containing table data, use the element
  ```
  <td>content</td>
  ```
  where *content* is the content of the table data.

> **Tip**
>
> To place an empty table cell anywhere within a row, insert the <td> </td> tag into the row.

The table you created for Kyle has three rows and eight columns. Remember that the number of columns is determined by the maximum number of cells within each row. If one row has four cells and another row has five, the table will have five columns. The row with only four cells will have an empty space at the end, where the fifth cell should be.

Adding a Table Border

By default, there are no gridlines displayed in a Web table, making it difficult to see the table structure. You decide the table would be easier to read with gridlines marking each cell in the table. To add gridlines, insert the attribute

```
<table border="value">
   ...
</table>
```

in the table element, where *value* is the width of the table border in pixels. Figure 5-7 shows how different border values affect the appearance of a sample table.

Tables with different border sizes | Figure 5-7

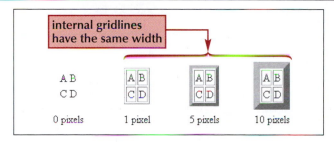

Note that the border attribute does not control the width of internal gridlines; however, to display internal gridlines you must add a border to the table. You can change the width of the internal gridlines by changing the space between the table cells, an issue you'll examine in the next session.

Adding a Table Border Using HTML

- To add a border to a Web table using HTML, use the border attribute
  ```
  <table border="value"> ... </table>
  ```
  where *value* is the size of the border in pixels.

You decide to add a 1-pixel border to the schedule table. Because of the border, your browser will also insert gridlines around each of the table cells.

To add a border to the schedule:

▶ 1. Return to the **schedule.htm** file in your text editor and add the attribute

   border="1"

   to the opening <table> tag, as shown in Figure 5-8.

Figure 5-8 ▶ **Adding a table border**

```
<table class="schedule" border="1">
    <tr>
        <th>Time</th>
        <th>Monday</th>
        <th>Tuesday</th>
        <th>Wednesday</th>
        <th>Thursday</th>
        <th>Friday</th>
        <th>Saturday</th>
        <th>Sunday</th>
    </tr>
```

table cells will be surrounded by a 1-pixel-wide border

▶ 2. Save your changes to the file, and then reload the schedule page in your Web browser. Figure 5-9 shows the revised table with the border and the internal gridlines added.

Figure 5-9 ▶ **Web table with cell borders** 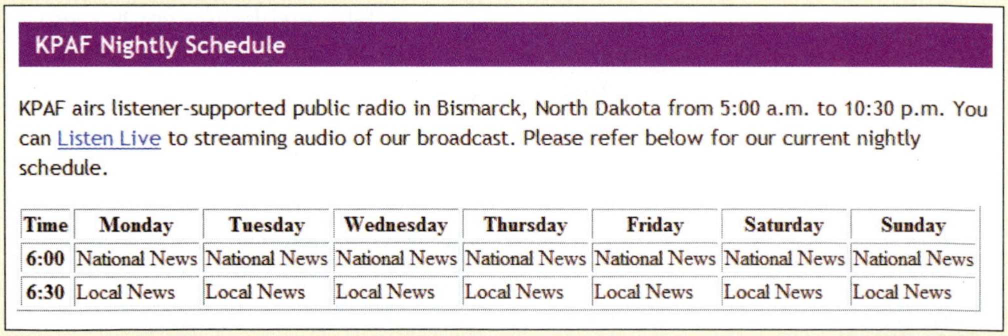

KPAF Nightly Schedule

KPAF airs listener-supported public radio in Bismarck, North Dakota from 5:00 a.m. to 10:30 p.m. You can Listen Live to streaming audio of our broadcast. Please refer below for our current nightly schedule.

Time	Monday	Tuesday	Wednesday	Thursday	Friday	Saturday	Sunday
6:00	National News	National News	National News	National News	National News	National News	National News
6:30	Local News	Local News	Local News	Local News	Local News	Local News	Local News

| Table Border Colors | | InSight |

Most browsers display the table border in gray in a raised style that gives the border a 3D effect. There is no HTML attribute to change the border style, but many browsers allow you to change the color by adding the bordercolor attribute

```
<table border="value" bordercolor="color"> ... </table>
```

to the table element, where *color* is either a recognized color name or a hexadecimal color value. For example, the following HTML code adds a 10-pixel blue border to a table:

```
<table border="10" bordercolor="blue"> ... </table>
```

The exact appearance of the table border differs among browsers. Internet Explorer and Safari display the border in a solid blue color, Firefox displays the border in a raised style using two shades of blue, and Opera does not support the bordercolor attribute at all. So you should not rely on getting a consistent border color across all browsers with this attribute.

The bordercolor attribute has been deprecated by the World Wide Web Consortium (W3C) and is being gradually phased out. The recommended method is to use one of the CSS border styles discussed in Tutorial 3, but you will still see this attribute used in many Web pages.

Spanning Rows and Columns

Reviewing the schedule from Figure 5-2, you notice that several programs are longer than a half hour, and some are repeated across several days. For example, every day of the week there is national and local news at 6:00 and 6:30, respectively. Likewise, from Monday through Thursday, the hour from 7:00 to 8:00 is needed for the shows Opera Fest, Radio U, Science Week, and The Living World. And finally, the Classical Music Connection airs Monday through Thursday for two hours from 8:00 to 10:00. Rather than repeat the names of programs in all of the half-hour slots, Kyle would prefer that the table cells stretch across those hours and days.

To do this, create a **spanning cell** in which a single cell occupies more than one row or one column in the table. Spanning cells are created by inserting a rowspan or colspan attribute into a <th> or <td> tag. The syntax is

```
<th rowspan="value" colspan="value"> ... </th>
```

or

```
<td rowspan="value" colspan="value"> ... </td>
```

where *value* is the number of rows or columns that you want the table cell to cover. The spanning starts in the cell where you put the rowspan and colspan attributes and goes downward and to the right from that cell. For example, to create a data cell that spans two columns and three rows, enter the <td> tag as:

```
<td colspan="2" rowspan="3"> ... </td>
```

It's important to remember that when a cell spans multiple rows or columns, you must adjust the number of cells used elsewhere in the table. For column-spanning cells, you have to reduce the number of cells in the current row. For example, if a row contains five columns but one of the cells in the row spans three columns, you need only three cell elements in the row: two cells that occupy a single column each and one cell that spans the remaining three columns.

To see how column-spanning cells works, you'll replace the cells for the National News and Local News programs that currently occupy seven cells a piece with two cells that each span seven columns in each row.

To create cells that span several columns:

▶ 1. Return to the **schedule.htm** file in your text editor and add the attribute

```
colspan="7"
```

to the second table cell in the second and third rows of the table.

▶ 2. Delete the remaining six table cells in both the second and the third table rows. Figure 5-10 shows the revised code for the schedule table.

Figure 5-10 **Creating cells to span several columns**

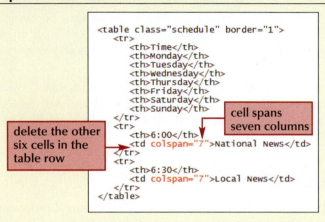

```
<table class="schedule" border="1">
    <tr>
        <th>Time</th>
        <th>Monday</th>
        <th>Tuesday</th>
        <th>Wednesday</th>
        <th>Thursday</th>
        <th>Friday</th>
        <th>Saturday</th>
        <th>Sunday</th>
    </tr>
    <tr>
        <th>6:00</th>
        <td colspan="7">National News</td>
    </tr>
    <tr>
        <th>6:30</th>
        <td colspan="7">Local News</td>
    </tr>
</table>
```

delete the other six cells in the table row

cell spans seven columns

▶ 3. Save your changes to the file, and then refresh the **schedule.htm** file in your Web browser. Figure 5-11 shows the revised appearance of the Web table.

Figure 5-11 **Column-spanning cell**

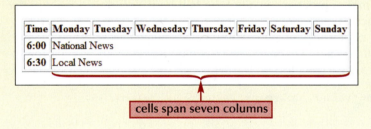

Time	Monday	Tuesday	Wednesday	Thursday	Friday	Saturday	Sunday
6:00	National News						
6:30	Local News						

cells span seven columns

To make the cell for the hour-long shows on Monday through Thursday, you'll need to span two rows, which lengthens the height of the cell. For row-spanning cells, you need to remove extra cells from the rows below the spanning cell. Consider the table shown in Figure 5-12, which contains three rows and four columns. The first cell spans three rows. You need four table cells in the first row, but only three in the second and third rows. This is because the spanning cell from row one occupies a position reserved for a cell that would normally appear in those rows.

Cells spanning several rows   Figure 5-12

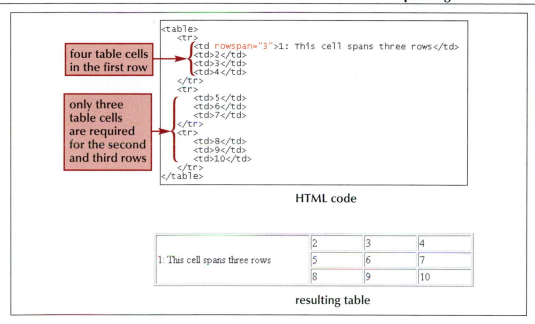

```
<table>
    <tr>
        <td rowspan="3">1: This cell spans three rows</td>
        <td>2</td>
        <td>3</td>
        <td>4</td>
    </tr>
    <tr>
        <td>5</td>
        <td>6</td>
        <td>7</td>
    </tr>
    <tr>
        <td>8</td>
        <td>9</td>
        <td>10</td>
    </tr>
</table>
```

four table cells in the first row

only three table cells are required for the second and third rows

HTML code

1: This cell spans three rows	2	3	4
	5	6	7
	8	9	10

resulting table

Creating a Spanning Cell | Reference Window

- To create a table cell that spans several columns, add the attribute
  `colspan="value"`
  to the cell, where *value* is the number of columns covered by the cell.
- To create a table cell that spans several rows, add the attribute
  `rowspan="value"`
  to the cell, where *value* is the number of rows covered by the cell.

The 7:00 to 8:00 section of the KPAF schedule contains several programs that run for an hour. To insert these programs, you'll create row-spanning cells that span two rows in the schedule table. To keep the columns lined up, you must reduce the number of cells entered in the subsequent row.

To span several table rows:

1. Return to the **schedule.htm** file in your text editor and add the following row to the bottom of the schedule table:

```
<tr>
    <th>7:00</th>
    <td rowspan="2">Opera Fest</td>
    <td rowspan="2">Radio U</td>
    <td rowspan="2">Science Week</td>
    <td rowspan="2">The Living World</td>
    <td>Word Play</td>
    <td>Agri-Week</td>
    <td rowspan="2">Folk Fest</td>
</tr>
```

2. The next row should display table cells only for the two programs that start at 7:30. The HTML code for this table row is:

```
<tr>
    <th>7:30</th>
    <td>Brain Stew</td>
    <td>Bismarck Forum</td>
</tr>
```

Figure 5-13 shows the code for the two new table rows.

Figure 5-13 | **Inserting cells that span two rows**

```
<tr>
    <th>6:30</th>
    <td colspan="7">Local News</td>
</tr>
<tr>
    <th>7:00</th>
    <td rowspan="2">Opera Fest</td>
    <td rowspan="2">Radio U</td>
    <td rowspan="2">Science Week</td>
    <td rowspan="2">The Living World</td>
    <td>Word Play</td>
    <td>Agri-Week</td>
    <td rowspan="2">Folk Fest</td>
</tr>
<tr>
    <th>7:30</th>
    <td>Brain Stew</td>
    <td>Bismarck Forum</td>
</tr>
</table>
```

3. Save your changes to the file, and then refresh the **schedule.htm** file in your Web browser. As shown in Figure 5-14, the Sunday through Thursday 7:00 p.m. programs each last an hour, spanning two table rows.

Figure 5-14 | **Schedule table with several one-hour programs spanning two table rows**

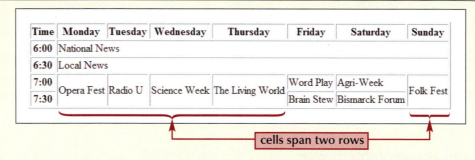

The final part of the evening schedule includes the program Classical Musical Connection, which spans two hours on Monday through Thursday. Like the news programs, you don't want to repeat the name of the show each day; and like the four hour-long programs you just entered, you don't want to repeat the name of the show in each half-hour cell. Kyle suggests that you use both the colspan and rowspan attributes to enter a table cell that spans four rows and four columns.

Other programs in the 8:00 to 10:00 time slots, such as Saturday Nite Jazz and The Indie Connection, also span four rows, but only one column. The last program aired before KPAF signs off is the World News Feed, which is played every night from 10:00 to 10:30. You'll add these and the other late evening programs to the schedule table now.

To add the remaining KPAF evening programs:

▶ 1. Return to the **schedule.htm** file in your text editor and enter the following table row for programs airing starting at 8:00:

```
<tr>
    <th>8:00</th>
    <td rowspan="4" colspan="4">The Classical Music Connection</td>
    <td>Old Time Radio</td>
    <td rowspan="4">Saturday Nite Jazz</td>
    <td rowspan="4">The Indie Connection</td>
</tr>
```

▶ 2. The Inner Mind is the only program that starts at 8:30 during the week. Add the 8:30 starting time to the table using the following row:

```
<tr>
    <th>8:30</th>
    <td>The Inner Mind</td>
</tr>
```

▶ 3. The only program that starts at 9:00 is Open Mike Nite. Add the following row to the table to display this program in the schedule:

```
<tr>
    <th>9:00</th>
    <td rowspan="2">Open Mike Nite</td>
</tr>
```

▶ 4. There are no programs that start at 9:30, so you'll add the table row but without any programs listed. Add the following row:

```
<tr>
    <th>9:30</th>
</tr>
```

▶ 5. Complete the schedule table by adding the last table row for the World News Feed occurring every night from 10:00 to 10:30. This single program occupies a single row and spans seven columns. Add the following row:

```
<tr>
    <th>10:00</th>
    <td colspan="7">World News Feed</td>
</tr>
```

Figure 5-15 shows the code completing the structure of the schedule table.

Adding the remaining KPAF evening programs ◀ **Figure 5-15**

```
<tr>
    <th>7:30</th>
    <td>Brain Stew</td>
    <td>Bismarck Forum</td>
</tr>
<tr>
    <th>8:00</th>
    <td rowspan="4" colspan="4">The Classical Music Connection</td>
    <td>Old Time Radio</td>
    <td rowspan="4">Saturday Nite Jazz</td>
    <td rowspan="4">The Indie Connection</td>
</tr>
<tr>
    <th>8:30</th>
    <td>The Inner Mind</td>
</tr>
<tr>
    <th>9:00</th>
    <td rowspan="2">Open Mike Nite</td>
</tr>
<tr>
    <th>9:30</th>
</tr>
<tr>
    <th>10:00</th>
    <td colspan="7">World News Feed</td>
</tr>
</table>
```

> **6.** Save your changes to the file, and refresh the **schedule.htm** file in your Web browser. Figure 5-16 shows the complete evening schedule of programs offered by KPAF.

Figure 5-16 ▶ **The complete KPAF evening schedule**

Time	Monday	Tuesday	Wednesday	Thursday	Friday	Saturday	Sunday
6:00	National News						
6:30	Local News						
7:00	Opera Fest	Radio U	Science Week	The Living World	Word Play	Agri-Week	Folk Fest
7:30					Brain Stew	Bismarck Forum	
8:00	The Classical Music Connection				Old Time Radio	Saturday Nite Jazz	The Indie Connection
8:30					The Inner Mind		
9:00					Open Mike Nite		
9:30							
10:00	World News Feed						

The Web table you created matches the printout of KPAF's evening schedule. Kyle likes the clear structure of the table. He notes that many KPAF listeners tune into the station over the Internet, listening to KPAF's streaming audio feed. Since those listeners might be located in different time zones, Kyle suggests that you add a caption to the table indicating that all times in the schedule are based on the Central time zone.

Creating a Table Caption

Table captions are another part of the basic table structure and are marked using the caption element

```
<table>
   <caption>content</caption>
   ...
</table>
```

where *content* is the content contained within the caption. You can nest inline elements within a caption element. For example, the following code marks the text *Program Schedule* using the em element:

```
<table>
   <caption><em>Program Schedule</em></caption>
   ...
</table>
```

Only one caption is allowed per Web table and the <caption> tag must be listed directly after the opening <table> tag. The caption is treated as a block-level element, placed directly above the table, but you can change the placement of the caption using the following align attribute:

```
<caption align="position">content</caption>
```

In this code, *position* equals top, bottom, left, or right, to place the caption either above, below, or to the left or right sides of the table.

The interpretation of the left and right align value is not consistent among the major browsers. Netscape and Firefox follow the W3C specifications and place the captions to the left or right of the Web table. Internet Explorer and Opera still place the caption above the table, but horizontally align the caption text to the left or right. The align attribute is another example of a presentational attribute that has been deprecated in favor of style sheets, though you'll still often find it used on Web sites, both old and new.

Tip

You can also use the CSS caption-side style to align caption text.

Creating a Table Caption | Reference Window

- To create a table caption, add the caption element directly below the opening <table> tag with the syntax
    ```
    <caption>content</caption>
    ```
    where content is the content of the table caption.

Add Kyle's suggested caption to the program schedule. You do not have to specify an align value because you want the caption to be above the table.

To create a caption for the program schedule:

1. Return to the **schedule.htm** file in your text editor and insert the following caption element directly below the opening tag, as shown in Figure 5-17.

    ```
    <caption>All times listed in central time</caption>
    ```

Inserting a table caption | Figure 5-17

```
<table class="schedule" border="1">
    <caption>All times listed in central time</caption>
    <tr>
        <th>Time</th>
        <th>Monday</th>
        <th>Tuesday</th>
        <th>Wednesday</th>
        <th>Thursday</th>
        <th>Friday</th>
        <th>Saturday</th>
        <th>Sunday</th>
    </tr>
```

2. Save your changes to the file and refresh the **schedule.htm** file in your Web browser. As shown in Figure 5-18, Kyle's suggested caption appears centered above the Web table.

Table caption for the KPAF programming schedule | Figure 5-18

All times listed in central time							
Time	**Monday**	**Tuesday**	**Wednesday**	**Thursday**	**Friday**	**Saturday**	**Sunday**
6:00	National News						
6:30	Local News						
7:00	Opera Fest	Radio U	Science Week	The Living World	Word Play	Agri-Week	Folk Fest
7:30					Brain Stew	Bismarck Forum	
8:00	The Classical Music Connection				Old Time Radio	Saturday Nite Jazz	The Indie Connection
8:30					The Inner Mind		
9:00					Open Mike Nite		
9:30							
10:00	World News Feed						

Although table captions might lie outside of the borders of the Web table, they are still part of the Web table's structure. This means that they'll inherit any styles associated with the table. For example, if you create a style for the table that sets the font color to red, the caption text will also be in a red font. You'll explore how to apply styles to table captions in the next session.

Marking Row Groups

You can divide a table's rows into **row groups**, in which each group element contains different types of content and can be formatted differently. HTML supports three row groups: one to mark the header rows, another for the body rows, and a third for the footer rows. The syntax to create these three row groups is:

```
<table>
   <thead>
      table rows
   </thead>
   <tfoot>
      table rows
   </tfoot>
   <tbody>
      table rows
   </tbody>
</table>
```

where *table rows* are rows from the Web table. For example, the following code marks two rows as belonging to the table header row group:

```
<thead>
   <tr>
      <th colspan="2">KPAF Programs</th>
   </tr>
   <tr>
      <th>Time</th>
      <th>Program</th>
   </tr>
</thead>
```

Tip

The table header, table body, and table footer must all contain the same number of columns.

Order is important. The thead element must appear first, and then the tfoot element, and finally the tbody element. A table can contain only one set of thead and tfoot elements, but it can have any number of tbody elements. The reason the body group appears last and not the footer group is to allow the browser to render the footer before receiving what might be numerous groups of table body rows.

One purpose of row groups is to allow you to create different styles for groups of rows in your table. Any style that you apply to the thead, tbody, or tfoot elements is inherited by the rows those elements contain. Row groups are also used for tables that import their data from external data sources such as databases or XML documents. In those situations, a single table can span several Web pages, and it's helpful to have the rows within the thead and tfoot elements repeated on every page.

Creating Row Groups | Reference Window

- Row groups must be entered in the following order: table header rows, table footer rows, and then table body rows.
- To create a row group consisting of header rows, add the element
  ```
  <thead>
      rows
  </thead>
  ```
  within the table, where *rows* are the row elements within the table header.
- To create a row group consisting of footer rows, add the following element:
  ```
  <tfoot>
      rows
  </tfoot>
  ```
- To create a row group consisting of rows used in the body of the table, add the following element:
  ```
  <tbody>
      rows
  </tbody>
  ```
  A table can have multiple table body row groups.

To indicate the structure of the schedule table, you decide to the use the thead element to mark the header row in the program schedule and the tbody element to mark the rows that include the broadcast times of each program. You do not need to specify a footer for this table.

To mark the row groups:

1. Return to the **schedule.htm** file in your text editor and enclose the first row of the table within an opening and closing set of **<thead>** tags.

2. Enclose the remaining rows of the table within an opening and closing set of **<tbody>** tags. Figure 5-19 shows the markup tags for the two new row groups.

Figure 5-19   **Marking the table header and table body row groups**

```
<table class="schedule" border="1">
    <caption>All times listed in central time</caption>

    <thead>
    <tr>
        <th>Time</th>
        <th>Monday</th>
        <th>Tuesday</th>
        <th>Wednesday</th>
        <th>Thursday</th>
        <th>Friday</th>
        <th>Saturday</th>
        <th>Sunday</th>
    </tr>
    </thead>

    <tbody>
    <tr>
        <th>6:00</th>
        <td colspan="7">National News</td>
    </tr>



    <tr>
        <th>9:30</th>
    </tr>
    <tr>
        <th>10:00</th>
        <td colspan="7">World News Feed</td>
    </tr>
    </tbody>

</table>
```

Marking Column Groups

As you've seen, there is no HTML tag to mark table columns—the columns are created implicitly from the number of cells within each row. However, once the columns have been determined by the browser, you can reference them through the use of **column groups**. Column groups give you the ability to assign a common format to all of the cells within a given column. Column groups are defined using the colgroup element

```
<colgroup>
    columns
</colgroup>
```

where *columns* are the individual columns with the group. The columns themselves are referenced using the following empty element:

```
<col />
```

The number of col elements must match the number of columns in the Web table. Once you create a column group, you can add id or class attributes to identify or classify individual columns. For example, the following code creates a column group consisting of three columns, each with a different class name:

```
<colgroup>
    <col class="column1" />
    <col class="column2" />
    <col class="column3" />
</colgroup>
```

The browser takes any style specified for the col element and applies it to cells within the column. So to create columns with different background colors, you could apply the inline styles

```
col.column1 {background-color: red}
col.column2 {background-color: blue}
col.column3 {background-color: yellow}
```

and the browser will display the first table column with a background color of red, the second with blue, and the third with yellow. Note that not all CSS styles can be applied to table columns. You'll explore column styles in more detail in the next session.

The col element also supports the span attribute, allowing a column reference to cover several table columns. The syntax of the span attribute is

```
<col span="value" />
```

where *value* is the number of columns referenced by the col element. The column structure

```
<colgroup>
   <col class="column1" />
   <col class="nextColumns" span="2" />
</colgroup>
```

references a group of three columns; the first column belongs to the column1 class and the next two columns belong to the nextColumns class. Note that you can also apply the span attribute to a column group itself. The following code uses two column groups to also reference three columns, the first belonging to the column1 class and the last two belonging to the nextColumns class:

```
<colgroup class="column1"></colgroup>
<colgroup class="nextColumns span="2"></colgroup>
```

Notice that in this case there are no col elements within the column group. The browser will assume the number of columns indicated by the span attribute; if no span attribute is present, the column group is assumed to have only one column.

Creating Column Groups

| Reference Window

- To create a column group, add the element
  ```
  <colgroup>
      columns
  </colgroup>
  ```
  to the Web table, where *columns* are individual columns within the group.
- To define a column or columns within a column group, use the element
  ```
  <col span="value" />
  ```
  where *value* is the number of defined columns. The span attribute is not required if only one column is defined.

Now that you've seen how columns can be referenced through the use of column groups, you'll create a column group for the programming table. You'll place the first column containing the broadcast times for the different KPAF programs in one column with the class name firstCol and the remaining seven columns containing the daily program listings in a column group with the class name dayCols. These groupings will allow you to format the two sets of columns in different ways later on.

To mark the column groups:

▶ 1. Return to the **schedule.htm** file in your text editor.

▶ 2. Directly below the table caption, insert the following code, as shown in Figure 5-20:

```
<colgroup>
   <col class="firstCol" />
   <col class="dayCols" span="7" />
</colgroup>
```

Figure 5-20	Inserting a column group

```
<table class="schedule" border="1">
    <caption>All times listed in central time</caption>

    <colgroup>
        <col class="firstCol" />
        <col class="dayCols" span="7" />
    </colgroup>
```
col element spans
seven columns

▶ 3. Save your changes to the file.

▶ 4. Creating row groups and column groups adds to the structure and flexibility of the table, but should not alter its appearance. To confirm that the row and column groups have not modified the table's appearance, refresh the **schedule.htm** file in your browser. Verify that the table layout is the same as that shown earlier in Figure 5-18.

Adding a Table Summary

Nonvisual browsers (such as aural browsers that are often used by visually impaired people) can't display tables, and it's cumbersome to listen to each cell being read. For these situations, it is useful to include a summary of a table's contents. While a caption and the surrounding page text usually provide clues about the table and its contents, the summary attribute allows you to include a more detailed description. The syntax of the summary attribute is

```
<table summary="description"> ... </table>
```

where *description* is a text string that describes the table's content and structure. The summary attribute fills the same role that the alt attribute fills for inline image: providing a textual (aural) alternative to what could be a long and complicated table. A user running a screen reader or other type of aural browser will first hear the summary of the table's contents, which can then aid in interpreting the subsequent reading of the table's content.

Kyle definitely wants the KPAF Web page to be accessible to users with all types of disabilities and asks that you include a summary description of the program schedule.

To add a summary to the table:

▶ 1. Return to the **schedule.htm** file in your text editor.

▶ 2. Within the opening <table> tag insert the following attribute as shown in Figure 5-21.

```
summary="This table contains the nightly KPAF program schedule aired
from Bismarck, North Dakota. Program times are laid out in
thirty-minute increments from 6:00 p.m. to 10:00 p.m., Monday through
Sunday night."
```

```
<table class="schedule" border="1"
       summary="This table contains the nightly KPAF program schedule aired
                from Bismarck, North Dakota. Program times are laid out in
                thirty-minute increments from 6:00 p.m. to 10:00 p.m., Monday
                through Sunday night.">

    <caption>All times listed in central time</caption>
```

3. Save your changes to the file, and then reload the **schedule.htm** file in your Web browser. Verify that the summary description does *not* appear in the browser window.

4. If you plan on taking a break before starting the next session, close your open files and programs now.

Tip

In some browsers, you can view the summary description by right-clicking the table and selecting Properties from the shortcut menu.

Creating Tables with Preformatted Text | InSight

As you learned in Tutorial 1, browsers strip out white space from the HTML code when they render Web pages. You can force the browser the keep certain white space by marking your document text as **preformatted text**, in which the browser displays the spacing and line breaks exactly as you enter it. Preformatted text is created using the tag

```
<pre>content</pre>
```

where *content* is the text that will appear preformatted in the browser. One use of preformatted text is to quickly create tables, neatly laid out in rows and columns. For example, the code

```
<pre>
Time    Friday      Saturday
====    ==========  ==============
7:30    Brain Stew  Bismarck Forum
</pre>
```

is displayed by the browser exactly as typed, with the spaces as shown:

```
Time    Friday      Saturday
====    ==========  ==============
7:30    Brain Stew  Bismarck Forum
```

Preformatted text is displayed by the browser in a **monospace font** in which each letter takes up the same amount of space. One of the advantages of monospace fonts that make them useful for entering tabular data is that the relative space between characters is unchanged as the font size increases or decreases. This means that if the font size of the above table were increased or decreased, the columns would still line up.

Although you should probably use Web tables to display most of your data, you might want to consider using preformatted text for simple and quick text tables.

You've completed your work in laying out the basic structure of the KPAF program schedule. The next thing Kyle wants you to focus on is formatting the table to be attractive and professional. In the next session you'll explore how to apply design styles to make an interesting and attractive Web table.

1. There is no HTML tag that marks a column; how is the number of columns in a Web table determined?
2. How does a browser usually render text marked with the <th> tag?
3. Specify the code to add a 10-pixel-wide border to a Web table.
4. A cell contains the text "Monday" and should stretch across 2 rows and 3 columns. Specify the HTML for the cell.
5. What adjustment do you have to make when a cell spans multiple columns?
6. Captions usually appear above or below their Web tables. Explain why a caption is still part of a table's structure.
7. What are the three table row groups, and in what order should they be specified in the code?
8. Specify the code to create a column group in which the first two columns belong to the introCol class and the next three columns belong to the col1, col2, and col3 classes, respectively.
9. What is the purpose of the table summary attribute?

Session 5.2

Formatting Tables with HTML Attributes

After specifying the content and structure of the program schedule, you and Kyle are ready to format the table's appearance. There are two approaches to formatting Web tables. One is to use HTML attributes, and the other is to use CSS styles. Because you'll see both approaches used on the Internet, you'll examine both techniques, starting with the HTML attribute approach.

Setting Cell Spacing with HTML

Web tables are one of the older HTML page elements, predating the introduction of cascading style sheets. Because of this, HTML has long supported several attributes controlling a table's layout and appearance. In the last session you used one of those attributes, the border attribute, to create a table border and display internal table gridlines. The next attribute you'll consider controls the amount of space between table cells, which is known as the **cell spacing**. By default, browsers set the cell spacing to 2 pixels. To set a different cell spacing value, add the cellspacing attribute

```
<table cellspacing="value"> ... </table>
```

to the table element, where *value* is the size of the cell spacing in pixels. If you have applied a border to your table, changing the cell spacing value also impacts the size of the internal gridlines. Figure 5-22 shows how different cell spacing values affect the appearance of the table border and internal gridlines. Note that if the cell spacing is set to 0 pixels, the browser will still display an internal gridline that comes from the drop shadow that browsers apply to cell and table borders.

Cell spacing values ◢ **Figure 5-22**

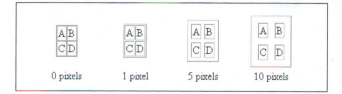

Cell spacing essentially sets the outside margins of the table cells. Unlike the CSS margin style, you can specify cell spacing values only in pixels and not other measuring units, nor can you set different cell spacing values for the different sides of the cell. Also, the effect of setting the cell spacing value is limited by the width allotted to the entire table. The browser ignores cell spacing values that would push the table beyond its defined width.

Setting Cell Padding with HTML

Related to cell spacing is **cell padding**, which is the space between the cell contents and the cell border. You set the padding using the attribute

```
<table cellpadding="value"> ... </table>
```

where *value* is the size of the cell padding. Like the cellspacing attribute, the cellpadding attribute applies to every cell in the table. Figure 5-23 shows the impact of various cell padding values on the table's appearance. Cell padding is similar to the CSS padding style, though there is no option to define padding values for different sides of the cell; and like the cellspacing attribute, cell padding values can only be expressed in pixels and not other units of measure.

Cell padding values ◢ **Figure 5-23**

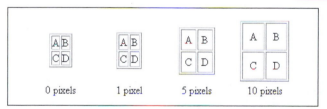

Kyle would like you to experiment with how the cellpadding and cellspacing attributes might affect the appearance of the program schedule, so you'll add these two attributes to the table element, setting the cell spacing to 3 pixels and the cell padding to 5 pixels.

To set the cell padding and cell spacing:

1. Return to the **schedule.htm** file in your text editor.

2. Within the opening <table> tag, insert the following attribute, as shown in Figure 5-24.

   ```
   cellspacing="3" cellpadding="5"
   ```

Figure 5-24   Setting the cell spacing and padding values

```
<table class="schedule" border="1" cellspacing="3" cellpadding="5"
       summary="This table contains the nightly KPAF program schedule aired
       from Bismarck, North Dakota. Program times are laid out in
       thirty-minute increments from 6:00 p.m. to 10:00 p.m., Monday
       through Sunday night.">
```

3. Save your changes to the file, and then open **schedule.htm** in your Web browser. As shown in Figure 5-25, the space between and within the table cells has been increased from their default values.

Figure 5-25   Table with increased cell spacing and padding

Time	Monday	Tuesday	Wednesday	Thursday	Friday	Saturday	Sunday
6:00	National News						
6:30	Local News						
7:00	Opera Fest	Radio U	Science Week	The Living World	Word Play	Agri-Week	Folk Fest
7:30					Brain Stew	Bismarck Forum	
8:00	The Classical Music Connection				Old Time Radio	Saturday Nite Jazz	The Indie Connection
8:30					The Inner Mind		
9:00					Open Mike Nite		
9:30							
10:00	World News Feed						

Setting Table Widths and Heights in HTML

You can use HTML to set the overall width and height of the table, and of the individual cells within the table. By default, the width of tables will range from the minimum necessary to display all the cell contents without the line wrapping up to the width of the container element. To set the width of the table to a specific value, add the width attribute

```
<table width="value"> ... </table>
```

to the table element, where *value* is the width either in pixels or as a percentage of the width of the containing element. If the containing element is the page itself, you can set the table to fill the entire page width by specifying a width value of 100%. You can still never reduce a table to a width smaller than is required to display the content or larger than the width of its container. For example, if the table content requires a width of 450 pixels, then the browser will ignore any width attribute that attempts to set a smaller table size.

Many browsers also support the height attribute, which has the syntax

```
<table height="value"> ... </table>
```

where *value* is the height of the table either in pixels or as a percentage of the height of the containing element. Even though the height attribute is widely supported, it is not part of the HTML specifications nor is it supported by XHTML. Like the width attribute, the height attribute indicates only the minimum height of the table. If the table content cannot fit into the specified height, the table height increases to match the content.

You can also set the width of individual columns by applying the width attribute to either an individual column or a column group. For example, the HTML code

```
<colgroup width="100" span="7">
</colgroup>
```

sets the width of each of seven columns from the table to 100 pixels. To specify different column widths, apply the width attribute to individual col elements as in the code

```
<colgroup>
   <col width="50" />
   <col width="100" span="5" />
   <col width="50" />
</colgroup>
```

which sets the widths of the five middle columns to 100 pixels, but sets the width of the first and seventh columns to 50 pixels each. Column widths can also be expressed as a percentage of the total width of the table. A column width of 50% causes a column to occupy half of the table width. Column widths are always limited by the total width of the table and the content that each cell contains. For example, if you try to set the width of each column in a five-column table to 200 pixels but only 800 pixels of space is available, the browser will adjust the column widths down to fit the content.

In the code for many Web tables, you might see the width attribute applied to individual table cells. This is another way to set the width of an entire column because the remaining cells in the column will adopt that width to keep the column cells aligned. Even so, the width value for a single cell might be overridden by the browser if other cells in the column require a larger width to display their content. With the introduction of column groups, there is little need to apply the width attribute to individual table cells. Also, the W3C has deprecated the use of the width attribute with the td and th elements. As you might expect, however, you will still see it supported by many of the current browsers.

Tip

Width and height values should always be thought of as minimum widths and heights because they will be overridden whenever the content of the table requires it.

Setting Row Heights with HTML

You can use HTML to set the row heights by applying the height attribute

```
<tr height="value"> ... </tr>
```

to the tr element, where *value* is the height of the row in pixels. Internet Explorer also allows you to specify height values as a percentage of the height of the table. The height attribute is not part of the W3C specifications, but most browsers support it. As with setting the column width by setting the width of an individual cell, you can also set the row height by applying the height attribute to an individual cell within the row. This approach is also supported by most browsers even though it has been deprecated by the W3C.

Formatting Table Borders with HTML

In the last session you used the border attribute to add a border around the table and each of the table cells. You can modify the placement of the table borders using table frames and table rules. A **table frame** specifies which sides of the table (or which sides of the table cells) will have borders. To apply a frame to a table, apply the frame attribute

```
<table border="value" frame="type"> ... </table>
```

to the table element, where *value* is the width of the table border and *type* is box (the default), above, border, below, hsides, vsides, lhs, rhs, or void. Figure 5-26 describes each of these frame options.

Figure 5-26 > **Values of the frame attribute**

Frame Value	Border Appearance
above	only above the table
below	only below the table
border	around all four sides of the table
box	around all four sides of the table
hsides	on the top and bottom sides of the table (the horizontal sides)
lhs	only on the left side
rhs	only on the right side
void	no border is drawn around the table
vsides	on the left and right sides of the table (the vertical sides)

Figure 5-27 shows the impact of these frame attribute values on a sample table grid.

Figure 5-27 > **Frame examples**

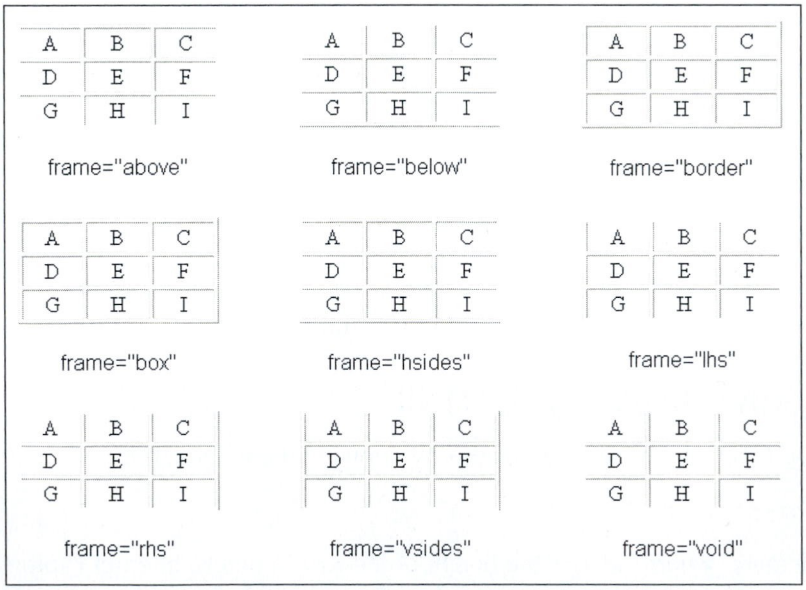

A **table rule** specifies how the internal gridlines are drawn within the table. To apply a table rule, add the rules attribute

```
<table border="value" rules="type"> ... </table>
```

to the table element, where *type* is all (the default), cols, groups, none, or rows. Figure 5-28 describes the impact of each of these rules attribute values on the placement of the internal table gridlines.

Values of the rules attribute | Figure 5-28

Rules Value	Description of Rules
all	places gridlines around all table cells
cols	places gridlines around columns
groups	places gridlines around row groups
none	displays no gridlines
rows	places gridlines around rows

Figure 5-29 shows how these rules values would appear in a sample table.

Rules examples | Figure 5-29

rules="all"   rules="cols"   rules="groups"

rules="none"   rules="rows"

By combining frame and rules values, you can duplicate many of the same effects you could achieve using the CSS border-style property, which you'll explore shortly. Some Web page authors prefer to work with these HTML attributes because they enable them to set the appearance of the table borders from within the <table> tag rather than through an external style sheet.

Aligning Cell Contents with HTML

The final set of HTML table attributes you'll examine before looking at CSS table styles are those attributes that control how content is aligned within each table cell. By default, browsers horizontally center the contents of table header cells and left-align the contents of table data cells. You can specify a different horizontal alignment using the align attribute

```
align="position"
```

where *position* is left, center, right, justify or char. The align attribute can be applied to table rows, row groups, columns, column groups, or individual table cells. For example, the code

```
<colgroup>
   <col align="left" />
   <col span="6" align="right" />
</colgroup>
```

left-aligns the first column of the Web table and right-aligns the remaining six columns. When you apply the align attribute to the table element, it aligns the entire table with the surrounding page content but does not affect the alignment of the cells within the table. The align attribute has been deprecated for use with the table element, but not for the row, column, and cell elements within the table.

InSight | **Character Alignment**

Another alignment option included with the align attribute is the char value, which tells the browser to align the values in a cell based on the position of a particular character. The default character is a decimal point, which is represented by a period in the English language and by commas in some European languages (such as French). To line up all of the data values within a column by their decimal points, enter the following code:

```
<col align="char" />
```

You can specify a different character by adding the char attribute to the tag. You can also specify how much the alignment character is offset from the cell borders using the charoff attribute. The syntax of these attributes is

```
align="char" char="character" charoff="position"
```

where *character* is the alignment character and *position* is the position of the character within the table cell either in pixels or as a percentage of the cell's width. So the HTML code

```
<col align="char" char="," charoff="50%" />
```

aligns all of the column values by the position of the comma character. The comma character itself will be placed in the center of each cell in the column.

While useful for displaying financial or scientific data, the character alignment attributes have not received much support in the browser market, so their potential is still mostly unfulfilled.

Vertical Alignment in HTML

You can also use HTML to vertically align the contents of each table cell. The default is to place the text in the middle of the cell. To choose a different placement, apply the valign attribute

```
valign="position"
```

where *position* is top, middle, bottom, or baseline. The top, middle, and bottom options align the content with the top, middle, and bottom borders of the cell. The baseline option places the text near the bottom of the cell but aligns the bases of each letter. The valign attribute can be applied to table rows, row groups, columns, and column groups to set the vertical alignment of several cells at once.

Kyle feels that having the program names placed in the middle of each cell makes the program schedule more difficult to read. He prefers having all of the program names lined up with the top of the cells. To change the cell alignment for all of the cells in the table body, you'll apply the valign attribute to the tbody row group.

To vertically align the text in the table:

▶ 1. Return to the **schedule.htm** file in your text editor.

▶ 2. Within the opening <tbody> tag, insert the following attribute, as shown in Figure 5-30:

```
valign="top"
```

Applying the valign attribute ▷ **Figure 5-30**

```
<tbody valign="top">
    <tr>
        <th>6:00</th>
        <td colspan="7">National News</td>
    </tr>
```

▶ **3.** Save your changes to the file, and then reload or refresh the **schedule.htm** file in your Web browser. As shown in Figure 5-31, the text is aligned at the top of the cells.

Cell content aligned with the top of each table cell ▷ **Figure 5-31**

Time	Monday	Tuesday	Wednesday	Thursday	Friday	Saturday	Sunday
6:00	National News						
6:30	Local News						
7:00	Opera Fest	Radio U	Science Week	The Living World	Word Play	Agri-Week	Folk Fest
7:30					Brain Stew	Bismarck Forum	
8:00	The Classical Music Connection				Old Time Radio	Saturday Nite Jazz	The Indie Connection
8:30					The Inner Mind		
9:00					Open Mike Nite		
9:30							
10:00	World News Feed						

Kyle likes the appearance of the program table. But he notes that this is only the evening schedule; he plans to create other Web pages for the morning and afternoon schedules. To have the tables match each other, you'll have to insert the various HTML attributes into each table's markup tags. Kyle would rather use CSS so he can easily apply the formatting he likes to all of the schedules at once. He suggests that you explore the CSS table styles before continuing your design of the evening schedule.

Formatting Tables with CSS

Starting with CSS2, Cascading Style Sheets included support for Web tables. With more browser support for these styles, CSS has gradually replaced the HTML attributes you've just reviewed (though you will still see those HTML attributes frequently used on the Web). Kyle suggests that you replace the HTML table attributes with an external style sheet that he can apply to all of the program schedule tables on the KPAF Web site.

To create the style sheet:

1. Open the **tablestxt.css** file from the tutorial.05\tutorial folder included with your Data Files. Enter *your name* and *the date* in the comment section of the file. Save the file as **tables.css** in the same folder.

2. Return to the **schedule.htm** file in your text editor and insert the following link element directly above the closing </head> tag:

   ```
   <link href="tables.css" rel="stylesheet" type="text/css" />
   ```

3. Because you'll be replacing the HTML attributes with CSS styles, delete the border, cellpadding, and cellspacing attributes from the opening <table> tag.

4. Delete the valign attribute from the opening <tbody> tag.

5. Save your changes to the file.

Now that you've linked the schedule.htm file to the tables.css style sheet and you've removed the old HTML table attributes, you are ready to begin creating the style sheet. You'll start with styles for the table border.

Table Border Styles

The first styles you'll apply to the program schedule are the border styles. Web tables use the same border styles you've already used with other page elements in previous tutorials. Unlike the HTML border attribute, you can apply one set of borders to the Web table itself and another set of borders to the individual cells within the table. You decide to add a 10-pixel purple border around the entire schedule table in the outset style. You'll also add a 1-pixel solid gray border around each cell within the table.

To add the table border styles:

1. Return to the **tables.css** file in your text editor. Add the following style to apply a border to the entire Web table:

   ```
   table.schedule {border: 10px outset rgb(153, 0, 153)}
   ```

2. Add the following style to apply borders to each table cell. See Figure 5-32.

   ```
   table.schedule th, table.schedule td
                   {border: 1px solid gray}
   ```

Figure 5-32 ▶ Setting the table border styles

```
table.schedule          {border: 10px outset rgb(153,0,153)}
table.schedule th, table.schedule td
                {border: 1px solid gray}
```

Notice that the style sheet uses contextual selectors to apply these styles only to the schedule table and not other tables that might exist on the KPAF Web site.

3. Save your changes to the style sheet and then reload the **schedule.htm** file in your Web browser. As shown in Figure 5-33, borders have now been added to the entire table and to each table cell.

Table and cell borders ◄ **Figure 5-33**

Time	Monday	Tuesday	Wednesday	Thursday	Friday	Saturday	Sunday
colspan: All times listed in central time							
6:00	National News						
6:30	Local News						
7:00	Opera Fest	Radio U	Science Week	The Living World	Word Play	Agri-Week	Folk Fest
7:30					Brain Stew	Bismarck Forum	
8:00	The Classical Music Connection				Old Time Radio	Saturday Nite Jazz	The Indie Connection
8:30					The Inner Mind		
9:00					Open Mike Nite		
9:30							
10:00	World News Feed						

CSS provides for two ways of drawing the table borders. The default, shown in Figure 5-33, is to draw separate borders around the table cells and the entire table. The other approach is to collapse the borders in upon each other as shown in Figure 5-34, removing any space between the borders.

Separate and collapsed borders ◄ **Figure 5-34**

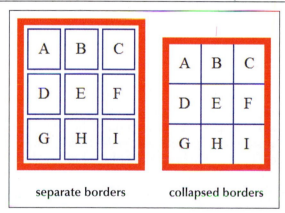

separate borders   collapsed borders

To determine whether to use the separate or collapsed border model, you apply the style

```
border-collapse: type
```

to the table element, where *type* is either separate (the default) or collapse. One of the key differences between the separate and collapse border models is that under the separate border model you can only apply borders to the table itself or to table cells. Under the collapse border model, any table object can have a border, including table rows, row groups, columns, and column groups. If the separate borders model is used, you can specify the distance between the borders by applying the style

```
border-spacing: value
```

to the table, where *value* is the space between the borders in one of the CSS units of measure. For example, the following style specifies that all borders within the table should be separated by a distance of 10 pixels:

```
table {border-collapse: separate; border-spacing: 10px}
```

The separate borders model, therefore, has the same effect as the HTML cellspacing attribute in providing additional space between table cells.

In the collapsed border model, there is no space between borders; in fact, the adjacent borders are merged together to form a single line. It's important to understand that the borders are not simply moved together, but rather they are combined into a single border. For example, if two adjacent 1-pixel-wide borders are collapsed together, the resulting border is not 2 pixels wide, but only 1 pixel wide. The situation is more complicated when the adjacent borders have different widths, styles, or colors. How would you merge a double red border and a solid blue border into a single border of only one color and style? Those kinds of differences must be reconciled before the two borders can be merged. CSS employs five rules to determine the style of the collapsed border. Listed in decreasing order of importance, the rules are:

1. If either border has a border style of hidden, the collapsed border is hidden.
2. A border style of none is overridden by any other border style.
3. If neither border is hidden, the style of the wider border takes priority over the narrower.
4. If the two borders have the same width but different styles, the border style with the highest priority is used. Double borders have the highest priority, followed by solid, dashed, dotted, ridge, outset, groove, and finally inset borders.
5. If the borders differ only in the color, the color from the table object with the highest priority is used. The highest priority color belongs to the border surrounding individual table cells, followed by the borders for table rows, row groups, columns, column groups, and finally the border around the entire table.

Any situation not covered by these rules is left to the browser to determine which border dominates when collapsing the two borders. Figure 5-35 provides an example of the first rule in action. In this example, the border around the entire table is hidden but a 1-pixel blue border is assigned to the cells within the table. When collapsed, any cell borders that are adjacent to the table border adopt the hidden border property.

| Figure 5-35 | Reconciling hidden borders |

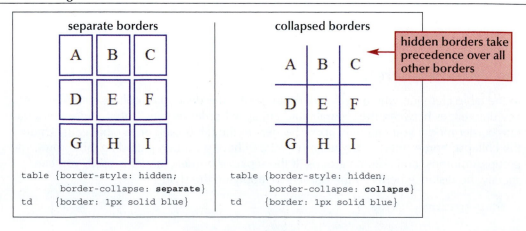

Figure 5-36 shows what happens when two borders of the same width but different styles meet. In this case, because of Rule 4, the table cell borders with the double blue lines have precedence over the solid red lines of the table border.

Reconciling different border styles   **Figure 5-36**

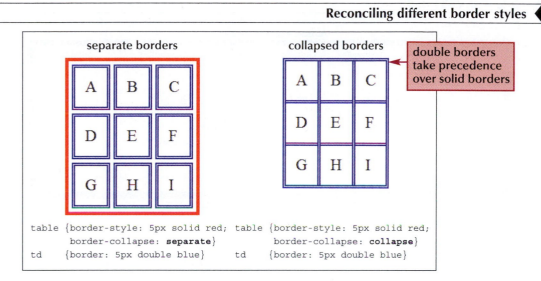

separate borders   collapsed borders   double borders take precedence over solid borders

```
table {border-style: 5px solid red;   table {border-style: 5px solid red;
       border-collapse: separate}            border-collapse: collapse}
td     {border: 5px double blue}      td     {border: 5px double blue}
```

Although the collapse model appears more complicated at first, the rules are reasonable and allow for a wide variety of border designs.

Setting Table Borders with CSS | Reference Window

- To define the border model used by the table, apply the table style
  ```
  border-collapse: type
  ```
  where *type* is separate (the default) to keep all borders around cells and the table itself, separate, or collapse to merge all adjacent borders.
- To set the space between separated borders, apply the table style
  ```
  border-spacing: value
  ```
  where *value* is the space between the borders in any of the CSS units of measure.

For the KPAF program schedule, Kyle thinks the table would look better if there were no space between the table cells. He asks you to collapse the borders.

To collapse the cell borders:

▶ 1. Return to the **tables.css** file in your text editor. Add the following style to the table element, as shown in Figure 5-37.

```
border-collapse: collapse
```

Adding the border-collapse style   **Figure 5-37**

```
table.schedule         {border: 10px outset rgb(153,0,153); border-collapse: collapse}

table.schedule th, table.schedule td
                       {border: 1px solid gray}
```

> **2.** Save your changes to the style sheet, and then reload **schedule.htm** in your Web browser. Figure 5-38 shows the revised table design with the collapsed border layout.

Figure 5-38 | **Table with collapsed borders**

Time	Monday	Tuesday	Wednesday	Thursday	Friday	Saturday	Sunday
			All times listed in central time				

Notice that the browser still uses the purple outset style for the border around the entire table. This is due to Rule 3 above. Because the border around the entire table is 10 pixels wide, it takes priority over the 1-pixel-wide borders around the individual table cells under the collapsed border model.

Applying Styles to Rows and Columns

Kyle doesn't like the appearance of the table text. He suggests changing the table text to a sans-serif font that is 0.7 em units in size. He also suggests that the text in the header row appear in a white font on a purple background and that the first column of the schedule, containing the program times, appear on a light yellow background.

You can apply these styles to the row groups and column groups you created in the last session. Recall that the header row is part of the thead row group (see Figure 5-19), and the first column of the table belongs to the firstCol class of columns (see Figure 5-20). So to apply Kyle's suggested styles, you could add the following declarations to the tables.css style sheet:

```
table.schedule                {font-family: Arial, Helvetica, sans-
                               serif; font-size: 0.7em}
table.schedule thead          {color: white; background-color:
                               rgb(203,50,203)}
table.schedule col.firstCol   {background-color: rgb(255,255,192)}
```

However, you notice a small problem. The first cell in the table belongs to both the header row and the first column. Will this cell have a purple background or a yellow background? Which style has precedence? Table objects, like other parts of CSS, have levels of precedence in which the more specific object has priority over the more general. Figure 5-39 shows a diagram of the different levels of precedence in the Web table structure.

Levels of precedence in Web table styles ◁ Figure 5-39

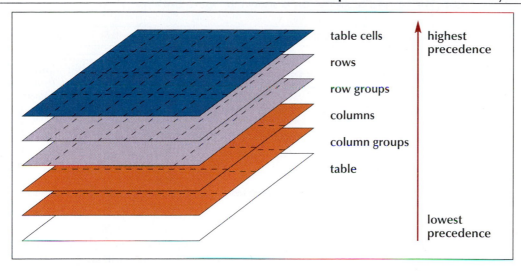

The most general styles are those applied to the entire table. Those styles are overruled by styles that are applied to column groups and then to columns. The next level up in precedence contains those styles applied to row groups and then rows. The highest level of precedence is given to those styles applied to table cells. Be aware that not all styles are supported by different layers of the table structure. In particular, columns and column groups accept only four styles: border, background, width, and visibility.

With Kyle's proposed design, the first cell should have a purple background because row groups take priority over columns or column groups. To see that this is the case, add Kyle's proposed styles to the tables.css style sheet.

To set the text and background styles in the schedule table:

▶ 1. Return to the **tables.css** file in your text editor. Add the following styles to the style declaration for the schedule table:

```
font-family: Arial, Helvetica, sans-serif; font-size: 0.7em
```

▶ 2. Go to the bottom of the style sheet and insert the following lines to create styles for the table's header row and first column as shown in Figure 5-40:

```
table.schedule thead          {color: white; background-color:
                               rgb(203,50,203)}
table.schedule col.firstCol {background-color: rgb(255,255,192)}
```

Adding font and color styles to the schedule table ◁ Figure 5-40

```
table.schedule        {border: 10px outset rgb(153,0,153); border-collapse: collapse;
                        font-family: Arial, Helvetica, sans-serif; font-size: 0.7em}
table.schedule th, table.schedule td
                      {border: 1px solid gray; font-family: Arial}          table font styles
table.schedule thead  {color: white; background-color: rgb(203,50,203)}
table.schedule col.firstCol
                      {background-color: rgb(255,255,192)}
```

style applied to thead row group

style applied to first table column

> ▶ **3.** Save your changes to the style sheet, and then reload **schedule.htm** in your Web browser. The revised table design is shown in Figure 5-41.

Figure 5-41 | **Applying styles to the header row and first column**

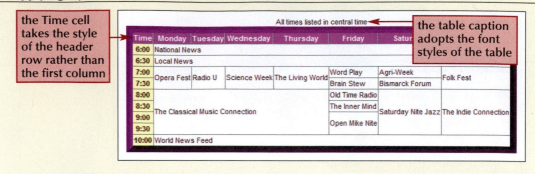

As you expected, the cell in the first column of the header row does indeed have a purple, and not a light yellow, background. Also note that all of the cells in the table and the table caption have adopted the smaller sans-serif font. This is because the font style you entered for the schedule table is inherited by all table objects unless a different font style is specified.

Using the Width and Height Styles

Reducing the font size and changing the font family has resulted in a more compact table, but Kyle thinks it could be difficult to read and wonders if you could enlarge the table. Recall that browsers will set the table width to efficiently use the page space, never making tables wider than necessary to display the content. You can use the CSS width style to specify a different table size. Widths are expressed in one of the CSS units of measure or as a percentage of the containing element. Kyle suggests that you set the width of the table to 100% so that it covers the entire width of its div container.

To set the width of the table:

> ▶ **1.** Return to the **tables.css** file in your text editor. Add the following style to the table element, as shown in Figure 5-42.
>
> `width: 100%`

Figure 5-42 | **Setting the width of the schedule table**

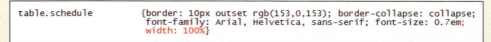

```
table.schedule          {border: 10px outset rgb(153,0,153); border-collapse: collapse;
                         font-family: Arial, Helvetica, sans-serif; font-size: 0.7em;
                         width: 100%}
```

> ▶ **2.** Save your changes to the file, and then reload **schedule.htm** in your Web browser. Figure 5-43 shows the layout of the enlarged table.

Table width set to 100% Figure 5-43

You notice that the column widths are inconsistent, with very little width given to the Time column and different widths given to different days of the week. This is because the space allotted to each column is a function of the column's content. The Web browser will attempt to fit the most content possible within each column without having the text wrap to a new line. This means that columns with more text are wider than those with less text. When the width of the entire table is increased, the added space is divided evenly among the table columns.

You can set column widths using the same width style you applied to the table itself. The column width is expressed either in a CSS unit of measure or as a percentage of the entire width of the table. You decide to set the width of the first column to 7% of the entire table width, while setting each of the seven remaining columns to 13% of the table width. Added together, 98% of the table width will be allotted to the eight table columns. The remaining table width is reserved for table and cell borders.

You can set the column widths by applying the width style to the two column groups. The width values are applied to the individual columns within those groups. The styles are:

```
table.schedule col.firstCol {width: 7%}
table.schedule col.dayCols  {width: 13%}
```

Add these styles to the tables.css style sheet.

> **Tip**
>
> Always set the total width of the table columns to be less than 100% of the table width to allow space for table borders and padding.

To set the width of the table columns:

▶ **1.** Return to the **tables.css** file in your text editor. Add the following style to the first-Col selector:

```
width: 7%
```

> **2.** Insert the following style declaration to set the widths of the columns in the day-Cols class to 13% as shown in Figure 5-44:
>
> ```
> table.schedule col.dayCols {width: 13%}
> ```

Figure 5-44   **Setting the width of the schedule table columns**

```
table.schedule col.firstCol
                        {background-color: rgb(255,255,192); width: 7%}
table.schedule col.dayCols
                        {width: 13%}
```

> **3.** Save your changes to the file, and then reload **schedule.htm** in your Web browser. Figure 5-45 shows the revised layout of the table.

Figure 5-45   **Revised table column widths**

widths for the day columns are equal

Kyle also wants you to increase the height of the table rows to provide more visual space for the table contents. Heights are set using the CSS height style. You can apply heights to entire table rows or individual table cells. You can also use the height style to set the height of the entire table. As with the width style, the height style should be interpreted as the minimum height for these table objects since the browser will enlarge the table, table row, or table cell if the content requires it.

You decide to set the height of the rows in the table header to 20 pixels and the height of the rows in the table body to 30 pixels. The styles to do this are:

```
table.schedule thead tr {height: 20px}
table.schedule tbody tr {height: 30px}
```

Note that you don't apply the height style to the row groups themselves because that would set the width of the entire group and not the individual rows within the group.

To set the height of the table rows:

> **1.** Return to the **tables.css** file in your text editor and add the following styles to the bottom of the style sheet, as shown in Figure 5-46.
>
> ```
> table.schedule thead tr {height: 20px}
> table.schedule tbody tr {height: 30px}
> ```

Figure 5-46   **Setting the height of the table rows**

```
table.schedule col.dayCols
                        {width: 13%}

table.schedule thead tr {height: 20px}
table.schedule tbody tr {height: 30px}
```

▶ **2.** Save your changes to the file, and then reload **schedule.htm** in your Web browser. Verify that the heights in the table header and table body have changed.

With the increased row height, Kyle would like all of the program names in the schedule to be vertically aligned with the top of the cell borders as you did earlier with the valign HTML attribute. The equivalent CSS style is the vertical-align property introduced in Tutorial 3. Kyle also wants to increase the padding within each cell to add more space between the program names and the cell border. You'll add the following style to the style sheet:

```
table.schedule tbody td {vertical-align: top; padding: 5px}
```

To place the program names at the top of each table cell:

▶ **1.** Return to the **tables.css** file in your text editor and add the following style as shown in Figure 5-47.

```
table.schedule tbody td {vertical-align: top; padding: 5px}
```

Aligning the data cells within the table body   **Figure 5-47**

```
table.schedule thead tr {height: 20px}
table.schedule tbody tr {height: 30px}
table.schedule tbody td {vertical-align: top; padding: 5px}
```

▶ **2.** Save your changes to the file, and then reload **schedule.htm** in your Web browser. As shown in Figure 5-48, the program names are now placed at the top of each cell and the padding space between the program names and the cell borders has been increased.

Revised table layout   **Figure 5-48**

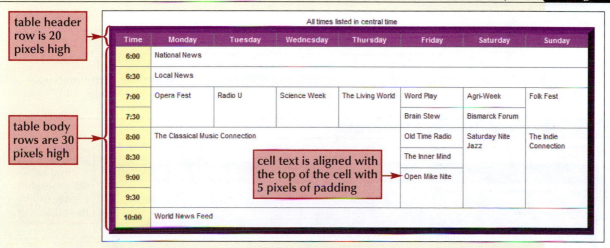

Notice that only the data cells within the tbody rows are placed at the top of the cell. The header cells are still centered vertically because they were not included in the contextual selector you specified in the style sheet.

Caption Styles

Kyle likes the new table design. His only remaining suggestion is that you align the table caption with the top-right corner of the table. Browsers usually place captions above the table, but you can specify the caption location using the caption-side style with the syntax

```
caption-side: position
```

Tip

Firefox supports caption-side values of left and right to place the caption directly to the left or right of the Web table.

where *position* is either top (the default) or bottom to place the caption below the Web table. To horizontally align the caption text you use the CSS text-align style. So to place the schedule caption at the top-right corner of the table, you would enter the following CSS style:

```
caption {caption-side: top; text-align: right}
```

Reference Window | **Formatting a Table Caption with CSS**

- To position a table caption, apply the style
  caption-side: *position*
  where *position* is top or bottom.

Add this style to the tables.css style sheet.

To apply a style to the table caption:

▶ 1. Return to the **tables.css** file in your text editor and add the following style, as shown in Figure 5-49:

```
table.schedule caption {caption-side: top; text-align: right}
```

Figure 5-49 ▶ Setting the caption position

```
table.schedule tbody td {vertical-align: top; padding: 5px}
table.schedule caption   {caption-side: top; text-align: right}
```

▶ 2. Close the file, saving your changes, and then reload the **schedule.htm** file in your Web browser. Figure 5-50 shows the final appearance of the Web table.

Figure 5-50 ▶ Final design of the schedule table

caption is aligned with the top-right corner of the table

3. If you want to take a break before starting the next session, close all of your files and programs now.

Applying Table Styles to Other Page Elements

As you can see, tables are useful for displaying information in an organized structure of rows and columns. Tables are so useful, in fact, that there's no reason to limit the table structure to Web tables. Using the CSS display style, you can apply the table layout to other HTML elements, such as paragraphs, block quotes, or lists. Figure 5-51 describes the various CSS table display styles and their HTML equivalents.

Table display styles   Figure 5-51

Display Style	Equivalent HTML Element
display: table	table (treated as a block-level element)
display: table-inline	table (treated as an inline element)
display: table-row	tr
display: table-row-group	tbody
display: table-header-group	thead
display: table-footer-group	tfoot
display: table-column	col
display: table-column-group	colgroup
display: table-cell	td or th
display: table-caption	caption

For example, the following definition list contains definitions of several networking terms:

```
<dl>
   <dt>bandwidth</dt>
   <dd>A measure of data transfer speed over a network</dd>
   <dt>HTTP</dt>
   <dd>The protocol used to communicate with Web servers</dd>
</dl>
```

Rather than accepting the default browser layout for this list, it might be useful to display the text in a table. But you don't want to lose the meaning of the markup tags. After all, HTML is designed to mark content, but not indicate how that content should be rendered by the browser. To display this definition list as a table, you first enclose each set of terms and definitions within a div container tag, as follows:

```
<dl>
   <div>
      <dt>bandwidth</dt>
      <dd>A measure of data transfer speed over a network</dd>
   </div>
   <div>
      <dt>HTTP</dt>
      <dd>The protocol used to communicate with Web servers</dd>
   </div>
</dl>
```

You then apply the following style sheet to the list, which treats the entire definition list as a table, the div elements as table rows, and the definition terms and descriptions as table cells within those rows:

```
dl      {display: table; border-collapse: collapse; width: 300px}
dl div {display: table-row}
dt, dd {display: table-cell; border: 1px solid black;
        vertical-align: top; padding: 5px}
```

When viewed in a Web browser, the definition list looks exactly as if it were created using the HTML table tags as shown in Figure 5-52.

Figure 5-52 ▶ **Applying table styles to a definition list**

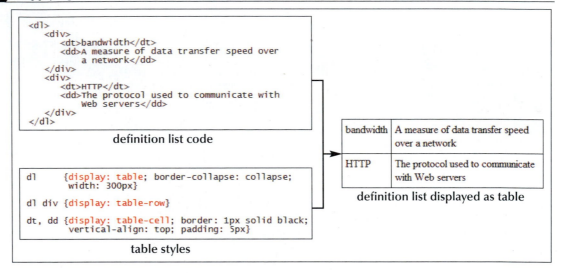

```
<dl>
    <div>
        <dt>bandwidth</dt>
        <dd>A measure of data transfer speed over
            a network</dd>
    </div>
    <div>
        <dt>HTTP</dt>
        <dd>The protocol used to communicate with
            web servers</dd>
    </div>
</dl>
```
definition list code

```
dl      {display: table; border-collapse: collapse;
        width: 300px}

dl div {display: table-row}

dt, dd {display: table-cell; border: 1px solid black;
        vertical-align: top; padding: 5px}
```
table styles

| bandwidth | A measure of data transfer speed over a network |
| HTTP | The protocol used to communicate with Web servers |

definition list displayed as table

In the same way, you can display other page elements in tabular form. As long as the markup tags are nested in a way that mimics the table structure, it doesn't matter if they're table tags or not. You can display them as tables using CSS.

Kyle is pleased with the work you've done on the programming schedule page. In the next session you'll explore how to use tables for page layout and you'll study various CSS layout designs.

Review | **Session 5.2 Quick Check**

1. What HTML attribute do you add to the table element to set the space between cells to 10 pixels?
2. What HTML attribute would you add to the table element to display a 1-pixel border around the table but no gridlines within the table?
3. What HTML attribute would you add to the table element to add borders around the table columns?
4. What CSS style would you enter to collapse all adjacent borders in the table into single borders?
5. Two table cells have adjacent borders. One cell has a 5-pixel-wide double border and the other cell has a 6-pixel-wide solid border. If the table borders are collapsed, what type of border will the two cells share?
6. In the case of conflicting styles, which has highest precedence: the style of the row group or the style of the column group?

7. What style should you enter to align the content of all table header cells with the bottom of the cell?
8. What style would you enter to display the table caption below the table?
9. Specify the style to display ordered lists as table elements and list items as table cells.

Session 5.3

Using Tables for Page Layout

Kyle is very pleased with the work you've done on the KPAF evening schedule. He thinks the page would look even better if it included summaries of upcoming broadcasts. Figure 5-53 shows a sketch of Kyle's proposed addition. He suggests placing the program summaries in a new column to the right of the schedule table.

Kyle's proposed addition to the evening schedule page — Figure 5-53

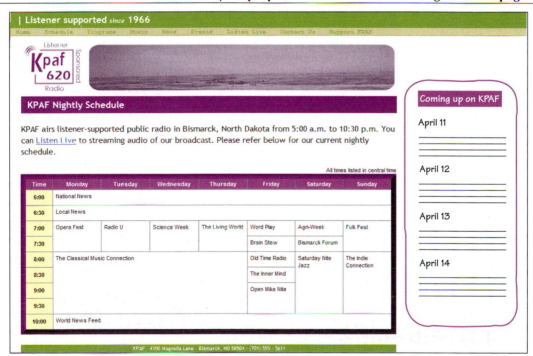

To create this new column, you'll add a new div container named right_col to the schedule.htm file.

To create the new column:

1. Return to the **schedule.htm** file in your text editor.

2. Scroll to the bottom of the file, and directly above the closing </body> tag, insert the following div container as shown in Figure 5-54.

```
<div id="right_col">
</div>
```

Figure 5-54 ▶ Inserting the right_col div element

```
<address>
   KPAF &#183;
   4300 Magnolia Lane &#183;
   Bismarck, ND 58504 &#183;
   (701) 555 - 5611
</address>

</div>

<div id="right_col">
</div>

</body>
```

▶ **3.** Save your changes to the file.

Now you'll add styles to the kpaf.css style sheet to set the width of this new column to 200 pixels. You'll use absolute positioning to place it alongside the nightly program schedule, creating a two-column layout.

To create styles for a two-column layout:

▶ **1.** Open the **kpaf.css** file in your text editor.

▶ **2.** Directly below the style declaration for the #page_content selector, insert the following style for the #right_col selector:

```
#right_col {width: 200px; position: absolute; top: 55px; left:
770px}
```

Figure 5-55 highlights the new style sheet code.

Figure 5-55 ▶ Adding styles to create a two-column layout

```
body            {margin: 0px}
#heading        {color: white; background-color: rgb(215, 205, 151);
                 border-bottom: 1px solid rgb(105, 177, 60)}
#page_content   {width: 730px; position: absolute; top: 55px; left: 20px}
#right_col      {width: 200px; position: absolute; top: 55px; left: 770px}
```

▶ **3.** Close the style sheet file, saving your changes.

Next you'll start creating the bar that lists upcoming programs. To avoid having this look too "boxy," Kyle has proposed that the list be placed in a rectangle with rounded corners. There is no HTML element or CSS style for rounded corners, but you can simulate the effect using background images and a Web table.

Introducing the Jigsaw Layout

So far in this tutorial you've only placed text into your Web tables; however, tables can contain any page content, including inline images, headings, paragraphs, lists, and other tables. Because of this, Web designers began using tables for page layout, allowing them to have more control over the placement of different page elements. For example, a three-column layout could be simulated by enclosing the entire page within a table containing a single row with three columns. The table borders would be hidden from the user, leaving only the table content visible.

Tables support a wide variety of possible page layouts. The one that you'll explore in this session is known as a **jigsaw layout**, so called because it involves breaking up the page content into separate table cells that are then joined together like pieces in a jigsaw puzzle. Figure 5-56 shows an example of a jigsaw layout in which the page content is broken into fourteen table cells, including an image file that has been sliced into nine distinct pieces and placed on the page as a background image. When the cells are reassembled in the complete table after removing the table borders, it appears that the page content flows naturally alongside and within the graphic images or other features of the page.

A jigsaw layout   Figure 5-56

table grid

Defining the Structure of a Jigsaw Table

Figure 5-57 shows a similar jigsaw layout for Kyle's list of upcoming programs. The cell borders have been added to make the table structure clear, but they are removed in the final version of the object. The table contains three rows and three columns with eight background images. Only the middle cell contains any actual content; the remaining cells are used to display the graphic images that constitute the rounded border. When rendered by the browser without the table gridlines, it appears like a rectangle with rounded borders.

Figure 5-57 ▶ **Creating a box with rounded corners**

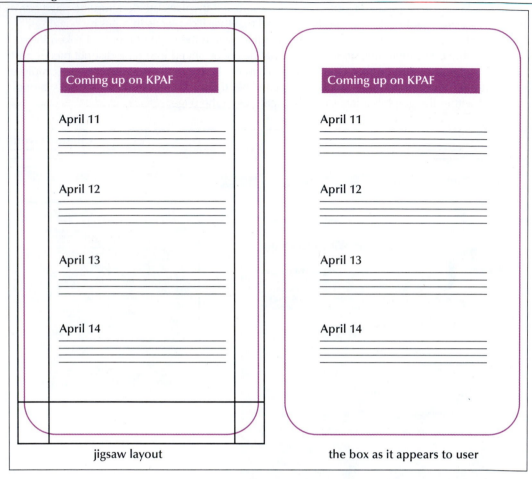

jigsaw layout   the box as it appears to user

Kyle is interested in this technique and asks you to add the structure for this 3x3 table to the schedule.htm file.

To create the table:

▶ 1. Return to the **schedule.htm** file in your Web browser.

▶ 2. Within the right_col container, insert the following table. See Figure 5-58.

```
<table class="roundedBox">
   <tr>
      <td></td>
      <td></td>
      <td></td>
   </tr>
   <tr>
      <td></td>
      <td></td>
      <td></td>
   </tr>
   <tr>
      <td></td>
      <td></td>
      <td></td>
   </tr>
</table>
```

Basic table structure for the roundedBox layout | **Figure 5-58**

```
<div id="right_col">
    <table class="roundedBox">
        <tr>
            <td></td>
            <td></td>
            <td></td>
        </tr>
        <tr>
            <td></td>
            <td></td>
            <td></td>
        </tr>
        <tr>
            <td></td>
            <td></td>
            <td></td>
        </tr>
    </table>
</div>
```

Next you have to assign class names to the nine cells contained within the table. Remember that only the center cell will contain any content. The remaining cells will be used to display the outside borders of the rounded box. You'll assign the outside cells the class names topLeft, top, topRight, left, right, bottomLeft, bottom, and bottomRight. You'll give the inside cell the class name boxContent.

To add class values to the table cells:

▶ 1. Return to the **schedule.htm** file and add the class values **topLeft**, **top**, **topRight**, **left**, **right**, **bottomLeft**, **bottom**, and **bottomRight** to the eight outside table cells.

▶ 2. Add the class value **boxContent** to the center table cell. Figure 5-59 shows the class values in the roundedBox table.

Inserting the class attributes | **Figure 5-59**

```
<div id="right_col">
    <table class="roundedBox">
        <tr>
            <td class="topLeft"></td>
            <td class="top"></td>
            <td class="topRight"></td>
        </tr>
        <tr>
            <td class="left"></td>
            <td class="boxContent"></td>
            <td class="right"></td>
        </tr>
        <tr>
            <td class="bottomLeft"></td>
            <td class="bottom"></td>
            <td class="bottomRight"></td>
        </tr>
    </table>
</div>
```

▶ 3. Save your changes to the file.

Now that you've created the basic structure of the roundedBox table, you can start working on the design. Rounded boxes are useful elements of page design that Kyle will probably want to repeat throughout the KPAF Web site. So you'll insert the styles for the roundedBox table in an external style sheet named rounded.css.

To open the style sheet file and link it to the schedule file:

▶ **1.** Use your text editor to open the **roundedtxt.css** file from the tutorial.05\tutorial folder included with your Data Files. Enter *your name* and *the date* in the comment section of the file. Save the file as **rounded.css**.

▶ **2.** Return to the **schedule.htm** file in your text editor.

▶ **3.** Directly above the closing </head> tag, insert the following link element:

```
<link href="rounded.css" rel="stylesheet" type="text/css" />
```

▶ **4.** Save your changes to the file.

In a jigsaw layout, you don't want any seams to appear between the cells, so you have to collapse the table borders and set the cell padding to 0 pixels. For the KPAF Web site you also want to add space between the table and any surrounding page content, so you'll set the margin space around the table to 5 pixels.

To set the table styles:

▶ **1.** Return to the **rounded.css** file in your text editor.

▶ **2.** Add the following styles to the sheet, as shown in Figure 5-60:

```
table.roundedBox     {margin: 5px; border-collapse: collapse}
table.roundedBox td {padding: 0px}
```

Figure 5-60 ▶ **Setting the table styles to control the spaces within the table**

```
table.roundedBox     {margin: 5px; border-collapse: collapse}
table.roundedBox td {padding: 0px}
```

▶ **3.** Save your changes to the file.

Next you must define the sizes of the eight cells that constitute the outer edges of the table. Because the box will vary in width and height depending on its content, the different cells need to be free to move in different directions. The left and right sides should expand in the vertical direction to accommodate the table content, while the top and bottom sides should expand horizontally. The four corner cells are fixed in size and should not expand or contract based on the table content. See Figure 5-61.

The outside table cells | Figure 5-61

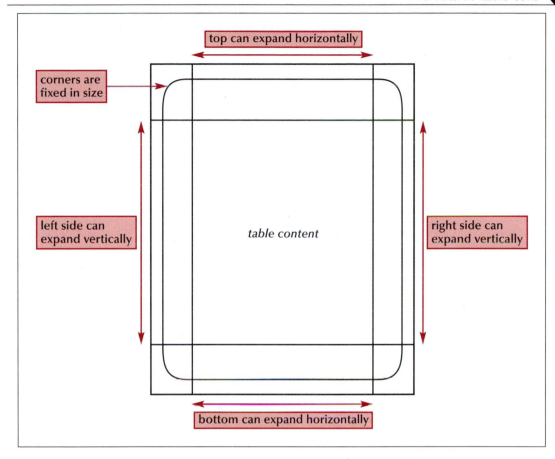

Each cell still must be large enough to display the border image files, which you'll add shortly. For example, the corner cells must be 16 pixels wide by 16 pixels high. The style for the top-left corner cell would therefore be:

```
table.roundedBox td.topLeft {width: 16px; height: 16px}
```

On the other hand, the top border is free to expand horizontally, but it must be tall enough to display the top border image. Its style would be:

```
table.roundedBox td.top {width: auto; height: 16px}
```

Remember that a width or height value of auto allows the browser to change the element to match the content. The other six border cells have similar width and height values. Add these styles to the rounded.css style sheet.

To set the dimensions of the outside cells:

▶ 1. To set the dimensions of the four corner cells, add the following styles to the bottom of the **rounded.css** style sheet:

```
table.roundedBox td.topLeft     {width: 16px; height: 16px}
table.roundedBox td.topRight    {width: 16px; height: 16px}
table.roundedBox td.bottomLeft  {width: 16px; height: 16px}
table.roundedBox td.bottomRight {width: 16px; height: 16px}
```

▶ 2. For the top and bottom cells, add the styles:

```
table.roundedBox td.top    {width: auto; height: 16px}
table.roundedBox td.bottom {width: auto; height: 16px}
```

▶ **3.** Finally, for the left and right cells, add the styles:

```
table.roundedBox td.left          {width: 16px; height: auto}
table.roundedBox td.right         {width: 16px; height: auto}
```

Figure 5-62 highlights the styles of the eight cells on the outside edge of the table.

Figure 5-62 ▶ **Setting cell widths and heights**

```
table.roundedBox      {margin: 5px; border-collapse: collapse}
table.roundedBox td {padding: 0px}

table.roundedBox td.topLeft       {width: 16px; height: 16px}
table.roundedBox td.topRight      {width: 16px; height: 16px}
table.roundedBox td.bottomLeft    {width: 16px; height: 16px}
table.roundedBox td.bottomRight   {width: 16px; height: 16px}

table.roundedBox td.top           {width: auto; height: 16px}
table.roundedBox td.bottom        {width: auto; height: 16px}

table.roundedBox td.left          {width: 16px; height: auto}
table.roundedBox td.right         {width: 16px; height: auto}
```

corner cells →
top and bottom cells →
left and right cells →

You won't set a width or height for the boxContent cell because that should expand to match whatever content you place inside.

Adding the Rounded Border

The last part of the jigsaw table is to put background images in the eight outside cells. Kyle has created eight separate files that cover the four corners and four sides of the box. The files—named topleft.png, top.png, topright.png, left.png, right.png, bottomleft.png, bottom.png, and bottomright.png—are shown in Figure 5-63.

Figure 5-63 ▶ **The layout of the eight border images**

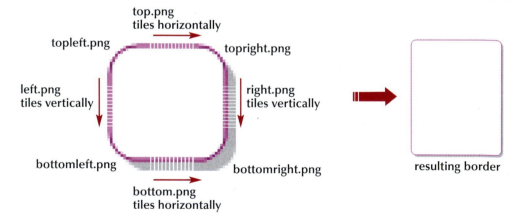

top.png
tiles horizontally

topleft.png   topright.png

left.png   right.png
tiles vertically   tiles vertically

bottomleft.png   bottomright.png

bottom.png
tiles horizontally

resulting border

Each background image is tiled in a different way. The left and right images are tiled only in the vertical direction, filling up the entire background of the left and right cells. The top and bottom images are tiled horizontally, filling up the backgrounds of the top and bottom cells. Finally, the corner cells do no tiling, remaining fixed.

So to set the background of the top-left corner cell, you would use the following background style:

```
.topLeft {background: url(topleft.png) no-repeat top left}
```

Note that this style places the topleft.png image without tiling and fixes it in the top-left corner of the cell (if you're unclear about the background style, review the material on background styles from Tutorial 3). The style for the top border would appear as:

```
.top {background: url(top.png) repeat-x top}
```

Here the background image starts at the top of the cell and tiles in the x or horizontal direction only. The style for the left border would appear as

```
.left {background: url(left.png) repeat-y left}
```

with the tiling done only in the y or vertical direction.

Notice this style is applied to any element belonging to the topLeft, top, or left classes. This is not an accident. Later in this session, you'll reuse these background image styles, applying them to page elements other than table cells.

Add these styles to the rounded.css style sheet to insert and tile the eight background images for the roundedBox table.

Tip

If you have an object with a fixed width and height, you can create a rounded border with a single background image. If the object can vary in size, break the border graphic into separate pieces in a jigsaw layout.

To add the table background images to the style sheet:

▶ **1.** Go to the bottom of the **rounded.css** style sheet and add the following styles to set the background images for the four corner cells:

```
.topLeft {background: url(topleft.png) no-repeat top left}
.topRight {background: url(topright.png) no-repeat top right}
.bottomLeft {background: url(bottomleft.png) no-repeat bottom left}
.bottomRight {background url(bottomright.png) no-repeat bottom right}
```

▶ **2.** Add the styles for the top and bottom cell backgrounds:

```
.top {background: url(top.png) repeat-x top}
.bottom {background: url(bottom.png) repeat-x bottom}
```

▶ **3.** Finally add the background images for the left and right cells:

```
.left {background: url(left.png) repeat-y left}
.right {background: url(right.png) repeat-y right}
```

Figure 5-64 shows the newly inserted style code.

Setting the background images for the eight corners ◄ **Figure 5-64**

```
table.roundedBox      {margin: 5px; border-collapse: collapse}
table.roundedBox td {padding: 0px}

table.roundedBox td.topLeft      {width: 16px; height: 16px}
table.roundedBox td.topRight     {width: 16px; height: 16px}
table.roundedBox td.bottomLeft   {width: 16px; height: 16px}
table.roundedBox td.bottomRight  {width: 16px; height: 16px}

table.roundedBox td.top          {width: auto; height: 16px}
table.roundedBox td.bottom       {width: auto; height: 16px}

table.roundedBox td.left         {width: 16px; height: auto}
table.roundedBox td.right        {width: 16px; height: auto}
```

corners →
```
.topLeft      {background: url(topleft.png) no-repeat top left}
.topRight     {background: url(topright.png) no-repeat top right}
.bottomLeft   {background: url(bottomleft.png) no-repeat bottom left}
.bottomRight  {background: url(bottomright.png) no-repeat bottom right}
```

top and bottom sides →
```
.top          {background: url(top.png) repeat-x top}
.bottom       {background: url(bottom.png) repeat-x bottom}
```

left and right sides →
```
.left         {background: url(left.png) repeat-y left}
.right        {background: url(right.png) repeat-y right}
```

▶ **4.** Save your changes to the file.

Adding the Box Content

Now that you've created the styles that define the size and backgrounds of the eight outside cells, you can enter sample text into the roundedBox table. You'll test your styles by first inserting some simple text to verify that you have not made any errors in entering the table tags or CSS styles.

To enter sample text into the box:

▶ 1. Return to the **schedule.htm** file in your text editor.

▶ 2. Locate the center cell in the roundedBox table and insert the following text, as shown in Figure 5-65.

```
Coming Up on KPAF
```

Figure 5-65 ▶ **Inserting the sample text**

```
            <address>
              KPAF &#183;
              4300 Magnolia Lane &#183;
              Bismarck, ND 58504 &#183;
              (701) 555 - 5611
            </address>

        </div>

            <div id="right_col">
              <table class="roundedBox">
                <tr>
                  <td class="topLeft"></td>
                  <td class="top"></td>
                  <td class="topRight"></td>
                </tr>
                <tr>
                  <td class="left"></td>
                  <td class="boxContent">Coming Up on KPAF</td>
                  <td class="right"></td>
                </tr>
                <tr>
                  <td class="bottomLeft"></td>
                  <td class="bottom"></td>
                  <td class="bottomRight"></td>
                </tr>
              </table>
            </div>

        </body>
```

▶ 3. Save your changes to the file, and then reload **schedule.htm** in your Web browser. As shown in Figure 5-66, the sample text is displayed within a rounded box that is tightly fit to the text.

Figure 5-66 ▶ **Sample text placed in a rounded box**

Coming Up on KPAF

Trouble? If your box does not resemble the box shown in Figure 5-66, check your style sheet code against the code shown in Figure 5-64. Make sure you have separated all of the style values with semicolons, that you have entered all of the background image file names correctly, and that you have the images correctly tiled.

The advantage of the table design you've created is that it's flexible and will expand to match the content you place in the center cell.

You've tested your code against the sample text; now you can replace that text with the complete list of upcoming KPAF programs. Kyle has already written HTML code listing upcoming KPAF programs and has created a style sheet for that list. You can copy and paste that code directly into the rounded box table and then link the page to Kyle's style sheet.

To insert the descriptions of upcoming programs at KPAF:

▶ 1. In your text editor, open the **newshows.txt** file from the tutorial.05\tutorial folder included with your Data Files.

▶ 2. Copy all of the HTML code describing upcoming KPAF programs.

▶ 3. Return to the **schedule.htm** file in your text editor and scroll down to the bottom of the file.

▶ 4. Paste the copied HTML code into the center table cell, replacing the sample text you just entered (you might want to insert a line break into your text file to make the new code easier to read). Figure 5-67 shows the newly inserted code.

Inserting the text of the upcoming KPAF programs ◀ Figure 5-67

```
<td class="boxContent">
<h1 class="newshows">Coming Up on KPAF</h1>

<ul class="newshows">
    <li>
        <h2 class="newshows">April 11 - 14</h2>
        <h3 class="newshows">The Classical Music Connection</h3>
        <p>Peter Thiesen shares his eclectic
            selections from the world of classical
            music.</p>
    </li>
    <li>
        <h2 class="newshows">April 11</h2>
        <h3 class="newshows">Opera Fest</h3>
        <p>Excerpts from <i>Turandot</i> by Giacomo Puccini.</p>
    </li>
    <li>
        <h2 class="newshows">April 12</h2>
        <h3 class="newshows">Radio U</h3>
        <p>Novelist Karen Graves reads from her latest
            work, <i>Hellion of Troy</i>.</p>
    </li>
    <li>
        <h2 class="newshows">April 13</h2>
        <h3 class="newshows">Science Week</h3>
        <p>Prof. Thomas Glass from UND discusses
            <i>String Theory and Spooky Action at a Distance</i>.</p>
    </li>
    <li>
        <h2 class="newshows">April 14</h2>
        <h3 class="newshows">The Living World</h3>
        <p>A panel discussion on
            the <i>Return of the Electric Car</i> and the latest
            in eco-news.</p>
    </li>
</ul>
</td>
```

Styles for the list of upcoming shows are contained in the newshows.css style sheet that Kyle created. You need to add a link to this style sheet to the schedule.htm file.

▶ 5. Scroll to the top of the file. Directly above the closing </head> tag, insert the following link element:

```
<link href="newshows.css" rel="stylesheet" type="text/css" />
```

▶ 6. Save your changes to the file, and then reload **schedule.htm** in your Web browser. As shown in Figure 5-68, the list of upcoming KPAF programs is presented in a box with rounded corners.

Figure 5-68 The upcoming programs sidebar

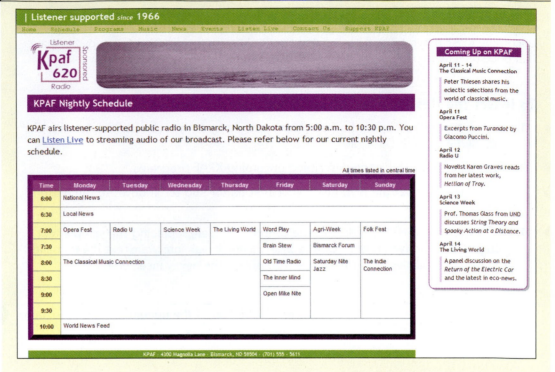

As you expected, the box expanded to fit the contents of the program list without showing any seams in the rounded border. Kyle is happy to know that this design can be easily adapted to any page content and complements you on your work.

Kyle wonders whether you should use Web tables to design other parts of his Web site. He asks you which is better for doing page layout: div containers or Web tables? You'll explore this question next.

Exploring the Controversy over Table Layouts

Using Web tables for page layout predates the introduction of CSS, and for many years the technique was one of the essential tools of the Web page designer. However, this changed with the introduction of CSS, which held the promise of simplifying the process of Web page design. But browser support for CSS was scattered and inconsistent at first, so many designers were reluctant to give up their Web table layouts. Then as more browsers began to support CSS and in particular the CSS positioning styles, Web designers began to advise against using Web tables for page layout—arguing that tables should be reserved for strictly tabular data, such as the KPAF program schedule. There are several good reasons for this:

• **Table layouts are not in the spirit of HTML**. A basic philosophy of Web page design is that the HTML code should indicate the structure of the document, but not how it should be rendered by the browser. Tables take control of layout from style sheets, putting page design back into the HTML file.

- **Table layouts are difficult to revise**. Imagine a complex table layout consisting of two columns with several levels of additional tables nested within each column. Now imagine having to revise that table structure, changing it into a three-column layout. This would not be an easy task because the page content is intertwined with the page layout. Now further imagine the difficulty of having to repeat that design change for dozens of pages across a large Web site. On the other hand, a layout created with a properly designed style sheet is much easier to maintain and revise because it is separate from the page content.

- **Tables take longer to render**. Unless the size of every element in the table is specified, the browser needs to first load the table content and then run an algorithm to determine how to size each element of the table. This can be time-consuming for a large, complex table that involves many cells and nested elements.

- **Tables can be code-heavy**. Creating a visually striking table layout often requires several table cells, rows, and columns, and some nested tables. This is particularly true if you create a jigsaw layout. Therefore, the ratio of HTML code to actual page content becomes more heavily weighted toward the HTML code, resulting in a longer file that takes longer to load and that can be difficult to interpret by people who need to edit the underlying code.

- **Tables can be inaccessible to users with disabilities**. People who use an aural or Braille browser to access a Web page formatted with a table layout can find it difficult to interpret the page content. The problem is that screen readers and speech output browsers read the HTML source code line-by-line in a linear direction, but tables sometimes convey information in several different directions. Figure 5-69 shows how a table whose content is quite clear visually becomes jumbled when presented aurally. This example shows the problems associated with a simple 3x3 table; comprehending a truly complex table layout with several levels of nested tables might be insurmountable to the visually impaired. On the other hand, an aural style sheet could be written that would more easily convey this information.

Aural browsers and tables   **Figure 5-69**

Time	Thursday	Friday
7:00	The Living World	Word Play
7:30		Brain Stew

table displayed visually

```
<table>
    <tr>
        <th>Time</th>
        <th>Thursday</th>
        <th>Friday</th>
    </tr>
    <tr>
        <th>7:00</th>
        <th colspan="2">The Living World</th>
        <th>World Play</th>
    </tr>
    <tr>
        <th>7:30</th>
        <th>Brain Stew</th>
    </tr>
</table>
```

HTML table code

"... Time ... Thursday ... Friday ... 7:00 ... The Living World ... Word Play ... 7:30 ... Brain Stew ..."

table read by an aural browser doesn't clearly convey the table contents

With the current strong browser support for CSS, there is less reason to use tables for page layout. In fact, the jigsaw layout shown earlier in Figure 5-56 could also be done using div containers positioned on the Web page with CSS. However, Web table layouts will not disappear immediately, so Web page designers must be conversant with both approaches, especially if they are called upon to support older browser versions or have the task of maintaining the code of an older Web site.

Creating a Rounded Box Using div Containers

You tell Kyle what you've learned about the controversy over Web table layouts and he agrees that the KPAF Web site should limit the use of tables to strictly tabular information. Kyle wants to add another rounded box to the schedule page, one that displays the name and description of the program currently running on KPAF. He understands your concern about using table layouts and asks whether you can create the same rounded box design using only div containers and CSS styles. As with your work on the table layout, whatever you create must be flexible enough to accommodate content of any size.

After researching the issue on the Internet, you discover there are actually hundreds of techniques that Web designers have developed over the years to create rounded borders without using tables. You decide to use one that was introduced by the Web designer Tedd Sperling (*www.sperling.com*).

Nesting div Containers

The basic idea of Tedd Sperling's approach is to nest several levels of div elements within one another. Since the div elements have no padding and no margin spaces, they will be completely superimposed upon one another—creating a stack of div elements that all occupy the same space on the Web page. Because they're stacked on top of each other, when these div elements are displayed by the browser, any background image from an element lower in the stack will be visible as long as it is not obstructed by another background image higher in the stack. Figure 5-70 shows how eight different background images from eight nested div elements would appear as a single curved border when rendered by the browser.

Figure 5-70 | **Creating a rounded border using nested div elements**

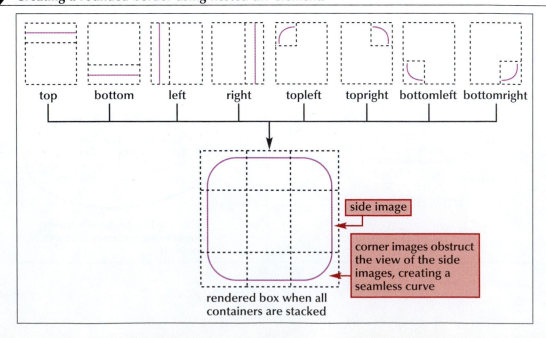

top   bottom   left   right   topleft   topright   bottomleft   bottomright

side image

corner images obstruct the view of the side images, creating a seamless curve

rendered box when all containers are stacked

Notice that the corner images obstruct the view of the side images, so that it appears as one seamless curve around the content. To create this effect in HTML, you can nest these eight div elements

```
<div class="top"><div class="bottom">
<div class="left"><div class="right">
<div class="topLeft"><div class="topRight">
<div class="bottomLeft"><div class="bottomRight">
   <div class="boxContent">
      content
   </div>
</div></div></div></div>
</div></div></div></div>
```

where *content* is the page content you would surrounded by the rounded border. The order of the div elements is important. The corner borders must be on top of the stack because they connect the side borders, and so you list the top, bottom, left, and right sides first. The div elements for the corners (topleft, topright, bottomleft, and bottomright) are nested within them. When the browser renders these elements, it starts from the outside and moves in. The corners are therefore displayed last, appearing on top of the side borders.

Add this basic structure of nested div elements to the schedule.htm page.

To insert the div containers:

▶ **1.** Return to the **schedule.htm** file in your text editor.

▶ **2.** Scroll down to the bottom of the file and directly after the opening tag

```
<div id="right_col">
```

insert the following code as shown in Figure 5-71:

```
<div class="roundedBox">
    <div class="top"><div class="bottom">
    <div class="left"><div class="right">
    <div class="topLeft"><div class="topRight">
    <div class="bottomLeft"><div class="bottomRight">

        <div class="boxContent">
        </div>

    </div></div></div></div>
        </div></div></div></div>
    </div>
```

Creating a set of nested div elements ◀ Figure 5-71

```
<div id="right_col">

    <div class="roundedBox">
        <div class="top"><div class="bottom">
        <div class="left"><div class="right">
        <div class="topLeft"><div class="topRight">
        <div class="bottomLeft"><div class="bottomRight">

        <div class="boxContent">
        </div>

        </div></div></div></div>
        </div></div></div></div>
    </div>

    <table class="roundedBox">
        <tr>
            <td class="topLeft"></td>
            <td class="top"></td>
            <td class="topRight"></td>
        </tr>
```

▶ **3.** Save your changes to the file.

You might have noticed that you repeated the same class names used earlier in Figure 5-58. That's no accident—the eight div elements fulfill the same role of creating the rounded border as the eight table cells did in the table layout. Also, because you assigned background images to any element belonging to the topLeft, topRight, and so forth classes, these div elements will have the same background images as the table cells did in the roundedBox table. The only thing you must add to this set of div elements is a style to place a 5-pixel margin around the roundedBox and 16 pixels of padding space to the boxContent element. Finally, because of how Internet Explorer treats nested div elements, you'll place the box using relative positioning to ensure that all of the nested div elements line up properly in that browser. Add these styles to the rounded.css file.

To define the style for the box and its contents:

▶ **1.** Return to the **rounded.css** file and insert the following style to define the appearance of the containing box:

```
div.roundedBox {margin: 5px; position: relative}
```

▶ **2.** Add the following style to set the display properties of the box's content:

```
div.boxContent {padding: 16px}
```

Figure 5-72 shows the final style definitions for the rounded box style sheet.

Figure 5-72 ▶ **Defining the styles for the box contents**

```
.topLeft      {background: url(topleft.png) no-repeat top left}
.topRight     {background: url(topright.png) no-repeat top right}
.bottomLeft   {background: url(bottomleft.png) no-repeat bottom left}
.bottomRight  {background: url(bottomright.png) no-repeat bottom right}

.top          {background: url(top.png) repeat-x top}
.bottom       {background: url(bottom.png) repeat-x bottom}

.left         {background: url(left.png) repeat-y left}
.right        {background: url(right.png) repeat-y right}

div.roundedBox {margin: 5px; position: relative}
div.boxContent {padding: 16px}
```

▶ **3.** Close the **rounded.css** file, saving your changes.

▶ **4.** Reload the **schedule.htm** file in your Web browser. The page should now show an empty rounded box directly above the list of upcoming programs.

Kyle asks that you add text to this box describing the program currently airing on KPAF.

▶ **5.** Return to the **schedule.htm** file in your text editor and insert the following code within the boxContent div element as shown in Figure 5-73:

```
<h1 class="newshows">On the Air Now</h1>
<h2 class="newshows">Folk Fest</h2>
<p class="newshows">Featuring the best of traditional and
          contemporary folk music</p>
```

Adding text for the current program | **Figure 5-73**

```
<div class="roundedBox">
   <div class="top"><div class="bottom">
   <div class="left"><div class="right">
   <div class="topLeft"><div class="topRight">
   <div class="bottomLeft"><div class="bottomRight">

   <div class="boxContent">
      <h1 class="newshows">On the Air Now</h1>
      <h2 class="newshows">Folk Fest</h2>
      <p  class="newshows">Featuring the best of traditional
         and contemporary folk music</p>
   </div>

   </div></div></div></div>
   </div></div></div></div>
</div>
```

6. Save your changes to the file, and then reload **schedule.htm** in your Web browser. As shown in Figure 5-74, the name of the program currently airing on KPAF is shown in a rounded box at the top of the page.

The final KPAF nightly schedule page | **Figure 5-74**

Trouble? If your rounded box does not resemble that shown in Figure 5-74, check your style code against that shown in Figure 5-72 and Figure 5-73. Common errors include misspelling class names, forgetting to separate style properties with semicolons, neglecting to close style declarations with right curly braces, and misspelling the names of style properties.

7. You can close any open files or programs now.

Kyle will talk to the KPAF programmers to write code that will automatically insert the name of the currently airing program into the rounded box you created, but for now this gives him a good idea of how the page will look to KPAF listeners.

| InSight | | Rounded Boxes and CSS3 |

The Web is a competitive environment in which designers are always looking for ways to make their pages stand out. One way is with specialized design elements like the rounded box you created in this session. Such designs can be challenging the first few times. One reason is that CSS 2.1 allows only one background image per element, so you have to "trick" browsers into displaying several images at once. How much easier the task would be if you could place multiple background images that automatically resized with the element!

This is starting to change with the introduction and adoption of CSS3 styles. In CSS3, you can define multiple backgrounds by entering them in a comma-separated list for the background-image style. The syntax is

```
background image: url(image1), url(image2), ...
```

where *image1*, *image2*, and so forth are the image files you want displayed as a background for the element. To position the images, you once again enter a comma-separated list of position values matching the background image. For example, the style

```
background-position: top left, center left
```

places the first background image in the top-left corner of the element and the second image on the center-left edge. As you increase the number of background images, you add more background-position values, one for each image.

Finally, you specify how the images are repeated by entering each repeat property in another list. The style

```
background-repeat: no-repeat, repeat-y
```

fixes the first background image in place and tiles the second image in the vertical direction.

You can see from these styles that what would require a Web table or several nested div elements can be accomplished in CSS3 with one element and a style sheet. CSS3 will also introduce styles to allow for more decorative borders, including rounded borders. To create a rounded border, you will be able to apply the style

```
border-radius: value
```

where *value* defines the curvature of the rounded corners of the border. This style has scattered browser support at the moment, though Firefox does support the following equivalent style:

```
-moz-border-radius: value
```

CSS3 is still in the development stage, so you cannot rely on it yet for designing Web sites. However, as these and other CSS3 styles are finalized and adopted by the browser market, designers will explore new possibilities for their Web sites.

You've completed your work on the design of the KPAF nightly schedule page. Kyle will discuss your final version with other people at the station and get back to you with future projects.

| Review | | **Session 5.3 Quick Check** |

1. What is a jigsaw layout?
2. You are creating a table structure for a table that will be used to develop a jigsaw layout. One of the cells in the table with the id midCell needs to have a height of 20 pixels, but the width can be calculated by the browser. Specify a style to apply to the midCell table cell.
3. Why are tables especially challenging for the visually impaired?
4. You want to use the image tlcorner.jpg as the top-left background corner image for a div element with the id mainLogo. What style would you enter?

5. A div element with the id name subLogo needs to use a background image for the left side border. The div element could be any height, so the image will need to tile vertically down the element. The image comes from the file lborder.jpg. Specify a style to apply this image to the element's background.

6. You want to use an image file named bborder.jpg as the bottom border for the div element mainContent. The width of the mainContent element can vary freely, so the image file will need to tile horizontally across the element. Specify the style you would use.

7. An old Web page uses a table with one row and two columns to create a two-column layout. The Web site manager wants to move away from using table layouts. Suggest two ways of creating a two-column layout without tables.

Tutorial Summary | Review

In this tutorial you learned how to create and design Web tables, and you explored the issues surrounding using tables for page layout. The first session introduced the basic structure of the Web table. You learned how to define table rows, table cells, row groups, column groups, and captions. The session also explored how to create cells that span multiple rows and columns. The session concluded by introducing the summary attribute as a way of making table content accessible in nonvisual browsers. The second session explored how to format a table's appearance. The first half of the session looked at various HTML attributes that have long been used to format tables. The second half of the session concentrated on the CSS styles that can be applied to tables. The session ended by showing how to use CSS to make almost any page element appear as a table. The third session looked at the special topic of creating page boxes with rounded borders. The first method examined was the use of a Web table to lay out the graphical borders of the box. The second method explored how to do the same thing with nested div elements. The third session discussed the advantages and disadvantages of using tables for page layout and examined the prevalence of table-based designs on the Web today.

Key Terms

cell padding	monospace font	table data cell
cell spacing	preformatted text	table frame
column group	row group	table heading
jigsaw layout	spanning cell	table rule

Practice	**Review Assignments**

Practice the skills you learned in the tutorial using the same case scenario.

Data Files needed for the Review Assignments: kpaf.css, kpaf.jpg, left.jpg, morningtxt.htm, programstxt.css, right.jpg, topleft.jpg, and topright.jpg

Kyle has had a chance to work with the KPAF nightly schedule page. He wants you to make a few changes to the layout and apply the new design to a page that displays the KPAF morning schedule. Kyle has already entered much of the Web page content and style. He wants you to complete his work by creating the Web table with the morning schedule. He wants you to add some rounded and shaped corners to the table to make it stand out more on the page. Figure 5-75 shows a preview of the table you'll create for Kyle.

Figure 5-75

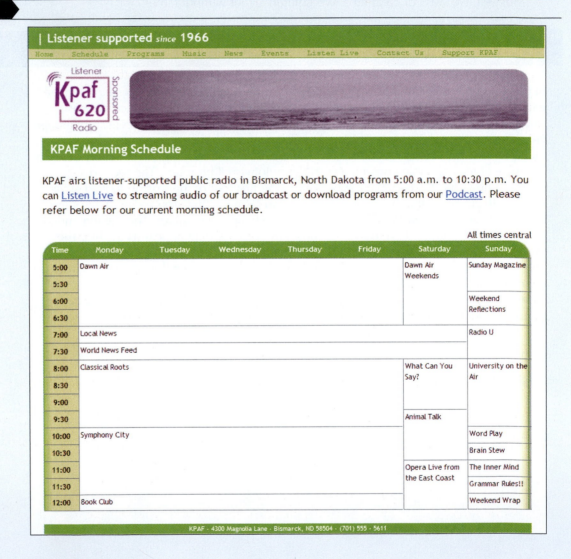

Complete the following:

1. Use your text editor to open the **morningtxt.htm** and **programstxt.css** files from the tutorial.05\review folder included with your Data Files. Enter *your name* and *the date* in the comment section of each file. Save the files as **morning.htm** and **programs.css**, respectively, in the same folder.

2. Go to the **morning.htm** file in your text editor. Insert a link to the **programs.css** style sheet.

3. Scroll down the file and directly below the paragraph element, insert a Web table with the class name programs.

4. Add a caption containing the text "All times central".

5. Below the caption, create a column group containing three columns. The first column element should have the class name timeColumn. The second column element should have the class name daysColumn and span six columns in the table. The last column element should have the class name lastColumn.

6. Insert the following summary for the table: "Lists the morning programs aired by KPAF from 5:00 a.m. to 12:00 p.m. (central time)".

7. Add the table header row group containing the headings shown in Figure 5-75.

8. Enter the tbody row group containing the times and names of the different KPAF programs from 5:00 a.m. to 12:00 p.m., Monday through Sunday, in half-hour intervals. Create row- and column-spanning cells to match the layout of the days and times shown in Figure 5-75.

9. Assign the cell in the top-left corner of the table the id name topLeft. Assign the cell in the top-right corner the id name topRight.

10. Close the **morning.htm** file, saving your changes.

11. Go to the **programs.css** file in your text editor. Create the following styles for the programs table:
    - Set the width of the table to 100%.
    - Display the table text according to the following list of fonts: Trebuchet MS, Arial, Verdana, and sans-serif.
    - Set the table borders to collapse.

12. Align the table caption with the bottom-right border of the table. Set the caption font size to 0.8 em.

13. Add the following styles for the table cells:
    - Set all table cells to a font size of 0.7 em.
    - Vertically align the text of all table data cells with the top of the cell.
    - Add a 1-pixel solid gray border to the left and bottom of every table data cell.
    - Add a 1-pixel solid gray border to the bottom of every table header cell.

14. Set the height of all table rows to 25 pixels.

15. Display the header row group in white font with a background color of (105, 177, 60).

16. Add the following styles for the three column types in the table:
    - Set the width of the timeColumn to 7%. Change the background color to the value (215, 205, 151). Add the background image file **left.jpg** to the column, repeated vertically and set against the left border of the column.
    - Set the width of the columns in the dayColumns group to 13%.
    - Set the width of the lastColumn column to 13%. Set the background color to white and add the background image file **right.jpg**, tiled vertically and set against the right border of the column.

17. For the table cell with the id topLeft, set the background color to the value (105, 177, 60) and add the background image file **topleft.jpg** set against the top-left corner of the cell. Do not tile the background image.

18. For the table cell with id topRight, set the background color also to the value (105, 177, 60) and add the background image file **topright.jpg**. Set the background image against the top-right border of the cell and do not tile the image.

19. Save your changes to the **programs.css** file.

20. Open the **morning.htm** file in your Web browser and verify that the table layout and design resembles that shown in Figure 5-75. (Note: If you are using Internet Explorer, you might see the caption aligned with the top-right corner of the table rather than the bottom-right.)

21. Submit your completed files to your instructor.

Apply	**Case Problem 1**

Apply your knowledge of Web tables and table styles to create a puzzle page.

Data Files needed for this Case Problem: gold.jpg, green.jpg, jpf.jpg, jpftxt.css, left.jpg, stabletxt.css, sudokutxt.htm, topleft.jpg, and topright.jpg

The Japanese Puzzle Factory Rebecca Peretz has a passion for riddles and puzzles. Her favorites are the Japanese logic puzzles that have become very popular in recent years. Rebecca and a few of her friends have begun work on a new Web site called The Japanese Puzzle Factory (JPF), where they plan to create and distribute Japanese-style puzzles. Eventually the JPF Web site will include interactive programs to enable users to solve the puzzles online, but for now Rebecca is interested only in the design and layout of the pages. You've been asked to help by creating a draft version of the Web page describing the Sudoku puzzle. Figure 5-76 shows a preview of the design and layout you'll create for Rebecca.

Figure 5-76

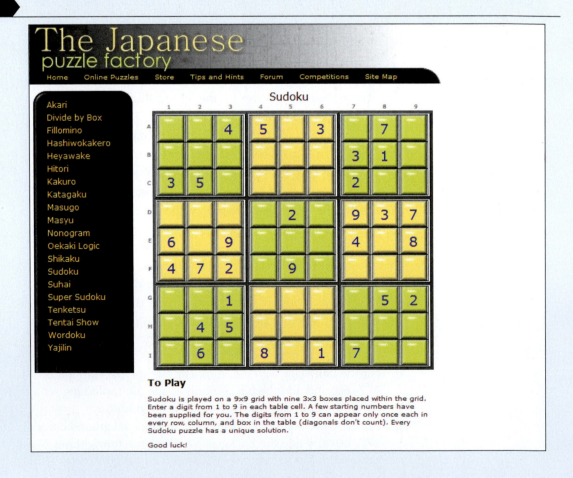

Rebecca has created some of the content and designs for this page. Your task is to complete the page by entering the code and styles for the Sudoku table as well as adding some background images to other sections of the page layout.

Complete the following:

1. Use your text editor to open the **jpftxt.css**, **stabletxt.css**, and **sudokutxt.htm** from the tutorial.05\case1 folder included with your Data Files. Enter *your name* and *the date* in the comment section of each file. Save the files as **jpf.css**, **stable.css**, and **sudoku.htm**, respectively, in the same folder.

2. Return to the **sudoku.htm** file in your text editor. Add a link to the **jpf.css** and **stable.css** style sheets.

3. Scroll down to the links div element. Rebecca wants the list of links to have rounded top corners and a shaded left corner. Mark the corner and sides by nesting the ul element within three div elements with class names of left, topLeft, and topRight.

4. Save your changes to the file, and then go to the **jpf.css** style sheet in your text editor. At the bottom of the style sheet, add the following styles:
   - For the div element belonging to the topLeft class, display the background image file **topleft.jpg** in the top-left corner of the element. Do not tile the image.
   - For the div element from the topRight class, display the background image file **topright.jpg** in the top-right corner without tiling.
   - For the div element from the left class, display the **left.jpg** background image file placed on the left border of the element and tiled in the vertical direction only.

5. Save your changes to the file, and then display the **sudoku.htm** file in your Web browser. Verify that the list of Japanese puzzles on the left margin of the page is displayed with rounded top corners and a shaded left border.

6. Return to the **sudoku.htm** file in your text editor. Scroll down to the rightColumn div element. Directly below the opening <div> tag, insert a table element that will be used to display the Sudoku puzzle. Give the table element the class name spuzzle.

7. Add a caption to the spuzzle table containing the text Sudoku.

8. Create a table head row group containing a single row. The row should display 10 heading cells. The first heading cell should be blank and the remaining nine cells should display the digits from 1 to 9.

9. Create the table body row group. The tbody should contain the following structure:
   - There are nine rows in the tbody.
   - The first cell in each row should contain a table heading cell displaying the letters A through I.
   - Starting with the first row, every third row should contain three table data cells with each cell spanning three rows and three columns. All together, these table cells will store the nine 3x3 boxes that are part of the Sudoku puzzle.
   - In the first row, put the three table data cells in the greenBox, goldBox, and greenBox classes, respectively. In the fourth row, the three data cells belong to the goldBox, greenBox, and goldBox classes. In the seventh row, the three data cells belong to the greenBox, goldBox, and greenBox classes.

⊕ **EXPLORE**   10. Go to each of the nine table data cells you created in the last step. Within each data cell, insert a nested table belonging to the subTable class. Within each nested table, insert three rows and three columns of data cells. Enter the digits from Figure 5-76 in the appropriate table cells. Where there is no digit, leave the table cell empty.

11. Save your changes to the file, and then go to the **stable.css** file in your text editor.

12. Collapse the borders of the spuzzle and subTable tables.

13. Add a 5-pixel outset gray border to the data cells within the spuzzle table. Set the font size of header cells within the spuzzle table to 8 pixels and the font color to gray. Set the height of header cells within the body row group of the spuzzle table to 40 pixels.

14. For data cells within the subTable table, add the following styles:
    - Set the font size to 20 pixels and the font color to blue.
    - Set the width and height to 40 pixels and center the cell text both horizontally and vertically.
    - Add a 1-pixel solid black border around the cell.

15. For table cells nested within the goldBox class of table cells, apply the background image file gold.jpg centered within the cell and not tiled (*Hint*: Use background position values of 50% for both the horizontal and vertical directions.) For cells nested within the greenBox class of table cells, set the background image to the green.jpg file, once again centered within the cell without tiling.

16. Save your changes to the file and then reload **sudoku.htm** in your Web browser. Verify that the layout and design of the Sudoku table resembles that shown in Figure 5-76.

17. Submit your completed files to your instructor.

| Apply | **Case Problem 2** |

Create a calendar table for a community civic center.

Data Files needed for this Case Problem: bottom.jpg, bottomleft.jpg, bottomright.jpg, caltxt.css, ccc.jpg, ccctxt.css, febtxt.htm, left.jpg, right.jpg, tab.jpg, top.jpg, topleft.jpg, and topright.jpg

The Chamberlain Civic Center   Lewis Kern is an events manager at the Chamberlain Civic Center in Chamberlain, South Dakota. The center is in the process of updating its Web site and Lewis has asked you to work on the pages detailing events in the upcoming year. He's asked you to create a calendar page for the month of February. Lewis wants the page design to catch the reader's eye and so he suggests that you create a Web table with a background showing a spiral binding. The spiral binding graphic must be flexible to accommodate calendars of different sizes, so you'll build the borders for this image by nesting the February calendar table within eight div elements. The February calendar must list the following events:
- Every Sunday, the Carson Quartet plays at 1:00 p.m. ($8)
- February 1, 8:00 p.m.: Taiwan Acrobats ($16/$24/$36)
- February 5, 8:00 p.m.: Joey Gallway ($16/$24/$36)
- February 7-8, 7:00 p.m.: West Side Story ($24/$36/$64)
- February 10, 8:00 p.m.: Jazz Masters ($18/$24/$32)
- February 13, 8:00 p.m.: Harlem Choir ($18/$24/$32)
- February 14, 8:00 p.m.: Chamberlain Symphony ($18/$24/$32)
- February 15, 8:00 p.m.: Edwin Drood ($24/$36/$44)
- February 19, 8:00 p.m.: The Yearling ($8/$14/$18)
- February 21, 8:00 p.m.: An Ellington Tribute ($24/$32/$48)
- February 22, 8:00 p.m.: Othello ($18/$28/$42)
- February 25, 8:00 p.m.: Madtown Jugglers ($12/$16/$20)
- February 28, 8:00 p.m.: Ralph Williams ($32/$48/$64)

Lewis wants the weekend events (Friday and Saturday night) to be displayed with a light red background. A preview of the page you'll create is shown in Figure 5-77.

Figure 5-77

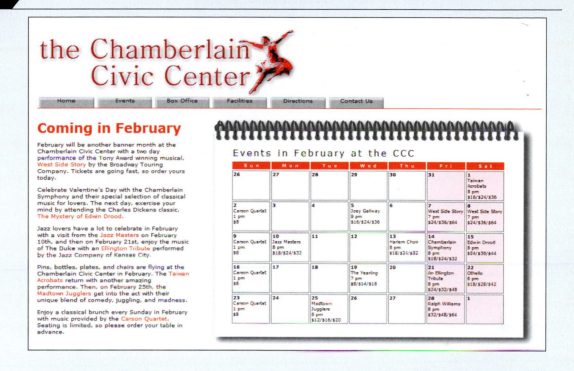

Complete the following:

1. Use your text editor to open the **caltxt.css**, **ccctxt.css**, and **febtxt.htm** from the tutorial.05\case2 folder included with your Data Files. Enter *your name* and *the date* in the comment section of each file. Save the files as **calendar.css**, **ccc.css**, and **feb.htm**, respectively, in the same folder.

2. Go to the **feb.htm** file in your text editor. Create links to the **calendar.css** and **ccc.css** style sheets.

3. Scroll down to the rightColumn div element. Within the div element, insert a table with the class name calendar. Add the caption "Events in February at the CCC" to the calendar.

4. Create a column group for the calendar consisting of two col elements. The first col element should belong to the weekdays class and span five columns. The second col element should belong to the weekends class and span two columns.

5. Create a table header row group consisting of one row of table headings displaying the three-letter abbreviations of the days of the week, starting with Sun and ending with Sat.

6. Create a table body row group containing the days in the month of February. The row group should contain five rows and seven columns of table data cells. There are no spanning cells in any of the rows or columns.

7. Each table data cell should have the following content:
   - The day of the month marked as an h3 heading (refer to Figure 5-77 for the starting and ending days in the calendar).
   - On the days in which there is a CCC event, enter the event information as a definition list with the name of the event marked as a dt element, and the time and price of the event each marked with dd elements.

8. Enclose the entire table within a set of nine nested div elements. The four outermost elements should have the ids tBorder, lBorder, rBorder, and bBorder. The next four innermost elements should have the ids tlCorner, trCorner, blCorner, and brCorner. The innermost div element should have the id boxContent.

9. Save your changes to the file, and then go to the **ccc.css** file in your text editor.

10. Apply the following background image styles to the eight div container elements:
    - For the tlCorner element, display the **topleft.jpg** image in the top-left corner of the element without tiling.
    - For the trCorner element, display the **topright.jpg** image in the top-right corner without tiling.
    - For the blCorner element, display the **bottomleft.jpg** image in the bottom-left corner without tiling.
    - For the brCorner element, display the **bottomright.jpg** image in the bottom-right corner without tiling.

⊕ EXPLORE
    - For the tBorder element, display the **top.jpg** image 39 pixels from the left edge aligned at the top border, tiling the image horizontally.
    - For the lBorder element, display the **left.jpg** image on the left border and tiled vertically.
    - For the rBorder element, display the **right.jpg** image on the right border and tiled vertically.
    - For the bBorder element, display the **bottom.jpg** image on the bottom border and tiled horizontally.

11. Set the padding space of the boxContent div element to 50 pixels.

12. Save your changes to the file, and then go to the **calendar.css** file in your text editor. Add the table styles described in the next steps to the style sheet.

⊕ EXPLORE
13. Display the borders of the table as separate borders with the space between the borders set to 5 pixels. Set the font size of the table text to 8 pixels.

14. Align the table caption with the top left of the calendar table. Set the font size of the caption to 16 pixels and the letter spacing to 3 pixels.

15. Set the width of the table columns to 14% of the width of the table. For columns belonging to the weekend class, change the background color to the value (255, 232, 232).

16. For table headings in the table header row group of the calendar table, set the background color to red, the font color to white, and the letter spacing to 5 pixels.

17. Set the height of the table row within the table header row group of the calendar table to 5%. Set the height of the table rows within the table body row group to 19% each.

18. Add a 1-pixel solid gray border to every table data cell within the calendar table. Set the vertical alignment of the cell content to the top of the cell.

19. Set the font size of h3 headings with the data table cells of the calendar table to 8 pixels and set the margin and padding spaces of the h3 headings to 0 pixels.

20. Set the margin and padding spaces of the definition list, definition descriptions, and definition terms within the tables to 0 pixels.

21. Save your changes to the file, and then open **feb.htm** in your Web browser. Verify that the layout and design of the page resemble that shown in Figure 5-77.

22. Submit your completed files to your instructor.

Challenge | **Case Problem 3**

Explore additional CSS table styles and image techniques by designing the home page for a manufacturer of geodesic domes.

Data Files needed for this Case Problem: blank.gif, bottom.jpg, bottomleft.jpg, bottomright.jpg, dhometxt.htm, dlogo.jpg, domepaper.css, dometxt.css, dtabletxt.css, left.jpg, leftbox.jpg, right.jpg, rightbox.jpg, tableback.jpg, top.jpg, topleft.jpg, and topright.jpg

dHome, Inc. Olivia Moore is the director of advertising for dHome, one of the nation's newest manufacturers of geodesic dome houses. She's hired you to work on the company's Web site. Olivia has provided you with all of the text you need for the Web page, and your job is to design the page's layout. You'll start by designing a draft of the company's home page. Olivia wants the page to include information about dHome's pricing structure for various dome models. The page should also contain links to other pages on the Web site. A preview of the design you'll create for Olivia is shown in Figure 5-78.

Figure 5-78

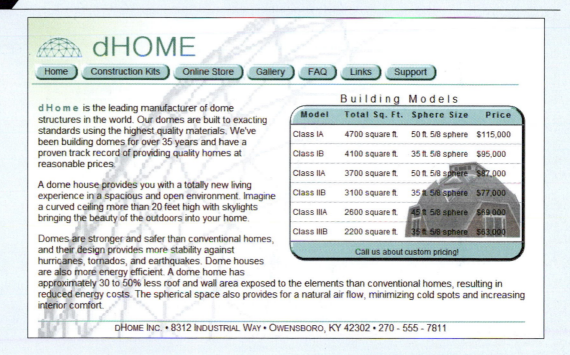

Complete the following:

1. Use your text editor to open **dhometxt.htm**, **dometxt.css**, and **dtabletxt.css** from the tutorial.05\case3 folder included with your Data Files. Enter *your name* and *the date* in the comment section of each file. Save the files as **dhome.htm**, **dome.css**, and **dtable.css**, respectively, in the same folder.

2. Go to the **dhome.htm** file in your text editor. Create links to the **dome.css** and **dtable.css** style sheets.

3. Scroll down to the pageContent div element, and above the paragraphs within that element, insert a table with the class name domeSpecs. Add the table summary, "A table describing six dome models sold by dHome, Inc." and add the caption, "Building Models".

4. Create a column group containing three col elements with class names of firstColumn, middleColumns, and lastColumn. The middleColumns element should span two columns in the table.

5. Create a table header row group containing a single table row with four table heading cells. The cells should contain the headings Model, Total Sq. Ft., Sphere Size, and Price. Mark the first cell with the id value topLeft and the last cell with the id value topRight.

EXPLORE

6. Insert a table footer row group containing a single row and three data cells. The first and third cells should be left blank. The middle cell should contain the text, "Call us about custom pricing!" and should span two columns. Mark the first cell with the id bottomleft and the last cell with the id bottomright.

7. Create the table body row group consisting of six table rows with four cells each. Insert the model, square feet, sphere size, and price values from Figure 5-78.

8. Save your changes to the **dhome.htm** file, and then go to the **dome.css** file in your text editor.

9. Many of the styles for the dHome Web page have been entered for you. Your job is to insert styles for the list of links. Make the following style changes to the unordered list within the links div element:
   - Remove the bullet marker.
   - Set the padding space to 0 pixels.
   - Set the top and left margins to 5 pixels and the right and bottom margins to 0 pixels.

10. Make the following style changes to the list elements:
    - Change the list items to inline objects, floating on the left margin.
    - Set the font size to 14 pixels and the right margin to 5 pixels.
    - Display the background image file **rightbox.jpg**, placed on the center of the right margin. Do not tile the image.

11. Make the following changes to hypertext links within list elements:
    - Display the hypertext links as block-level elements.
    - Set the font color to black and remove underlining from the links.
    - Set the top and bottom padding space to 10 pixels and the left and right padding spaces to 15 pixels.
    - Display the background image file **leftbox.jpg**, placed on the center of the left margin. Do not tile the image.

12. Change the font color of the hyperlinks within the list element to blue whenever the mouse pointer hovers over the link.

13. Save your changes to the file, and then load **dhome.htm** in your Web browser. Verify that the list of links is displayed in a single line below the dHome logo and that each link is enclosed within a rounded box of varying lengths.

EXPLORE

14. The technique used to create the rounded box behind the links is known as the *sliding door* technique. Open the **rightbox.jpg** and **leftbox.jpg** files in a graphics program and notice that the rightbox.jpg image file is extremely long compared to the text it lies behind. Why is the entire image not displayed? (Hint: Think about how the hypertext links are nested within list elements.) Look up the sliding door technique on the Web to learn more about this approach.

15. Go to **dtable.css** in your text editor. Create a style for the domeSpecs table that floats the table on the right border, sets the font size to 12 pixels, and sets the top and right margins to 0 pixels, the bottom margin to 10 pixels, and the left margin to 20 pixels. Collapse all the borders in the table.

16. Create a style for the caption, setting the font size to 16 pixels and the kerning to 5 pixels. Center the caption horizontally above the table.

17. Set the width of the first and last columns to 22% of the width of the table. Set the width of the middle columns to 28% of the table width.

18. Make the following style changes to the table row groups:

EXPLORE

- Add a 2-pixel-wide solid gray border to the bottom of the table head row group.
- Add a 2-pixel-wide solid gray border to the top of the table footer row group and center the text of the table footer.
- Add a 1-pixel dotted gray border to the table rows within the table body row group.

19. Make the following style changes to individual table cells and rows:

- Set the padding of all table cells to 0 pixels above and 5 pixels on the sides.
- Set the kerning of the table heading cells to 2 pixels.
- Set the height of all table rows to 30 pixels.

EXPLORE

20. Add the following background images to the table:

- Apply the **left.jpg** image as a background for the first table column, placed on the left border of the column and tiled vertically.
- Apply the **blank.gif** image as a background for the middle table columns tiled in all directions.
- Apply the **right.jpg** image as a background for the last column, placed on the right border and tiled vertically.
- Apply the **top.jpg** image to the table header row group, placed on the top border of the object and tiled horizontally.
- Add the **tableback.jpg** image to the background of the entire table, placed at the 98%, 70% position with no tiling.
- Add the **topleft.jpg**, **topright.jpg**, **bottomleft.jpg**, and **bottomright.jpg** image files to the background corners of the topLeft, topRight, bottomLeft, and bottomRight table cells. Do not tile the images.

21. Save your changes to the **dtable.css** file, and then open the **dhome.htm** file in the Firefox, Opera, or Safari browsers. Verify that the design of the table resembles that shown in Figure 5-78. (Note: Internet Explorer is unable to display the borders within the three row groups.)

22. Submit your completed files to your instructor.

Create | **Case Problem 4**

Create a Web page describing room reservations at a popular conference center.

Data Files needed for this Case Problem: bottom.png, bottomleft.png, bottomright.png, hcclogo.jpg, left.png, right.png, rooms.txt, top.png, topleft.png, and topright.png

Hamilton Conference Center Yancy Inwe is the facilities manager at the Hamilton Conference Center in Hamilton, Ohio. The conference center, a general-use facility for the community, hosts several organizations and clubs as well as special events and shows by local vendors. The center has recently upgraded its intranet capabilities and Yancy would like to create a Web site where employees and guests can easily track which conference rooms are available and which are being used. She would like this information displayed in a table that lays out the room use from 8:00 a.m. to 5:00 p.m. for seven rooms and halls. Eventually this process will be automated by the conference's Web server, but for now she has come to you for help in setting up a sample Web page layout and design.

Complete the following:

1. Use your text editor to create an HTML file named **conference.htm** and two style sheets named **hcc.css** and **schedule.css**. Enter *your name* and *the date* in a comment section of each file. Include any other comments you think aptly document the purpose and content of the files. Save the files in the tutorial.05\case4 folder included with your Data Files.

2. Use the text files provided to create a Web page containing the reservation information. The design of the Web page is up to you and you may supplement your Web page with any material you feel is appropriate. Place any CSS styles you design for the page in the **hcc.css** style sheet.

3. Create a table containing the room reservation information. The table structure should contain the following elements:
   - A table caption and summary
   - Table row and column groups
   - Examples of row- and/or column-spanning cells
   - Examples of both table heading and table data cells

4. Create a style for your table in the **schedule.css** style sheet. The layout and appearance of the table is up to you, but it should include the following:
   - A border style applied to one or more table objects
   - Multiple background colors
   - Use of horizontal and vertical alignment of the table cell contents
   - Different widths applied to different table columns
   - Styles applied to the table caption

5. Add a rounded-box object to your final Web page. You may use nested div elements, a Web table, or another approach to create the rounded border effect. You may use the border style graphics included in the tutorial.05\case4 folder included with your Data Files, or you may find or create your own.

6. Test your Web site on a variety of browsers to ensure your design works under different conditions.

7. Submit your completed files to your instructor.

Review | **Quick Check Answers**

Session 5.1

1. The number of columns is determined by the maximum number of cells within the table rows.
2. Horizontally centered and in a bold font
3. `<table border="10"> ... </table>`
4. `<td colspan="3" rowspan="2">Monday</td>`
5. You have to reduce the number of cells in the row to accommodate the spanning cell.
6. Because styles that are applied to the table element will be inherited by the caption.
7. thead, tfoot, and tbody (they should be specified in that order).
8.
```
<colgroup>
<col span="2" class="introCol" />
<col class="col1" />
<col class="col2" />
<col class="col3" />
</colgroup>
```

9. To provide more information to visually impaired users whose browsers have difficulty interpreting text in a tabular form.

Session 5.2

1. `<table cellspacing="10"> ... </table>`
2. `<table border="1" rules="none"> ... </table>`
3. `rules="cols"`
4. `border-collapse: collapse`
5. 6-pixel solid border because it is the border with the larger width
6. the row group
7. `th {vertical-align: bottom}`
8. `caption {caption-side: bottom}`
9. `ul {display: table}`
   `ul li {display: table-cell}`

Session 5.3

1. A layout in which the page content is broken down into smaller pieces which are then reassembled like pieces from a jigsaw puzzle
2. `#midCell {height: 20px; width: auto}`
3. Table text is read as it appears in the browser code, which can be confusing to users who cannot see the relationship between the rows and columns of the table.
4. `#mainLogo {background: url(tlcorner.jpg) no-repeat 0% 0%}`
5. `#subLogo {background: url(lborder.jpg) repeat-y 0% 0%}`
6. `#mainContent {background: url(bborder.jpg) repeat-x 0% 100%}`
7. You could float two div elements on the page's left page or you could place the div elements using absolute positioning.

Ending Data Files

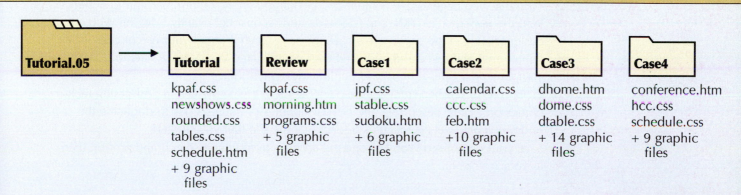

| Tutorial.05 | → | Tutorial | Review | Case1 | Case2 | Case3 | Case4 |

Tutorial
kpaf.css
newshows.css
rounded.css
tables.css
schedule.htm
+ 9 graphic
files

Review
kpaf.css
morning.htm
programs.css
+ 5 graphic
files

Case1
jpf.css
stable.css
sudoku.htm
+ 6 graphic
files

Case2
calendar.css
ccc.css
feb.htm
+10 graphic
files

Case3
dhome.htm
dome.css
dtable.css
+ 14 graphic
files

Case4
conference.htm
hcc.css
schedule.css
+ 9 graphic
files

Reality Check

The Web is a valuable source of information and it is particularly valuable for those who want to learn how to write Web pages. Each Web site presents an opportunity to study how other Web page designers solved problems involving layout and design. And most Web designers are eager to share the methods, techniques, and sometimes tricks they've used to get the most out of HTML, CSS, and an occasional uncooperative browser. In this exercise, you'll use the skills and tasks you learned in Tutorials 3 through 5 to create a Web site on a hobby or personal interest of yours. First you'll research and evaluate the techniques of published Web page designers.

Please be sure *not* to include any personal information of a sensitive nature in the files you create to be submitted to your instructor for this exercise. Later on, you can update the files with such information for your personal use.

1. Web designers have come up with a variety of approaches to creating two-, three-, and four-column layouts. Search the Web for designer pages and report on the different techniques designers have used to create these classic layouts.

2. In the course of your research, you'll come across information on fixed and liquid layouts. Summarize the two approaches and compare each one's advantages and disadvantages.

3. The W3C specifications for HTML and CSS represent a "gold standard" by which all browsers are rated. Do a Web search to determine the browsers that provide the best support for the W3C specifications. Which browsers provide the poorest level of support?

4. Designers must come up with work-arounds or "hacks" to deal with the incompatibilities between browsers in implementing HTML and CSS. Search the Web and come up with three different hacks that designers use in their Web sites. Describe each hack and the problem it solves.

5. Locate a Web page whose content and layout you enjoy. Take some time to download the underlying HTML and CSS code and reconstruct exactly how the Web designer created the page. A few caveats: be respectful about your use of copyrighted material and avoid large and over-complicated Web sites. A site for a large company or organization would be difficult to interpret.

6. When you're finished studying the page's code, recreate the layout and design techniques on a page describing one of your hobbies or interests. Try to duplicate the same look and feel (as much as possible) of the site that you studied.

7. Save your completed Web site and the answers from your research and present them to your instructor.

Color Names and Color Values

Appendix A

Both HTML and XHTML allow you to define colors using either color names or color values. HTML and XHTML support a list of 16 basic color names. Most browsers also support an extended list of color names, which are listed in the following table along with their RGB and hexadecimal values. The 16 color names supported by HTML and XHTML appear highlighted in the table. Web-safe colors appear in a bold font.

If you want to use only Web-safe colors, limit your RGB values to 0, 51, 153, 204, and 255 (or limit your hexadecimal values to 00, 33, 66, 99, CC, and FF). For example, an RGB color value of (255, 51, 204) would be Web safe, while an RGB color value of (255, 192, 128) would not.

Color Name	RGB Value	Hexadecimal Value
aliceblue	(240,248,255)	#F0F8FF
antiquewhite	(250,235,215)	#FAEBD7
aqua	**(0,255,255)**	**#00FFFF**
aquamarine	(127,255,212)	#7FFFD4
azure	(240,255,255)	#F0FFFF
beige	(245,245,220)	#F5F5DC
bisque	(255,228,196)	#FFE4C4
black	**(0,0,0)**	**#000000**
blanchedalmond	(255,235,205)	#FFEBCD
blue	**(0,0,255)**	**#0000FF**
blueviolet	(138,43,226)	#8A2BE2
brown	(165,42,42)	#A52A2A
burlywood	(222,184,135)	#DEB887
cadetblue	(95,158,160)	#5F9EA0
chartreuse	(127,255,0)	#7FFF00
chocolate	(210,105,30)	#D2691E
coral	(255,127,80)	#FF7F50
cornflowerblue	(100,149,237)	#6495ED
cornsilk	(255,248,220)	#FFF8DC
crimson	(220,20,54)	#DC1436
cyan	**(0,255,255)**	**#00FFFF**
darkblue	(0,0,139)	#00008B
darkcyan	(0,139,139)	#008B8B
darkgoldenrod	(184,134,11)	#B8860B
darkgray	(169,169,169)	#A9A9A9
darkgreen	(0,100,0)	#006400

Color Name	RGB Value	Hexadecimal Value
darkkhaki	(189,183,107)	#BDB76B
darkmagenta	(139,0,139)	#8B008B
darkolivegreen	(85,107,47)	#556B2F
darkorange	(255,140,0)	#FF8C00
darkorchid	(153,50,204)	#9932CC
darkred	(139,0,0)	#8B0000
darksalmon	(233,150,122)	#E9967A
darkseagreen	(143,188,143)	#8FBC8F
darkslateblue	(72,61,139)	#483D8B
darkslategray	(47,79,79)	#2F4F4F
darkturquoise	(0,206,209)	#00CED1
darkviolet	(148,0,211)	#9400D3
deeppink	(255,20,147)	#FF1493
deepskyblue	(0,191,255)	#00BFFF
dimgray	(105,105,105)	#696969
dodgerblue	(30,144,255)	#1E90FF
firebrick	(178,34,34)	#B22222
floralwhite	(255,250,240)	#FFFAF0
forestgreen	(34,139,34)	#228B22
fuchsia	**(255,0,255)**	**#FF00FF**
gainsboro	(220,220,220)	#DCDCDC
ghostwhite	(248,248,255)	#F8F8FF
gold	(255,215,0)	#FFD700
goldenrod	(218,165,32)	#DAA520
gray	(128,128,128)	#808080
green	(0,128,0)	#008000
greenyellow	(173,255,47)	#ADFF2F
honeydew	(240,255,240)	#F0FFF0
hotpink	(255,105,180)	#FF69B4

Color Name	RGB Value	Hexadecimal Value
indianred	(205,92,92)	#CD5C5C
indigo	(75,0,130)	#4B0082
ivory	(255,255,240)	#FFFFF0
khaki	(240,230,140)	#F0E68C
lavender	(230,230,250)	#E6E6FA
lavenderblush	(255,240,245)	#FFF0F5
lawngreen	(124,252,0)	#7CFC00
lemonchiffon	(255,250,205)	#FFFACD
lightblue	(173,216,230)	#ADD8E6
lightcoral	(240,128,128)	#F08080
lightcyan	(224,255,255)	#E0FFFF
lightgoldenrodyellow	(250,250,210)	#FAFAD2
lightgreen	(144,238,144)	#90EE90
lightgrey	(211,211,211)	#D3D3D3
lightpink	(255,182,193)	#FFB6C1
lightsalmon	(255,160,122)	#FFA07A
lightseagreen	(32,178,170)	#20B2AA
lightskyblue	(135,206,250)	#87CEFA
lightslategray	(119,136,153)	#778899
lightsteelblue	(176,196,222)	#B0C4DE
lightyellow	(255,255,224)	#FFFFE0
lime	**(0,255,0)**	**#00FF00**
limegreen	(50,205,50)	#32CD32
linen	(250,240,230)	#FAF0E6
magenta	**(255,0,255)**	**#FF00FF**
maroon	(128,0,0)	#800000
mediumaquamarine	(102,205,170)	#66CDAA
mediumblue	(0,0,205)	#0000CD
mediumorchid	(186,85,211)	#BA55D3

Color Name	RGB Value	Hexadecimal Value
mediumpurple	(147,112,219)	#9370DB
mediumseagreen	(60,179,113)	#3CB371
mediumslateblue	(123,104,238)	#7B68EE
mediumspringgreen	(0,250,154)	#00FA9A
mediumturquoise	(72,209,204)	#48D1CC
mediumvioletred	(199,21,133)	#C71585
midnightblue	(25,25,112)	#191970
mintcream	(245,255,250)	#F5FFFA
mistyrose	(255,228,225)	#FFE4E1
moccasin	(255,228,181)	#FFE4B5
navajowhite	(255,222,173)	#FFDEAD
navy	**(0,0,128)**	**#000080**
oldlace	(253,245,230)	#FDF5E6
olive	(128,128,0)	#808000
olivedrab	(107,142,35)	#6B8E23
orange	(255,165,0)	#FFA500
orangered	(255,69,0)	#FF4500
orchid	(218,112,214)	#DA70D6
palegoldenrod	(238,232,170)	#EEE8AA
palegreen	(152,251,152)	#98FB98
paleturquoise	(175,238,238)	#AFEEEE
palevioletred	(219,112,147)	#DB7093
papayawhip	(255,239,213)	#FFEFD5
peachpuff	(255,218,185)	#FFDAB9
peru	(205,133,63)	#CD853F
pink	(255,192,203)	#FFC0CB
plum	(221,160,221)	#DDA0DD
powderblue	(176,224,230)	#B0E0E6
purple	**(128,0,128)**	**#808080**

Color Name	RGB Value	Hexadecimal Value
red	**(255,0,0)**	**#FF0000**
rosybrown	(188,143,143)	#BC8F8F
royalblue	(65,105,0)	#4169E1
saddlebrown	(139,69,19)	#8B4513
salmon	(250,128,114)	#FA8072
sandybrown	(244,164,96)	#F4A460
seagreen	(46,139,87)	#2E8B57
seashell	(255,245,238)	#FFF5EE
sienna	(160,82,45)	#A0522D
silver	(192,192,192)	#C0C0C0
skyblue	(135,206,235)	#87CEEB
slateblue	(106,90,205)	#6A5ACD
slategray	(112,128,144)	#708090
snow	(255,250,250)	#FFFAFA
springgreen	(0,255,127)	#00FF7F
steelblue	(70,130,180)	#4682B4
tan	(210,180,140)	#D2B48C
teal	(0,128,128)	#008080
thistle	(216,191,216)	#D8BFD8
tomato	(255,99,71)	#FF6347
turquoise	(64,224,208)	#40E0D0
violet	(238,130,238)	#EE82EE
wheat	(245,222,179)	#F5DEB3
white	**(255,255,255)**	**#FFFFFF**
whitesmoke	(245,245,245)	#F5F5F5
yellow	**(255,255,0)**	**#FFFF00**
yellowgreen	(154,205,50)	#9ACD32

HTML Character Entities

Appendix B

The following table lists the extended character set for HTML, also known as the ISO Latin-1 Character Set. You can specify characters by name or by numeric value. For example, you can use either ® or ® to specify the registered trademark symbol, ®.

Not all browsers recognize all code names. Some older browsers that support only the HTML 2.0 standard do not recognize × as a code name, for instance. Code names that older browsers may not recognize are marked with an asterisk in the following table.

There are no starting Data Files needed for this appendix.

CHARACTER	CODE	CODE NAME	DESCRIPTION
	&#09;		Tab
	&#10;		Line feed
	&#32;		Space
!	&#33;		Exclamation mark
"	&#34;	&quot;	Double quotation mark
#	&#35;		Pound sign
$	&#36;		Dollar sign
%	&#37;		Percent sign
&	&#38;	&amp;	Ampersand
'	&#39;		Apostrophe
(	&#40;		Left parenthesis
)	&#41;		Right parenthesis
*	&#42;		Asterisk
+	&#43;		Plus sign
,	&#44;		Comma
-	&#45;		Hyphen
.	&#46;		Period
/	&#47;		Forward slash
0 - 9	0–9		Numbers 0–9
:	&#58;		Colon
;	&#59;		Semicolon
<	&#60;	&lt;	Less than sign

CHARACTER	CODE	CODE NAME	DESCRIPTION
=	&#61;		Equal sign
>	&#62;	&gt;	Greater than sign
?	&#63;		Question mark
@	&#64;		Commercial at sign
A – Z	A–Z		Letters A–Z
[	&#91;		Left square bracket
\	&#92;		Back slash
]	&#93;		Right square bracket
^	&#94;		Caret
_	&#95;		Horizontal bar (underscore)
`	&#96;		Grave accent
a – z	a–z		Letters a–z
{	&#123;		Left curly brace
|	|		Vertical bar
}	&#125;		Right curly brace
~	&#126;		Tilde
,	&#130;		Comma
ƒ	&#131;		Function sign (florin)
"	&#132;		Double quotation mark
…	&#133;		Ellipsis
†	&#134;		Dagger
‡	&#135;		Double dagger
ˆ	&#136;		Circumflex

CHARACTER	CODE	CODE NAME	DESCRIPTION
‰	&#137;		Permil
Š	&#138;		Capital S with hacek
‹	&#139;		Left single angle
Œ	&#140;		Capital OE ligature
	–		Unused
'	&#145;		Single beginning quotation mark
'	&#146;		Single ending quotation mark
"	&#147;		Double beginning quotation mark
"	&#148;		Double ending quotation mark
•	&#149;		Bullet
–	&#150;		En dash
—	&#151;		Em dash
~	&#152;		Tilde
™	&#153;	™*	Trademark symbol
š	&#154;		Small s with hacek
›	&#155;		Right single angle
œ	&#156;		Lowercase oe ligature
Ÿ	&#159;		Capital Y with umlaut
		*	Non-breaking space
¡	&#161;	¡*	Inverted exclamation mark
¢	&#162;	¢*	Cent sign
£	&#163;	£*	Pound sterling
¤	&#164;	¤*	General currency symbol

CHARACTER	CODE	CODE NAME	DESCRIPTION
¥	&#165;	¥*	Yen sign
¦	&#166;	¦*	Broken vertical bar
§	&#167;	§*	Section sign
¨	&#168;	¨*	Umlaut
©	&#169;	©*	Copyright symbol
ª	&#170;	ª*	Feminine ordinal
«	&#171;	«*	Left angle quotation mark
¬	&#172;	¬*	Not sign
	&#173;	­*	Soft hyphen
®	&#174;	®*	Registered trademark
¯	&#175;	¯*	Macron
°	&#176;	°*	Degree sign
±	&#177;	±*	Plus/minus symbol
^{2}	&#178;	²*	Superscript 2
^{3}	&#179;	³*	Superscript 3
´	&#180;	´*	Acute accent
µ	&#181;	µ*	Micro sign
¶	&#182;	¶*	Paragraph sign
·	&#183;	·*	Middle dot
ç	&#184;	¸*	Cedilla
^{1}	&#185;	¹*	Superscript 1
º	&#186;	º*	Masculine ordinal
»	&#187;	»*	Right angle quotation mark

CHARACTER	CODE	CODE NAME	DESCRIPTION
¼	&#188;	¼*	Fraction one-quarter
½	&#189;	½*	Fraction one-half
¾	&#190;	¾*	Fraction three-quarters
¿	&#191;	¿*	Inverted question mark
À	&#192;	&Agrave;	Capital A, grave accent
Á	&#193;	&Aacute;	Capital A, acute accent
Â	&#194;	&Acirc;	Capital A, circumflex accent
Ã	&#195;	&Atilde;	Capital A, tilde
Ä	&#196;	&Auml;	Capital A, umlaut
Å	&#197;	&Aring;	Capital A, ring
Æ	&#198;	&Aelig;	Capital AE ligature
Ç	&#199;	&Ccedil;	Capital C, cedilla
È	&#200;	&Egrave;	Capital E, grave accent
É	&#201;	&Eacute;	Capital E, acute accent
Ê	&#202;	&Ecirc;	Capital E, circumflex accent
Ë	&#203;	&Euml;	Capital E, umlaut
Ì	&#204;	&Igrave;	Capital I, grave accent
Í	&#205;	&Iacute;	Capital I, acute accent
Î	&#206;	&Icirc;	Capital I, circumflex accent
Ï	&#207;	&Iuml;	Capital I, umlaut
F	&#208;	Ð*	Capital ETH, Icelandic
Ñ	&#209;	&Ntilde;	Capital N, tilde
Ò	&#210;	&Ograve;	Capital O, grave accent

CHARACTER	CODE	CODE NAME	DESCRIPTION
Ó	&#211;	&Oacute;	Capital O, acute accent
Ô	&#212;	&Ocirc;	Capital O, circumflex accent
Õ	&#213;	&Otilde;	Capital O, tilde
Ö	&#214;	&Ouml;	Capital O, umlaut
×	&#215;	×*	Multiplication sign
Ø	&#216;	&Oslash;	Capital O slash
Ù	&#217;	&Ugrave;	Capital U, grave accent
Ú	&#218;	&Uacute;	Capital U, acute accent
Û	&#219;	&Ucirc;	Capital U, circumflex accent
Ü	&#220;	&Uuml;	Capital U, umlaut
Ý	&#221;	&Yacute;	Capital Y, acute accent
Þ	&#222;	&THORN;	Capital THORN, Icelandic
ß	&#223;	&szlig;	Small sz ligature
à	&#224;	&agrave;	Small a, grave accent
á	&#225;	&aacute;	Small a, acute accent
â	&#226;	&acirc;	Small a, circumflex accent
ã	&#227;	&atilde;	Small a, tilde
ä	&#228;	&auml;	Small a, umlaut
å	&#229;	&aring;	Small a, ring
æ	&#230;	&aelig;	Small ae ligature
ç	&#231;	&ccedil;	Small c, cedilla
è	&#232;	&egrave;	Small e, grave accent
é	&#233;	&eacute;	Small e, acute accent

CHARACTER	CODE	CODE NAME	DESCRIPTION
ê	&#234;	&ecirc;	Small e, circumflex accent
ë	&#235;	&euml;	Small e, umlaut
ì	&#236;	&igrave;	Small i, grave accent
í	&#237;	&iacute;	Small i, acute accent
î	&#238;	&icirc;	Small i, circumflex accent
ï	&#239;	&iuml;	Small i, umlaut
ð	&#240;	&eth;	Small eth, Icelandic
ñ	&#241;	&ntilde;	Small n, tilde
ò	&#242;	&ograve;	Small o, grave accent
ó	&#243;	&oacute;	Small o, acute accent
ô	&#244;	&ocirc;	Small o, circumflex accent
õ	&#245;	&otilde;	Small o, tilde
ö	&#246;	&ouml;	Small o, umlaut
÷	&#247;	÷*	Division sign
ø	&#248;	&oslash;	Small o slash
ù	&#249;	&ugrave;	Small u, grave accent
ú	&#250;	&uacute;	Small u, acute accent
û	&#251;	&ucirc;	Small u, circumflex accent
ü	&#252;	&uuml;	Small u, umlaut
ý	&#253;	&yacute;	Small y, acute accent
þ	&#254;	&thorn;	Small thorn, Icelandic
ÿ	&#255;	&yuml;	Small y, umlaut

Placing a Document on the World Wide Web

Appendix C

Once you complete work on a Web page, you're probably ready to place it on the World Wide Web for others to see. To make a file available on the World Wide Web, it must be located on a computer connected to the Web called a **Web server**.

Your **Internet Service Provider (ISP)**—the company or institution through which you have Internet access—probably has a Web server available for your use. Because each Internet Service Provider has a different procedure for storing Web pages, you should contact your ISP to learn its policies and procedures. Generally you should be prepared to do the following:

- Extensively test your files with a variety of browsers and under different display conditions. Eliminate any errors and design problems before you place the page on the Web.
- Check the links and inline objects in each of your documents to verify that they point to the correct filenames. Verify your filename capitalization—some Web servers distinguish between a file named "Image.gif" and one named "image.gif." To be safe, use only lowercase letters in all your filenames.
- If your links use absolute pathnames, change them to relative pathnames.
- Find out from your ISP the name of the folder into which you'll be placing your HTML documents. You may also need a special user name and password to access this folder.
- Use FTP, an Internet protocol for transferring files, or e-mail to place your pages in the appropriate folder on your ISP's Web server. This capability is built in to some Web browsers, including Internet Explorer and Netscape, allowing you to easily transfer files to your Web server.
- Decide on a name for your Web site (such as "http://www.jackson_electronics.com"). Choose a name that will be easy for customers and interested parties to remember and return to.
- If you select a special name for your Web site, you may have to register it. Registration information can be found at http://www.internic.net. Your ISP may also provide this service for a fee. Registration is necessary to ensure that any name you give to your site is unique and not already in use. Usually you will have to pay a yearly fee to use a special name for your Web site.

Once you've completed these steps, your work will be available on the World Wide Web in a form that is easy for users to access.

There are no starting Data Files needed for this appendix.

Making the Web More Accessible

Appendix D

Studies indicate that about 20% of the population has some type of disability. Many of these disabilities do not affect an individual's ability to interact with the Web. However, other disabilities can severely affect an individual's ability to participate in the Web community. For example, on a news Web site, a blind user could not see the latest headlines. A deaf user would not be able to hear a news clip embedded in the site's main page. A user with motor disabilities might not be able to move a mouse pointer to activate important links featured on the site's home page.

Disabilities that inhibit an individual's ability to use the Web fall into four main categories:

- **Visual disability:** A visual disability can include complete blindness, color-blindness, or an untreatable visual impairment.
- **Hearing disability:** A hearing disability can include complete deafness or the inability to distinguish sounds of certain frequencies.
- **Motor disability:** A motor disability can include the inability to use a mouse, to exhibit fine motor control, or to respond in a timely manner to computer prompts and queries.
- **Cognitive disability:** A cognitive disability can include a learning disability, attention deficit disorder, or the inability to focus on large amounts of information.

While the Web includes some significant obstacles to full use by disabled people, it also offers the potential for contact with a great amount of information that is not otherwise cheaply or easily accessible. For example, before the Web, in order to read a newspaper, a blind person was constrained by the expense of Braille printouts and audio tapes, as well as the limited availability of sighted people willing to read the news out loud. As a result, blind people would often only be able to read newspapers after the news was no longer new. The Web, however, makes news available in an electronic format and in real-time. A blind user can use a browser that converts electronic text into speech, known as a **screen reader**, to read a newspaper Web site. Combined with the Web, screen readers provide access to a broader array of information than was possible through Braille publications alone.

> "The power of the Web is in its universality. Access by everyone regardless of disability is an essential aspect."
>
> — Tim Berners-Lee, W3C Director and inventor of the World Wide Web

Starting Data Files

There are no starting Data Files needed for this appendix.

In addition to screen readers, many other programs and devices—known collectively as assistive technology or adaptive technology—are available to enable people with different disabilities to use the Web. The challenge for the Web designer, then, is to create Web pages that are accessible to everyone, including (and perhaps especially) to people with disabilities. In addition to being a design challenge, for some designers, Web accessibility is the law.

Working with Section 508 Guidelines

In 1973, Congress passed the Rehabilitation Act, which aimed to foster economic independence for people with disabilities. Congress amended the act in 1998 to reflect the latest changes in information technology. Part of the amendment, **Section 508**, requires that any electronic information developed, procured, maintained, or used by the federal government be accessible to people with disabilities. Because the Web is one of the main sources of electronic information, Section 508 has had a profound impact on how Web pages are designed and how Web code is written. Note that the standards apply to federal Web sites, but not to private sector Web sites; however, if a site is provided under contract to a federal agency, the Web site or portion covered by the contract has to comply. Required or not, though, you should follow the Section 508 guidelines not only to make your Web site more accessible, but also to make your HTML code more consistent and reliable. The Section 508 guidelines are of interest not just to Web designers who work for the federal government, but to all Web designers.

The Section 508 guidelines encompass a wide range of topics, covering several types of disabilities. The part of Section 508 that impacts Web design is sub-section 1194.22, titled

§ 1194.22   Web-based intranet and internet information and applications.

Within this section are 15 paragraphs, numbered (a) through (p), which describe how each facet of a Web site should be designed so as to maximize accessibility. Let's examine each of these paragraphs in detail.

Graphics and Images

The first paragraph in sub-section 1194.22 deals with graphic images. The standard for the use of graphic images is that

§1194.22 (a)   A text equivalent for every nontext element shall be provided (e.g., via "alt", "longdesc", or in element content).

In other words, any graphic image that contains page content needs to include a text alternative to make the page accessible to visually impaired people. One of the simplest ways to do this is to use the alt attribute with every inline image that displays page content. For example, in Figure D-1, the alt attribute provides the text of a graphical logo for users who can't see the graphic.

Figure D-1 ▷ **Using the alt attribute**

```
<img src="jkson.jpg" alt="Jackson Electronics" />
```

Not every graphic image requires a text alternative. For example, a decorative image such as a bullet does not need a text equivalent. In those cases, you should include the alt attribute, but set its value to an empty text string. You should never neglect to include the alt attribute. If you are writing XHTML-compliant code, the alt attribute is required. In other cases, screen readers and other nonvisual browsers will recite the filename of a graphic image file if no value is specified for the alt attribute. Since the filename is usually of no interest to the end-user, this results in needless irritation.

The alt attribute is best used for short descriptions that involve five words or less. It is less effective for images that require long descriptive text. You can instead link these images to a document containing a more detailed description. One way to do this is with the longdesc attribute, which uses the syntax

```
<img src="url" longdesc="url" />
```

where *url* for the longdesc attribute points to a document containing a detailed description of the image. Figure D-2 shows an example that uses the longdesc attribute to point to a Web page containing a detailed description of a sales chart.

Using the alt attribute ◀ **Figure D-2**

```
<img src="chart.jpg" alt="Sales Chart"
     longdesc="sales.html" />
```

In browsers that support the longdesc attribute, the attribute's value is presented as a link to the specified document. However, since many browsers do not yet support this attribute, many Web designers currently use a D-link. A **D-link** is an unobtrusive "D" placed next to the image on the page, which is linked to an external document containing a fuller description of the image. Figure D-3 shows how the sales chart data can be presented using a D-link.

| Figure D-3 | Using a D-link |

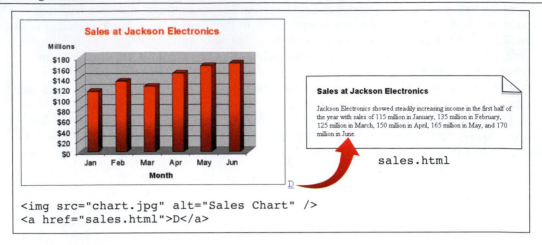

```
<img src="chart.jpg" alt="Sales Chart" />
<a href="sales.html">D</a>
```

To make your page accessible to visually-impaired users, you will probably use a combination of alternative text and linked documents.

Multimedia

Audio and video have become important ways of conveying information on the Web. However, creators of multimedia presentations should also consider the needs of deaf users and users who are hard of hearing. The standard for multimedia accessibility is

§1194.22 (b)   Equivalent alternatives for any multimedia presentation shall be synchronized with the presentation.

This means that any audio clip needs to be accompanied by a transcript of the audio's content, and any video clip needs to include closed captioning. Refer to your multimedia software's documentation on creating closed captioning and transcripts for your video and audio clips.

Color

Color is useful for emphasis and conveying information, but when color becomes an essential part of the site's content, you run the risk of shutting out people who are color blind. For this reason the third Section 508 standard states that

§1194.22 (c)   Web pages shall be designed so that all information conveyed with color is also available without color, for example from context or markup.

About 8% of men and 0.5% of women are afflicted with some type of color blindness. The most serious forms of color blindness are:

- **deuteranopia**: an absence of green sensitivity; deuteranopia is one example of red-green color blindness, in which the colors red and green cannot be easily distinguished.
- **protanopia**: an absence of red sensitivity; protanopia is another example of red-green color blindness.
- **tritanopia**: an absence of blue sensitivity. People with tritanopia have much less loss of color sensitivity than other types of color blindness.
- **achromatopsia**: absence of any color sensitivity.

The most common form of serious color blindness is red-green color blindness. Figure D-4 shows how each type of serious color blindness would affect a person's view of a basic color wheel.

Types of color blindness | **Figure D-4**

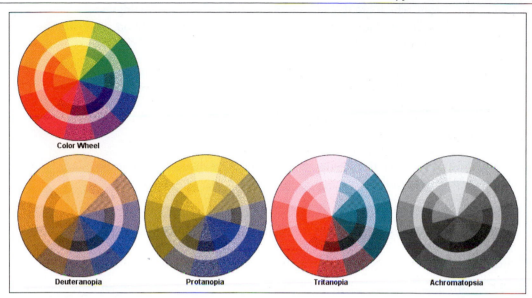

Color combinations that are easily readable for most people may be totally unreadable for users with certain types of color blindness. Figure D-5 demonstrates the accessibility problems that can occur with a graphical logo that contains green text on a red background. For people who have deuteranopia, protanopia, or achromatopsia, the logo is much more difficult to read.

The effect of color blindness on graphical content | **Figure D-5**

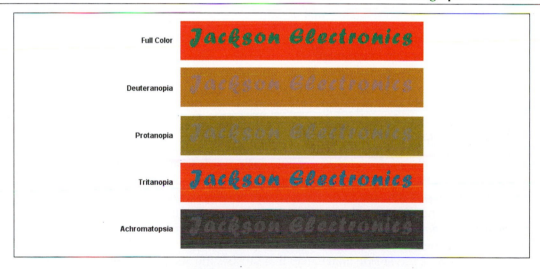

To make your page more accessible to people with color blindness, you can do the following:

- Provide noncolor clues to access your page's content. For example, some Web forms indicate required entry fields by displaying the field names in a red font. You can supplement this for color blind users by marking required fields with a red font *and* with an asterisk or other special symbol.
- Avoid explicit references to color. Don't instruct your users to click a red button in a Web form when some users are unable to distinguish red from other colors.
- Avoid known areas of color difficulty. Since most color blindness involves red-green color blindness, you should avoid red and green text combinations.

- Use bright colors, which are the easiest for color blind users to distinguish.
- Provide a grayscale or black and white alternative for your color blind users, and be sure that your link to that page is easily viewable.

Several sites on the Web include tools you can use to test your Web site for color blind accessibility. You can also load color palettes into your graphics software to see how your images will appear to users with different types of color blindness.

Style Sheets

By controlling how a page is rendered in a browser, style sheets play an important role in making the Web accessible to users with disabilities. Many browsers, such as Internet Explorer, allow a user to apply their own customized style sheet in place of the style sheet specified by a Web page's designer. This is particularly useful for visually impaired users who need to display text in extra large fonts with a high contrast between the text and the background color (yellow text on a black background is a common color scheme for such users). In order to make your pages accessible to those users, Section 508 guidelines state that

§1194.22 (d)   **Documents shall be organized so they are readable without requiring an associated style sheet.**

To test whether your site fulfills this guideline, you should view the site without the style sheet. Some browsers allow you to turn off style sheets; alternately, you can redirect a page to an empty style sheet. You should modify any page that is unreadable without its style sheet to conform with this guideline.

Image Maps

Section 508 provides two standards that pertain to image maps:

§1194.22 (e)   **Redundant text links shall be provided for each active region of a server-side image map.**

and

§1194.22 (f)   **Client-side image maps shall be provided instead of server-side image maps except where the regions cannot be defined with an available geometric shape.**

In other words, the *preferred* image map is a client-side image map, unless the map uses a shape that cannot be defined on the client side. Since client-side image maps allow for polygonal shapes, this should not be an issue; however if you must use a server-side image map, you need to provide a text alternative for each of the map's links. Because server-side image maps provide only map coordinates to the server, this text is necessary in order to provide link information that is accessible to blind or visually impaired users. Figure D-6 shows a server-side image map that satisfies the Section 508 guidelines by repeating the graphical links in the image map with text links placed below the image.

Figure D-6   **Making a server-side image map accessible**

Client-side image maps do not have the same limitations as server-side maps because they allow you to specify alternate text for each hotspot within the map. For example, if the image map shown in Figure D-6 were a client-side map, you could make it accessible using the following HTML code:

```
<img src="servermap.jpg" alt="Jackson Electronics"
usemap="#links" />
<map name="links">
<area shape="rect" href="home.html" alt="home"
coords="21,69,123,117" />
<area shape="rect" href="products.html" alt="products"
coords="156,69,258,117" />
<area shape="rect" href="stores.html" alt="stores"
coords="302,69,404,117" />
<area shape="rect" href="support.html" alt="support"
coords="445,69,547,117" />
</map>
```

Screen readers or other nonvisual browsers use the value of the alt attribute within each <area /> tag to give users access to each area. However, because some older browsers cannot work with the alt attribute in this way, you should also include the text alternative used for server-side image maps.

Tables

Tables can present a challenge for disabled users, in particular those who employ screen readers or other nonvisual browsers. To render a Web page, these browsers employ a technique called **linearizing**, which processes Web page content using a few general rules:

1. Convert all images to their alternative text.
2. Present the contents of each table one cell at a time, working from left to right across each row before moving down to the next row.
3. If a cell contains a nested table, that table is linearized before proceeding to the next cell.

Figure D-7 shows how a nonvisual browser might linearize a sample table.

Figure D-7 ▷ **Linearizing a table**

table						linearized content

Desktop PCs	Model	Processor	Memory	DVD Burner	Modem	Network Adapter
	Paragon 2.4	Intel 2.4GHz	256MB	No	Yes	No
	Paragon 3.7	Intel 3.7GHz	512MB	Yes	Yes	No
	Paragon 5.9	Intel 5.9GHz	1024MB	Yes	Yes	Yes

linearized content:

Desktop PCs
Model
Processor
Memory
DVD Burner
Modem
Network Adapter
Paragon 2.4
Intel 2.4 GHz
256MB
No
Yes
No
Paragon 3.7
Intel 3.7GHz
512MB
Yes
Yes
No
Paragon 5.9
Intel 5.9GHz
1024MB
Yes
Yes
Yes

One way of dealing with the challenge of linearizing is to structure your tables so that they are easily interpreted even when linearized. However, this is not always possible, especially for tables that have several rows and columns or may contain several levels of nested tables. The Section 508 guidelines for table creation state that

§1194.22 (g)   Row and column headers shall be identified for data tables.

and

§1194.22 (h)   Markup shall be used to associate data cells and header cells for data tables that have two or more logical levels of row or column headers.

To fulfill the 1194.22 (g) guideline, you should use the <th> tag for any table cell that contains a row or column header. By default, header text appears in a bold centered font; however, you can override this format using a style sheet. Many nonvisual browsers can search for header cells. Also, as a user moves from cell to cell in a table, these browsers can announce the row and column headers associated with each cell. So, using the <th> tag can significantly reduce some of the problems associated with linearizing.

You can also use the scope attribute to explicitly associate a header with a row, column, row group, or column group. The syntax of the scope attribute is

```
<th scope="type"> … </th>
```

where *type* is either row, column, rowgroup, or colgroup. Figure D-8 shows how to use the scope attribute to associate the headers with the rows and columns of a table.

Using the scope attribute **Figure D-8**

```
<table border="1" cellpadding="5">
<tr>
  <th scope="col">Model</th>
  <th scope="col">Processor</th>
  <th scope="col">Memory</th>
</tr>
<tr>
  <th scope="row">Paragon 2.4</th>
  <td>Intel 2.4GHz</td>
  <td>256MB</td>
</tr>
<tr>
  <th scope="row">Paragon 3.7</th>
  <td>Intel 3.7GHz</td>
  <td>512MB</td>
</tr>
</table>
```

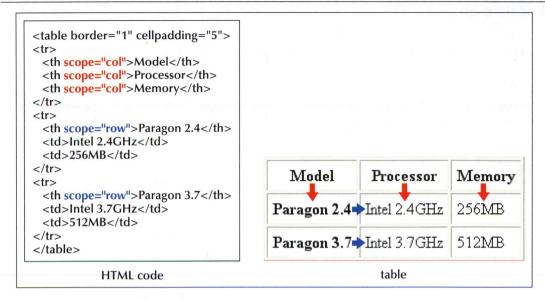

HTML code   table

A nonvisual browser that encounters the table in Figure D-8 can indicate to users which rows and columns are associated with each data cell. For example, the browser could indicate that the cell value, "512MB" is associated with the Memory column and the Paragon 3.7 row.

For more explicit references, HTML also supports the headers attribute, which specifies the cell or cells that contain header information for a particular cell. The syntax of the headers attribute is

```
<td headers="ids"> … </td>
```

where *ids* is a list of id values associated with header cells in the table. Figure D-9 demonstrates how to use the headers attribute.

Using the headers attribute **Figure D-9**

```
<table>
<tr>
  <th id="c1">Model</th>
  <th id="c2">Processor</th>
  <th id="c3">Memory</th>
</tr>
<tr>
  <th id="r1" headers="c1">Paragon 2.4</th>
  <td headers="r1 c2">Intel 2.4GHz</td>
  <td headers="r1 c3">256MB</td>
</tr>
<tr>
  <th id="r2" headers="c1">Paragon 3.7</th>
  <td headers="r2 c2">Intel 3.7GHz</td>
  <td headers="r2 c3">512MB</td>
</tr>
</table>
```

Model	Processor	Memory
Paragon 2.4	Intel 2.4GHz	256MB
Paragon 3.7	Intel 3.7GHz	512MB

HTML code   table

Note that some older browsers do not support the scope and headers attributes. For this reason, it can be useful to supplement your tables with caption and summary attributes in order to provide even more information to blind and visually impaired users. See Tutorial 4 for a more detailed discussion of these elements and attributes.

Frame Sites

When a nonvisual browser opens a frame site, it can render the contents of only one frame at a time. Users are given a choice of which frame to open. So, it's important that the name given to a frame indicate the frame's content. For this reason, the Section 508 guideline for frames states that

§1194.22 (i) Frames shall be titled with text that facilitates frame identification and navigation.

Frames can be identified using either the title attribute or the name attribute, and different nonvisual browsers use different attributes. For example, the Lynx browser uses the name attribute, while the IBM Home Page Reader uses the title attribute. For this reason, you should use both attributes in your framed sites. If you don't include a title or name attribute in the frame element, some nonvisual browsers retrieve the document specified as the frame's source and then use that page's title as the name for the frame.

The following code demonstrates how to make a frame site accessible to users with disabilities.

```
<frameset cols="25%, *">
   <frame src="title.htm" title="banner" name="banner" />
   <frameset rows="100, *">
      <frame src="links.htm" title="links" name="links" />
      <frame src="home.htm" title="documents" name="documents" />
   </frameset>
</frameset>
```

Naturally, you should make sure that any document displayed in a frame follows the Section 508 guidelines.

Animation and Scrolling Text

Animated GIFs, scrolling marquees, and other special features can be a source of irritation for any Web user; however, they can cause serious problems for certain users. For example, people with photosensitive epilepsy can experience seizures when exposed to a screen or portion of a screen that flickers or flashes within the range of 2 to 55 flashes per second (2 to 55 Hertz). For this reason, the Section 508 guidelines state that

§1194.22 (j) Pages shall be designed to avoid causing the screen to flicker with a frequency greater than 2 Hz and lower than 55 Hz.

In addition to problems associated with photosensitive epilepsy, users with cognitive or visual disabilities may find it difficult to read moving text, and most screen readers are unable to read moving text. Therefore, if you decide to use animated elements, you must ensure that each element's flickering and flashing is outside of the prohibited range, and you should not place essential page content within these elements.

Scripts, Applets and Plug-ins

Scripts, applets, and plug-ins are widely used to make Web pages more dynamic and interesting. The Section 508 guidelines for scripts state that

§1194.22 (l) When pages utilize scripting languages to display content, or to create interface elements, the information provided by the script shall be identified with functional text that can be read by adaptive technology.

Scripts are used for a wide variety of purposes. The following list describes some of the more popular uses of scripts and how to modify them for accessibility:

- **Pull-down menus**: Many Web designers use scripts to save screen space by inserting pull-down menus containing links to other pages in the site. Pull-down menus are usually accessed with a mouse. To assist users who cannot manipulate a mouse, include keyboard shortcuts to all pull-down menus. In addition, the links in a pull-down menu should be repeated elsewhere on the page or on the site in a text format.
- **Image rollovers**: Image rollovers are used to highlight linked elements. However, since image rollovers rely on the ability to use a mouse, pages should be designed so that rollover effects are not essential for navigating a site or for understanding a page's content.
- **Dynamic content**: Scripts can be used to insert new text and page content. Because some browsers designed for users with disabilities have scripting turned off by default, you should either not include any crucial content in dynamic text, or you should provide an alternate method for users with disabilities to access that information.

Applets and plug-ins are programs external to a Web page or browser that add special features to a Web site. The Section 508 guideline for applets and plug-ins is

§1194.22 (m)   When a Web page requires that an applet, plug-in or other application be present on the client system to interpret page content, the page must provide a link to a plug-in or applet that complies with §1994.21(a) through (i).

This guideline means that any applet or plug-in used with your Web site must be compliant with sections §1994.21(a) through (i) of the Section 508 accessibility law, which deal with accessibility issues for software applications and operating systems. If the default applet or plug-in does not comply with Section 508, you need to provide a link to a version of that applet or plug-in which does. For example, a Web page containing a Real Audio clip should have a link to a source for the necessary player. This places the responsibility on the Web page designer to know that a compliant application is available before requiring the clip to work with the page.

Web Forms

The Section 508 standard for Web page forms states that

§1194.22 (n)   When electronic forms are designed to be completed on-line, the form shall allow people using assistive technology to access the information, field elements, and functionality required for completion and submission of the form, including all directions and cues.

This is a general statement that instructs designers to make forms accessible, but it doesn't supply any specific instructions. The following techniques can help you make Web forms that comply with Section 508:

- **Push buttons** should always include value attributes. The value attribute contains the text displayed on a button, and is rendered by different types of assistive technology.
- **Image buttons** should always include alternate text that can be rendered by nonvisual browsers.
- **Labels** should be associated with any input box, text area box, option button, checkbox, or selection list. The labels should be placed in close proximity to the input field and should be linked to the field using the label element.
- **Input boxes** and **text area boxes** should, when appropriate, include either default text or a prompt that indicates to the user what text to enter into the input box.
- **Interactive form elements** should be triggered by either the mouse or the keyboard.

The other parts of a Web form should comply with other Section 508 standards. For example, if you use a table to lay out the elements of a form, make sure that the form still makes sense when the table is linearized.

Links

It is common for Web designers to place links at the top, bottom, and sides of every page in their Web sites. This is generally a good idea, because those links enable users to move quickly and easily through a site. However, this technique can make it difficult to navigate a page using a screen reader, because screen readers move through a page from the top to bottom, reading each line of text. Users of screen readers may have to wait several minutes before they even get to the main body of a page, and the use of repetitive links forces such users to reread the same links on each page as they move through a site. To address this problem, the Section 508 guidelines state that

§1194.22 (o) **A method shall be provided that permits users to skip repetitive navigation links.**

One way of complying with this rule is to place a link at the very top of each page that allows users to jump to the page's main content. In order to make the link unobtrusive, it can be attached to a transparent image that is one pixel wide by one pixel high. For example, the following code lets users of screen readers jump to the main content of the page without needing to go through the content navigation links on the page; however, the image itself is invisible to other users and so does not affect the page's layout or appearance.

```
<a href="#main">
   <img src="spacer.gif" height="1" width="1" alt="Skip to main
content" />
</a>

...

<a name="main"> </a>
page content goes here ...
```

One advantage to this approach is that a template can be easily written to add this code to each page of the Web site.

Timed Responses

For security reasons, the login pages of some Web sites automatically log users out after a period of inactivity, or if users are unable to log in quickly. Because disabilities may prevent some users from being able to complete a login procedure within the prescribed time limit, the Section 508 guidelines state that

§1194.22 (p) **When a timed response is required, the user shall be alerted and given sufficient time to indicate that more time is required.**

The guideline does not suggest a time interval. To satisfy Section 508, your page should notify users when a process is about to time out and prompt users whether additional time is needed before proceeding.

Providing a Text-Only Equivalent

If you cannot modify a page to match the previous accessibility guidelines, as a last resort you can create a text-only page:

§1194.22 (k) **A text-only page, with equivalent information or functionality, shall be provided to make a Web site comply with the provisions of this part, when compliance cannot be accomplished in any other way. The content of the text-only pages shall be updated whenever the primary page changes.**

To satisfy this requirement, you should:

- Provide an easily accessible link to the text-only page.
- Make sure that the text-only page satisfies the Section 508 guidelines.
- Duplicate the essential content of the original page.
- Update the alternate page when you update the original page.

By using the Section 508 guidelines, you can work towards making your Web site accessible to everyone, regardless of disabilities.

Understanding the Web Accessibility Initiative

In 1999, the World Wide Web Consortium (W3C) developed its own set of guidelines for Web accessibility called the **Web Accessibility Initiative (WAI)**. The WAI covers many of the same points as the Section 508 rules, and expands on them to cover basic Web site design issues. The overall goal of the WAI is to facilitate the creation of Web sites that are accessible to all, and to encourage designers to implement HTML in a consistent way.

The WAI sets forth 14 guidelines for Web designers. Within each guideline is a collection of checkpoints indicating how to apply the guideline to specific features of a Web site. Each checkpoint is also given a priority score that indicates how important the guideline is for proper Web design:

- **Priority 1:** A Web content developer **must** satisfy this checkpoint. Otherwise, one or more groups will find it impossible to access information in the document. Satisfying this checkpoint is a basic requirement for some groups to be able to use Web documents.
- **Priority 2:** A Web content developer **should** satisfy this checkpoint. Otherwise, one or more groups will find it difficult to access information in the document. Satisfying this checkpoint will remove significant barriers to accessing Web documents.
- **Priority 3:** A Web content developer **may** address this checkpoint. Otherwise, one or more groups will find it somewhat difficult to access information in the document. Satisfying this checkpoint will improve access to Web documents.

The following table lists WAI guidelines with each checkpoint and its corresponding priority value. You can learn more about the WAI guidelines and how to implement them by going to the World Wide Web Consortium Web site at *www.w3.org*.

WAI Guidelines	Priority
1. Provide equivalent alternatives to auditory and visual content	
1.1 Provide a text equivalent for every nontext element (e.g., via "alt", "longdesc", or in element content). *This includes:* images, graphical representations of text (including symbols), image map regions, animations (e.g., animated GIFs), applets and programmatic objects, ascii art, frames, scripts, images used as list bullets, spacers, graphical buttons, sounds (played with or without user interaction), stand-alone audio files, audio tracks of video, and video.	1
1.2 Provide redundant text links for each active region of a server-side image map.	1
1.3 Until user agents can automatically read aloud the text equivalent of a visual track, provide an auditory description of the important information of the visual track of a multimedia presentation.	1
1.4 For any time-based multimedia presentation (e.g., a movie or animation), synchronize equivalent alternatives (e.g., captions or auditory descriptions of the visual track) with the presentation.	1
1.5 Until user agents render text equivalents for client-side image map links, provide redundant text links for each active region of a client-side image map.	3
2. Don't rely on color alone	
2.1 Ensure that all information conveyed with color is also available without color, for example from context or markup.	1
2.2 Ensure that foreground and background color combinations provide sufficient contrast when viewed by someone having color deficits or when viewed on a black and white screen. [Priority 2 for images, Priority 3 for text].	2
3. Use markup and style sheets and do so properly	
3.1 When an appropriate markup language exists, use markup rather than images to convey information.	2
3.2 Create documents that validate to published formal grammars.	2
3.3 Use style sheets to control layout and presentation.	2
3.4 Use relative rather than absolute units in markup language attribute values and style sheet property values.	2
3.5 Use header elements to convey document structure and use them according to specification.	2
3.6 Mark up lists and list items properly.	2
3.7 Mark up quotations. Do not use quotation markup for formatting effects such as indentation.	2
4. Clarify natural language usage	
4.1 Clearly identify changes in the natural language of a document's text and any text equivalents (e.g., captions).	1
4.2 Specify the expansion of each abbreviation or acronym in a document where it first occurs.	3
4.3 Identify the primary natural language of a document.	3
5. Create tables that transform gracefully	
5.1 For data tables, identify row and column headers.	1
5.2 For data tables that have two or more logical levels of row or column headers, use markup to associate data cells and header cells.	1
5.3 Do not use a table for layout unless the table makes sense when linearized. If a table does not make sense, provide an alternative equivalent (which may be a linearized version).	2
5.4 If a table is used for layout, do not use any structural markup for the purpose of visual formatting.	2
5.5 Provide summaries for tables.	3
5.6 Provide abbreviations for header labels.	3

WAI Guidelines	Priority
6. Ensure that pages featuring new technologies transform gracefully	
6.1 Organize documents so they may be read without style sheets. For example, when an HTML document is rendered without associated style sheets, it must still be possible to read the document.	1
6.2 Ensure that equivalents for dynamic content are updated when the dynamic content changes.	1
6.3 Ensure that pages are usable when scripts, applets, or other programmatic objects are turned off or not supported. If this is not possible, then provide equivalent information on an alternative accessible page.	1
6.4 For scripts and applets, ensure that event handlers are input device-independent.	2
6.5 Ensure that dynamic content is accessible or provide an alternative presentation or page.	2
7. Ensure user control of time-sensitive content changes	
7.1 Until user agents allow users to control flickering, avoid causing the screen to flicker.	1
7.2 Until user agents allow users to control blinking, avoid causing content to blink (i.e., change presentation at a regular rate, such as turning on and off).	2
7.3 Until user agents allow users to freeze moving content, avoid movement in pages.	2
7.4 Until user agents provide the ability to stop the refresh, do not create periodically auto-refreshing pages.	2
7.5 Until user agents provide the ability to stop auto-redirect, do not use markup to redirect pages automatically. Instead, configure the server to perform redirects.	2
8. Ensure direct accessibility of embedded user interfaces	
8.1 Make programmatic elements such as scripts and applets directly accessible or compatible with assistive technologies [Priority 1 if functionality is important and not presented elsewhere, otherwise Priority 2.]	2
9. Design for device-independence	
9.1 Provide client-side image maps instead of server-side image maps except where the regions cannot be defined with an available geometric shape.	1
9.2 Ensure that any element with its own interface can be operated in a device-independent manner.	2
9.3 For scripts, specify logical event handlers rather than device-dependent event handlers.	2
9.4 Create a logical tab order through links, form controls, and objects.	3
9.5 Provide keyboard shortcuts to important links (including those in client-side image maps), form controls, and groups of form controls.	3
10. Use interim solutions	
10.1 Until user agents allow users to turn off spawned windows, do not cause pop-ups or other windows to appear and do not change the current window without informing the user.	2
10.2 Until user agents support explicit associations between labels and form controls, ensure that labels are properly positioned for all form controls with implicitly associated labels.	2
10.3 Until user agents (including assistive technologies) render side-by-side text correctly, provide a linear text alternative (on the current page or some other) for *all* tables that lay out text in parallel, word-wrapped columns.	3
10.4 Until user agents handle empty controls correctly, include default, place-holding characters in edit boxes and text areas.	3
10.5 Until user agents (including assistive technologies) render adjacent links distinctly, include nonlink, printable characters (surrounded by spaces) between adjacent links.	3
11. Use W3C technologies and guidelines	
11.1 Use W3C technologies when they are available and appropriate for a task and use the latest versions when supported.	2
11.2 Avoid deprecated features of W3C technologies.	2
11.3 Provide information so that users may receive documents according to their preferences (e.g., language, content type, etc.)	3
11.4 If, after best efforts, you cannot create an accessible page, provide a link to an alternative page that uses W3C technologies, is accessible, has equivalent information (or functionality), and is updated as often as the inaccessible (original) page.	1

WAI Guidelines	Priority
12. Provide context and orientation information	
12.1 Title each frame to facilitate frame identification and navigation.	1
12.2 Describe the purpose of frames and how frames relate to each other if this is not obvious from frame titles alone.	2
12.3 Divide large blocks of information into more manageable groups where natural and appropriate.	2
12.4 Associate labels explicitly with their controls.	2
13. Provide clear navigation mechanisms	
13.1 Clearly identify the target of each link.	2
13.2 Provide metadata to add semantic information to pages and sites.	2
13.3 Provide information about the general layout of a site (e.g., a site map or table of contents).	2
13.4 Use navigation mechanisms in a consistent manner.	2
13.5 Provide navigation bars to highlight and give access to the navigation mechanism.	3
13.6 Group related links, identify the group (for user agents), and, until user agents do so, provide a way to bypass the group.	3
13.7 If search functions are provided, enable different types of searches for different skill levels and preferences.	3
13.8 Place distinguishing information at the beginning of headings, paragraphs, lists, etc.	3
13.9 Provide information about document collections (i.e., documents comprising multiple pages).	3
13.10 Provide a means to skip over multiline ASCII art.	3
14. Ensure that documents are clear and simple	
14.1 Use the clearest and simplest language appropriate for a site's content.	1
14.2 Supplement text with graphic or auditory presentations where they will facilitate comprehension of the page.	3
14.3 Create a style of presentation that is consistent across pages.	3

Checking Your Web Site for Accessibility

As you develop your Web site, you should periodically check it for accessibility. In addition to reviewing the Section 508 and WAI guidelines, you can do several things to verify that your site is accessible to everyone:

- Set up your browser to suppress the display of images. Does each page still convey all of the necessary information?
- Set your browser to display pages in extra large fonts and with a different color scheme. Are your pages still readable under these conditions?
- Try to navigate your pages using only your keyboard. Can you access all of the links and form elements?
- View your page in a text-only browser. (You can use the Lynx browser for this task, located at *www.lynx.browser.org.*)
- Open your page in a screen reader or other nonvisual browser. (The W3C Web site contains links to several alternative browsers that you can download as freeware or on a short-term trial basis in order to evaluate your site.)
- Use tools that test your site for accessibility. (The WAI pages at the W3C Web site contains links to a wide variety of tools that report on how well your site complies with the WAI and Section 508 guidelines.)

Following the accessibility guidelines laid out by Section 508 and the WAI will result in a Web site that is not only more accessible to a wider audience, but whose design is also cleaner, easier to work with, and easier to maintain.

HTML and XHTML Elements and Attributes

Appendix E

This appendix provides descriptions of the major elements and attributes of HTML and XHTML. The elements and attributes represent the specifications of the W3C; therefore, they might not all be supported by the major browsers. Also, in some cases, an element or attribute is not part of the W3C specifications, but instead is an extension offered by a particular browser. Where this is the case, the element or attribute is listed with the supporting browser indicated in parentheses. Likewise, many elements and attributes have been deprecated by the W3C. Deprecated elements and attributes are supported by most browsers, but their use is discouraged.

Where appropriate, the appendix lists the version number in which each element and attribute was introduced. For example, an HTML version number of 2.0 for the <base /> tag means that it is supported by HTML 2.0 *and above*. Version numbers for XHTML refer to the support under the XHTML strict DTD. An asterisk next to the XHTML version number means that the element or attribute is supported under the XHTML transitional or frameset DTD, but not the strict DTD.

The following data types are used throughout this appendix:

- *char*   A single text character
- *char code*   A character encoding
- *color*   An HTML color name or hexadecimal color value
- *date*   A date and time in the format: *yyyy-mm-ddThh:mm:ssTIMEZONE*
- *integer*   An integer value
- *mime-type*   A MIME data type, such as "text/css", "audio/wav", or "video/x-msvideo"
- *mime-type list*   A comma-separated list of mime-types
- **option1**|option2| ...   The value is limited to the specified list of *options*; a default value, if it exists, is displayed in **bold**
- *script*   A script or a reference to a script
- *styles*   A list of style declarations
- *text*   A text string
- *text list*   A comma-separated list of text strings
- *url*   The URL for a Web page or file
- *value*   A numeric value
- *value list*   A comma-separated list of numeric values

Starting Data Files

There are no starting Data Files needed for this appendix.

General Attributes

Several attributes are common to many page elements. Rather than repeating this information each time it occurs, the following tables summarize these attributes.

Core Attributes

The following four attributes, which are laid out in the specifications for HTML and XHTML, apply to all page elements and are supported by most browser versions.

Attribute	Description	HTML	XHTML
class="*text*"	Specifies the class or group to which an element belongs	4.0	1.0
id="*text*"	Specifies a unique identifier to be associated with the element	4.0	1.0
style="*styles*"	Defines an inline style for the element	4.0	1.0
title="*text*"	Provides an advisory title for the element	2.0	1.0

Language Attributes

The Web is designed to be universal and has to be adaptable to languages other than English. So, another set of attributes provides language support. This set of attributes is not as widely supported by browsers as the core attributes are. As with the core attributes, they can be applied to most page elements.

Attribute	Description	HTML	XHTML
dir="**ltr**|rtl"	Indicates the text direction as related to the lang attribute; a value of ltr displays text from left to right; a value of rtl displays text from right to left	4.0	1.0
lang="*text*"	Identifies the language used in the page content	4.0	1.0

Form Attributes

The following attributes can be applied to most form elements or to a Web form itself, but not to other page elements.

Attribute	Description	HTML	XHTML
accesskey="*char*"	Indicates the keyboard character that can be pressed along with the accelerator key to access a form element	4.0	1.0
disabled="disabled"	Disables a form field for input	4.0	1.0
tabindex="*integer*"	Specifies a form element's position in a document's tabbing order	4.0	1.0

Internet Explorer Attributes

Internet Explorer supports a collection of attributes that can be applied to almost all page elements. Other browsers do not support these attributes or support them only for a more limited collection of elements.

Attribute	Description
accesskey="*char*"	Indicates the keyboard character that can be pressed along with the accelerator key to access the page element
contenteditable="true|false|**inherit**"	Specifies whether the element's content can be modified online by the user
disabled="disabled"	Disables the page element for input
hidefocus="true|**false**"	Controls whether the element provides a visual indication of whether the element is in focus
tabindex="*integer*"	Specifies the position of the page element in the tabbing order of the document
unselectable="on|**off**"	Specifies whether the element can be selected by the user

Event Attributes

To make Web pages more dynamic, HTML and XHTML support event attributes that identify scripts to be run in response to an event occurring within an element. For example, clicking a main heading with a mouse can cause a browser to run a program that hides or expands a table of contents. Each event attribute has the form

```
event = "script"
```

where *event* is the name of the event attribute and *script* is the name of the script or command to be run by the browser in response to the occurrence of the event within the element.

Core Events

The general event attributes are part of the specifications for HTML and XHTML. They apply to almost all page elements.

Attribute	Description	HTML	XHTML
onclick	The mouse button is clicked.	4.0	1.0
ondblclick	The mouse button is double-clicked.	4.0	1.0
onkeydown	A key is pressed down.	4.0	1.0
onkeypress	A key is initially pressed.	4.0	1.0
onkeyup	A key is released.	4.0	1.0
onmousedown	The mouse button is pressed down.	4.0	1.0
onmousemove	The mouse pointer is moved within the element's boundaries.	4.0	1.0
onmouseout	The mouse pointer is moved out of the element's boundaries.	4.0	1.0
onmouseover	The mouse pointer hovers over the element.	4.0	1.0
onmouseup	The mouse button is released.	4.0	1.0

Document Events

The following list of event attributes applies not to individual elements within the page, but to the entire document as it is displayed within the browser window or frame.

Attribute	Description	HTML	XHTML
onafterprint	The document has finished printing (IE only).		
onbeforeprint	The document is about to be printed (IE only).		
onload	The page is finished being loaded.	4.0	1.0
onunload	The page is finished unloading.	4.0	1.0

Form Events

The following list of event attributes applies either to the entire Web form or fields within the form.

Attribute	Description	HTML	XHTML
onblur	The form field has lost the focus.	4.0	1.0
onchange	The value of the form field has been changed.	4.0	1.0
onfocus	The form field has received the focus.	4.0	1.0
onreset	The form has been reset.	4.0	1.0
onselect	Text content has been selected in the form field.	4.0	1.0
onsubmit	The form has been submitted for processing.	4.0	1.0

Internet Explorer Data Events

The following list of event attributes applies to elements within the Web page capable of data binding. Note that these events are supported only by the Internet Explorer browser.

Attribute	Description
oncellchange	Data has changed in the data source.
ondataavailable	Data has arrived from the data source.
ondatasetchange	The data in the data source has changed.
ondatasetcomplete	All data from the data source has been loaded.
onrowenter	The current row in the data source has changed.
onrowexit	The current row is about to be changed in the data source.
onrowsdelete	Rows have been deleted from the data source.
onrowsinserted	Rows have been inserted into the data source.

Internet Explorer Events

The Internet Explorer browser supports a wide collection of customized event attributes. Unless otherwise noted, these event attributes can be applied to any page element and are not supported by other browsers or included in the HTML or XHTML specifications.

Attribute	Description
onactive	The element is set to an active state.
onafterupdate	Data has been transferred from the element to a data source.
onbeforeactivate	The element is about to be set to an active state.
onbeforecopy	A selection from the element is about to be copied to the Clipboard.
onbeforecut	A selection from the element is about to be cut to the Clipboard.
onbeforedeactivate	The element is about to be deactivated.
onbeforeeditfocus	The element is about to become active.
onbeforepaste	Data from the Clipboard is about to be pasted into the element.
onbeforeunload	The page is about to be unloaded.
onbeforeupdate	The element's data is about to be updated.
onblur	The element has lost the focus.
oncontextmenu	The right mouse button is activated.
oncontrolselect	Selection using a modifier key (Ctrl for Windows, Command for Macintosh) has begun within the element.
oncopy	Data from the element has been copied to the Clipboard.
oncut	Data from the element has been cut to the Clipboard.
ondrag	The element is being dragged.
ondragdrop	The element has been dropped into the window or frame.
ondragend	The element is no longer being dragged.
ondragenter	The dragged element has entered a target area.
ondragleave	The dragged element has left a target area.
ondragover	The dragged element is over a target area.
ondragstart	The element has begun to be dragged.
ondrop	The dragged element has been dropped.
onerrorupdate	The data transfer to the element has been cancelled.
onfocus	The element has received the focus.
onfocusin	The element is about to receive the focus.
onfocusout	The form element has just lost the focus.
onhelp	The user has selected online help from the browser.
oninput	Text has just been entered into the form field.
onlosecapture	The element has been captured by the mouse selection.
onmouseenter	The mouse pointer enters the element's boundaries.
onmouseleave	The mouse pointer leaves the element's boundaries.
onmousewheel	The mouse wheel is moved.
onmove	The browser window or element has been moved by the user.
onmoveend	Movement of the element has ended.
onmovestart	The element has begun to move.
onpaste	Data has been pasted from the Clipboard into the element.

Attribute	Description
onpropertychange	One or more of the element's properties has changed.
onreadystatechange	The element has changed its ready state.
onresize	The browser window or element has been resized by the user.
onscroll	The scroll bar position within the element has been changed (also supported by other browsers).
onselectstart	Selection has begun within the element.
onstop	The page is finished loading.

HTML and XHTML Elements and Attributes

The following table contains an alphabetic listing of the elements and attributes supported by HTML, XHTML, and the major browsers. Some attributes are not listed in this table, but are described instead in the general attributes tables presented in the previous section of this appendix.

Element/Attribute	Description	HTML	XHTML
`<!-- text -->`	Inserts a comment into the document (comments are not displayed in therendered page)	2.0	1.0
`<!doctype>`	Specifies the Document Type Definition for a document	2.0	1.0
`<a> </a>`	Marks the beginning and end of a link	2.0	1.0
`accesskey="char"`	Indicates the keyboard character that can be pressed along with the accelerator key to activate the link	4.0	1.0
`charset="text"`	Specifies the character encoding of the linked document	4.0	1.0
`coords="value list"`	Specifies the coordinates of a hotspot in a client-side image map; the value list depends on the shape of the hotspot: shape="rect" "left, right, top, bottom"shape="circle" "x_center, y_center, radius"shape="poly" "x1, y1, x2, y2, x3, y3, ..."	4.0	1.0
`href="url"`	Specifies the URL of the link	3.2	1.0
`hreflang="text"`	Specifies the language of the linked document	4.0	1.0
`name="text"`	Specifies a name for the enclosed text, allowing it to be a link target	2.0	1.0
`rel="text"`	Specifies the relationship between the current page and the link specified by the href attribute	2.0	1.0
`rev="text"`	Specifies the reverse relationship between the current page and the linkspecified by the href attribute	2.0	1.0
`shape="rect|circle| polygon"`	Specifies the shape of the hotspot	4.0	1.0
`title="text"`	Specifies the pop-up text for the link	2.0	1.0
`target="text"`	Specifies the target window or frame for the link	4.0	1.0
`type="mime-type"`	Specifies the data type of the linked document	4.0	1.0
`<abbr> </abbr>`	Marks abbreviated text	4.0	1.0
`<acronym> </acronym>`	Marks acronym text	3.0	1.0
`<address> </address>`	Marks address text	2.0	1.0

Element/Attribute	Description	HTML	XHTML
`<applet> </applet>`	Embeds an applet into the browser (deprecated)	3.2	1.0*

`align="absmiddle|`
`absbottom|baseline|`
`bottom|center`
`|left|middle`
`|right|texttop`
`|top"`
	Specifies the alignment of the applet with the surrounding text	3.2	1.0*

`alt="text"`	Specifies alternate text for the applet (deprecated)	3.2	1.0*
`archive="url"`	Specifies the URL of an archive containing classes and other resources to be used with the applet (deprecated)	4.0	1.0*
`code="url"`	Specifies the URL of the applet's code/class (deprecated)	3.2	1.0*
`codebase="url"`	Specifies the URL of all class files for the applet (deprecated)	3.2	1.0*
`datafld="text"`	Specifies the data source that supplies bound data for use with the applet	4.0	
`datasrc="text"`	Specifies the ID or URL of the applet's data source	4.0	
`height="integer"`	Specifies the height of the applet in pixels	3.2	1.0*
`hspace="integer"`	Specifies the horizontal space around the applet in pixels (deprecated)	3.2	1.0*
`mayscript="mayscript"`	Permits access to the applet by programs embedded in the document		
`name="text"`	Specifies the name assigned to the applet (deprecated)	3.2	1.0*
`object="text"`	Specifies the name of the resource that contains a serialized representation of the applet (deprecated)	4.0	1.0*
`src="url"`	Specifies an external URL reference to the applet		
`vspace="integer"`	Specifies the vertical space around the applet in pixels (deprecated)	3.2	1.0*
`width="integer"`	Specifies the width of the applet in pixels (deprecated)	3.2	1.0*
`<area />`	Marks an image map hotspot	3.2	1.0
`alt="text"`	Specifies alternate text for the hotspot	3.2	1.0
`coords="value list"`	Specifies the coordinates of the hotspot; the value list depends on the shape of the hotspot: shape="rect" "left, right, top, bottom" shape="circle" "x_center, y_center, radius" shape="poly" "x1, y1, x2, y2, x3, y3, ..."	3.2	1.0
`href="url"`	Specifies the URL of the document to which the hotspot points	3.2	1.0
`nohref="nohref"`	Specifies that the hotspot does not point to a link	3.2	1.0
`shape="rect|circle|` `polygon"`	Specifies the shape of the hotspot	3.2	1.0
`target="text"`	Specifies the target window or frame for the link	3.2	1.0*
`<b> </b>`	Marks text as bold	2.0	1.0
`<base />`	Specifies global reference information for the document	2.0	1.0
`href="url"`	Specifies the URL from which all relative links in the document are based	2.0	1.0
`target="text"`	Specifies the target window or frame for links in the document	2.0	1.0*
`<basefont />`	Specifies the font setting for the document text (deprecated)	3.2	1.0*
`color="color"`	Specifies the text color (deprecated)	3.2	1.0*
`face="text list"`	Specifies a list of fonts to be applied to the text (deprecated)	3.2	1.0*
`size="integer"`	Specifies the size of the font range from 1 (smallest) to 7 (largest) (deprecated)	3.2	1.0*

Element/Attribute	Description	HTML	XHTML
`<bdo> </bdo>`	Indicates that the enclosed text should be rendered with the direction specified by the dir attribute	4.0	1.0
`<bgsound />`	Plays a background sound clip when the page is opened (IE and Opera only)		
`balance="integer"`	Specifies the balance of the volume between the left and right speakers where balance ranges from -10,000 to 10,000 (IE and Opera only)		
`loop="integer| infinite"`	Specifies the number of times the clip will be played (a positive integeror infinite) (IE and Opera only)		
`src="url"`	Specifies the URL of the sound clip file (IE and Opera only)		
`volume="integer"`	Specifies the volume of the sound clip, where the volume ranges from -10,000 to 0 (IE and Opera only)		
`<big> </big>`	Increases the size of the enclosed text relative to the default font size	3.0	1.0
`<blink> </blink>`	Blinks the enclosed text on and off		
`<blockquote> </blockquote>`	Marks content as quoted from another source	2.0	1.0
`align="left| center|right"`	Specifies the horizontal alignment of the content		
`cite="url"`	Provides the source URL of the quoted content	4.0	1.0
`clear="none|left| right|all"`	Prevents content from rendering until the specified margin is clear	3.0*	
`<body> </body>`	Marks the page content to be rendered by the browser	2.0	1.0
`alink="color"`	Specifies the color of activated links in the document (deprecated)	3.2	1.0*
`background="url"`	Specifies the background image file used for the page (deprecated)	3.0	1.0*
`bgcolor="color"`	Specifies the background color of the page (deprecated)	3.2	1.0*
`bgproperties="fixed"`	Fixes the background image in the browser window (IE only)		
`bottommargin="integer"`	Specifies the size of the bottom margin in pixels (IE only)		
`leftmargin="integer"`	Specifies the size of the left margin in pixels		
`link="color"`	Specifies the color of unvisited links (deprecated)	3.2	1.0*
`marginheight="integer"`	Specifies the size of the margin above and below the page (Netscape 4 only)		
`marginwidth="integer"`	Specifies the size of the margin to the left and right of the page (Netscape 4 only)		
`nowrap="false|true"`	Specifies whether the content wraps using normal HTML line-wrapping conventions (IE only)		
`rightmargin="integer"`	Specifies the size of the right margin in pixels (IE only)		
`scroll="yes|no"`	Specifies whether to display a scroll bar (IE only)		
`text="color"`	Specifies the color of page text (deprecated)	3.2	1.0*
`topmargin="integer"`	Specifies the size of the top page margin in pixels (IE only)		
`vlink="color"`	Specifies the color of previously visited links (deprecated)	3.2	1.0*
` `	Inserts a line break into the page	2.0	1.0
`clear="none|left| right|all"`	Displays the line break only when the specified margin is clear (deprecated)	3.2	1.0*
`<button> </button>`	Creates a form button	4.0	1.0
`datafld="text"`	Specifies the column from a data source that supplies bound data for the button (IE only)		
`dataformatas="html| plaintext|text"`	Specifies the format of the data in the data source bound with the button (IE only)		

Element/Attribute	Description	HTML	XHTML
`datasrc="url"`	Specifies the URL or ID of the data source bound with the button (IE only)		
`name="text"`	Provides the name assigned to the form button	4.0	1.0
`type="submit| reset|button"`	Specifies the type of form button	4.0	1.0
`value="text"`	Provides the value associated with the form button	4.0	1.0
`<caption> </caption>`	Creates a table caption	3.0	1.0
`align="bottom| center|left| right|top"`	Specifies the alignment of the caption (deprecated)	3.0	1.0*
`valign="top|bottom"`	Specifies the vertical alignment of the caption		
`<center> </center>`	Centers content horizontally on the page (deprecated)	3.2	1.0*
`<cite> </cite>`	Marks citation text	2.0	1.0
`<code> </code>`	Marks text used for code samples	2.0	1.0
`<col> </col>`	Defines the settings for a column or group of columns	4.0	1.0
`align="left|right| center"`	Specifies the alignment of the content of the column(s)	4.0	1.0
`bgcolor="color"`	Specifies the background color of the column(s)		
`char="char"`	Specifies a character in the column used to align column values	4.0	1.0
`charoff="integer"`	Specifies the offset in pixels from the alignment character specified in the char attribute	4.0	1.0
`span="integer"`	Specifies the number of columns in the group	4.0	1.0
`valign="top| middle|bottom| baseline"`	Specifies the vertical alignment of the content in the column(s)	4.0	1.0
`width="integer"`	Specifies the width of the column(s) in pixels	4.0	1.0
`<colgroup> </colgroup>`	Creates a container for a group of columns	4.0	1.0
`align="left|right center"`	Specifies the alignment of the content of the column group	4.0	1.0
`bgcolor="color"`	Specifies the background color of the column group		
`char="char"`	Specifies a character in the column used to align column group values	4.0	1.0
`charoff="integer"`	Specifies the offset in pixels from the alignment character specified in the char attribute	4.0	1.0
`span="integer"`	Specifies the number of columns in the group	4.0	1.0
`valign="top|middle |bottom|baseline"`	Specifies the vertical alignment of the content in the column group	4.0	1.0
`width="integer"`	Specifies the width of the columns in the group in pixels	4.0	1.0
`<dd> </dd>`	Marks text as a definition within a definition list	2.0	1.0
`<del> </del>`	Marks text as deleted from the document	3.0	1.0
`cite="url"`	Provides the URL for the document that has additional information about the deleted text	3.0	1.0
`datetime="date"`	Specifies the date and time of the text deletion	3.0	1.0
`<dfn> </dfn>`	Marks the defining instance of a term	3.0	1.0
`<dir> </dir>`	Contains a directory listing (deprecated)	2.0	1.0*
`compact="compact"`	Permits use of compact rendering, if available (deprecated)	2.0	1.0*

Element/Attribute	Description	HTML	XHTML
`<div> </div>`	Creates a generic block-level element	3.0	1.0
`align="left|center right|justify"`	Specifies the horizontal alignment of the content (deprecated)	3.0	1.0*
`datafld="text"`	Indicates the column from a data source that supplies bound data for the block (IE only)		
`dataformatas="html |plaintext|text"`	Specifies the format of the data in the data source bound with the block (IE only)		
`datasrc="url"`	Provides the URL or ID of the data source bound with the block (IE only)		
`nowrap="nowrap"`	Specifies whether the content wraps using normal HTML line-wrapping conventions	3.0*	
`<dl> </dl>`	Encloses a definition list using the dd and dt elements	2.0	1.0
`compact="compact"`	Permits use of compact rendering, if available (deprecated)	2.0	1.0*
`<dt> </dt>`	Marks a definition term in a definition list	2.0	1.0
`nowrap="nowrap"`	Specifies whether the content wraps using normal HTML line-wrapping conventions		
`<em> </em>`	Marks emphasized text	2.0	1.0
`<embed> </embed>`	Places an embedded object into the page (not part of the W3C specifications, but supported by most major browsers)		
`align="bottom|left |right|top"`	Specifies the alignment of the object with the surrounding content		
`autostart="true |false"`	Starts the embedded object automatically when the page is loaded		
`height="integer"`	Specifies the height of the object in pixels		
`hidden="true|false"`	Hides the object on the page		
`hspace="integer"`	Specifies the horizontal space around the object in pixels		
`name="text"`	Provides the name of the embedded object		
`pluginspage="url"`	Provides the URL of the page containing information on the object		
`pluginurl="url"`	Provides the URL of the page for directly installing the object		
`src="url"`	Provides the location of the file containing the object		
`type="mime-type"`	Specifies the mime-type of the embedded object		
`units="text"`	Specifies the measurement units of the object		
`vspace="integer"`	Specifies the vertical space around the object in pixels		
`width="integer"`	Specifies the width of the object in pixels		
`<fieldset> </fieldset>`	Places form fields in a common group	4.0	1.0
`align="left|center |right"`	Specifies the alignment of the contents of the field set (IE only)		
`datafld="text"`	Indicates the column from a data source that supplies bound data for the field set (IE only)		
`dataformatas="html| plaintext|text"`	Specifies the format of the data in the data source bound with the field set (IE only)		
`datasrc="url"`	Provides the URL or ID of the data source bound with the field set (IE only)		
`<font> </font>`	Formats the enclosed text (deprecated)	3.2	1.0*
`color="color"`	Specifies the color of the enclosed text (deprecated)	3.2	1.0*
`face="text list"`	Specifies the font face(s) of the enclosed text (deprecated)	3.2	1.0*
`size="integer"`	Specifies the size of the enclosed text, with values ranging from 1 (smallest) to 7 (largest); a value of +integer increases the font size relative to the font size specified in the basefont element (deprecated)	3.2	1.0*

Element/Attribute	Description	HTML	XHTML
`<form> </form>`	Encloses the contents of a Web form	2.0	1.0
`accept="mime-type list"`	Lists mime-types that the server processing the form will handle	4.0	1.0
`accept-charset= "char code"`	Specifies the character encoding that the server processing the form will handle	4.0	1.0
`action="url"`	Provides the URL to which the form values are to be sent	2.0	1.0
`autocomplete="on|off"`	Enables automatic insertion of information in fields in which the user has previously entered data (IE only)		
`enctype="mime-type"`	Specifies the mime-type of the data to be sent to the server for processing; the default is "application/x-www-form-urlencoded"	2.0	1.0
`method="get|post"`	Specifies the method of accessing the URL specified in the action attribute	2.0	1.0
`name="text"`	Specifies the name of the form	2.0	1.0
`target="text"`	Specifies the frame or window in which output from the form should appear	4.0	1.0
`<frame> </frame>`	Marks a single frame within a set of frames	4.0	1.0*
`border="integer"`	Specifies the thickness of the frame border in pixels (Netscape 4 only)		
`bordercolor="color"`	Specifies the color of the frame border		
`frameborder="1|0"`	Determines whether the frame border is visible (1) or invisible (0); Netscape also supports values of yes or no	4.0	1.0*
`longdesc="url"`	Provides the URL of a document containing a long description of the frame's contents	4.0	1.0*
`marginheight= "integer"`	Specifies the space above and below the frame object and the frame's borders, in pixels	4.0	1.0*
`marginwidth="integer"`	Specifies the space to the left and right of the frame object and the frame's borders, in pixels	4.0	1.0*
`name="text"`	Specifies the name of the frame	4.0	1.0*
`noresize="noresize"`	Prevents users from resizing the frame	4.0	1.0*
`scrolling="auto| yes|no"`	Specifies whether the browser will display a scroll bar with the frame	4.0	1.0*
`src="url"`	Provides the URL of the document to be displayed in the frame	4.0	1.0*
`<frameset> </frameset>`	Creates a collection of frames	4.0	1.0*
`border="integer"`	Specifies the thickness of the frame borders in the frameset in pixels (not part of the W3C specifications, but supported by most browsers)		
`bordercolor="color"`	Specifies the color of the frame borders		
`cols="value list"`	Arranges the frames in columns with the width of each column expressed either in pixels, as a percentage, or using an asterisk (to allow the browser to choose the width)	4.0	1.0*
`frameborder="1|0"`	Determines whether frame borders are visible (1) or invisible (0); (not part of the W3C specifications, but supported by most browsers; Netscape also supports values of yes or no)		
`framespacing="integer"`	Specifies the amount of space between frames in pixels (IE only)		
`rows="value list"`	Arranges the frames in rows with the height of each column expressed either in pixels, as a percentage, or using an asterisk (to allow the browser to choose the height)	4.0	1.0*

Element/Attribute	Description	HTML	XHTML
`<hi> </hi>`	Marks the enclosed text as a heading, where i is an integer from 1 (the largest heading) to 6 (the smallest heading)	2.0	1.0
`align="left|center|right|justify"`	Specifies the alignment of the heading text (deprecated)	3.0	1.0*
`<head> </head>`	Encloses the document head, containing information about the document	2.0	1.0
`profile="url"`	Provides the location of metadata about the document	4.0	1.0
`<hr />`	Draws a horizontal line (rule) in the rendered page	2.0	1.0
`align="left|center|right"`	Specifies the horizontal alignment of the line (deprecated)	3.2	1.0*
`color="color"`	Specifies the color of the line		
`noshade="noshade"`	Removes 3-D shading from the line (deprecated)	3.2	1.0*
`size="integer"`	Specifies the height of the line in pixels or as a percentage of the enclosing element's height (deprecated)	3.2	1.0*
`width="integer"`	Specifies the width of the line in pixels or as a percentage of the enclosing element's width (deprecated)	3.2	1.0*
`<html> </html>`	Encloses the entire content of the HTML document	2.0	1.0
`version="text"`	Specifies the version of HTML being used	2.0	1.1
`xmlns="text"`	Specifies the namespace prefix for the document		1.0
`<i> </i>`	Displays the enclosed text in italics	2.0	1.0
`<iframe> </iframe>`	Creates an inline frame in the document	4.0	1.0*
`align="bottom|left|middle|top|right"`	Specifies the horizontal alignment of the frame with the surrounding content (deprecated)	4.0	1.0*
`datafld="text"`	Indicates the column from a data source that supplies bound data for the inline frame (IE only)		4.0
`dataformatas="html|plaintext|text"`	Specifies the format of the data in the data source bound with the inline frame (IE only)		4.0
`datasrc="url"`	Provides the URL or ID of the data source bound with the inline frame (IE only)		4.0
`frameborder="1|0"`	Specifies whether to display a frame border (1) or not (0)	4.0	1.0*
`height="integer"`	Specifies the height of the frame in pixels	4.0	1.0*
`hspace="integer"`	Specifies the space to the left and right of the frame in pixels	4.0	1.0*
`longdesc="url"`	Indicates the document containing a long description of the frame's content	4.0	1.0*
`marginheight="integer"`	Specifies the space above and below the frame object and the frame's borders, in pixels	4.0	1.0*
`marginwidth="integer"`	Specifies the space to the left and right of the frame object and the frame's borders, in pixels	4.0	1.0*
`name="text"`	Specifies the name of the frame	4.0	1.0*
`scrolling="auto|yes|no"`	Determines whether the browser displays a scroll bar with the frame	4.0	1.0*
`src="url"`	Indicates the document displayed within the frame	4.0	1.0*
`vspace="integer"`	Specifies the space to the top and bottom of the frame in pixels	4.0	1.0*
`width="integer"`	Specifies the width of the frame in pixels	4.0	1.0*

Element/Attribute	Description	HTML	XHTML
`<ilayer> </ilayer>`	Creates an inline layer used to display the content of an external document (Netscape 4 only)		
`above="text"`	Specifies the name of the layer displayed above the current layer (IE only)		
`background="url"`	Provides the URL of the file containing the background image (IE only)		
`below="text"`	Specifies the name of the layer displayed below the current layer (IE only)		
`bgcolor="color"`	Specifies the layer's background color (IE only)		
`clip="top, left, bottom, right"`	Specifies the coordinates of the viewable region of the layer (IE only)		
`height="integer"`	Specifies the height of the layer in pixels (IE only)		
`left="integer"`	Specifies the horizontal offset of the layer in pixels (IE only)		
`pagex="integer"`	Specifies the horizontal position of the layer in pixels (IE only)		
`pagey="integer"`	Specifies the vertical position of the layer in pixels (IE only)		
`src="url"`	Provides the URL of the document displayed in the layer (IE only)		
`top="integer"`	Specifies the vertical offset of the layer in pixels (IE only)		
`visibility="hide|inherit|show"`	Specifies the visibility of the layer (IE only)		
`width="integer"`	Specifies the width of the layer in pixels (IE only)		
`z-index="integer"`	Specifies the stacking order of the layer (IE only)		
`<img> </img>`	Inserts an inline image into the document	2.0	1.0
`align="left|right|top|texttop|middle|absmiddle|baselines|bottom|absbottom"`	Specifies the alignment of the image with the surrounding content (deprecated)	2.0	1.0*
`alt="text"`	Specifies alternate text to be displayed in place of the image	2.0	1.0
`border="integer"`	Specifies the width of the image border (deprecated)	3.2	1.0*
`controls="control"`	For video images, displays a playback control below the image (IE only)		
`datafld="text"`	Names the column from a data source that supplies bound data for the image (IE only)		
`dataformatas="html|plaintext|text"`	Specifies the format of the data in the data source bound with the image (IE only)		
`datasrc="url"`	Provides the URL or ID of the data source bound with the image (IE only)		
`dynsrc="url"`	Provides the URL of a video or VRML file (IE and Opera only)		
`height="integer"`	Specifies the height of the image in pixels	3.0	1.0
`hspace="integer"`	Specifies the horizontal space around the image in pixels (deprecated)	3.0	1.0*
`ismap="ismap"`	Indicates that the image can be used as a server-side image map	2.0	1.0
`longdesc="url"`	Provides the URL of a document containing a long description of the image	4.0	1.0
`loop="integer"`	Specifies the number of times the video will play (IE and Opera only)		
`lowsrc="url"`	Provides the URL of the low-resolution version of the image (IE and Netscape only)		
`name="text"`	Specifies the image name	4.0	1.0*

Element/Attribute	Description	HTML	XHTML
src="*url*"	Specifies the image source file	2.0	1.0
start="fileopen| mouseover"	Indicates when to start the video clip (either when the file is opened or when the mouse hovers over the image) (IE and Opera only)		
suppress="true| false"	Suppresses the display of the alternate text and the placeholder icon until the image file is located (Netscape 4 only)		
usemap="*url*"	Provides the location of a client-side image associated with the image (not well-supported when the URL points to an external file)	3.2	1.0
vspace="*integer*"	Specifies the vertical space around the image in pixels (deprecated)	3.2	1.0*
width="*integer*"	Specifies the width of the image in pixels	3.0	1.0
<input> </input>	Marks an input field in a Web form	2.0	1.0
align="left|right| top|texttop| middle|absmiddle| baseline|bottom| absbottom"	Specifies the alignment of the input field with the surrounding content (deprecated)	2.0	1.0*
alt="*text*"	Specifies alternate text for image buttons and image input fields	4.0	1.0
checked="checked"	Specifies that the input check box or input radio button is selected	2.0	1.0
datafld="*text*"	Indicates the column from a data source that supplies bound data for the input field	4.0	
dataformatas="html| plaintext|text"	Specifies the format of the data in the data source bound with the input field	4.0	
datasrc="*url*"	Provides the URL or ID of the data source bound with the input field	4.0	
height="*integer*"	Specifies the height of the image input field in pixels (not part of the W3C specifications, but supported by many browsers)		
hspace="*integer*"	Specifies the horizontal space around the image input field in pixels (not part of the W3C specifications, but supported by many browsers)		
ismap="ismap"	Enables the image input field to be used as a server-side image map	4.0	1.1
maxlength="*integer*"	Specifies the maximum number of characters that can be inserted into a text input field	2.0	1.0
name="text"	Specifies the name of the input field	2.0	1.0
readonly="readonly"	Prevents the value of the input field from being modified	2.0	1.0
size="*integer*"	Specifies the number of characters that can be displayed at one time in an input text field	2.0	1.0
src="*url*"	Indicates the source file of an input image field	2.0	1.0
type="button| checkbox|file| hidden|image| password|radio| reset|submit| text"	Specifies the type of input field	2.0	1.0
usemap="url"	Provides the location of a client-side image associated with the image input field (not well-supported when the URL points to an external file)	4.0	1.0
value="*text*"	Specifies the default value of the input field	2.0	1.0
vspace="*integer*"	Specifies the vertical space around the image input field in pixels (not part of the W3C specifications, but supported by many browsers)		
width="*integer*"	Specifies the width of an image input field in pixels (not part of the W3C specifications, but supported by many browsers)		

Element/Attribute	Description	HTML	XHTML
`<ins> </ins>`	Marks inserted text	3.0	1.0
`cite="url"`	Provides the URL for the document that has additional information about the inserted text	3.0	1.0
`datetime="date"`	Specifies the date and time of the text insertion	3.0	1.0
`<isindex />`	Inserts an input field into the document for search queries (deprecated)	2.0	1.0*
`action="url"`	Provides the URL of the script used to process the sindex data		1.0
`prompt="text"`	Specifies the text to be used for the input prompt (deprecated)	3.0	1.0*
`<kbd> </kbd>`	Marks keyboard-style text	2.0	1.0
`<label> </label>`	Associates the enclosed content with a form field	4.0	1.0
`datafld="text"`	Indicates the column from a data source that supplies bound data for the label (IE only)		
`dataformatas="html|plaintext|text"`	Specifies the format of the data in the data source bound with the label (IE only)		
`datasrc="url"`	Provides the URL or ID of the data source bound with the label (IE only)		
`for="text"`	Provides the ID of the field associated with the label	4.0	1.0
`<layer> </layer>`	Creates a layer used to display the content of external documents; unlike the ilayer element, layer elements are absolutely positioned in the page (Netscape 4 only)		
`above="text"`	Specifies the name of the layer displayed above the current layer (Netscape 4 only)		
`background="url"`	Provides the URL of the file containing the background image (Netscape 4 only)		
`below="text"`	Specifies the name of the layer displayed below the current layer (Netscape 4 only)		
`bgcolor="color"`	Specifies the layer's background color (Netscape 4 only)		
`clip="top, left, bottom, right"`	Specifies the coordinates of the viewable region of the layer (Netscape 4 only)		
`height="integer"`	Specifies the height of the layer in pixels (Netscape 4 only)		
`left="integer"`	Specifies the horizontal offset of the layer in pixels (Netscape 4 only)		
`pagex="integer"`	Specifies the horizontal position of the layer in pixels (Netscape 4 only)		
`pagey="integer"`	Specifies the vertical position of the layer in pixels (Netscape 4 only)		
`src="url"`	Provides the URL of the document displayed in the layer (Netscape 4 only)		
`top="integer"`	Specifies the vertical offset of the layer in pixels (Netscape 4 only)		
`visibility="hide|inherit|show"`	Specifies the visibility of the layer (Netscape 4 only)		
`width="integer"`	Specifies the width of the layer in pixels (Netscape 4 only)		
`z-index="integer"`	Specifies the stacking order of the layer (Netscape 4 only)		
`<legend> </legend>`	Marks the enclosed text as a caption for a field set	4.0	1.0
`align="bottom|left|top|right"`	Specifies the alignment of the legend with the field set; Internet Explorer also supports the center option (deprecated)	4.0	1.0*

Element/Attribute	Description	HTML	XHTML
`<li> </li>`	Marks an item in an ordered (ol), unordered (ul), menu (menu), or directory (dir) list	2.0	1.0
`type="A|a|I|i|1|disc|square|circle"`	Specifies the bullet type associated with the list item: a value of "1" is the default for ordered list; a value of "disc" is the default for unordered list (deprecated)	3.2	1.0*
`value="integer"`	Sets the value for the current list item in an ordered list; subsequent list items are numbered from that value (deprecated)	3.2	1.0*
`<link />`	Creates an element in the document head that establishes the relationship between the current document and external documents or objects	2.0	1.0
`charset="char code"`	Specifies the character encoding of the external document	4.0	1.0
`href="url"`	Provides the URL of the external document	2.0	1.0
`hreflang="text"`	Indicates the language of the external document	4.0	1.0
`media="all|aural|braille|handheld|print|projection|screen|tty|tv"`	Indicates the media in which the external document is presented	4.0	1.0
`name="text"`	Specifies the name of the link		
`rel="text"`	Specifies the relationship between the current page and the link specified by the href attribute	2.0	
`rev="text"`	Specifies the reverse relationship between the current page and the link specified by the href attribute	2.0	1.0
`target="text"`	Specifies the target window or frame for the link	4.0	1.0*
`title="text"`	Specifies the title of the external document	2.0	1.0
`type="mime-type"`	Specifies the mime-type of the external document	4.0	1.0
`<map> </map>`	Creates an element that contains client-side image map hotspots	3.2	1.0
`name="text"`	Specifies the name of the image map	3.2	1.0*
`<marquee> </marquee>`	Displays the enclosed text as a scrolling marquee (not part of the W3C specifications, but supported by most browsers)		
`behavior="alternate|scroll|slide"`	Specifies how the marquee should move		
`bgcolor="color"`	Specifies the background color of the marquee		
`datafld="text"`	Indicates the column from a data source that supplies bound data for the marquee		
`dataformatas="html|plaintext|text"`	Indicates the format of the data in the data source bound with the marquee		
`datasrc="url"`	Provides the URL or ID of the data source bound with the marquee		
`direction="down|left|right|up"`	Specifies the direction of the marquee		
`height="integer"`	Specifies the height of the marquee in pixels		
`hspace="integer"`	Specifies the horizontal space around the marquee in pixels		
`loop="integer|infinite"`	Specifies the number of times the marquee motion is repeated		
`scrollamount="integer"`	Specifies the amount of space, in pixels, between successive draws of the marquee text		
`scrolldelay="integer"`	Specifies the amount of time, in milliseconds, between marquee actions		
`truespeed="truespeed"`	Indicates whether the scrolldelay value should be set to its exact value; otherwise any value less than 60 milliseconds is rounded up		

Element/Attribute	Description	HTML	XHTML
vspace="*integer*"	Specifies the vertical space around the marquee in pixels		
width="*integer*"	Specifies the width of the marquee in pixels		
<menu> </menu>	Contains a menu list (deprecated)	2.0	1.0*
compact="compact"	Reduces the space between menu items (deprecated)	2.0	1.0*
start="*integer*"	Specifies the starting value of the items in the menu list		
type="A|a|I|i |1|disc|square| circle|none"	Specifies the bullet type associated with the list items	3.2	1.0*
<meta> </meta>	Creates an element in the document's head section that contains information and special instructions for processing the document	2.0	1.0
content="*text*"	Provides information associated with the name or http-equiv attributes	2.0	1.0
http-equiv="*text*"	Provides instructions to the browser to request the server to perform different http operations	2.0	1.0
name="*text*"	Specifies the type of information specified in the content attribute	2.0	1.0
scheme="*text*"	Supplies additional information about the scheme used to interpret the content attribute	4.0	1.0
<nobr> </nobr>	Disables line wrapping for the enclosed content (not part of the W3C specifications, but supported by most browsers)		
<noembed> </noembed>	Encloses alternate content for browsers that do not support the embed element (not part of the W3C specifications, but supported by most browsers)		
<noframe> </noframe>	Encloses alternate content for browsers that do not support frames	4.0	1.0*
<nolayer> </nolayer>	Encloses alternate content for browsers that do not support the layer or ilayer elements (Netscape 4 only)		
<noscript> </noscript>	Encloses alternate content for browsers that do not support client-side scripts	4.0	1.0
<object> </object>	Places an embedded object (image, applet, sound clip, video clip, etc.) into the page	4.0	1.0
archive="*url*"	Specifies the URL of an archive containing classes and other resources preloaded for use with the object	4.0	1.0
align="absbottom| absmiddle|baseline |bottom|left| middle|right| texttop|top"	Aligns the object with the surrounding content (deprecated)	4.0	1.0*
border="*integer*"	Specifies the width of the border around the object (deprecated)	4.0	1.0*
classid="*url*"	Provides the URL of the object	4.0	1.0
codebase="*url*"	Specifies the base path used to resolve relative references within the embedded object	4.0	1.0
codetype="*mime-type*"	Indicates the mime-type of the embedded object's code	4.0	1.0
data="*url*"	Provides the URL of the object's data file	4.0	1.0
datafld="*text*"	Identifies the column from a data source that supplies bound data for the embedded object	4.0	
dataformatas="html| plaintext|text"	Specifies the format of the data in the data source bound with the embedded object	4.0	
datasrc="*url*"	Provides the URL or ID of the data source bound with the embedded object	4.0	

Element/Attribute	Description	HTML	XHTML
declare="declare"	Declares the object without embedding it on the page	4.0	1.0
height="*integer*"	Specifies the height of the object in pixels	4.0	1.0
hspace="*integer*"	Specifies the horizontal space around the image in pixels	4.0	1.0
name="*text*"	Specifies the name of the embedded object	4.0	1.0
standby="*text*"	Specifies the message displayed by the browser while loading the embedded object	4.0	1.0
type="*mime-type*"	Indicates the mime-type of the embedded object	4.0	1.0
vspace="*integer*"	Specifies the vertical space around the embedded object	4.0	1.0
width="*integer*"	Specifies the width of the object in pixels	4.0	1.0
<ol> </ol>	Contains an ordered list of items	2.0	1.0
compact="compact"	Reduces the space between ordered list items (deprecated)	2.0	1.0*
start="*integer*"	Specifies the starting value in the list (deprecated)	3.2	1.0
type="A|a|I|i|1"	Specifies the bullet type associated with the list items (deprecated)	3.2	1.0*
<optgroup> </optgroup>	Contains a group of option elements in a selection field	4.0	1.0
label="*text*"	Specifies the label for the option group	4.0	1.0
<option> </option>	Formats an option within a selection field	2.0	1.0
label="*text*"	Supplies the text label associated with the option	4.0	1.0
selected="selected"	Selects the option by default	2.0	1.0
value="*text*"	Specifies the value associated with the option	2.0	1.0
<p> </p>	Marks the enclosed content as a paragraph	2.0	1.0
align="**left**|center|right|justify"	Horizontally aligns the contents of the paragraph (deprecated)	3.0	1.0*
<param> </param>	Marks parameter values sent to an object element or an applet element	3.2	1.0
name="*text*"	Specifies the parameter name	3.2	1.0
type="*mime-type*"	Specifies the mime-type of the resource indicated by the value attribute	4.0	1.0
value="*text*"	Specifies the parameter value	3.2	1.0
valuetype="**data**|ref|object"	Specifies the data type of the value attribute	4.0	1.0
<plaintext> </plaintext>	Marks the enclosed text as plain text (not part of the W3C specifications, but supported by most browsers)		
<pre> </pre>	Marks the enclosed text as preformatted text, retaining white space from the document	2.0	1.0
width="*integer*"	Specifies the width of preformatted text, in number of characters (deprecated)	2.0	1.0*
<q> </q>	Marks the enclosed text as a quotation	3.0	1.0
cite="*url*"	Provides the source URL of the quoted content	4.0	1.0
<s> </s>	Marks the enclosed text as strikethrough text (deprecated)	3.0	1.0*
<samp> </samp>	Marks the enclosed text as a sequence of literal characters	2.0	1.0
<script> </script>	Encloses client-side scripts within the document; this element can be placed within the head or the body element or it can refer to an external script file	3.2	1.0
charset="*char code*"	Specifies the character encoding of the script	4.0	1.0
defer="defer"	Defers execution of the script	4.0	1.0
event="*text*"	Specifies the event that the script should be run in response to	4.0	

Element/Attribute	Description	HTML	XHTML
`for="text"`	Indicates the name or ID of the element to which the event attribute refers to	4.0	
`language="text"`	Specifies the language of the script (deprecated)	4.0	1.0*
`src="url"`	Provides the URL of an external script file	4.0	1.0
`type="mime-type"`	Specifies the mime-type of the script	4.0	1.0
`<select> </select>`	Creates a selection field (drop-down list box) in a Web form	2.0	1.0
`align="left|right| top|texttop| middle|absmiddle| baseline|bottom| absbottom"`	Specifies the alignment of the selection field with the surrounding content (deprecated)	3.0*	
`datafld="text"`	Identifies the column from a data source that supplies bound data for the selection field	4.0	
`dataformatas="html| plaintext|text"`	Specifies the format of the data in the data source bound with the selection field	4.0	
`datasrc="url"`	Provides the URL or ID of the data source bound with the selection field	4.0	
`multiple="multiple"`	Allows multiple sections from the field	2.0	1.0
`name="text"`	Specifies the selection field name	2.0	1.0
`size="integer"`	Specifies the number of visible items in the selection list	2.0	1.0
`<small> </small>`	Decreases the size of the enclosed text relative to the default font size	3.0	1.0
`<span> </span>`	Creates a generic inline element	3.0	1.0
`datafld="text"`	Identifies the column from a data source that supplies bound data for the inline element (IE only)		
`dataformatas="html| plaintext|text"`	Specifies the format of the data in the data source bound with the inline element (IE only)		
`datasrc="url"`	Provides the URL or ID of the data source bound with the inline element (IE only)		
`<strike> </strike>`	Marks the enclosed text as strikethrough text (deprecated)	3.0	1.0*
`<strong> </strong>`	Marks the enclosed text as strongly emphasized text	2.0	1.0
`<style> </style>`	Encloses global style declarations for the document	3.0	1.0
`media="all|aural| braille|handheld| print|projection| screen|tty|tv|"`	Indicates the media of the enclosed style definitions	4.0	1.0
`title="text"`	Specifies the style of the style definitions	4.0	1.0
`type="mime-type"`	Specifies the mime-type of the style definitions	4.0	1.0
`<sub> </sub>`	Marks the enclosed text as subscript text	3.0	1.0
`<sup> </sup>`	Marks the enclosed text as superscript text	3.0	1.0
`<table> </table>`	Encloses the contents of a Web table	3.0	1.0
`align="left|center |right"`	Aligns the table with the surrounding content (deprecated)	3.0	1.0*
`background="url"`	Provides the URL of the table's background image (not part of the W3C specifications, but supported by most browsers)		
`bgcolor="color"`	Specifies the background color of the table (deprecated)	4.0	1.0*
`border="integer"`	Specifies the width of the table border in pixels	3.0	1.0
`bordercolor="color"`	Specifies the table border color (IE and Netscape 4 only)		

Element/Attribute	Description	HTML	XHTML
bordercolordark= "*color*"	Specifies the color of the table border's shaded edge (IE only)		
bordercolorlight= "*color*"	Specifies the color of the table border's unshaded edge (IE only)		
cellpadding= "*integer*"	Specifies the space between the table data and the cell borders in pixels	3.2	1.0
cellspacing= "*integer*"	Specifies the space between table cells in pixels	3.2	1.0
cols="*integer*"	Specifies the number of columns in the table		
datafld="*text*"	Indicates the column from a data source that supplies bound data for the table	4.0	
dataformatas="html| plaintext|text"	Specifies the format of the data in the data source bound with the table	4.0	
datapagesize= "*integer*"	Sets the number of records displayed within the table	4.0	1.1
datasrc="*url*"	Provides the URL or ID of the data source bound with the table	4.0	
frame="above|below |**border**|box| hsides|lhs|rhs| void|vside"	Specifies the format of the borders around the table	4.0	1.0
height="*integer*"	Specifies the height of the table in pixels (not part of the W3C specifications, but supported by most browsers)		
hspace="*integer*"	Specifies the horizontal space around the table in pixels (not part of the W3C specifications, but supported by most browsers)		
rules="**all**|cols| groups|none|rows"	Specifies the format of the table's internal borders or gridlines	4.0	1.0
summary="*text*"	Supplies a text summary of the table's content	4.0	1.0
vspace="*integer*"	Specifies the vertical space around the table in pixels		
width="*integer*"	Specifies the width of the table in pixels	3.0	1.0
<tbody> </tbody>	Encloses the content of the Web table body	4.0	1.0
align="left|center |right|justify|char"	Specifies the alignment of the contents in the cells of the table body	4.0	1.0
bgcolor="*color*"	Specifies the background color of the table body		
char="*char*"	Specifies the character used for aligning the table body contents when the align attribute is set to "char"	4.0	1.0
charoff="*integer*"	Specifies the offset in pixels from the alignment character specified in the char attribute	4.0	1.0
valign="baseline| bottom|middle|top"	Specifies the vertical alignment of the contents in the cells of the table body	4.0	1.0
<td> </td>	Encloses the data of a table cell	3.0	1.0
abbr="*text*"	Supplies an abbreviated version of the contents of the table cell	4.0	1.0
align="**left**|center |right"	Specifies the horizontal alignment of the table cell data	3.0	1.0
background="*url*"	Provides the URL of the background image file		
bgcolor="*color*"	Specifies the background color of the table cell (deprecated)	4.0	1.0*
bordercolor="*color*"	Specifies the color of the table cell border (IE only)		
bordercolordark="*color*"	Specifies the color of the table cell border's shaded edge (IE only)		

Element/Attribute	Description	HTML	XHTML
bordercolorlight= "*color*"	Specifies the color of the table cell border's unshaded edge (IE only)		
char="*char*"	Specifies the character used for aligning the table cell contents when the align attribute is set to "char"	4.0	1.0
charoff="*integer*"	Specifies the offset in pixels from the alignment character specified in the char attribute	4.0	1.0
colspan="*integer*"	Specifies the number of columns the table cell spans	3.0	1.0
headers="*text*"	Supplies a space-separated list of table headers associated with the table cell	4.0	1.0
height="*integer*"	Specifies the height of the table cell in pixels (deprecated)	3.2	1.0*
nowrap="nowrap"	Disables line-wrapping within the table cell (deprecated)	3.0	1.0*
rowspan="*integer*"	Specifies the number of rows the table cell spans	3.0	1.0
scope="col|colgroup |row|rowgroup"	Specifies the scope of the table for which the cell provides data	4.0	1.0
valign="top|**middle** |bottom"	Specifies the vertical alignment of the contents of the table cell	3.0	1.0
width="*integer*"	Specifies the width of the cell in pixels (deprecated)	3.2	1.0*
<textarea> </textarea>	Marks the enclosed text as a text area input box in a Web form	2.0	1.0
datafld="*text*"	Specifies the column from a data source that supplies bound data for the text area box	4.0	
dataformatas="html| plaintext|text"	Specifies the format of the data in the data source bound with the text area box	4.0	
datasrc="*url*"	Provides the URL or ID of the data source bound with the text area box	4.0	
cols="*integer*"	Specifies the width of the text area box in characters	2.0	1.0
name="*text*"	Specifies the name of the text area box	2.0	1.0
readonly="readonly"	Specifies the value of the text area box, cannot be modified	4.0	1.0
rows="*integer*"	Specifies the number of visible rows in the text area box	2.0	1.0
wrap="off|**soft**|hard"	Specifies how text is wrapped within the text area box and how that text-wrapping information is sent to the server-side program; in earlier versions of Netscape Navigator, the default value is "off" (Netscape accepts the values "off," "virtual," and "physical.")		
<tfoot> </tfoot>	Encloses the content of the Web table footer	4.0	1.0
align="left|center |right|justify|char"	Specifies the alignment of the contents in the cells of the table footer	4.0	1.0
bgcolor="*color*"	Specifies the background color of the table body (not part of the W3C specifications, but supported by many browsers)		
char="*char*"	Specifies the character used for aligning the table footer contents when the align attribute is set to "char"	4.0	1.0
charoff="*integer*"	Specifies the offset in pixels from the alignment character specified in the char attribute	4.0	1.0
valign="baseline| bottom|middle|top"	Specifies the vertical alignment of the contents in the cells of the table footer	4.0	1.0
<th> </th>	Encloses the data of a table header cell	3.0	1.0
abbr="*text*"	Supplies an abbreviated version of the contents of the table cell	4.0	1.0
align="**left**|center |right"	Specifies the horizontal alignment of the table cell data	3.0	1.0
axis="*text list*"	Provides a list of table categories that can be mapped to a table hierarchy	3.0	1.0

Element/Attribute	Description	HTML	XHTML
background="*url*"	Provides the URL of the background image file (not part of the W3C specifications, but supported by many browsers)		
bgcolor="*color*"	Specifies the background color of the table cell (deprecated)	4.0	1.0*
bordercolor="*color*"	Specifies the color of the table cell border (IE only)		
bordercolordark="*color*"	Specifies the color of the table cell border's shaded edge (IE only)		
bordercolorlight="*color*"	Specifies the color of the table cell border's unshaded edge (IE only)		
char="*char*"	Specifies the character used for aligning the table cell contents when the align attribute is set to "char"	4.0	1.0
charoff="*integer*"	Specifies the offset in pixels from the alignment character specified in the char attribute	4.0	1.0
colspan="*integer*"	Specifies the number of columns the table cell spans	3.0	1.0
headers="*text*"	A space-separated list of table headers associated with the table cell	4.0	1.0
height="*integer*"	Specifies the height of the table cell in pixels (deprecated)	3.2	1.0*
nowrap="nowrap"	Disables line-wrapping within the table cell (deprecated)	3.0	1.0*
rowspan="*integer*"	Specifies the number of rows the table cell spans	3.0	1.0
scope="col|colgroup|row|rowgroup"	Specifies the scope of the table for which the cell provides data	4.0	1.0
valign="top|**middle**|bottom"	Specifies the vertical alignment of the contents of the table cell	3.0	1.0
width="*integer*"	Specifies the width of the cell in pixels (deprecated)	3.2	1.0*
<thead> </thead>	Encloses the content of the Web table header	4.0	1.0
align="left|center|right|justify|char"	Specifies the alignment of the contents in the cells of the table header	4.0	1.0
bgcolor="*color*"	Specifies the background color of the table body		
char="*char*"	Specifies the character used for aligning the table header contents when the align attribute is set to "char"	4.0	1.0
charoff="*integer*"	Specifies the offset in pixels from the alignment character specified in the char attribute	4.0	1.0
valign="baseline|bottom|middle|top"	Specifies the vertical alignment of the contents in the cells of the table header	4.0	1.0
<title> </title>	Specifies the title of the document, placed in the head section of the document	2.0	1.0
<tr> </tr>	Encloses the content of a row within a Web table	3.0	1.0
align="left|center|right"	Specifies the horizontal alignment of the data in the row's cells	3.0	1.0
background="*url*"	Provides the URL of the background image file for the row		
bgcolor="*color*"	Specifies the background color of the row (deprecated)	4.0	1.0*
bordercolor="*color*"	Specifies the color of the table row border (IE only)		
bordercolordark="*color*"	Specifies the color of the table row border's shaded edge (IE only)		
bordercolorlight="*color*"	Specifies the color of the table row border's unshaded edge (IE only)		
char="*char*"	Specifies the character used for aligning the table row contents when the align attribute is set to "char"	4.0	1.0
charoff="*integer*"	Specifies the offset in pixels from the alignment character specified in the char attribute	4.0	1.0

Element/Attribute	Description	HTML	XHTML
height="*integer*"	Specifies the height of the table row in pixels		
valign="baseline|bottom|*middle*|top"	Specifies the vertical alignment of the contents of the table row	3.0	1.0
`<tt> </tt>`	Marks the enclosed text as teletype or monospaced text	2.0	1.0
`<u> </u>`	Marks the enclosed text as underlined text (deprecated)	3.0	1.0*
`<ul> </ul>`	Contains an unordered list of items	2.0	1.0
compact="compact"	Reduces the space between unordered list items (deprecated)	2.0	1.0*
type="disc|square|circle"	Specifies the bullet type associated with the list items (deprecated)	3.2	1.0*
`<var> </var>`	Marks the enclosed text as containing a variable name	2.0	1.0
`<wbr />`	Forces a line-break in the rendered page (not part of the W3C specifications, but supported by many browsers)		
`<xml> </xml>`	Encloses XML content (also referred to as a "data island") or references an external XML document (IE only)		
ns="*url*"	Provides the URL of the XML data island (IE only)		
prefix="*text*"	Specifies the namespace prefix of the XML content (IE only)		
src="*url*"	Provides the URL of an external XML document (IE only)		
`<xmp> </xmp>`	Marks the enclosed text as preformatted text, preserving the white space of the source document; replaced by the pre element (deprecated)	2.0	

Cascading Style Sheets

Appendix F

This appendix describes the selectors, units, and attributes supported by Cascading Style Sheets (CSS). Version numbers indicate the lowest version that supports the given selector, unit, or attribute. This appendix focuses on CSS1 and CSS2 styles. It does not include all of the CSS3 styles due to the state of CSS3's development and current level of browser support for CSS3. You should always check your code against different browsers and browser versions to ensure that your page is being rendered correctly. Additional information about CSS can be found at the World Wide Web Consortium Web site at *www.w3.org*.

Starting Data Files

There are no starting Data Files needed for this appendix.

Selectors

The general form of a style declaration is:

selector {attribute1:value1; attribute2:value2; ...}

where *selector* is the selection of elements within the document to which the style will be applied; *attribute1*, *attribute2*, etc. are the different style attributes; and *value1*, *value2*, etc. are values associated with those styles. The following table shows some of the different forms that a selector can take.

Selector	Matches	CSS
*	All elements in the document	2.0
e	An element, *e*, in the document	1.0
e1, e2, e3, …	A group of elements, *e1*, *e2*, *e3*, in the document	1.0
e1 e2	An element *e2* nested within the parent element, *e1*	1.0
e1 > e2	An element *e2* that is a child of the parent element, *e1*	2.0
e1+e2	An element, *e2*, that is adjacent to element *e1*	2.0
e1.class	An element, *e1*, belonging to the *class* class	1.0
.class	Any element belonging to the *class* class	1.0
#id	An element with the id value *id*	1.0
[att]	The element contains the *att* attribute	2.0
[att="val"]	The element's *att* attribute equals "*val*"	2.0
[att~="val"]	The element's *att* attribute value is a space-separated list of "words," one of which is exactly "*val*"	2.0
[att|="val"]	The element's *att* attribute value is a hyphen-separated list of "words" beginning with "val"	3.0
[att^="val"]	The element's *att* attribute begins with "*val*"	3.0
[att$="val"]	The element's *att* attribute ends with "*val*"	3.0
[att*="val"]	The element's *att* attribute contains the value "*val*"	3.0
[ns|att]	References all *att* attributes in the *ns* namespace	3.0

Pseudo-Elements and Pseudo-Classes

Pseudo-elements are elements that do not exist in HTML code but whose attributes can be set with CSS. Many pseudo-elements were introduced in CSS2.

Pseudo-Element	Matches	CSS
e:after {content: "text"}	Text content, *text*, that is inserted at the end of an element, *e*	2.0
e:before {content: "text"}	Text content, *text*, that is inserted at the beginning of an element, *e*	2.0
e:first-letter	The first letter in the element, *e*	1.0
e:first-line	The first line in the element, *e*	1.0

Pseudo-classes are classes of HTML elements that define the condition or state of the element in the Web page. Many pseudo-classes were introduced in CSS2.

Pseudo-Class	Matches	CSS
:canvas	The rendering canvas of the document	
:first	The first printed page of the document (used only with print styles created with the @print rule)	2.0
:last	The last printed page of the document (used only with print styles created with the @print rule)	2.0
:left	The left side of a two-sided printout (used only with print styles created with the @print rule)	2.0
:right	The right side of a two-sided printout (used only with print styles created with the @print rule)	2.0
:root	The root element of the document (the html element in HTML and XHTML documents)	
:scrolled-content	The content that is scrolled in the rendering viewport (Netscape only)	
:viewport	The rendering viewport of the document (Netscape only)	
:viewport-scroll	The rendering viewport of the document plus the scroll bar region (Netscape only)	
e:active	The element, e, is being activated by the user (usually applies only to hyperlinks)	1.0
e:empty	The element, e, has no content (Netscape only)	
e:first-child	The element, e, which is the first child of its parent element	2.0
e:first-node	The first occurrence of the element, e, in the document tree	
e:focus	The element, e, has received the focus of the cursor (usually applies only to Web form elements)	2.0
e:hover	The mouse pointer is hovering over the element, e (usually applies only to hyperlinks)	2.0
e:lang(text)	Sets the language, text, associated with the element, e	2.0
e:last-child	The element, e, that is the last child of its parent element	2.0
e:last-node	The last occurrence of the element, e, in the document tree (Netscape only)	
e:link	The element, e, has not been visited yet by the user (applies only to hyperlinks)	1.0
e:not	Negate the selector rule for the element, e, applying the style to all e elements that do not match the selector rules (Netscape only)	
e:visited	The element, e, has been already visited by the user (to only the hyperlinks)	1.0

@ Rules

CSS supports different "@ rules" designed to run commands within a style sheet. These commands can be used to import other styles, download font definitions, or define the format of printed output.

@ Rule	Description	CSS
`@charset "encoding"`	Defines the character set encoding used in the style sheet (this must be the very first line in the style sheet document)	2.0
`@import url(url) media`	Imports an external style sheet document into the current style sheet, where *url* is the location of the external style sheet and *media* is a comma-separated list of media types (optional)	1.0
`@media media {style declaration}`	Defines the media for the styles in the *style declaration* block, where *media* is a comma-separated list of media types	2.0
`@namespace prefix url(url)`	Defines the namespace used by selectors in the style sheet, where *prefix* is the local namespace prefix (optional) and *url* is the unique namespace identifier; the @namespace rule must come before all CSS selectors (Netscape only)	
`@page label pseudo-class {styles}`	Defines the properties of a printed page, where *label* is a label given to the page (optional), *pseudo-class* is one of the CSS pseudo-classes designed for printed pages, and *styles* are the styles associated with the page	2.0

Miscellaneous Syntax

The following syntax elements do not fit into the previous categories but are useful in constructing CSS style sheets.

Item	Description	CSS
`style !important`	Places high importance on the preceding *style*, overriding the usual rules for inheritance and cascading	1.0
`/* comment */`	Attaches a *comment* to the style sheet	1.0

Units

Many style attribute values use units of measurement to indicate color, length, angles, time, and frequencies. The following table describes the measuring units used in CSS.

Units	Description	CSS
Color	**Units of color**	
name	A color name; all browsers recognize 16 base color names: aqua, black, blue, fuchsia, gray, green, lime, maroon, navy, olive, purple, red, silver, teal, white, and yellow	1.0
#*rrggbb*	The hexadecimal color value, where *rr* is the red value, *gg* is the green value, and *bb* is the blue value	1.0
#*rgb*	A compressed hexadecimal value, where the *r*, *g*, and *b* values are doubled so that, for example, #A2F = #AA22FF	1.0
rgb(*red*, *green*, *blue*)	The decimal color value, where *red* is the red value, *green* is the green value, and *blue* is the blue value	1.0
rgb(*red%*, *green%*, *blue%*)	The color value percentage, where *red%* is the percent of maximum red, *green%* is the percent of maximum green, and *blue%* is the percent of maximum blue	1.0
Length	**Units of length**	
auto	Keyword which allows the browser to automatically determine the size of the length	1.0
em	A relative unit indicating the width and the height of the capital "M" character for the browser's default font	1.0
ex	A relative unit indicating the height of the small "x" character for the browser's default font	1.0
px	A pixel, representing the smallest unit of length on the output device	1.0
in	An inch	1.0
cm	A centimeter	1.0
mm	A millimeter	1.0
pt	A point, approximately 1/72 inch	1.0
pc	A pica, approximately 1/12 inch	1.0
%	A percent of the width or height of the parent element	1.0
xx-small	Keyword representing an extremely small font size	1.0
x-small	Keyword representing a very small font size	1.0
small	Keyword representing a small font size	1.0
medium	Keyword representing a medium-sized font	1.0
large	Keyword representing a large font	1.0
x-large	Keyword representing a very large font	1.0
xx-large	Keyword representing an extremely large font	1.0
Angle	**Units of angles**	
deg	The angle in degrees	2.0
grad	The angle in gradients	2.0
rad	The angle in radians	2.0

Units	Description	CSS
Time	**Units of time**	
ms	Time in milliseconds	2.0
s	Time in seconds	2.0
Frequency	**Units of frequency**	
hz	The frequency in hertz	2.0
khz	The frequency in kilohertz	2.0

Attributes and Values

The following table describes the attributes and values for different types of elements. The attributes are grouped into categories to help you locate the features relevant to your particular design task.

Attribute	Description	CSS
Aural	**Styles for Aural Browsers**	
azimuth: *location*	Defines the location of the sound, where *location* is left-side, far-left, left, center-left, center, center-right, right, far-right, right-side, leftward, rightward, or an angle value	2.0
cue: url(*url1*) url(*url2*)	Adds a sound to an element: if a single value is present, the sound is played before and after the element; if two values are present, the first is played before and the second is played after	2.0
cue-after: url(*url*)	Specifies a sound to be played immediately after an element	2.0
cue-before: url(*url*)	Specifies a sound to be played immediately before an element	2.0
elevation: *location*	Defines the vertical location of the sound, where *location* is below, level, above, lower, higher, or an angle value	2.0
pause: *time1 time2*	Adds a pause to an element: if a single value is present, the pause occurs before and after the element; if two values are present, the first pause occurs before and the second occurs after	2.0
pause-after: *time*	Adds a pause after an element	2.0
pause-before: *time*	Adds a pause before an element	2.0
pitch: *value*	Defines the pitch of a speaking voice, where *value* is x-low, low, medium, high, x-high, or a frequency value	2.0
pitch-range: *value*	Defines the pitch range for a speaking voice, where *value* ranges from 0 to 100; a low pitch range results in a monotone voice, whereas a high pitch range sounds very animated	2.0
play-during: url(*url*) mix repeat *type*	Defines a sound to be played behind an element, where *url* is the URL of the sound file; mix overlays the sound file with the sound of the parent element; repeat causes the sound to be repeated, filling up the available time; and *type* is auto to play the sound only once, none to play nothing but the sound file, or inherit	2.0
richness: *value*	Specifies the richness of the speaking voice, where *value* ranges from 0 to 100; a low value indicates a softer voice, whereas a high value indicates a brighter voice	2.0
speak: *type*	Defines how element content is to be spoken, where *type* is normal (for normal punctuation rules), spell-out (to pronounce one character at a time), none (to suppress the aural rendering), or inherit	2.0

Attribute	Description	CSS
`speak-numeral: type`	Defines how numeric content should be spoken, where *type* is digits (to pronounce one digit at a time), continuous (to pronounce the full number), or inherit	2.0
`speak-punctuation: type`	Defines how punctuation characters are spoken, where *type* is code (to speak the punctuation literally), none (to not speak the punctuation), or inherit	2.0
`speech-rate: value`	Defines the rate of speech, where *value* is x-slow, slow, medium, fast, x-fast, slower, faster, or a value in words per minute	2.0
`stress: value`	Defines the maximum pitch, where *value* ranges from 0 to 100; a value of 50 is normal stress for a speaking voice	2.0
`voice-family: text`	Defines the name of the speaking voice, where *text* is male, female, child, or a text string indicating a specific speaking voice	2.0
`volume: value`	Defines the volume of a voice, where *value* is silent, x-soft, soft, medium, loud, x-loud, or a number from 0 (lowest) to 100 (highest)	2.0
Backgrounds	**Styles applied to an element's background**	
`background: color url(url) repeat attachment position`	Defines the background of the element, where *color* is a CSS color name or value, *url* is the location of an image file, *repeat* defines how the background image should be repeated, *attachment* defines how the background image should be attached, and *position* defines the position of the background image	1.0
`background-attachment: type`	Specifies how the background image is attached, where *type* is inherit, scroll (move the image with the page content), or fixed (fix the image and not scroll)	1.0
`background-color: color`	Defines the color of the background, where *color* is a CSS color name or value; the keyword "inherit" can be used to inherit the background color of the parent element, or "transparent" can be used to allow the parent element background image to show through	1.0
`background-image: url(url)`	Specifies the image file used for the element's background, where *url* is the URL of the image file	1.0
`background-position: x y`	Sets the position of a background image, where *x* is the horizontal location in pixels, as a percentage of the width of the parent element, or the keyword "left", "center", or "right", *y* is the vertical location in pixels, as a percentage of the height and of the parent element, or the keyword, "top", "center", or "bottom"	1.0
`background-repeat: type`	Defines the method for repeating the background image, where *type* is no-repeat, repeat (to tile the image in both directions), repeat-x (to tile the image in the horizontal direction only), or repeat-y (to tile the image in the vertical direction only)	1.0
Block-Level Styles	**Styles applied to block-level elements**	
`border: length style color`	Defines the border style of the element, where *length* is the border width, *style* is the border design, and *color* is the border color	1.0
`border-bottom: length style color`	Defines the border style of the bottom edge of the element	1.0
`border-left: length style color`	Defines the border style of the left edge of the element	1.0
`border-right: length style color`	Defines the border style of the right edge of the element	1.0
`border-top: length style color`	Defines the border style of the top edge of the element	1.0

Attribute	Description	CSS
border-color: *color*	Defines the color applied to the element's border using a CSS color unit	1.0
border-bottom-color: *color*	Defines the color applied to the bottom edge of the element	1.0
border-left-color: *color*	Defines the color applied to the left edge of the element	1.0
border-right-color: *color*	Defines the color applied to the right edge of the element	1.0
border-top-color: *color*	Defines the color applied to the top edge of the element	1.0
border-style: *style*	Specifies the design of the element's border (dashed, dotted, double, groove, inset, none, outset, ridge, or solid)	1.0
border-style-bottom: *style*	Specifies the design of the element's bottom edge	1.0
border-style-left: *style*	Specifies the design of the element's left edge	1.0
border-style-right: *style*	Specifies the design of the element's right edge	1.0
border-style-top: *style*	Specifies the design of the element's top edge	1.0
border-width: *length*	Defines the width of the element's border, in a unit of measure or using the keyword "thick", "medium", or "thin"	1.0
border-width-bottom: *length*	Defines the width of the element's bottom edge	1.0
border-width-left: *length*	Defines the width of the element's left edge	1.0
border-width-right: *length*	Defines the width of the element's right edge	1.0
border-width-top: *length*	Defines the width of the element's top edge	1.0
margin: *top right bottom left*	Defines the size of the margins around the top, right, bottom, and left edges of the element, in one of the CSS units of length	1.0
margin-bottom: *length*	Defines the size of the element's bottom margin	1.0
margin-left: *length*	Defines the size of the element's left margin	1.0
margin-right: *length*	Defines the size of the element's right margin	1.0
margin-top: *length*	Defines the size of the element's top margin	1.0
padding: *top right bottom left*	Defines the size of the padding space within the top, right, bottom, and left edges of the element, in one of the CSS units of length	1.0
padding-bottom: *length*	Defines the size of the element's bottom padding	1.0
padding-left: *length*	Defines the size of the element's left padding	1.0
padding-right: *length*	Defines the size of the element's right padding	1.0
padding-top: *length*	Defines the size of the element's top padding	1.0

Attribute	Description	CSS
Content	**Styles to attach additional content to elements**	
content: *text*	Generates a text string to attach to the content of the element	2.0
content: attr(*attr*)	Returns the value of the *attr* attribute from the element	2.0
content: close-quote	Attaches a close quote using the characters specified in the quotes style	2.0
content: counter(*text*)	Generates a counter using the text string *text* attached to the content (most often used with list items)	2.0
content: counters(*text*)	Generates a string of counters using the comma-separated text string *text* attached to the content (most often used with list items)	2.0
content: no-close-quote	Prevents the attachment of a close quote to an element	2.0
content: no-open-quote	Prevents the attachment of an open quote to an element	2.0
content: open-quote	Attaches an open quote using the characters specified in the quotes style	2.0
content: url(*url*)	Attaches the content of an external file indicated in the *url* to the element	2.0
counter-increment: *id integer*	Defines the element to be automatically incremented and the amount by which it is to be incremented, where *id* is an identifier of the element and *integer* defines by how much	2.0
counter-reset: *id integer*	Defines the element whose counter is to be reset and the amount by which it is to be reset, where *id* is an identifier of the element and *integer* defines by how much	2.0
quotes: *text1 text2*	Defines the text strings for the open quotes (*text1*) and the close quotes (*text2*)	2.0
Display Styles	**Styles that control the display of the element's content**	
clip: rect(*top, right, bottom, left*)	Defines what portion of the content is displayed, where *top*, *right*, *bottom*, and *left* are distances of the top, right, bottom, and left edges from the element's top-left corner; use a value of auto to allow the browser to determine the clipping region	2.0
display: *type*	Specifies the display type of the element, where *type* is one of the following: block, inline, inline-block, inherit, list-item, none, run-in, table, inline-table, table-caption, table-column, table-cell, table-column-group, table-header-group, table-footer-group, table-row, or table-row-group	1.0

Attribute	Description	CSS
height: *length*	Specifies the height of the element in one of the CSS units of length	1.0
min-height: *length*	Specifies the minimum height of the element	2.0
min-width: *length*	Specifies the minimum width of the element	2.0
max-height: *length*	Specifies the maximum height of the element	2.0
max-width: *length*	Specifies the maximum width of the element	2.0
overflow: *type*	Instructs the browser how to handle content that overflows the dimensions of the element, where *type* is auto, inherit, visible, hidden, or scroll	2.0
overflow-x: *type*	Instructs the browser how to handle content that overflows the element's width, where *type* is auto, inherit, visible, hidden, or scroll (IE only)	
overflow-y: *type*	Instructs the browser on how to handle content that overflows the element's height, where *type* is auto, inherit, visible, hidden, or scroll (IE only)	
text-overflow: *type*	Instructs the browser on how to handle text overflow, where *type* is clip (to hide the overflow text) or ellipsis (to display the … text string) (IE only)	
visibility: *type*	Defines the element's visibility, where *type* is hidden, visible, or inherit	2.0
width: *length*	Specifies the width of the element in one of the CSS units of length	1.0
Fonts and Text	**Styles that format the appearance of fonts and text**	
color: *color*	Specifies the color of the element's foreground (usually the font color)	1.0
font: *style variant weight size/line-height family*	Defines the appearance of the font, where *style* is the font's style, *variant* is the font variant, *weight* is the weight of the font, *size* is the size of the font, *line-height* is the height of the lines, and *family* is the font face; the only required attributes are *size* and *family*	1.0
font-family: *family*	Specifies the font face used to display text, where *family* is sans-serif, serif, fantasy, monospace, cursive, or the name of an installed font	1.0
font-size: *value*	Specifies the size of the font in one of the CSS units of length	1.0
font-size-adjust: *value*	Specifies the aspect *value* (which is the ratio of the font size to the font's ex unit height)	2.0
font-stretch: *type*	Expands or contracts the font, where *type* is narrower, wider, ultra-condensed, extra-condensed, condensed, semi-condensed, normal, semi-expanded, extra-expanded, or ultra-expanded	2.0
font-style: *type*	Specifies a style applied to the font, where *type* is normal, italic, or oblique	1.0
font-variant: *type*	Specifies a variant of the font, where *type* is inherit, normal, or small-caps	1.0
font-weight: *value*	Defines the weight of the font, where *value* is 100, 200, 300, 400, 500, 600, 700, 800, 900, normal, lighter, bolder, or bold	1.0
letter-spacing: *value*	Specifies the space between letters, where *value* is a unit of length or the keyword "normal"	1.0
line-height: *value*	Specifies the height of the lines, where *value* is a unit of length or the keyword, "normal"	1.0

Attribute	Description	CSS
text-align: *type*	Specifies the horizontal alignment of text within the element, where *type* is inherit, left, right, center, or justify	1.0
text-decoration: *type*	Specifies the decoration applied to the text, where *type* is blink, line-through, none, overline, or underline	1.0
text-indent: *length*	Specifies the amount of indentation in the first line of the text, where *length* is a CSS unit of length	1.0
text-shadow: *color* *x y blur*	Applies a shadow effect to the text, where *color* is the color of the shadow, *x* is the horizontal offset in pixels, *y* is the vertical offset in pixels, and *blur* is the size of the blur radius (optional); multiple shadows can be added with shadow effects separated by commas	2.0
text-transform: *type*	Defines a transformation applied to the text, where *type* is capitalize, lowercase, none, or uppercase	1.0
vertical-align: *type*	Specifies how to vertically align the text with the surrounding content, where *type* is baseline, middle, top, bottom, text-top, text-bottom, super, sub, or one of the CSS units of length	1.0
white-space: *type*	Specifies the handling of white space (blank spaces, tabs, and new lines), where *type* is inherit, normal, pre (to treat the text as preformatted text), or nowrap (to prevent line-wrapping)	1.0
word-spacing: *length*	Specifies the amount of space between words in the text, where *length* is either a CSS unit of length or the keyword "normal" to use normal word spacing	1.0
Layout	**Styles that define the layout of elements**	
bottom: *y*	Defines the vertical offset of the element's bottom edge, where *y* is either a CSS unit of length or the keyword "auto" or "inherit"	2.0
clear: *type*	Places the element only after the specified margin is clear of floating elements, where *type* is inherit, none, left, right, or both	1.0
float: *type*	Floats the element on the specified margin with subsequent content wrapping around the element, where *type* is inherit, none, left, right, or both	1.0
left: *x*	Defines the horizontal offset of the element's left edge, where *x* is either a CSS unit of length or the keyword "auto" or "inherit"	2.0
position: *type*	Defines how the element is positioned on the page, where *type* is absolute, relative, fixed, static, and inherit	1.0
right: *x*	Defines the horizontal offset of the element's right edge, where *x* is either a CSS unit of length or the keyword "auto" or "inherit"	2.0
top: *y*	Defines the vertical offset of the element's top edge, where *y* is a CSS unit of length or the keyword "auto" or "inherit"	2.0
z-index: *value*	Defines how overlapping elements are stacked, where *value* is either the stacking number (elements with higher stacking numbers are placed on top) or the keyword "auto" to allow the browser to determine the stacking order	2.0
Lists	**Styles that format lists**	
list-style: *type image position*	Defines the appearance of a list item, where *type* is the marker type, *image* is the URL of the location of an image file used for the marker, and *position* is the position of the marker	1.0
list-style-image: url(*url*)	Defines image used for the list marker, where *url* is the location of the image file	1.0

Attribute	Description	CSS
list-style-type: *type*	Defines the marker type used in the list, where *type* is disc, circle, square, decimal, decimal-leading-zero, lower-roman, upper-roman, lower-alpha, upper-alpha, or none	1.0
list-style-position: *type*	Defines the location of the list marker, where *type* is inside or outside	1.0
marker-offset: *length*	Defines the distance between the marker and the enclosing list box, where *length* is either a CSS unit of length or the keyword "auto" or "inherit"	2.0
Outlines	**Styles to create and format outlines**	
outline: *color style width*	Creates an outline around the element content, where *color* is the color of the outline, *style* is the outline style, and *width* is the width of the outline	2.0
outline-color: *color*	Defines the color of the outline	2.0
outline-style: *type*	Defines the style of the outline, where *type* is dashed, dotted, double, groove, inset, none, outset, ridge, solid, or inherit	2.0
outline-width: *length*	Defines the width of the outline, where *length* is expressed in a CSS unit of length	2.0
Printing	**Styles for printed output**	
page: *label*	Specifies the page design to apply, where *label* is a page design created with the @page rule	2.0
page-break-after: *type*	Defines how to control page breaks after the element, where *type* is avoid (to avoid page breaks), left (to insert a page break until a left page is displayed), right (to insert a page break until a right page is displayed), always (to always insert a page break), auto, or inherit	2.0
page-break-before: *type*	Defines how to control page breaks before the element, where *type* is avoid left, always, auto, or inherit	2.0
page-break-inside: *type*	Defines how to control page breaks within the element, where *type* is avoid, auto, or inherit	2.0
marks: *type*	Defines how to display crop marks, where *type* is crop, cross, none, or inherit	2.0
size: *width height orientation*	Defines the size of the page, where *width* and *height* are the width and the height of the page and *orientation* is the orientation of the page (portrait or landscape)	2.0
orphans: *value*	Defines how to handle orphaned text, where *value* is the number of lines that must appear within the element before a page break is inserted	2.0
widows: *value*	Defines how to handle widowed text, where *value* is the number of lines that must appear within the element after a page break is inserted	2.0
Scrollbars and Cursors	**Styles to format the appearance of scrollbars and cursors**	
cursor: *type*	Defines the cursor image used, where *type* is n-resize, ne-resize, e-resize, se-resize, s-resize, sw-resize, w-resize, nw-resize, crosshair, pointer, move, text, wait, help, auto, default, inherit, or a URL pointing to an image file; individual browsers also support dozens of other cursor types	2.0
scrollbar-3dlight-color: *color*	Defines the *color* of the outer top and left edge of the slider (IE only)	
scrollbar-arrow-color: *color*	Defines the *color* of the scroll bar directional arrows (IE only)	

Attribute	Description	CSS
scrollbar-base-color: *color*	Defines the *color* of the scroll bar button face, arrow, slider, and slider tray (IE only)	
scrollbar-darkshadow-color: *color*	Defines the *color* of the outer bottom and right edges of the slider (IE only)	
scrollbar-face-color: *color*	Defines the *color* of the button face of the scroll bar arrow and slider (IE only)	
scrollbar-highlight-color: *color*	Defines the *color* of the inner top and left edges of the slider (IE only)	
scrollbar-shadow-color: *color*	Defines the *color* of the inner bottom and right edges of the slider (IE only)	
Special Effects	**Styles to create special visual effects**	
filter: *type parameters*	Applies transition and filter effects to elements, where *type* is the type of filter and *parameters* are parameter values specific to the filter (IE only)	
Tables	**Styles to format the appearance of tables**	
border-collapse: *type*	Determines whether table cell borders are separate or collapsed into a single border, where *type* is separate, collapse, or inherit	2.0
border-spacing: *length*	If separate borders are used for table cells, defines the distance between borders, where *length* is a CSS unit of length or inherit	2.0
caption-side: *type*	Defines the position of the caption element, where *type* is bottom, left, right, top, or inherit	2.0
empty-cells: *type*	If separate borders are used for table cells, defines whether to display borders for empty cells, where *type* is hide, show, or inherit	2.0
speak-header: *type*	Defines how table headers are spoken in relation to the data cells, where *type* is always, once, or inherit	2.0
table-layout: *type*	Defines the algorithm used for the table layout, where *type* is auto (to define the layout once all table cells have been read), fixed (to define the layout after the first table row has been read), or inherit	2.0

Glossary/Index

Note: Boldface entries include definitions.

World Wide Web (Web) An interface designed to make the resources of the Internet accessible to the general public. HTML 3

history, HTML 2–4

World Wide Web Consortium (W3C) A group of Web developers, programmers, and authors who set the standards or specifications that all browser manufacturers follow; the W3C has no enforcement power, but because a uniform language is in everyone's best interest, the recommendations are usually followed, though not always right away. HTML 5

X

XHTML. *See* Extensible Hypertext Markup Language

XHTML 2.0 A version of XHTML still in the draft stage; it has proved to be controversial because it is not backward-compatible with earlier versions of HTML and XHTML. HTML 7

XHTML 5.0 A working draft of HTML in the draft stage; it provides greater support for emerging online technology while still providing support for older browsers. HTML 7

XML. *See* Extensible Markup Language